WRITING
TO THE RHYTHM
OF LABOR

WRITING TO THE RHYTHM OF LABOR

Cultural Politics of the Chinese Revolution, 1942–1976

BENJAMIN KINDLER

Columbia University Press
New York

Columbia University Press
Publishers Since 1893
New York   Chichester, West Sussex

Copyright © 2025 Columbia University Press
All rights reserved

Library of Congress Cataloging-in-Publication Data
Names: Kindler, Benjamin, author.
Title: Writing to the rhythm of labor : cultural politics of the Chinese revolution, 1942–1976 / Benjamin Kindler.
Description: New York City : Columbia University Press, 2025. | Includes bibliographical references and index.
Identifiers: LCCN 2024033968 (print) | LCCN 2024033969 (ebook) | ISBN 9780231219310 (hardback) | ISBN 9780231219327 (trade paperback) | ISBN 9780231562638 (ebook)
Subjects: LCSH: Chinese literature—20th century—History and criticism. | Labor in literature. | Socialism in literature. | Literature and revolutions—China—History—20th century. | Politics and literature—China—History—20th century. | Politics and culture—China—History—20th century.
Classification: LCC PL2303 .K545 2025 (print) | LCC PL2303 (ebook) | DDC 895.109/0052—dc23/eng/20240923

Cover design: Chang Jae Lee
Cover images: © Shutterstock & 毛泽东,《在延安文艺座谈会上的讲话》,《解放日报》, 1943年10月19日 (Mao Zedong, "Zai Yan'an wenyi zuotan hui shang de jianghua," Jiefang Ribao, October 19, 1943)

GPSR Authorized Representative: Easy Access System Europe, Mustamäe tee 50, 10621 Tallinn, Estonia, gpsr.requests@easproject.com

And then we shall have the free reign of the margin on the beach of communism: there will be no more written texts, no more written right, no more written law, no more written orders, no more writing . . .

—Louis Althusser, *How to Be a Marxist in Philosophy*

CONTENTS

Acknowledgments   ix

Introduction   1

1. Learning to Write, Learning to Labor: The Yan'an Way and the Birth of the Culture Worker   20

2. Lazy Peasants, Productive Proletarians: The Developmental Logic of Cultural Labor and Uneven Development   61

3. Time for Communism: Mass Writing, Revolutionary Form, and "Bourgeois Right"   96

4. Reproducing Revolution: Cultural Reconstruction and the Aesthetics of Communist Heroism   136

5. In and Out of Petersburg: Soul and Writing Under Late Maoism   177

Thermidor (By Way of Conclusion)   217

Notes   235
Selected Bibliography   265
Index   269

ACKNOWLEDGMENTS

This is a book about writing. It is, for that reason, also a book animated by the problem of loneliness. The writers who emerge from the pages of this book operated in conditions unfathomably different from those of our present, as they were part of a political project building a better world. Yet they struggled to bridge the gap between their collective lives as communist militants, located in mass struggles and the lives of working people, and the individual, lonely conditions of writing. So too is academic writing an often desperately lonely affair, above all under the conditions of the neoliberal university and the repression of possibilities for collective political endeavor, a condition common to Hong Kong, mainland China, and the United States.

It is for this reason that I am deeply grateful for those friends and comrades who have made the process of writing this book a little less lonely, and who have, in multiple senses, enabled me to write this book. I am grateful, in the first place, for the support of the editorial team at Columbia University Press, especially Christine Dunbar, who has been central to the publication process from its inception. I thank the journal *Modern China* for permission to reuse previously published material in chapter 3.

Lydia Liu has been indispensable for my ability to read literary texts with the closeness and care they deserve. The landmarks of her scholarship—the problems of language, modernity and writing—continue to inform everything that I do. Qian Ying allowed me to discover the pleasures of Chinese cinema, but more than that, she alerted me to the contradictions of Chinese socialism and assisted me with advice on her own book publishing journey. They and many others made for an enriching experience at Columbia.

A little way beyond the Columbia campus, it was my great privilege to meet Laurence Coderre. Her work on how to understand the complex mediations between political economy and cultural production has been a constant inspiration. Tani Barlow's scholarship on Chinese feminism, incisive advice, and good humor has been key over recent years, above all during our time teaching together at Lingnan, when she endured my early-career anxieties about reader reports and much more besides. Above all, Rebecca Karl has been not only an indispensable intellectual advisor but also a caring friend. She has supported me through academic and personal difficulties and teaches me every day what it means to be a critical, political intellectual. Thank you, Rebecca. I further thank Fabio Lanza, Mindy Smith and Sigrid Schmalzer for their personal support and academic work, as they have done much to allow me and others to work on Chinese socialism. Cai Xiang and Wang Hui supported me during my periods of archival research in China, and their respective intellectual projects have done much to inform my work here.

I have been lucky to receive the care of friends scattered across the world. Michi Ebihara has been by my side even across vast distances during this project and has sustained me during the stresses and disappointments that life inevitably brings. Faye Cheung remains among the most intellectually brilliant people that I know, and I treasure the rare moments that we see each other. Achas Burin constantly reminds me of the search for justice that necessarily informs all good research in the humanities and was central to making Oxford a personal and intellectual home. Through the loving times we spent together, Minh Ha Nguyen is also part of this book. For that, and much else, I will always be deeply grateful.

In New York, Chloe Estep and Chris Peacock were central to my research. John Thompson has been a caring friend, in New York and Shanghai, and this book owes much to our conversations and friendship. Joanna Lee became a close friend when the world was falling apart and has remained as such, not least through the evenings of riotous conversation at her apartment. Harlan Chambers has been the first comrade in arms over many years. His brilliant work and sincere friendship made my graduate studies endurable, and I trust our bond will endure for many years to come.

It has been my privilege to return to the city of my upbringing, Hong Kong, as this book moved into existence. I am grateful in the first place to my friends and colleagues at the Department of Cultural Studies at Lingnan University, who have provided me with a new academic community, above all Pun Ngai, who has welcomed me into her home and shown true comradeship on countless occasions, as well as my fellow junior scholars in the department—Daren Leung, Jamie Chau, Lu Miao, and Zhou Yang—who have given me encouragement along the way. Pang Laikwan at CUHK has been a welcome familiar face in the city and a further source of encouragement. I am also lucky to have found friends here from earlier in my life, above all Lisa Lee and Elio Cunico, and I thank them for their support over these years. Beyond those I know directly in Hong Kong, I thank those millions of others who, in times of laughter or in times of sadness, make this city what it is against all the odds. It is thanks to them that this city will always remain my home, that place of boundless oceans and vast skies.

My academic career would not be possible without my family. My mother has always encouraged me to think without fear and has been a friend as well as parent over recent years. It has been a joy to see my younger brother, Sam, find the things that inspire him, and I hope we will spend more time together in the future. My grandparents, Evelyn and Reg Dixon, did not live to see this book reach completion, yet they live within its pages.

Wai Wing Yun entered my life during the final stages of this book and has been the cause of vibrancy and laughter ever since. Thank you, Wai, for your Hong Kong heart.

WRITING TO THE RHYTHM OF LABOR

INTRODUCTION

I feel as if I am growing, as if I am flying, I want to speak, I want to sing, I want to write. A voice fills my heart, which I must shout: I want to labor!

—Ding Ling 丁玲

These words, of veteran revolutionary writer Ding Ling 丁玲, were written in 1955, amidst China's First Five-Year Plan. By that moment, Ding Ling had been involved in left-wing cultural circles for more than two decades. She had also been among those intellectuals who had undertaken the long and difficult journey to the communist wartime base of Yan'an, where she participated in the Yan'an Forum on Literature and Art, which sought to provide a new theoretical and practical basis for the problem of writing amid an evolving revolutionary process. The sentiments expressed by these words were not unique to Ding Ling nor to the mid-1950s, yet they are strange to the contemporary moment from which this book is written, because they embody a mode of desire, a desire for labor, meaning physical labor among the workers and peasants, that calls into question accepted ideas about the relative autonomy of writing itself as a mode of cultural practice. Ding Ling's desire, that she might suspend her separation from the workers and peasants as an intellectual and come to labor among them, emerges as a mode of communist desire, one orientated towards a totalizing transformation of the writer. The serial articulation of different kinds of desire, connected to different modes of cultural practice—"I want to speak, I want to sing, I want to write"—coalesce into that singular desire, "I want to labor," which thereby provides the site of possibility from which cultural practice itself might emerge. Within two years of these words, Ding Ling suffered a drastic fall from authority amid the bureaucratic antagonisms of the socialist state. She was exiled to undertake an extended period of debilitating labor in China's Northeast. Reflecting on these episodes at the end of the socialist period, she recalled her initial arrival at a state-run farm and the task of having to deal with unruly chickens. Refusing the interpellation of "victim" offered to her by the postsocialist intellectual scene, she wrote: "I wanted to labor, so how could I be afraid of those chickens?"[1] A different time, different conditions of writing, yet that repeated desire: I want to labor.

These historical landmarks, of the Yan'an base area, the socialist construction of the 1950s, and the end of the socialist experiment in the late 1970s mark the outlines of a revolutionary process in which writers such as Ding Ling sought to transform the most fundamental coordinates of what it means to write. They did so as part of the movement toward a different, more egalitarian kind of society, in which cultural production was no longer the property of the intellectual, positioned apart from the masses as the arbiter of enlightenment and pedagogy, but organized according to a different logic entirely: the culture worker. Theirs was the desire that their pens and bodies might move to a new rhythm, a rhythm that would mark the supersession of the debilitating division between those who wrote and those who worked with their hands: the rhythm of labor.

Writing revolution, revolutionizing writing

This book argues that Ding Ling's mode of communist desire poses, in concentrated form, the question of how to devise relations of cultural production adequate to the demands of an extended revolutionary process. This marked the challenge of how to radically remake the relations between cultural labor and the totality of social relations of labor in a socialist society as part of a generalized process of overcoming the division between mental and manual labor. The basic but by no means definitive relation of cultural production in the Chinese Revolution was designated early on in the revolutionary process as the culture worker 文艺工作者.[2]

This relation was defined by its departure from the model of the petty-bourgeois intellectual and other categories of cultural production designated by conventional terms such as author and its equivalents. The culture worker was, instead, a model of cultural production whose adequacy for a socialist experiment was determined by a series of specific practices and modes of social organization that sought to overturn the privileged position of the author in favor of a new set of relations between the producers of culture and the masses, as part of a systematic defetishization and deindividuation of writing. These practices were theorized through the crucial Maoist vocabulary of *life* as *shenghuo*/生活, and formalized as "entering into life" 深入生活 or "experiencing life" 体验生活, whereby writers spent prolonged periods of time among the laboring masses, toiling in conditions that would wrench the culture worker apart from the social environments of their bourgeois class background and transform 改造 their entire emotional, intellectual, and embodied experience so that they could adequately produce culture in the service of socialism. They did so not only in order to entertain but also with the understanding, central to the Chinese Revolution, that culture itself would instead actively intervene in the transformation and reconstitution of social relations. The status of the culture worker as laborer was central to the entire socialist project, because these culture workers were tasked with being laborers of society and reorganizers of the social. Chinese socialist culture was an experiment irreducible to its Soviet antecedents, based around a complex dynamic between the ongoing transformation of cultural producers through immersion in the life of the masses, in order that culture would be able to intervene in the transformation of social life itself.

This study is addressed to the intersections between different sectors of social practice—the organization of cultural production, the powers of narrative texts to instantiate the aims and contradictions of Chinese socialism, and the totality of social life in a socialist society. Central to this argument is the understanding, from the work of the Chinese scholar Cai Xiang, *Revolution and Its Narratives*, that the Chinese Revolution itself was, in the words of his translators, "an ongoing cultural narrative event, whose logic, tensions, localizations and so on all needed to be worked out in concert with the economic building of socialism and the socialist transformation of everyday life. That is, the revolution was embedded in narrative just as it was narrativized in multiple different ways."[3]

In other words, the very contents of what a socialist society would look like were by no means determined in advance by a static vision to which cultural production was made to conform but were rather the product of precisely that dynamic between culture workers, the material system of social relations, and the transformative capacities of texts themselves. It is in its emphasis on the productive, transformative capacity of culture in relation to the social organization of labor, together with the demand to transform writers into culture workers, that this study contributes to the growing field of English-language scholarship concerned with Chinese socialist culture. It attends, ultimately, to the question of what it means to write under conditions of social transformation and how writing can be reorganized in the interests of revolution. Consistent with the central problem of writing, this book focuses especially on written narratives, namely in the form of novels, novellas, and short stories in its choice of cultural texts. While cultural production under Chinese socialism and indeed the figure of the culture worker encompassed a range of forms of cultural production—ranging from film through to dramatic performance and folk culture—the orientation here toward writing and its corollary of prose narrative lies in the final analysis in the difficulty of overcoming or transforming writing as a practice and its location in an individual modality of writing, that of the author, that constantly reproduces its difference from other forms of labor. To engage with this history, then, means to ask what it meant to write in the midst of a social revolution. So too does it mean to question the division between those who write and those who engage in physical labor, and whether we might imagine a condition in which that and other sites of alienating division have been transcended. In its orientation toward the productive and transformative tasks that were devolved on socialist culture, and in the dynamic mapped out earlier, this study is not concerned with the sociology of cultural production in revolutionary China, and least of all does it pose a typology of representations of labor in individual works. It does not treat labor as explicable in terms of the formal etymologies of *laodong*/劳动 or *gongzuo*/工作. It is, rather, concerned with cultural production within the production and reproduction of social relations whereby the constitution of the culture worker via immersion in relations of social labor opened the possibility of the organized transformation of those same relations. In the understanding of Chinese revolutionaries themselves, the mediations between these different sets of relations were explored through the vocabulary of life 生活 itself—life as the moment of possibility and return for the totality of cultural production.

In addressing itself to the politics of writing in the Chinese revolutionary project, this book cannot but be aware of the politics that attends its own writing. The scholarly conjuncture in which this project intervenes is one where scholars have increasingly begun to take the socialist period seriously as a site of cultural production.[4] That this trend is a relatively new phenomenon within Chinese literary studies in the English-speaking world reflects the institutional history of the discipline, in which the commitment to a modernist notion of textual autonomy and corresponding notions of aesthetic merit, formed amid the political conjunctures of the Cold War, have allowed for the consistent exclusion of Chinese socialist culture from academic study, all the while supported by a depoliticized notion of "modernity" in which the Chinese Revolution is configured as a mere historical aberration on the path toward integration with the capitalist world-system. That the Chinese intellectual space affords other interpretive possibilities—emblematized by the interventions not only of Cai Xiang but also of Li Tuo, Han Shaogong, He Guimei, Dai Jinhua, and many others—surely reflects the fact of these intellectuals having participated in that very process of transformation that underpins this book, not least in its final premutation as the Cultural Revolution. In keeping with the stubborn refusal of revolutionary legacies to die, the thread that informs this study is that not only is the cultural legacy of the Chinese Revolution of 1942–1976 rich and worthy of reexamination but also that this cultural legacy actively engendered the very horizons of Chinese socialism itself, as a historical process always in motion, always producing its own moments of self-critique. To read these horizons seriously, above all as they emerged in narrative form through literary texts, means to understand that the Chinese Revolution was also a sustained process of exploration, one that emerged out of the specific conditions of the revolution itself but that also came to ask more fundamental questions about building a different kind of society. The self-reflexive process of building socialism that emerges from the cultural texts of the Chinese Revolution encompasses such varied problems as the bifurcation between rural and urban spaces, the problem of gendered labor, and the compatibility of the wage with the transition to a communist society. These problems were posed and reposed in the narrative forms generated by culture workers, whose capacity to do so was a result of their immersion and transformation amid the life of the masses. The category of narrative here and elsewhere allows me, together with Cai Xiang, to understand the revolution itself as always already implicated in its processes of narrative imagination, such that it becomes possible to read cultural works from this period not in terms of their factual accuracy as determined by a "reality" that is already prior to narrative imagination, and not in terms of cultural works being determined by an always coherent and homogenous political discourse, but rather in terms of the active productivity of narrative as a force for the generation of new desires and visions of the future. To insist on narrative practice thereby opens up a space of complexity and heterogeneity between different dimensions of the revolutionary process and to underscore the Chinese Revolution as one that constantly produced its own contradictions, contradictions that served to generate new debates, ruptures, and deepenings of the revolutionary process, which in turn generated new demands for cultural narrative.

My insistence here on the radical productivity of narrative and its irreducibility to any already existing set of social relations calls for a theoretical concept that can think the relations between the social practice of writing, the transformative capacities of narrative at the level of cultural texts, and the social relations of labor that were to undergo further transformations, without reducing these terms to a homogenous totality, or abstracting textuality from materiality and social relations. The category that serves this function for me is that of *temporality*, specifically as a way of understanding practices of writing, narrative and labor as practices that take place *in time* and occupy heterogenous rhythms and temporalities. The problem of writing, in the last instance, is therefore determined by its particularly uneven rhythm, which makes it difficult to synchronize with other forms of social practice. Thus, understood in temporal terms, the problem behind the formation of a new practice of writing was how to articulate the rhythmic temporality of cultural production, including writing in the most basic and literal sense, with that of other kinds of social labor. The question of the mediations between writing and other forms of production, in other words, is, above all, a temporal one, and more specifically still one of *rhythm*, or the relation between distinct temporalities. The problem of how to theorize differential temporalities, arising from the articulation of different modes of production within a social formation, and how, through political struggle, to transform the relation of these temporalities to one another, is central to the Althusserian segment of the Marxist tradition. Louis Althusser's project was formed in explicit opposition to those currents of Marxist thought that sought to reduce the varied sectors of the social totality to a single moment or point of causation, or the imposition of a singular, teleological temporality, rendering such currents unable to think the problem of temporal unevenness and differential rhythms. In his own articulation of the problem of rhythm, in his contribution to *Reading Capital*, Althusser seeks to articulate a theory of historical time that is resolutely opposed to the Hegelian notion of a unified temporality based on the emergent self-consciousness of absolute spirit, as well as its neo-Hegelian Marxist analogues. For Althusser history is not comprehensible as a unified temporality in which any aspect of the whole may be understood with reference to a singular originating principle, but must rather be understood in terms of the temporal unevenness of its constituent elements, that is, the possibility of thinking the divergent times and rhythms of different histories and practices. To a Hegelian notion of "continuous and homogenous time" Althusser opposes a notion of time in which the different levels and dimensions of the social totality each possess a "peculiar time, relatively autonomous and hence relatively independent, even in its dependence, of the 'times' of the other levels," such that, with a social formation therefore comprising varied modes of production that are uneven with other, for each such mode "there is a peculiar time and history, punctured in a specific way by the development of the productive forces; the relations of production have their peculiar time and history, punctuated in a specific way." So too does art, such that "aesthetic productions have their own time and history." In the most striking invocation of rhythm, Althusser asserts that each peculiar history "is punctuated with peculiar rhythms and can only be known on condition that we have defined the concept of the specificity of its historical temporality and its punctuations (continuous development, revolutions, breaks etc.)."[5]

Althusser is therefore able to think of each time as based on a multiplicity of rhythms that resist assimilation to a single temporal logic. Even while his critique operates at a high level of theoretical abstraction, Althusser reveals that his articulation of the problem of uneven temporalities arises from a material and political context, which is unevenness as a lived problem of political economy and revolutionary strategy, so that he himself recognizes that the theorization of uneven temporalities derives its necessity from "the status of a whole series of notions which have a major strategic role in the language of the century's economic and political thought, e.g., the notions of unevenness of development, of survivals, of backwardness (in consciousness) in Marxism itself, or the notion of 'under-development' in contemporary economic and political practice."[6]

Althusser's intervention here and elsewhere across his work has a larger reference for this book. His thesis of the epistemological break and critique of readings of Marx based on a humanist anthropology of labor also feed into the positions taken here on how to understand the utopian potentiality of labor within a revolutionary project, as well as the complex intellectual legacies of humanism in the vicissitudes of the Chinese Revolution, in ways that will become clear shortly. But for now, thinking more strictly with reference to temporality as a problem of cultural production, Althusser's emphasis on *aesthetic production* having its own rhythm, and indeed its own history, sets out the problem of producing new practices of cultural production as well as the incredible challenge this task represented, that is, of making the body of the writer move to the rhythm of the temporalities of labor and manual production. For Althusser, the reference to aesthetic production having its own time and history refers largely to the suprahistorical level in which aesthetics does not follow the same historical temporality as politics. Yet so too does his emphasis on aesthetic production having its own time allow us to stretch his formulations to mark the time of writing in its most anodyne but also revolutionary sense, that is, consisting of the multiple, uneven, and recursive processes temporal processes that inform literary production, including not only of the material process of writerly production itself but also of those associated processes of preparation, revision, and so on. To write means to work according to a complex rhythm of labor that cannot be easily synchronized with the labor of factory or field. It is therefore in terms of a process of a series of ongoing temporal disjunctures and tensions that this study approaches the transformation of writing in the Chinese Revolution. The persistence of these disjunctures, that is, the resistance of writing to synchronization according to any totalizing logic, marks that very specificity of the temporal logic of writing that Althusser himself recognized. This specificity was, in a profoundly contradictory sense, also the site of productive possibility, which is to say that prose narrative itself, understood as the product of the labor of writing, possesses a particular orientation toward the problem of time and indeed a capacity to transform lived temporalities. If, in other words, cultural production as writing has its own rhythm and temporality, or as Althusser puts it, its own history, then so too do texts themselves possess a distinctive temporality, namely the temporality of narrative form. This further informs the orientation toward writing as a specific form of cultural production in this book. If writing is negatively defined by the difficulty of overcoming its status as an individuated and atomized form of cultural production, then so too does writing have an ultimately unique capacity to instantiate alternative temporalities and therefore alternative social relations through the flexibility of prose narrative.

Through narrating the production and emergence of new kinds of social relations, that is, new temporalities and rhythms of labor, it becomes possible to intervene in the social relations of life as *shenghuo* that serve as the grounds of cultural production. The time of narrative and the concrete effectivity of culture intervene between the time of writing (and other forms of cultural production) and the complex times of relations of labor (structured within a complex structure of unevenness and temporal heterogeneity) to form a complex time of times, or ensemble of temporalities. It is in this sense that temporality, in its specific modality as rhythm, serves as the general category for this study, one that can think together the time of writing, the time of labor, and the capacity of narrative to intervene in the social totality. Althusser's emphasis on the specific temporality of different practices including that of the aesthetic has, in turn, created the conditions for other theorists in Althusser's circle to further advance these formulations, and so too do his formulations receive echoes in more recent work in narratology. In Caroline Levine's brilliant formulation, "rhythm is therefore a category that always refuses the distention between aesthetic form and other forms of lived experience" even while narrative retains a special capacity to reconfigure lived rhythms of social practice, such that the rhythms of literary texts may be understood "not as an epiphenomenal effect of social realities, but capable itself of exerting or transmitting power."[7] For this reason also, my practice of reading in this study owes a great deal to recent formalist attempts like that of Levine to link the formal characteristics of texts with their social effectivities, as against any notion of mere representation. The very heterogeneity of these temporalities underscores, on the one hand, the transformative possibilities of cultural production in and through its relative autonomy from the immediate conditions of social relations, and yet on the other also points toward the problem, internal to the socialist project, of how to organize these temporalities into an effective unity, which bears on the institutional configuration of writing and culture.

This is also the question of how to inaugurate not merely a plurality of times, but rather how to envisage and produce a coherent *time of socialism*. The "answer," such as it was, emerged in the socialist period in the form of the Writers Association, thinkable in Althusserian terms as an ideological state apparatus (ISA), that is, as a set of institutions combining ideological and coercive functions but ultimately geared toward organizing the forces of cultural production so as to reproduce and expand the conditions of socialism. The Writers Association had as its formal task the process of aligning the practice of its members with the demands of the socialist project so that culture could participate in the *reproduction* of socialist social relations. In his own, classic account of the role of ISAs, Althusser recognized that the articulation of new ISAs under socialist conditions was an experimental process: "In this matter, Lenin, who abhorred 'decrees,' was perfectly well aware that things could not be settled by 'decree' or from on high. He also knew that there existed no prefabricated, ready-made, a priori plan or line for establishing these new ISAs. He knew that it was a task that had to be worked on every minute; better, that it was a long experimentation involving huge risks."[8] The emphasis here on the articulation of new, socialist ISAs as a risky and experimental process can just as effectively serve as a summation of the process undertaken in the Chinese Revolution insofar as it comprised a search for practices and institutions capable of organizing writing in the service of a project of emancipation while avoiding the reemergence of the hierarchy between mental and manual labor embodied in the professional author. Yet in and through these experiments, so too did Althusser recognize the omnipresent danger that "even under the official facade of socialist state institutions (formally and officially socialist)," the force of bourgeois ideology may yet "survive, reproduce itself, and spawn a terribly dangerous effect—insinuating itself for good and all into one or another weak spot in the relations of production or the political relations of the socialist state."[9] Problems precisely of this order emerged in China strictly after 1949 through the Writers Association, as that formal body allocated the task of coordinating and organizing writing, such that just this ostensibly socialist ISA also became a major site of struggle and critique, not least because of the ways that it came—under socialist conditions, no less—to reinstitutionalize the corresponding division of mental and manual labor.

The trajectory of these critiques and crises comprises much of the book that follows, including their eventual moment of explosion in the Cultural Revolution. Yet the significance of these crises lay precisely in the forging of new social relations of labor, beyond the specific sphere of cultural production, by intervening in the conditions of *life* as *shenghuo* that also served as the basis for the transformation of writing itself.

Realms of freedom

The problems of temporality that inform the intersecting challenges of the fashioning of the culture worker and the production of socialist narrative in this book are at the same time central to my conceptualization of labor as such, insofar as the transformation of social relations of production in China also emerged amid conditions of uneven colonial development, characterized by heterogenous and conflicting temporalities and a diversity of social forms and modes of production.

"Labor" as a conceptual category remains closely contested in contemporary Marxist thought.[10] This book refuses both the contemporary Marxist currents of the repudiation of the emancipation of labor as a demand *and* the humanist invocation of labor as the basis of human flourishing in favor of a Marxist-feminist conception of labor as (re)productive, in the first place, of the very conditions of life itself, which emerged in the Maoist imagination precisely as the problem of *shenghuo*/生活. Labor, then, designates the practices that engage in the production and reproduction not only of biological life but also of the very conditions of the social. A conception of life along these lines was present in Chinese revolutionary thought in its earliest iterations at the beginning of the century, namely the brilliant theorist He-Yin Zhen 何殷震 and her associates around the journal *Natural Justice*, who, as an anarchist, advanced labor as the basis of a reshaping of the social, expressed through her formulation of the universalization of labor 人人劳动. He-Yin Zhen's varied essays provide a point of intervention through which to theorize the articulation of labor under capital, with a view to how the gendered dimensions of labor provide a standpoint from which to understand the totality of exploitative social relations under capitalism. For He-Yin Zhen, as for other more recent feminists, the organization of capital around the wage-relation also rests, for its functioning, on the existence of other, less visible forms of social production that are formally outside the circuits of commodity production, meaning, in the first place, the unwaged forms of reproductive labor that fall to women.

The sweep of He-Yin Zhen's vision, then, comprises a rereading of the historical configuration of gender relations in China as well as the reorganization of women's labor and bodies under global capitalist modernity to understand how the experience of women offers the point of departure for a totalizing social revolution. Her long 1907 essay "On the Question of Women's Labor" offers the ideal starting point for a reconstruction of her theoretical insights. He-Yin Zhen combines a critique of the exploitation of female bodies under precapitalist conditions of an awareness of the ways in which capital itself also produces new modes of exploitation that are centered on the factory and the wage system. For He-Yin Zhen, the distinction between these two historical moments lies in the fact that the employment of women in premodern society, especially as domestic labor, is not yet part of a process of accumulation, and so she distinguishes premodern female labor as part of the "problem of livelihood 生计" rather than the "class system."[11] That the premodern familial system embodies its own forms of gendered violence and exploitation is, for He-Yin Zhen, beyond doubt. In her 1907 "Feminist Manifesto" she glosses the character for women, "*fu*," 妇 in terms of its relationship to "*fu*" 服 meaning "to serve" in order to argue that in premodern families of means, "ancient women considered serving and obeying to be their obligation," which provided the textual and ideological foundation for the restriction of women to their inner quarters and the limitation of their responsibilities to "managing the household."[12] Yet the sophistication of her arguments is also demonstrated by her understanding that the premodern family was a site of both production and consumption, and that these practices of production consisted not only of the role of women as the agents of the reproduction of labor power, but also other forms of material production that provided a certain degree of autonomy. She writes, then, of "premodern times," that "machine industry was not yet developed and women had to spin and weave in their homes. This can be seen as free or voluntary employment. The materials that they produced were sold in the market. This was the condition for the freedom of [labor] and the condition for the freedom of trade."[13]

The valorization of domestic labor as "free or voluntary employment" in these terms marks a strategic appropriation of the past, and gendered practices of labor, as the basis of a possible future, in which free or voluntary employment might come to regulate the totality of human labor rather than simply being a liminal site of autonomy for women within the premodern household. Yet it also functions as the basis for a contrast with the tendencies of capitalist modernity, insofar as the conditions for the exploitation of gendered labor as wage labor, that is, within a process of *capitalist* transition, arose from the destruction of household and agrarian industries and the concomitant transformation of women into a reserve army of labor, premised on a violent separation of workers from the conditions of life and the incorporation of life into the logic of capital.[14] The effect of factory production, He-Yin Zhen writes, was for women to become mere "instruments of wealth accumulation," registering the ways in which wage labor not only constitutes the basis of a structural process of exploitation but also registers daily humiliations against the female body. The transformation of labor into capitalist wage labor, then, engendered a series of bifurcations. The household was no longer a locus of autonomous production organized by women but rather of forms of unwaged social reproduction orientated toward the provision of labor power for factory production outside the home, such that the new position of housewife was itself integral to capital. The understanding of capitalist modernity as engendering a process of bifurcation in these terms, or more specifically a logic of *difference*, locates the division between public factory labor and the privatized, largely invisible status of the labor of social reproduction as itself a product of capitalist modernity. In place of the relative autonomy afforded by premodern production, then, the condition of women under capital is one of being both integrated into factory production and being the agents of social reproduction inside a newly privatized domestic space, with neither providing a meaningful basis for women's liberation. In this sense, the distinction drawn between labor as "livelihood" and wage labor does not mark a strict historical transition that can ever be completed, but rather a rearticulation, in which modern, capitalist labor as mediated by the wage nonetheless continues to encompass and depend on unwaged household labor as the production and reproduction of life. So too, in He-Yin Zhen's account, does the incorporation of female labor into capital accumulation pose the problem of knowledge and the division between mental and manual labor in a new way. The deployment of modern machinery results in the reorganization of technical knowledge, such that "Western skills are being transmitted as specializations in schools" and "poor women have no money for tuition." This being the case, for He-Yin Zhen the problem of the division between mental and manual labor always already contains a gendered dimension, such that the separation of mental from manual labor may be seen to coconstitute, with the separation of production from reproduction, a shared historical problematic. At the most fundamental level, the introduction of wage labor as an arbiter of social existence is seen to transform the conditions of the social, such that the affective relations between laborers, including women, come to be mediated by the wage and degraded as a result. She notes, quoting the Japanese socialist Tazoe Tetsuji, that "as long as the responsibility of a family's livelihood is shared by both men and women, the bitterness of competing for survival will permeate family relations. Between wife and husband, between sons and their elders, as well as between parents and children, all will vie with one another on the basis of the wages each pulls in."[15]

The reorganization of social life around capital and more specifically the wage form is therefore said to introduce bifurcations and sites of destructive difference at the level of the everyday relations of the family. The wage form, in other words, also comes to penetrate and restructure the spaces and times of unwaged social life. To these processes of bifurcation—on the basis of gender difference, factory and domestic space, as well as that between mental and manual labor, and ultimately at the level of the social—may be added the bifurcation between rural and urban spaces. For Liu Shipei, He-Yin Zhen's collaborator, capitalist development entailed a deindustrialization of the countryside and its subsequent transformation into a reserve army of labor. In his 1908 essay "Concerning the Desirability of an Association of the Laboring Masses in China," Liu Shipei explicitly pointed toward the production of new antagonistic social, temporal and spatial relationships, arguing:

> The industries operated by the peasants have gradually been annexed by the capitalists. For example, the Chinese peasants have always had a system of family-based textile manufacture, and so too have they also raised eggs, and so too in the intervals between agriculture have they also engaged in fishing and firewood industries. But today, various kinds of weaving and cloth companies have set themselves up in the treaty ports, and are making use of machines and various kinds of advanced techniques, which means that they are able to produce goods quickly and sell them at a low cost, which means that the kinds of textile products produced by the peasants find their markets constantly diminishing, and so too do we find that the fishing and firewood occupations of the peasants are being faced with the establishment of fisheries and forestry companies, such that they cannot overcome these free enterprises, and so too do they suffer a decline in income.[16]

The effect of this transitional process, Liu understood, was to destroy what had hitherto been a set of integrated social relations within the countryside and to thrust the countryside into a new structure of global capital, one that, having destroyed the folk industries of the peasants, forced them to migrate to the cities and make themselves available for capitalist wage labor. In a separate essay, also published in 1908, entitled "Concerning the Possibility of Implementing a Unified System of Agriculture and Industry in China," Liu Shipei further emphasizes the ruptural, violent quality of this process and the way it produces a new set of antinomies and antagonisms: "in past days industry was largely amalgamated with agricultural production, and yet today agriculture and industry have become bifurcated from one another."[17] In later, Marxist terms to which He-Yin Zhen did not have access, these intersecting processes of bifurcation and the violent reorganization of social life may be understood as modes of primitive accumulation, a term that Marx used to identify the necessary and ongoing forms of violence that create the conditions for capital accumulation. In this theoretical framework, therefore, colonial capitalist development takes place through the production of varied forms of temporal unevenness. Yet the overcoming of these antinomies did not comprise the limit of He-Yin Zhen's politics or the visions of the Chinese Revolution. At the end of her essay "On the Question of Women's Labor" she articulates a future horizon of emancipation:

> Labor is a natural calling for women. But everyone, not just poor women, should labor. When labor is borne only by some poor women, then it is a kind

of subservient labor. So, in our opinion if there were the implementation of a system of communalized property, then everyone, whether man or woman, would labor equally. Those who expended a certain amount of labor toward [the production of] things of daily necessity to the people would enjoy the right of free use [of these products]. When employed labor is transformed into equal labor, then some people would no longer be dependent on other people; everyone would be independent—no one would have to rely on others, and no one would have to serve others. This would indeed be fortunate for the world. How could it be fortunate only for women?[18]

He-Yin Zhen's demand for a universalization of labor marks the supersession of all those violent forms of bifurcation and difference that attend capitalist development and a recouping of the universality of labor against the abstract form of universality that it assumes under capital, in which all forms of labor are rendered commensurable with each other under the wage form. This future horizon, of equal and independent labor, emerges as an extension and universalization of those liminal modes of autonomous household labor that He-Yin Zhen located in the premodern family. In these terms, He-Yin Zhen's projection of a future horizon of equal or free labor enacts a short-circuiting of the then-emerging ideological mystification of "free labor" as determined by the formal freedom of contractual wage labor at the site of factory production—described ironically by Marx as "a very Eden of the innate rights of man"—and its separation from precapitalist forms of coercive (or unfree) labor. Far from being "free," capitalist wage labor is, for He-Yin Zhen, precisely a mode of dependence on others, to no less an extent than unwaged labor within the home, and so simply moving into the factory cannot provide any meaningful basis for women's liberation. He-Yin Zhen's short-circuiting of the capitalist notion of "free labor" as wage labor, counterpoised to chattel slavery, also marks a rejection of the liberal state, with its reliance on the ideological fictions of contract and the abstract individual agent as its basic categories.[19] Her vision therefore usurps the language of freedom, so that it comes to mark not the buying and sale of labor power under the aegis of the formal freedom of the capitalist market but rather a future horizon, in which the freedom of communist labor lies in its universalization and rupture with the wage form.

This freedom depends on a dual movement defined by the abolition of both those forms of labor that are defined by the capitalist wage form *and* those unwaged forms of reproductive labor that are necessary for the reproduction of those bodies of labor power that are deployed in the service of capital. The formulation of free labor in these terms, as an incipient communist universalism—indeed, what Massimiliano Tomba terms a form of "insurgent universality," disjunctured from the state form—allows He-Yin Zhen to explicitly critique reformist projects that projected women in the home as "unproductive" by virtue of their exclusion from external, waged labor, including the possibility that a minority of women might derive their emancipation from labor by displacing household labor on to other women.[20] Among the translations undertaken by *Natural Justice* was the chapter "Agreeable Work" from Peter Kropotkin's *The Conquest of Bread*, in which the treatment of reproductive labor is far in advance of that of Marxist theorizing at the time. The passage from Kropotkin translated in *Natural Justice* in 1907 reads as follows: "To emancipate woman is not only to open the gates of the university, the law courts, or the parliaments, for her, for the 'emancipated' woman will always throw domestic toil on to another woman. To emancipate woman is to free her from the brutalizing toil of kitchen and washhouse; it is to organize your household in such a way as to enable her to rear her children, if she be so minded, while still retaining sufficient leisure to take her share of social life."[21]

Read in light of Kropotkin's insistence on the socialization of reproductive labor, the site of free labor as conceived by He-Yin Zhen is not, therefore, the autonomous rights-bearing subject of liberalism or bourgeois feminism, for whom nondomestic factory labor under capitalism provides the arbiter of liberation, nor is she the subject of creative labor that arises from humanist forms of Marxism. This anticipated abolition of the wage as a mediator of social relations in conjunction with the socialization of reproductive labor emerges directly from her envisioning of people having "the right of free use" of the fruits of social production, and so too does it emerge in her other texts. In her further essay "What Women Should Know About Communism," written in the vernacular, then, she describes the communist society as one in which "the things required for eating, clothing, and daily use, will all be available in one place, and all, regardless of whether they be men or women, provided that they participate in work 做一点工, will be able to take whatever they want, in whatever quantities, like collecting water from the ocean."[22]

This vision is precisely that of Marx's notion of "from each according to his ability, to each according to his needs." To the contractual subject of capitalist wage-labor He-Yin Zhen poses a feminist figure, in which labor is not the realization of a human essence but "an immanent creative principle in the service of specific historical problematics"[23] whereby the laboring practices associated with women, those, for example, of care, may yet provide a vision or standpoint of a practice of labor that can and should be universalized. How to make this transition, whereby laboring practices of women might undergo a process of universalization such that they cease to be implicated in or premised on a gendered division of labor sustained by violence, marks a question or a contradiction to which He Yin-Zhen herself gave no answer. The project of a universalization of that mode of labor such that it is no longer a force of repression marks a constellation of challenges to which this book will repeatedly return in its engagements with literary texts. Its contradictions notwithstanding, the expansive and integrated conception of labor as posed by He-Yin Zhen has an echo in those sectors of contemporary Marxist theorizing that have been described in terms of the problem of "social reproduction," which, often drawing on the Althusserian tradition, designates their attention to the problem of the reproduction of labor power, as that sector of social practice that generally falls outside the formal domain of wage-labor. The power of these theoretical projects is intimated by Susan Ferguson, who delineates a category of labor adequate to social reproduction in the following terms:

> At the heart of social-reproduction feminism is the conception of labor as broadly productive—creative not just of economic values, but of society (and thus of *life*) itself. It comprises "the activities and attitudes, behaviours and emotions, responsibilities and relationships directly involved in the maintenance of life on a daily basis, and intergenerationally." This is not "labor" as it has been understood in mainstream economics and vulgar Marxism. Rather, it is the "practical human activity" that creates all the things, practices, people, relations, and ideas constituting the wider social totality—that which Marx and Engels identify as "the first premise of all human history."[24]

Ferguson's identification of labor as the production and reproduction of society and of life itself provides a point of overlap with He-Yin Zhen's own concept of livelihood as the substratum of labor even under capitalism. Ferguson explicitly argues for this conception of labor to be understood as an "ontology" in the form of a concrete unity of diverse practices. It is on this basis that, following the larger trajectory of feminists in this tradition, she critiques Marx for his focus on "developing just one side of this ontology—that of value-creating labor" with the result that "the full rich diversity of labor and laboring bodies is sidelined from Marx's theory of capitalism."[25] The sidelining that Ferguson identifies here would frequently pass into the Chinese socialist project in the form of a failure to adequately account for reproductive labor at a theoretical level, and yet so too did this provide a space for narrative texts to intervene as they addressed themselves to the tensions internal to Chinese socialism. The vision of a totalizing reconfiguration of *life*, based on the universalization of labor, marks the subterranean horizon of the Chinese Revolution.

Make the world new

These points of theoretical departure—an Althusserian conception of differentiated historical time, in which cultural production and writing possess their own temporality and effectivity, and labor as the complex production and reproduction of life itself, derived from He-Yin Zhen and the insights of social reproduction theory—serve as the theoretical matrix for this book. They coincide in the problematics of *reproduction* and *transition*. The role of cultural production as the basis for the reproduction of socialist social relations encountered the complex of relations of waged production and unwaged reproduction engendered by China's prerevolutionary social formation. There thence emerged the challenge of transition as one of remaking social relations, transition understood here not as a teleological process, but rather in terms of the process of transforming the heterogeneous ensemble of temporalities that characterized China's historical situation, and the persistence-in-reproduction of those temporalities throughout the revolutionary process. The ultimate object of this common process of transition consisted of remediating and overcoming the separation of mental and manual labor, and the separation of production and reproduction, both of these *modes of separation* being the product of China's colonial capitalist development. This conception of transition hews closest to the work of Etienne Balibar as a result of his involvement in Althusser's project. For Balibar, in the formulation of Alberto Toscano, revolutions and transitions in the twentieth century "were marked by the absence of a totalizing social homogeneity—they were transitions in and of unevenness." Toscano goes on to stress that "it is the question of continuity and discontinuity that permeates Balibar's protracted struggle to elucidate the theoretical and political meanings of 'transition.'"[26] The insistence on the persistence and reproduction of unevenness and contradiction through a whole process of transition ultimately bears on Balibar's rejection, with Lenin, of any notion of "socialism" as a classless society, or else a society entirely even with itself as a homogenous totality of social relations: "Against the conviction, both Stalinist and social-democratic, that something like a stable socialist society should be envisaged, in Balibar's interpretation of Lenin it is simply incoherent to consider socialism as a classless society. Though the transition period combines mongrel transition social relations with capitalist ones, it is not in any way an independent economic and social formation, or a mode of production. Neither evolutionary staging post nor stable phase, socialism is the organization, under the political control of the party and the state of this contradictory co-existence."[27]

The designation of socialism and of the Chinese Revolution as an ensemble of contradictory forms is true not only of social forms as categories of political economy, such as the wage, the commodity, and the law of value, so too, for this book, is it true of the culture workers as well as the problem of literary-cultural forms themselves, insofar as the practices and laborers of culture, actualized specifically by the culture workers, marked both the possibility of a further development in the revolutionary process via the transformative powers of culture, and at the same time were themselves in need of further transformation, marking, then, a dynamic of exceptional complexity. It is in this sense that the "culture worker" emerges under Chinese socialism as a *figure of transition*, whereby the culture worker was called upon to *assist* in the process of socialist transition through the transformation of the social, and yet was at the same time *itself* a transitional *form*, as a figure of writing drawn into Chinese socialism from the prerevolutionary period, one whose remaking was always an experimental and often precarious process. Whether, and under what conditions, intellectuals could be transformed so that they might come to write in the service of revolution always remained an open question—indeed, a *wager*—and a site of intense struggle across the whole of this period. With its focus on the problem of the relations of cultural production and the transformative powers of culture, each chapter of this book focuses on moments at which the relationship between cultural production and the totality of social relations was thrown into contestation in the mode of a self-critique, through new attempts at articulation, transformation, and ultimately the negation of the writer as a professional arbiter of culture. The organization of this book is as follows.

Chapter 1 takes up the Yan'an period as central to the reconstruction of writing and the writer, based around Mao's Yan'an Talks and the key theoretical role of Zhou Yang as an attempt to develop the Maoist concept of *life* as *shenghuo*/生活. It attends to the one of the first attempts at the renewal of the novel form in the socialist period, through Liu Qing's A Record of Sowing Grain for its narrative depiction of the transformation of rural labor, and also examines Ding Ling's complex engagements with the Maoist project through her reportage and essay writing.

Chapter 2 examines the period of the early People's Republic, including, above all, the First Five Year Plan of 1953–1957. The practice of cultural labor during this period was deeply implicated with the uneven temporalities between city and countryside. It investigates the narrative production of the proletarian through novels, especially Zhou Libo's *Rivulets of Steel* and Bai Lang's *For a Happy Tomorrow*, which disclose the contradictions surrounding the factory and its female proletarian laborers. It also takes up the state-led promotion of proletarian writers, notably the Shanghai-based worker-writer Tang Kexin.

Chapter 3 examines the first of several crises of the culture worker. It returns to the problem of the appropriate narrative form for socialist cultural production through a close engagement with the short short story as that textual form adequate to accelerated temporalities of labor. It also examines long-form texts, especially the work of Li Zhun, and their relation to the problem of the wage, which, from this moment onward, became a central concern of the revolutionary process, associated closely with the Maoist theorist Zhang Chunqiao.

Chapter 4 interrogates the post-Leap interregnum through the multiple problems of reproduction, including the reproduction of labor power and the emergent problem of ideological reproduction. The shift to the figure of the "revolutionary successor" in this period posed, in a deflected form, the challenge of the household as a site of social reproduction. The chapter also shows how the crisis of the Writers Association yielded a shift to the PLA as an alternative institutional locus of cultural production.

Chapter 5 takes up the late Cultural Revolution as the period in which the contradictions of cultural labor became most intense and contributed toward the end of the revolutionary process itself. It does so above all through examples of the sent-down-youth novel, most notably Zhang Chenggong's *Youth*. The insurmountable contradictions of this moment finally contributed to the exhaustion of the revolutionary process, expressed through a lapse of narrative time.

The conclusion interrogates the afterlives of the Chinese Revolution through the depoliticizing effects of labor humanism in the 1980s, as well as through an engagement with Ding Ling's attempts to interrogate the promise of Chinese socialism from a communist-feminist standpoint of care as a basis for envisaging what communist labor might be, developed most acutely through her posthumous biographical texts and her short story "Du Wanxiang."

CHAPTER 1

LEARNING TO WRITE, LEARNING TO LABOR

The Yan'an Way and the Birth of the Culture Worker

Writers and artists must draw their materials from the workers, soldiers and peasants, but so too must they become friends with the workers, soldiers and peasants, they must be like brothers and sisters

—Mao Zedong 毛泽东

These lines are taken from Mao Zedong's report "The Culture Workers Must Amalgamate with the Workers, Peasants and Soldiers." The report followed his more famous "Talks at the Yan'an Forum on Literature and Art" of May 1942. Mao's vision of friendship between culture workers and the masses set the basis for a revolutionary program of cultural labor, which sought to reconfigure the social relations between those who worked with their hands and those who wrote. The site for this radical project was the then-isolated border region of Yan'an, which formed the base of activities for the revolution from the end of the Long March in 1936 up until the exit from the region in 1947. From 1941 onward, under the conditions of the War of Resistance Against Japan, different forces and tendencies converged, giving impetus to the transformation of social relations within the border region. The uneasy alliance between the CPC and the Nationalists against Japanese aggression began to break down as a result of armed conflicts between the two sides. In January 1941 the New Fourth Army Incident, in which the forces of the two sides clashed with each other in central China, resulted in a tightening of the existing blockade around the border region. There arose the challenges of increased inflation, reduced access to vital necessities such as food and cloth, and the need for an increased tax burden on the peasantry.[1] These imperatives came to generate, in turn, the pressing challenge of how to reconfigure the role of intellectuals who had come to Yan'an since the start of the war.

The attempted solution assumed the form of the Rectification Campaign 整风 and the Mass Production Movement 生产运动, both taking place over the period from 1941 to 1944. The two movements were linked to one another through the shared problem of labor. On the one hand, the isolation of intellectuals from the workers and peasants who accounted for most of Yan'an's population and the accumulation of criticism from these intellectuals during the early stages of the Rectification Campaign compelled Mao to question the adequacy of the position of the author, along with its associated modes of writing and creative practice. The answer—first proposed in Mao's 1942 Yan'an Talks—was a wholesale transformation of intellectuals and the retheorization of what it meant to write. The new conception of literature which emerged out of these talks posed labor as a transformative force, enabling intellectuals to enter into new sets of social relations with workers and peasants, summed up by the figure of the culture worker 文艺工作者. On the other hand, the workers and peasants were located within relations of labor that demanded transformation, not least as a response to the economic dislocation caused by the Nationalist blockade. The Mass Production Movement had as its immediate objective the expansion of production. However, in order to achieve this mission, it became necessary to transform the quotidian life of the masses along a range of axes, not least the reorganization of production along cooperative lines. The result was nothing less than a new life, one based on new cooperative relations of labor. In this sense, the changes that were introduced in Yan'an, whether with respect to the role of intellectuals or the quotidian life of those who worked in the fields, established labor as the basis for all social relationships, indeed as the content of the social itself. The relationship between the reshaping of writing and the transformation of social relations was a dialectical one. The demand for the transformation of intellectuals through their immersion in the working lives of the masses carried with it the understanding that the process and practice of cultural labor itself would participate in the transformation of social relations.

Getting a life, making friends

Mao's Yan'an Talks formulated practices and categories that allowed for cultural production to be posed as labor within the context of a larger revolutionary project, and for the writer to be reconstructed as a culture worker. The ideological transformations enacted by Mao's Talks emerged against the background of the literary movements that had emerged from the outbreak of the New Culture Movement in the 1910s up to the Sino-Japanese War in the late 1930s. Specifically, the conceptions of the intellectual and culture on which these varied movements had been based were premised on a hierarchical relation between intellectuals and mass audiences. From the perspective of Mao and others, before the Yan'an Talks, Chinese intellectuals had been unable to move beyond the professional position of intellectual charged with the task of liberal enlightenment. From their choice of literary forms, to their language, and above all, in the ways their relationships with the masses were limited to a politics of representation, intellectuals occupied a position that prohibited relations of equality with the masses, let alone the possibility that the working masses might develop their own modes of cultural production.[2] The significance of Mao's Talks goes far beyond any role as a source of legitimation for the party-led control of literature and authors, or as an extension of a ready-formed Soviet notion of socialist realism;[3] instead, they marked the way out of a real political impasse. The position of the culture worker, as distinct from the author, generated a suspension of the politics of representation between the intellectual and the masses via the inversion of the practice of pedagogy. Cultural production, as the concrete labor of the culture worker, would be experienced not as intellectual labor or writing divorced from material production, but as an imminently embodied and material process. It would no longer be a practice of individual genius, but rather a collaborative process in which the individual culture worker was a mediator between the life of the masses and cultural production.

The singular category that made the culture worker possible as a new practice of writing was the demand that writers "enter into life"—or more simply, *life* as such. The theoretical genealogy of "life" as it underpins Mao's cultural politics is therefore a matter of vital importance. "Life," as a keyword of Maoist cultural politics, marks the intersection of theoretical vocabularies of aesthetics, literary creation, and social relations. Crucial, in these terms, was the Russian aesthetician Nikolai Chernyshevsky. The influence of Chernyshevsky is most clearly indicated by the eventual translation into Chinese of Chernyshevsky's *The Aesthetic Relations of Art to Reality*, in 1942, in the months immediately prior to the Yan'an Talks. This translation was carried out according to the English translation of Chernyshevsky's work that had appeared in the Soviet literary journal *International Literature* in 1935. Chernyshevsky argued for a realist aesthetics, emerging in opposition to the prevalence of neo-Hegelian idealist aesthetics in the Russia of the nineteenth century. The concept of "life" that informed Chernyshevsky revealed the influence of a thoroughgoing materialism. He critiqued the whole edifice of idealist conceptions of beauty from the perspective of embodied experience in the world, taking the form, therefore, of a demystification of aesthetics in its Hegelian or Kantian mode.

As his basic maxim, Chernyshevsky argued "that is beautiful in which we see life such as it should be according to our conceptions; that is beautiful which expresses by itself life or reminds of life." In the first section of his work, published in *International Literature*, his materialist conception of beauty was lent a historical and political character by the understanding that the conception of "life"—rendered in the 1942 Chinese translation as *shenghuo*/生活—that informs beauty is itself sundered by the different aesthetic horizons attached to different classes. Chernyshevsky counterpoised the aesthetic horizons of peasants and the ruling class, arguing, for the former: "The description of beauty in folk songs will not contain a single attribute of beauty which would not be a sign of flourishing health and balanced strength of body, the consequence always of a life of plenty with constant hard, though not excessive, work."[4]

For the bourgeoisie, by contrast, their conception of beauty is an ethereal one, arising from and validating "a life without physical labor."[5] The problem of life is here posed as one of social relationships, and beauty as site of struggle and contending class forces, each informed by divergent experiences of "life" itself. The publication of Chernyshevsky's text in *International Literature* can, to be sure, hardly be separated from the Soviet canonisation of socialist realism as the guiding theoretical literature for socialist literature and arts. In the 1930s and subsequent decades, Chernyshevsky was canonized as one of several revolutionary-democrat writers, being frequently positioned alongside Vissarion Belinsky and Nikolai Dobrolyubov as a triumvirate of nineteenth-century writers and critics who were said to have anticipated the development of socialist realism. Yet the ultimate trajectory of Chernyshevsky in China cannot simply be reduced to the promulgation of socialist realism, however, but was rather inextricable from a set of conceptual possibilities opened by his ideas. The mediated introduction to Chernyshevsky to Chinese cultural politics, moreover, was indebted to an altogether maligned figure, Zhou Yang 周扬, who was the translator of the Chinese 1942 edition of Chernyshevsky's treatise.[6] Zhou is usually treated by as a cultural bureaucrat, not least in his capacity as the dean of the Lu Xun Academy of Art and Literature at Yan'an, or else as a mediator in the introduction of Soviet literary discourses during the period of the League of Left-Wing Writers after the formal adoption of that body of thought in the Soviet Union itself in 1934, and then as the main force behind the institutionalization of Mao's Talks after 1942.

Zhou's relevance to Mao's Talks, however, cannot be reduced to a purely organizational role. Zhou was an important theoretical protagonist on account of his articulation of the fundamental concept of life as *shenghuo*, which emerges as *the* theoretical category of Chinese revolutionary culture. Mao's

Yan'an Talks would expand the theoretical scope of this concept of life by demanding a wholesale transformation of the life of authors, in which life would come to be understood as collective labor. Zhou Yang's responses to Chernyshevsky, from the mid-1930s through to the eventual Chinese translation in 1942, took the form of a progressive elaboration of the social dimension of life. "Life" came to refer to a system of social relationships with an indissoluble relation to aesthetics, encompassing, therefore, a transformative notion of "life" as the origin of cultural practice itself, as well as antagonistic demarcation of the different aesthetic horizons of class formations, which held out the possibility of transforming the class status of intellectuals.

The Maoist category of "life" as *shenghuo* was not given from the introduction of Chernyshevsky in Yan'an, but rather passed through a set of complex trajectories from the mid-1930s onward, in which Zhou Yang had the decisive role. Central to this process, and indicative of the shifting theoretical contents of "life" itself, are the multiple renderings of the English term "life" that pervaded Zhou's translations of Chernyshevsky. In his first two essays in which he referred explicitly to Chernyshevsky and cited at considerable length from Chernyshevsky's treatise, entitled "Art and Life" and "We Need A New Aesthetics," both published in 1937, Zhou Yang rendered "life" as *rensheng*/人生, including within the title of the first essay, only to change subsequently to the more precise *shenghuo* in his 1941 and 1942 treatments, including in the preface to his translation of Chernyshevsky in 1942. These two renderings carry their own connotations and nuances. *Rensheng* echoed earlier set of debates between the Literary Research Association 文学研究会 and the Creation Society 创造社 during the 1920s over the tasks of literature, with the association committing itself to a project of "literature for life" 文学为人生. In this context, *rensheng* maintained a fundamentally metaphysical register. The shift in translation after 1937, in Zhou's writings, to *shenghuo*, therefore, marked a shift away from the conceptions of writing of the May Fourth context and an emergent understanding of life in terms of social relations. The context for Zhou Yang's earlier renderings of life comprised the fraught literary scene of Shanghai in 1937, and in particular, the polemics exchanged between Zhou Yang and the idealist aestheticians, Zhu Guangqian and Liang Shiqiu. In response to both of these figures, in the essay "We Need a New Aesthetics," Zhou invoked Chernyshevsky to demand that aesthetics, as the scientific study of the beautiful, be understood not in terms of permanent differentiations between the ugly and beautiful such as might be derived from a Hegelian idealist aesthetics, nor in terms of the subjective perceptions of individual subjects but rather in terms of conceptions of beauty as the product of historical conditions, indeed transformations in the relations of life. Zhou made explicit, furthermore, in a gesture that draws unmistakably from Chernyshevsky, that aesthetic horizons were particular to specific class formations, such that "in any given epoch the conceptions of beauty on the part of different social strata are radically different from one another, and are indeed directly opposite."⁷

The formation of the work of art, was, similarly, for Zhou, not the product of a flash of individual inspiration, but rather a concretization of the forms of beauty that are said to correspond to particular social strata. In the same terms, the relationship between the creator and the work of art was not, for Zhou Yang, a disinterested one, but rather required a process of engagement, one that could allow for the rendering of life but in such a way as to avoid merely replicating a series of external appearances and epiphenomena: "The artist should enter into life 人生 and undergo a deep amalgamation with present existence 现实生活 he should not be a bystander, and cannot raise himself above life, he must instead be closely linked to the direction of historical development and with the pains, sufferings and joys of the numerous masses of the epoch."⁸

Enclosed in Zhou's statements was the rejection of art conceived in solipsistic terms and instead the demand for a materialist science of aesthetics that could lend theoretical justification to realism, one that was distinguished from a naïve or photographic naturalism in the requirement that artists discern the essential relations that determine the shape of their era. At the end of "We Need a New Aesthetics," Zhou invoked Chernyshevsky explicitly as one of the theorists belonging to the aesthetics of the previous century who might be recruited to the task of constructing a new science of aesthetics. Zhou acknowledged Chernyshevsky as having derived his theoretical impetus from Feuerbach and cited Chernyshevsky's formulation of "beauty is life" 人生即美 as the appropriate theoretical maxim for Zhou's own theoretical project.⁹ Zhou's invocation of Chernyshevsky's thesis concerning the divergent conceptions of beauty among different strata lent a double valence to the demand for a "new aesthetics" that is the title of his text, consisting not only of the demand to construct a new science of aesthetics as the study of the beautiful on the basis of a materialist conception of artistic creation, but also the formulation of a new aesthetic in the sense of that horizon of beauty that was appropriate to a revolutionary project and an emergent set of class forces. Moreover, even at this stage, Zhou offered intimations of a transformed conception of the author, through his slogan that the artist should enter into life, albeit with life here still rendered in relatively metaphysical terms as *rensheng*.

Zhou Yang's 1937 investigations "Art and Life" and "We Need A New Aesthetics" concerning the formulation of a new aesthetics, and his later theorizations of the problem of writing and the role of art and literature in a socialist revolution in the early 1940s, are demarcated from one another by the outbreak of the War of Resistance and Zhou's move to Yan'an at the end of 1937. He was part of a large-scale movement of intellectuals and writers from the coastal areas and urban metropolises to the border region. In Yan'an, Zhou

Yang's institutional base was the Lu Xun Academy of Arts and Literature, subsequent to the formation of the Academy in 1938. In this capacity Zhou delivered a course on the history of the New Culture Movement, in which he sought to trace the relations between the literary experiments of the 1920s with the emergent demands of literature and art in the base area by arguing that the historical importance of the May Fourth period lay in its realist literary aesthetics and orientation toward the masses. He observed that "the pioneers of the May Fourth literary movement advocated a realist theory, and with respect to creation they carried out this theory. Concerning the masses, although there was unavoidably an attitude of looking at the masses from up high, yet there was always some degree of resonance between authors and the spirit of the masses, and to a greater or lesser degree these authors expressed the life and struggles of the masses, their pain and their hopes."[10]

Zhou's invocation of the life of the masses here must be read in terms of the problematics of Chernyshevsky's aesthetics and the fundamental role of life in literary creation, and one that indicated an emergent rejection of the isolated position of the intellectual. Whereas in 1937 Zhou Yang introduced the problem of life and discussed it only in the context of more extended treatments on Chernyshevsky's aesthetics, without granting it the status of a theoretical category related to political and social practice, in 1941, the problem of life came to take on a more productive set of valences, directly orientated toward a specific political and cultural conjuncture. In this context, Zhou's 1941 essay "A Casual Discussion on Literature and Life" may be read as the singularly most important document in raising the categories of Mao's Talks before the Talks themselves. Through this essay, Zhou addressed the relationship between art and life with a new conception of cultural practice. He made the origins of this relationship explicit, proclaiming that "with respect to aesthetics, I am a loyal follower of Chernyshevsky. His famous formula of 'beauty is life' 美即生活 carries a fundamental truth." The rendering here, for the first time, of Chernyshevsky's formula of life as *shenghuo* marks an important shift in the theorization of life away from a metaphysical and phenomenological concept and toward a materialist conception of life as a system of social relations. The importance of life, then, lies in the fact that it provides the author with the materials and experiences which are the ultimate source of cultural production, and that it is a system of social relations and practices that are at once material and affective. Zhou Yang's "A Casual Discussion on Literature and Life" was, however, by no means a mechanical folding of literature into life but rather an examination of the complex dialectical relations that obtain between the two. No simple equivalence could be drawn between what Zhou described as "the practice of life" and "the practice of creation." Instead, according to Zhou, the problem of the author is that of mediation, namely how the writer *mediates* between the material substance of social relations and life and the transformation of life into the work of art. That process of mediation is described by Zhou as the problem of "how to draw materials, and how to work them up 加工," comprising, in his own words, the work of writing itself.[11] For this reason, the problem of how the writer should relate to life, and especially the life of the masses, assumes a position of fundamental importance.

Zhou Yang poses the entry of the writer into life as the radical abnegation of the professional position of writing. He states, then, that "a truly outstanding writer" will pursue entry into life "until they attain the merging of subjectivity 主观 and objectivity 客观." In these terms, Zhou Yang states, "if we use a certain Wang Guowei–style mode of expression, this can be called the 'merging of the artistic sense and the environment, the abnegation of the subject-object distinction.'"[12] In view of these demands, the formation of a relationship between the writer and the life of the masses of a kind that can yield artistic creation is, for Zhou, a long and painful process. His imagery anticipates Mao's Yan'an Talks:

> To be suited [to life] is not the kind of thing that can be done in a moment. It requires a relative period of time amidst this life. To go everywhere and observe flowers from horseback is rather easy, but it cannot yield any real results. It is necessary to participate in some actual work, and in order to do this, you shouldn't fear any difficulties. . . . Merge into one with the people around you, study from them, and ask for guidance from them. Don't blame them for not understanding you, instead you should seek to understand them.[13]

In light of his own comments with regard to the May Fourth movement, Zhou Yang's demand that writers study from the masses instead of positioning themselves in a subject-position of enlightenment in order to reform the masses carried great significance. The significance of "life" for literary creation became something other than merely being that which is reflected in the artwork, even in a highly mediated or technical form. It became the basis for the transformation of the position of the writer himself. This transformation in turn rested on and enabled a new set of social relationships, in which the inequalities that arose from a conception of the author as a force of enlightenment were suspended. Crucially, the process of entering into life also posed, for Zhou Yang, the problem of *time*. The purpose of entering into life was not to provide opportunities for writing, but to compel the transformation of the writer. He therefore insisted that as they experience life, writers should "not have any thoughts of finding any time 时间 or an environment for creation 创作." The transformation of writers amid the conditions of mass life were such as to require suspension even of the practice of writing, pending the formation of a new system of social relations. Life, then, emerged as the site at which a revolutionary project becomes lived through a new set of relations. He asserted that "a creator must broadly, in many respects and deeply merge with people in everyday life, you must become friends with them, talk about family matters, intimate affairs of the heart, so that between you there is no longer any kind of psychological forbearance or distance."[14] Having done so, "at this time the true masses will become visible to you, what you understand will no longer be an abstract concept of the masses, but concrete individuals of flesh and blood."[15] Zhou Yang's formulation of "making friends" likely provided the basis for Mao's adoption of this phrase, with which the chapter began. Zhou Yang's subsequent 1942 translation of Chernyshevsky's aesthetic treatise was accompanied by an essay in *Liberation Daily* (used as the introduction for Zhou's translation in its 1957 edition), "Materialist Aesthetics—An Introduction to Chernyshevsky's Aesthetics," in which Zhou reprised the orientation between social class and horizons of aesthetic beauty.[16] More important, Zhou also brought a critical light to bear on the limits of Chernyshevsky's conception of realism, arguing that Chernyshevsky maintained a passive, Feuerbachian conception of the process through which art may be said to reflect reality, and that he therefore ignores the active function of art in the transformation of society. This included, for Zhou, the problem of artistic appreciation and its relation to the production of a new horizon of sensory experience. He therefore drew on Marx's *A Contribution to the Critique of Political Economy* to argue that the function of the work of art lay in its capacity to create the audience that is appropriate for its own appreciation, by engendering the transformation of aesthetic perception. The work of art, in other words, achieved its social effects in large part through a mode of labor on the terrain of sensory experience.[17] This marked both the culmination of a process of theoretical development and a set of theoretical resources directly proximate to the Yan'an Talks. Although delivered at a high level of abstraction, Zhou Yang provided an outline of the ways in which culture workers would undergo aesthetic transformation through the life of the masses but were at the same time charged with the transformation of those very same social relations via the transformative powers of culture.

The search for an adequate conception of "life" in Zhou's texts was matched by the increasingly tumultuous state of literary politics in April 1942. The publication of his earlier text, "A Casual Discussion," had already produced a response on the part of the core group of intellectuals who had traveled to Yan'an, in which they objected to Zhou's program for the transformation of the intellectual. The formation of these lines of antagonism reflected some of the factional divergences in Yan'an between different groups of intellectuals and theorists. These groups were themselves affiliated with the different institutional bases of, on the one hand, the Lu Xun Academy of Arts and Literature, of which Zhou was himself the leading representative, and, on the other, the Yan'an branch of the National Resistance Association of Literary and Art Workers. These institutional allegiances were based on divergences concerning the nature of literary production. The writers of the Association were insistent on the autonomous role of the artist as an agent of social criticism, which contrasted with the emergent understanding of the author as a mediator between artistic production and the life of the masses which Zhou posed in his interventions.[18] In the interim period between the announcement of the Rectification Campaign in February 1942, through Mao's speech "Rectify the Party's Style of Work" and the Talks over the course of May the same year, these lines of antagonism deepened. Authors associated with the Resistance Association, including several who had earlier responded to Zhou's essays concerning the transformation of authors in 1941, used the license for critique granted by the beginning of the Rectification Movement to criticise bureaucracy and inequality within the base areas, giving rise to essays such as Ding Ling's "Thoughts on March 8," Ai Qing's "Understand Authors, Respect Authors," or Wang Shiwei's varied essays on the relationships between politics and culture. At issue was the fundamental question of the position of the writer and the nature of writing itself.

Following the formal announcement in April 1942 of Mao's decision to hold a forum on art and literature, Mao undertook a series of visits with individual authors to discuss their concerns about literary freedom in the base area, before the convening of the first session of the forum on May 2, followed by its closing session on May 23. Mao's speeches during these two sessions comprised his famous Yan'an Talks, the first edition of which was published in *Liberation Daily* in October 1943. The Talks drew on the multifaceted conception of life that had been developed by Zhou through his engagements with Chernyshevsky. For Chernyshevsky, Zhou and subsequently, for Mao, life provided the grounds and materials for art and literature, and of the culture worker. This was true most basically in terms of Chernyshevsky's conception of life as the origin of art. In no other terms can one understand Mao's argument that "rich deposits of literature and art actually exist in popular life itself: they are things in their natural forms, crude but also extremely lively, rich and fundamental; they make all processed forms of literature pale in comparison, they are the sole and inexhaustible source of processed forms of literature and art."[19]

Yet this was crucially not only a matter of life as origin, but one of social practice. The political significance of this concept of life lay in its transformative potential and that it was able to provide an answer of how to transform the relationship between the masses and the cultural producer. The then-existing condition of writers in Yan'an, for Mao, was based on the constant reproduction of their status as petty-bourgeois intellectuals who are isolated from the masses. The task was therefore transforming the "stand" 立场 of these authors.

An immersion in the conditions of mass life or the lived social relations of workers and peasants would provide the conditions for the transformation of the class stand of petty-bourgeois authors. Mao recalled his own experience as a scholar in which he held the bodies of workers and peasants in disdain, believing that "intellectuals were the only clean people in the world." Only having lived with the workers and peasants in the context of the revolution, Mao said, did he come to understand that "I came to feel that intellectuals are not only unclean in many respects but even physically unclean, while the cleanest people are workers and peasants; their hands may be dirty and their feet soiled with cow dung, but they are still cleaner than the big and petty bourgeoisie."[20] Here, Mao registers the extent to which the problem of "stand" is affective and aesthetic, insofar as it pertains to the ways that embodiment itself is structured by class difference. For this reason, Mao summarized the process of transformation that intellectuals are required to undergo in order that they be reconstituted as culture workers and therefore as full participants in a revolutionary project: "That is what is meant by a change in feelings 感情, a change from one class to another. If our writers and artists who come from the intelligentsia want their works to be well received by the masses, they must change and remold their thinking and their feelings. Without such a change, without such remolding, they can do nothing well and will be misfits."[21]

Mao's confident statement concerning the transformation of writers from one class to another marked a departure from a theorization of class as a simple sociological category.[22] He instead understood class to encompass a whole set of dispositions, attitudes, and emotions, including, implicitly, the connection with aesthetics and beauty raised by Chernyshevsky and Zhou. The fact that this crucial extract followed directly from Mao's long anecdote about the body was no coincidence because what ultimately defined the process of entering into life was a transition from a merely intellectual understanding of the masses, in which they figured as abstract categories that are divorced from lived experience, to an experience that was felt at the most intimate levels of the body. Here, too, the influence of Chernyshevsky may be felt, as Chernyshevsky saw the different attitudes of class formations toward the aesthetics of beauty to be manifested above all in the valuation or devaluation of bodies that bear the visible signs of labor, encompassing a set of embodied standpoints, aesthetic orientations and modes of thought that would need to become the writer's own.

In Mao's cultural politics, therefore, class always encompasses an affective dimension, which, being related to aesthetics in its sensorial and embodied immediacy, can on no account be enclosed within any notion of mere ideology or idealism. To this extent, therefore, the Maoist project must be rigorously distinguished from any notion of a merely intellectual or formal transformation in cultural consciousness, or indeed any disembodied notion of subjectivity. The process of entering life necessarily has a coercive dimension in the form of the total abnegation of the preexisting writerly subject and even subjectivity *as such*, insofar as the intellectual must be made into an *object* of transformation, and restructured according to a different set of class aesthetics, before they can become a *participant* in the revolutionary project. Only having done so can their writing become operative in the further transformation of social relations. In his concluding address, therefore, Mao further reinforced that writers must "go to the sole, the broadest, the richest source, to observe, experience, study and analyse all the different kinds of people, all the classes and all the masses, all the vivid patterns of life and struggle, and all literature and art in their natural from, and only then can they engage in working-up 加工, that is to say, creation, whereby they integrate raw materials with production, and the process of study with the process of creation."[23]

The presentation of writing here in terms of a process of "working-up" marks yet a further crucial point of intersection between Mao's Talks and Zhou Yang's work, whereby the task of the culture worker is understood as a site of mediation. Strikingly, this part of Mao's Talks as published and disseminated in Yan'an underwent edits prior to their inclusion in the 1953 version of his *Collected Works*, in which the references to "working-up" were replaced by the category of the "creative process" 创作过程. This shift was part of an emergent professionalization of cultural work that came to distinguish the 1950s from the more egalitarian practices of Yan'an. In the Yan'an context, however, the formulation of "working-up" marked a departure from the bourgeois conception of writing as dependent on the individual genius or autonomous creativity of the author, and a figuring of writing instead as a process of mediation between the imminent conditions of "life" and the audience to whom the literary work is directed. The role of the culture worker as mediator who "works up" the existing conditions of life opens up the possibility of the reciprocal interaction between life, writing and culture, then, such that, in Mao's expanded formulation, "literature and art that have been worked-up are more organized and concentrated than literature and art in their natural form,"[24] and this higher-level mode of organization provides the impetus for culture to reorganize social relations themselves.[25]

Having emerged on the basis of Zhou Yang's early explorations of the problem of life, the Talks themselves produced a set of categories that were rapidly implemented at the level of policy. The forum at which Mao gave his Talks was followed over the remainder of 1942 by a period of intense study based around the Talks and other texts issuing from the Rectification movement. The shift from the theoretical demands of the Talks to a new system of lived practices came in March 1943 through a further conference of literary workers called by the Central Committee and the Central Organization Department. This meeting announced the imminent dispatch of culture workers to villages in the countryside 下乡 and other base units. Although the movement of authors to the countryside predated the Talks, Kai Feng emphasized at the conference how the Talks had transformed this practice so that it could become truly transformative, and not merely a temporary exercise in "collecting materials" for literary creation. He emphasized that, in going down, intellectuals should "put aside their qualifications as men and women of culture 文化人." So too, in this context, did Kai anticipate that the transformation of intellectuals would engender new methods of writing and language adequate to the changed conception of their tasks: "When you gain new things 新事物 after participating in work, you will likely cast aside your old methods of writing 旧写作方式 and create a whole new set of methods of writing."[26]

In the immediate aftermath of the conference of literary workers called by the Central Committee and the Central Organization Department, the first major wave of dispatching authors took place. The basic format of this dispatching set the precedent for repeated and regularized campaigns throughout the subsequent history of revolutionary China, in which writers, at the same time as undergoing transformation, would also assist in local cultural work and draw materials from the protean life of the masses as the basis for cultural production. Following their publication in October 1943 in *Liberation Daily*, in November 1943 the CPC established the Talks' status as the key text for the further development of cultural policy through the document "Concerning a Decision to Implement the Party's Policy in Art and Culture." These decisions marked the institutionalization of the Talks as the basis of the Maoist cultural project, a position that they were to maintain into the 1970s.

Raising a new army of labor

The reorganization of cultural practice on the basis of Mao's Talks made itself visible above all at the level of literary form, in the way that texts came to stage the formation of new, collective temporalities of labor through the capacities of narrative. Among the authors whose work best stages this reorganization of narrative time is Liu Qing, who subsequently emerged as one of the central authors of the socialist period, not least through his epic *The Creators*. In the period immediately prior to the Talks, however, Liu Qing's texts are distinguished precisely by their fidelity to the May Fourth tradition and its narrative devices. This is true especially of his work "In the Home Village" (1942), which, having been published in the literary journal *Spring Rain* in 1942 just as Mao's Talks unfolded, marks a limit case of the May Fourth paradigm of writing. The title of the text provides an echo of Lu Xun's "Hometown," yet, at the level of narrative form and content, the proximate textual reference for Liu Qing's story is undoubtedly Lu Xun's "New Year's Sacrifice." Like that earlier and more famous story, Liu Qing's "In the Home Village" is also organized around the event of the return on the part of an I-narrator who is comparatively well educated and serves as the center through which the events of the narrative are processed. Crucially, the opening paragraph inaugurates a temporality that structures the narrative as a whole, consisting not merely of the act of return, but a return after a prolonged absence as marked by the incorporation of the village into the border region: "Several days before the New Year, it was with a heart approaching curiosity that I returned to my hometown. This was my first time returning since the village had been incorporated into the border region; and it had been a whole ten years since I had spent the new year in my hometown."[27]

The "curiosity" that the I-narrator protagonist articulates as their emotional basis for the act of return is quickly explained in terms of the imagined transformations that the village might have undergone since its incorporation into the border region, yet this imaginary is quickly frustrated when it emerges that—with the exception of "some slogans about public grain and elections daubed in wonky script on the door to the temple"—the village in fact "showed little difference compared to the previous time that I was there."[28] In these terms, through the temporal staging of the narrative in its opening paragraph, combined with the absence of visual signs of change, the narrative establishes itself in terms that render the possibility of a radical future hard to conceive. The absence of the future comes quickly to be actualized around a poorer villager, Old Seven, who serves as the motivating figure for the remainder of the text. The emergence of Old Seven—who, while born as the seventh son of a landlord family, has fallen into penury—takes place through a series of discussions that the narrator enjoys with their immediate family shortly after their arrival. While the protagonist's older uncle insists that there has been an improvement in the base-level living conditions of the village, a younger uncle interjects. The fragment of dialogue thereby gives way to a movement into the internal consciousness of the I-narrator in the form of a subjective analepsis that draws the narrative back in time to their previous encounter with the village:

"It's good," I said, "that everyone is able to get by now, in the village."
"Well" exclaimed my Third Uncle in laughter, who was smoking his pipe in the shadows, as if he had suddenly thought of something funny, "Old Seven still has a pretty rough time of it, you should get a look at his pitiable face . . ."
At that moment, an old person, with a sparse yellow beard, a dirty hat revealing hair that had not been cut for a long time, wearing clothes that had been repeatedly patched and yet which still appeared split at the seams, staggering along, suddenly flashed into my mind. "Ah, Fourth Master has returned." This old person, resembling a beggar, called out to me, and yet

because many of his teeth had fallen out, he always stumbled over certain words, pronouncing "zhe" as "de," and "gao" as "dao." "You've been out of the village for some time, surely you've gone up in the world? Ha, ha . . ." And like this, there followed a great deal of coughing and spluttering, and after wiping down the tears brought about by this coughing with the sleeve of his jacket, he would mutter to himself "I'm old, old . . ." and then slowly, gently sit my side, exchanging some idle chat, taking his leave only after having eaten his fill at my house.[29]

The relevance of this passage lies in the arrangement of time, whereby the comments of Third Uncle provide the basis for a wholly subjective analepsis in reference to the previous occasion on which the I-narrator returned to their village. In fact, the use of subjective analepsis emerges in this text as the primary narrative strategy, in which the narrator is drawn into long reveries, which has the additional effect of slowing down the pace of events in the actual narrative present. These analepses are themselves most often the result of Old Seven being mentioned by others, such that Old Seven is constantly invoked as the object of discourse. The narrator almost obsessively invokes the fragmented memories of Old Seven, including the disclosure that "the last time that I came back from the provincial city, because I hadn't arrived quite as late as I had on this occasion, he came over right away on that day to see me, and only left after dinner"[30]. Yet further back in time, the protagonist's earliest knowledge of Old Seven is said to arise from their grandmother, who admonished him to beware of Old Seven as a cautionary tale of the decline of a landlord family, only for the I-narrator to emphasize the fragmentary character of these childhood memories, noting that "from the landlord Chen Dengbao to his son Old Seven, there had been a series of twisting changes, but at that time I had been a kid playing around at home, without understanding any of those things, and then when I grew up I left the village to go to school, so that now, with someone mentioning Old Seven, I only had some fragmented, murky memories."[31] There follows several pages of dense description both of the backstory of Old Seven as a son of the previous landlord family of the village, as well as descriptions of iterative narrative events consisting of the various ruses by which Old Seven gains food from others without going so far as to degrade themselves to the level of a straightforward beggar, all being ascribed to the fragmented recollections of the I-narrator: "in my memory, Old Seven was always staggering around the village bent at the waist, going from this house to that house." Only following these several pages of description, all of which fall into the subjective analepsis of the I-narrator, does the time of the narrative return to the present scene constituted by the I-narrator and their assembled family and the context of their most recent return home. It is therefore the individual psyche and memory of this I-narrator that organizes the narrative with reference to different time frames, marked explicitly when the I-narrator comments to themselves that "Third Uncle having casually mentioned him in conversation made my memories about him suddenly rush to the surface. I had originally quite forgotten this old man. Returning home, I had asked after quite a number of people, just like a child, but I hadn't thought at all about him."[32]

Crucially, across these extended pages of reverie, Old Seven remains consistently absent from the actual narrative present, and in fact does so across the larger part of the narrative, being only spoken of, or emerging in the memory of the protagonist. He functions, therefore, as a provocation to memory, the mere mention of whom provides the pretext for falling back into the past, whether the previous visit of the protagonist, or their childhood memories. Even when the I-narrator's brother informs them at length of a happier instance of a previous rural proletarian who has managed to acquire their own land, Old Seven cannot help but reemerge, and again in the form of a present absence, whose real person remains thus far a specter of the lingering force of the past in the present: "yet despite myself I fell into a deep silence, having called to mind that 'pathetic landlord' Old Seven; because, having turned a corner, we had to pass by the road in front of his dilapidated old hovel. Old Seven was not, in fact, at home." There is, here, a formal parallel with Lu Xun's own "Hometown," where the extended memorialization of Runtu also precedes and anticipates their emergence in the narrative present, but with this anticipation in Liu Qing's text being much longer as compared to Lu Xun's relative economy in this regard. The occasion of the eventual meeting—given shortly after the I-narrator passes by their house and comes across a wretched figure on the threshing ground—between the I-narrator and Old Seven is given in terms that reinforce the pathos of Old Seven as that singular figure who has as of yet failed to "get by" in the village. and which in turn provokes a failure of communication on the part of the I-narrator: "In this wretched atmosphere I felt an overwhelming spiritual pressure. Although I had a certain amount of pity for him, there were no appropriate words that I could say. What's more, some other people saw that I was chatting to Old Seven, and came over, and how could that not make me even more ill at ease?"[33]

The conversion of the encounter with Old Seven into a moment of self-pathos on the part of the I-narrator and the failure of communication between the two narrative figures dramatizes the formal narrative structure of the entire text, based as it is on the psychic interiority and fraught subjectivity of its narrator, one that, as we have seen, also marks the organizing principle behind the temporality of the narrative, namely through the use of subjective analepsis. The psychological drawing-back into the past embodied by this temporality persists even at this scene of present meeting, as when the I-narrator recalls upon witnessing Old Seven's wretched state that "I remembered that on previous occasions when he was also unable to pass the new year, he would come to us seeking help, and on those past occasions we had given him some millet, some vegetables and sweet potato as an act of generosity. I wondered to myself whether this was also what he wanted at that moment."[34]

The brief emergence of Old Seven in the narrative present at this juncture is followed by his yet again becoming absent, which leads the I-narrator to ponder, in the midst of family gatherings, why he does not come seeking food: "at this moment, I thought to myself that Old Seven had not come to my home during these few days. Knowing as I did about his past conduct, I had assumed that he would indeed come."[35] The explanation for Old Seven's renewed absence and the ultimate, tragic denouement of the story comes with the news of his death from suicide, told to the I-narrator by his younger uncle:

> As I came out of the latrine, I saw my Fifth Uncle, who lived in the same courtyard as us, coming back after having picked up manure in the village, his felt cap covering his ears and brow, only exposing a small part, and his moustache beneath his nose showing some shards of frost. When he saw me, he told me in a strange tone: Old Seven had already croaked. He said that last night there had still been some people who had seen him go back to his hovel after "doing the rounds," and so people could not believe he had actually died, thinking it was someone making a joke. Therefore, Fifth Uncle said, he had seen a group of people crowding round Old Seven's hovel that morning. "Basically," Fifth Uncle said, "Old Seven didn't see any way to keep on living, and so he hanged himself."[36]

This denouement is followed by a tragicomic funeral service and the I-narrator's departure from the village. The temporal duration encompassed by the narrative, then, lasts only across the course of the New Year, and within that duration, Old Seven makes only a single fleeting appearance. His central role in the narrative, however, emerges through a combination of extensive subjective analepses on the part of the narrator, and his being spoken of through a combination of mockery and gossip on the part of the collective villagers. Insofar as Old Seven is that figure who constantly reemerges as a figure of the discourse of others, so too does he register a narrative temporality that threatens to constantly fall backward in time, foreclosing any narrative orientation toward the future. In much the same way, he, as a wholly isolated figure in the village, also dramatizes the ways that the I-narrator has themselves become a figure apart from the village community as a whole, due to their prolonged absence and experience of education. The final line of the story—"as I left my beautiful hometown, it gradually grew distant; yet from time to time I still looked backward, looking with affection on the landscape, the trees and the people"[37]—can, in this context, only be read as an ironic gesture.

In formal terms, therefore, through the use of an intellectual I-narrator, the narrative trope of a return to the native place, constant subjective analepsis, and the absence of a forward, future-oriented temporality, "In the Home Village" stages the limits of the kinds of narrative practices that had comprised the May Fourth tradition and which the Yan'an period sought to overcome. With the conclusion of the post-talks period of rectification in February 1943, therefore, Liu Qing was dispatched to Mizhi County to serve as the secretary at the village government level. He described this shift as an abnegation of his previous mode of work:

> In February of 1943, the organization decided that party culture workers should enter into real work among the workers, peasants, and soldiers, thereby bringing an end to the previous style of work in which we had planned to spend long times in literary organizations, except for taking some short trips, where we would collect some impressions in the manner of guests, before returning to add some "imagination," and then prepare a plan to write up these impressions. In these sorts of organizations, there were people to collect water and clean the floors, prepare budgets and dispatch materials, so it was possible to discuss a plan for half a year, without even beginning to write; or even if you ended up writing ten thousand characters, it didn't matter.[38]

The integration of Liu Qing into the post-talks conjuncture was accompanied by a radical shift in textual form, consisting in the first place of an abandonment of the literary as such in favor of the investigation of social conditions at the base as part of his role as a village secretary. Liu Qing's report, published in *Liberation Daily* under the title "Experience in Leading Labor Exchange Teams" in March 1945, marked not only the displacement of its writer from the privileged conditions that had existed before Mao's Talks but also the ways that the tasks of cultural production were integrated into the demand for the production of new social forms of production. The "labor-exchange team" 变工 that underpinned Liu Qing's report had, by 1946, already gained the recognition of Mao as the privileged form of incipient rural cooperative labor that would allow peasants to enter into short-term cooperative organizations during the busiest parts of the agricultural calendar. Mao's 1943 talk "Get Organized!" provided a new set of insights in the problem of reorganizing peasant labor. In this speech, delivered in November 1943, Mao appealed to peasants to undertake the transformation of their production relations: "Among the peasant masses a system of individual economy has prevailed for thousands of years, with each family or household forming a productive unit. This scattered, individual form of production is the economic foundation of feudal rule and keeps the peasants in perpetual poverty. The only way to change it is gradual collectivization, and the only way to bring about collectivization, according to Lenin, is through cooperatives."[39]

To "get organized" meant taking the first steps toward a transformation in the social relations of labor, one that would, in Mao's terms, enable the formation of a new "army of labor."[40] In view of the specifically nonsocialist character of the political project that the party was pursuing in Yan'an, theorized as the new-democratic stage of a prolonged revolutionary process, it would be necessary, Mao said, to develop cooperative forms of labor "based on an individual economy (on private property)," that is, without yet violating the central place of private property and commodity production.[41] The basis of the strategy that emerged over 1943 and which was given formal sanction by Mao's speech rested on the use and development of forms of cooperative labor already present as part of the lifeworld of the peasantry in the base area.[42] The possibility that these forms provided was consistently theorized in terms of the Marxist category of labor power, whereby cooperative forms would come to engender a new, collective mode of labor power whose capacities exceeded its dispersed, atomized components. The superior productive capacities of collective labor lay, to a large extent, in the way it also marked the transition from a wholly private, individuated temporality, to a collective or social temporality based on the self-supervision over its constituent members. The call for "organization" advanced by Mao, then, was nothing less than a demand for the reorganization of *time*, in which time becomes social. The editorial "Organize Labor Power" stated explicitly that "in farming, the most important thing is 'not to violate the agricultural calendar.' Whether you plant early or late, there will be different results, and so too with harvesting. It is difficult to avoid 'violating' by relying only on atomized and dispersed labor. But with labor mutual aid, things are quite different."[43]

The specifically temporal dimension of the construction of new social relations and modes of labor power recurred elsewhere. In "Labor Mutual Aid in the Shan-Gan-Ning Border Region," the author argued that the rhythmic temporality of agricultural labor, based around the variation of the seasons and the need to perform particular tasks at specific times, demonstrated the advantages of collective labor: "In the case of collective labor, everyone will feel that with so many people laboring together at the same time there is a definite need to grasp time closely, such that, whereas when you previously had one person working it wasn't so important if they wasted some time, this isn't possible with a lot of people."[44]

Furthermore, these authors enthused, "when someone works on their own, there is no specified length of time for rest, but with collective labor there are people who take responsibility [for this matter], so that the time for rest is reduced." Altogether, "the result of mutual aid in labor is that people get going early, come back late, reduce their time spend resting, reduce the time spent traveling, reduce their neglect of work, and in actual fact they can prolong the amount of effective labor time."[45] At the heart of these and other texts was the problem of how to forge the otherwise fragmentary character of peasant labor into a collective body of *labor power*. It is also precisely this problem that underpinned Liu Qing's own 1945 report, above all in the form of how to render different instances of individual labor power commensurate with one another in the organization of labor brigades, recognizing that "different instances of labor power 劳动力 differ in their capacity, which can easily result in problems surrounding the calculation of work."[46] Liu's involvement in work at the base in the furthering of mutual aid, then, discloses the tensions and contradictions that would recur in the process of building new relations of labor, namely, the uneasy relationship between the expanded productive powers of collective labor on the one hand and its disciplinary function on the other, as well as the related problem of how to render different bodies of labor power commensurable or comparable with one another. This central problem, emerging as it did from the quest for new social forms of labor, provided the impetus for Liu Qing's resumption of fictional writing and the search for new practices of narration which might stage, in temporal terms, the shift to a collective mode of labor power. This meant locating a new language, or, in Kai Feng's formulation, new methods of writing, to narrate the transformation of social relations among peasants.

Liu Qing's post-talks novel *A Record of Sowing Grain* (1947) was in fact derived precisely from the experience of real-world investigation that he introduced in his 1945 report, being concerned with the protracted process of organizing labor-exchange teams in the village community to which Liu Qing had been dispatched as secretary, including the challenges of negotiating between the complexities of family disagreements, personal animosities, and class divisions. Liu's novel marks that process of "working-up," whereby participation in labor would be transmuted into narrative form. The arresting opening of the novel immediately foregrounds the problem of time in the form of a series of temporal incompatibilities between a major character, Wang Kejian, and both his wife and the demands of the household, and other cadres in the village. Wang Kejian is late coming home for the midday meal, much to the consternation of his wife. Whereas in the middle of the day all the other male peasants have returned home to eat, Kejian's wife suffers the ignominy of his whereabouts remaining unknown: "this wife of Wang Kejian kept raising up her arms, and going outside to take a look, taking quick but minute steps on her ancient pair of bound feet. As the time bore on, she went over to the door ever more frequently."[47] The problem of lateness and temporal dysfunction resulting from Wang Kejian not having yet returned from the fields, its reason being as of yet unknown to the reader, is doubled by the fact that Wang Kejian also seems to be absconding from his public responsibilities. When young students enquire with Wang Kejian's wife about whether he has yet returned home, the student reports: "'Our teacher said that they really can't wait. He and "peasant association" have already gone ahead, and they asked that when he gets back, he should go to the village administration as soon as possible to start the meeting.' Having recited the message and completed their task, the two students merrily skipped back to school."[48]

Within this opening chapter, the initial scene is delivered in terms strictly focalized around Wang Kejian's wife, but the narrative subsequently withdraws from its immediate context to give the reader a justification for Wang Kejian's lateness, namely that he refuses to take part in labor-exchange teams, above all because of his attachment to his donkey, which, being regularly pregnant, he refuses to share with other villagers, even while the speed of the donkey slows down his pace of labor. The result is the need for an extension of the time in labor to make up for a relative absence of intensity in order that Wang Kejian can match the output of peasants working collectively: "He could, of course, have planted rather less and then come back earlier, but he was a stubborn fellow, he swore that he wanted to match the labor-exchange teams, so every day he planted a *shang*, using it to prove that even if he wasn't a member of a labor-exchange team, he planted the same as the others! The result, then, was that he often returned home significantly after midday."[49] Subsequent to this summary, the return to the narrative present—the scene of agonizing waiting on the part of Wang Kejian's wife—coincides with Wang Kejian's return home, and then a subsequent shift in narrative focalization to Wang Kejian himself, evoked when he is reminded of the meeting that he has failed to attend, via a minor analepsis:

> The previous day he had already been told of the meeting. Although the letter of the village government was at the school, but the chairman of the peasant association had told him in person, and when his younger son had come back from school, so too had he passed on the reminder from the teacher. But, having slept a night, any memory of this had vanished along with his bodily fatigue. When he went to the field and took his tools in hand, he wouldn't think of anything else. When his eyes were fixed on the moist soil that turned over with the ease of water, it was as if the rest of the world didn't exist for him.[50]

The dramatic opening of the novel inaugurates the central thematic concerns to which the text is addressed, namely how an atomized mode of labor generates temporal disjunctures that can only be remedied by a collective organization of labor power. Yet so too does this opening also generate this problem in formal terms. The character introduction of Wang Kejian, who remains the primary object of social critique and farce, in the opening chapter anticipates the replication of the same formal device in the chapters that follow, in that the first series of chapters operate according to a series of analepses, in which the narrator follows the trajectory of one individual character up to the time of the meeting, accompanied by a summary introduction of that character's backstory, only, in the following chapter, to break off and introduce another character up to the time of the same narrative moment. This narrative strategy serves as a device with an obvious rationale insofar as it produces an array of characters who will, in various ways, remain central to the larger narrative that follows, but so too does it encompass a distinct temporal form in the way the meeting—the meeting for which Wang Kejian is late—comes to comprise a present moment beyond which the narrative cannot as of yet proceed, due to the absence of a shared future horizon that can unite all the characters and the village as a whole. The characters so introduced are referred to here and throughout the novel primarily by their formal positions in the village. Just as Wang Kejian is referred to as "administrator," then, so too is Wang Jiafu "peasant association," Wang Cunqi "model," and Zhao Deming, the "teacher."

Of these, Zhao Deming invokes a suggestive parallel with Wang Kejian insofar as he also approximates a figure of farce in the novel, albeit given in terms relating to his role as an intellectual. Having been dispatched to the village to work as a school teacher, Zhao's commitment to inaugurating a new collective temporality in the village is invoked by his relation to the crucial narrative trope and structuring device of the village bell, which, having formerly been deployed only in a religious context, periodically emerges throughout the narrative as a reminder of the scope of social transformations in the life of the village. The deployment of the bell to organize collective meetings and structure production is ascribed to Zhao Deming in the form of an analepsis relating to previous attempts to reorganize the village: "In order to get each family to work as one on the land, Zhao had put forward a proposal, which, having gone through a furious discussion, finally decided that the bell which had previously been kept in the almost collapsed spirit official temple would be moved to the village, and so was a system of keeping time established."[51]

Yet, it is revealed, the introduction of such a coordinated device did not itself produce a transformation in the temporality of the village, with work teams remaining in an unstable state. The farcical element of Zhao Deming's introduction comes from the way that his enthusiasm in the village also poses the problem of writing, being the only member of the village possessed of the capacity to write. He therefore functions in the narrative as a metaliterary device, capable of drawing attention to the problem of writing and language as such. Directly after his role in the introduction of the bell as a new timekeeping device has been described in the mode of an analepsis, a return to the narrative present, with Zhao Deming waiting for the convening of the meeting, constructs his role in a more humorous, albeit negative capacity:

> He again took out from his drawer the two copies of the Border Region Mass News that he had brought back from the county government. For the third time, the newspaper had carried a report of his, and he had written about the process of setting up the bell system in Wang village. He had originally written in very detailed terms: how the spirit official temple had been about to collapse, how the spirit medium Wang Cungui had already been reformed, how the knives that had been used to summon spirits had been turned into agricultural implements, how the labor exchange team had felt the inconvenience of the time spent preparing food in each home being out of alignment, and how he had put forward ideas, how the old fogies had resisted him, how the masses had supported him, and how finally, with the bell, there had been a good response, all of this he had written in exacting detail. Yet when his report was published, half of it had been edited away, and his report had been turned into a simple notice.[52]

The shift between an initial narrative report, in which the incorporation of the bell into a new temporality is described in brief terms, with only the amount of information necessary for narrative context provided, compared to the written account generated by Zhao Deming and summarized from his perspective, serves a function within the narrative in the way it gestures toward the problem of the language of writing itself, whereby the mockery of Zhao Deming contained in this passage revolves around his continued pursuit of a mode of writing that can enhance his own cultural authority. The practice of editing that is a cause of such disappointment of Zhao Deming thereby emerges as the practice by which language can be wrested away from the self-regard of intellectuals and pressed into the demands of a revolutionary project. Across the characters who comprise the core leadership of the village, then, Wang Kejian and Zhao Deming emerge as the primary objects of farce in the novel, each corresponding to a form of labor, agricultural or intellectual, that remains stubbornly individuated. The serial introduction of these characters in the opening chapter is followed by the inauguration of the narrative proper when Wang Kejian finally arrives at the meeting. There is, in this respect, a homology between waiting at the level of content, whereby Zhao Deming and others are made to wait, and the formal construction of the narrative itself, whereby the narrative must await the serial introduction of its protagonists before it can proceed properly.

The meeting itself, therefore, takes on the role of an attempt at a new beginning, with respect both to the social organization of the village and the narrative itself. Yet the role of the meeting as a leaping-off point is upset by moments of utter farce, which in turn provide the basis for further analepses in which the narrative is drawn back into the past. When, for example, Wang Kejian displays misgivings about speaking on the recent higher-level directives, the narrative immediately falls into an analepsis concerning his embarrassment at a county-level meeting the month prior:

> There was plenty of time allocated for him on the schedule, and the district propaganda chief sat with him during meetings, accompanied him during eating and sleeping, and spent night and day giving him instruction on many occasions. He even asked Wang Kejian to do a practice run with him more than once, in order that he would be able to win glory for the work in the district. Yet, when Wang Kejian finally ascended to the podium, his face was completely red, his legs shook violently, as if he was drunk, so that he could not even keep still.[53]

The close association between the formal use of analepsis and the farcical treatment of Wang Kejian from this point onward foreshadows his role in the narrative as he who will ultimately disturb the commitment to the inauguration of new temporalities in the sphere of social relations. The meeting ends with the decision to convene a village-wide assembly in order that peasants can be mobilized to take part in work teams, whereby they will agree on a shared day to undertake planting, and the children being granted holiday from school at the same time to assist with agricultural labor. Yet in the chapter immediately following this initial, cadre-level meeting, there is a dramatic refocalization around Wang Kejian himself, whereby Wang Kejian already resolves, in tandem with his wife, not to take part in collective work-team planting but instead to persist in using the labor of his extended family without regard for any collective temporality: "So, he made up his mind: he wouldn't take part in any work team! He had seen the results of their discussion, and how they couldn't get anything good from organizing; at least they had followed Wang Jiafu's way of doing things, if they had followed the proposal of the teacher, then things would have been even worse."[54]

Therefore, "he resolved that he would find a reason to start planting before the date decided by the whole of the village. There wasn't much time left before that date, so he would say, politely 'You go off and have your work teams, I don't need any work team.'"[55] From this moment henceforth, Wang Kejian's persistence in an individual mode of production creates the effect of a dramatic irony, in which his irresolution is known to the reader but not to the more optimistic village cadres. The discrepancy in knowledge on the part of the reader in relation to Wang Kejian's intentions and the enthusiasm of the cadres, even in the face of a relative lack of activism on the part of the other villagers, is the consequence in the shifts of focalization that occur across the novel, beginning with the close focalization around Wang Kejian himself immediately after the initial cadre meeting. Much of Liu Qing's skill in the chapters that follow consists in the expansion of this technique, where the shift in focalization allows for the recounting of the trajectories of one or more of the cadre characters in the narrative, only for that narrative trajectory to reencounter eventually the central story of Wang Kejian, with the reader benefiting from the knowledge that accompanies the various shifts in focalization. For example, the larger part of chapter 6 is concerned with the efforts on the part of Wang Jiafu to get the aid teams in order in preparation for planting. At the end of this episode, however, Wang Jiafu and another villager catch sight of Wang Kejian from afar, in a moment of clear focalization:

> As they reached the top of the hill, they turned around to take a look, the whole of Wang Village arrayed before them. The village was beginning a day of loneliness beneath the red glare of the sun. Suddenly, Mao Dan discovered that Wang Kejian was leading his donkey out of the main gate of his house, the donkey laden with a red mattress, and its owner wearing his outfit for visiting relatives, one hand holding a whip, the other leading the donkey down the ridge. "Look, look," said Mao Dan, "where is the administrator going off to?"[56]

The significance of this sighting is already known to the reader on account of the previous chapter, which concludes with the reader having learned of Wang Kejian's plan to recruit his relatives to assist in the planting outside of the organizational patterns of the aid team. The reliance on familial labor marks not only the collapse of any village-wide collective temporality but also a falling back into a familial-patriarchal mode of labor. In these terms, the crisscrossing of narrative trajectories as produced through skillful shifts in focalization produce an image of totality and ironic anticipation, whereby the reader is granted advance knowledge of the likely failure of the village-wide campaign to form aid teams while that knowledge is denied to any individual characters. This failure is intimated, however, by the fact that when the village-wide meeting is convened, as that event which is supposed to inaugurate a collective temporality, it can only descend into farce and is described as such, with villagers dragooned into agreement despite being asleep:

> When the counting was done, it turned out that around one hundred people had turned up to the meeting. Among them, there were quite a few who had been leaning against the wall sleeping but had just been awoken. Wang Cungao with his bad eyes pretty much became deaf and mute as soon as it got dark, so that it was as if he hadn't even come, little Lazybones and Lanzhu

were apparently sleeping quite peacefully next to the mouth of the latrine. The group leader thought that to wake them up would put them in a bad mood, so he said that they had already given their agreement in the fields that day, there would be no point in forcing them to raise their hands...[57]

In view of the lurking probability of Wang Kejian's refusal to form an aid team, and the elements of farce that attach to even putatively collective, future-oriented gatherings by the villagers, the larger part of the novel is marked by an almost achingly slow narrative temporality, consisting of attempts by the activist cadres to forge work teams that will be acceptable to their participants, and Wang Kejian's wavering over whether to agree to a village-wide planting schedule. It is worth pointing out, here, that the story time of the novel—the actual temporal extent of the events described, not taking into account analepses relating to events prior to the beginning of the narrative—is short, encompassing a matter of weeks for a novel of this length, as contemporary critics were closely aware.[58] The urge to accelerate the pace of the social transformations and the narrative itself becomes visible at yet a further cadre meeting, in which the head of the peasant association, Wang Jiafu, enters into flights of fantasy as to what the future might bring: "There then naturally arose in his mind a scene of soldiers, schools and official bodies working together. The great mass of the people would excavate the ground on the mountains, and would rest together, with their hoes flying wildly on the air, and thus would the earth beneath their feet rapidly change color, from light gray to dark brown, yes, before long just this sort of scene would appear amid the mountains of Wang Family Village!"[59]

The emergence of this kind of dream-image marks a device that is to reappear in subsequent rural narratives, such as Zhao Shuli's more famous *San Li Wan*, in which the literal imagining of the future village through a painting provides the villagers with the imaginative possibility of a vastly transformed social existence. Yet here, in view of the epistemological gap that separates the reader from these protagonists, it underscores the temporal disjuncture between the future-oriented aspirations of the cadres, Wang Kejian's private misgivings, and the overall farcical character of the villagers. This is also a formal, narrative problem insofar as it produces the need for a force that can overcome these otherwise separate temporalities and the accompanying slow narrative pace through a device that can force a reckoning, either through the progressive reorganization of the village or through a making-visible of the irreconcilability of the disparate aims of the varied villagers. Such a device, or in fact a set of such devices, do emerge in the form of forces that arise from beyond the village itself, first in the form of the eruption of conflict in the areas surrounding the border region, which, through the circulation of rumor in the villages, compels Wang Kejian, together with other recalcitrant elements in the village, to publicly begin their own planting schedule in violation of the collective planting on which the cadres have agreed up to this point. When Wang Kejian's rejection of the carefully wrought plans for village-wide labor organization is revealed to the villagers for the first time, having been known to the reader since the early stages of the novel, the consequence is a collapse in any semblance of village solidarity, which causes an angry outburst on the part of Zhao Deming: "He ran over to criticize the stupidity, selfishness and lack of organization of those who had broken the resolution [to collectively engage in planting], and all of the words which he knew to describe the backwardness of the peasantry were, at this point, applied to these sorts of people."[60]

The collapse of any possible temporality of collective labor, in these terms, not only is an impediment to the possibility of a development in the material conditions of village life but also marks a renewed bifurcation between the conditions of physical labor and the transformation of writing, as Zhao makes use of an unquoted language of peasant backwardness in order to demarcate the difference between himself and the unruly peasants, of whom Wang Kejian is the foremost exemplar. The peasants here comprise not a collective historical or narrative subject but rather a rabble, and therefore fall radically short of the ambitions envisaged by Wang Jiafu, given explicitly in the form of a collapse of any horizon of futurity, or a falling back into the present: "the sight that arose before him, far from being any future vision of a farm, was rather the prospect of the collapse of the planting teams." Yet the invocation of this device to impart dynamism to the narrative through the exposure of the precariousness of the aspirations toward collective labor produces, in turn, the need for a second, supplementary device that can restore order to the narrative and produce narrative closure. This supplementary device also emerges in the form of an external force in the modality of the district chief, who puts in place the conditions for Wang Kejian to be removed from his post, and the reorganization of the narrative on a stable, unified temporal basis. The actuality of this reorganization becomes visible at the end of the narrative through a new descriptive mode that renders what had hitherto been simply a set of dream-images comprehensible within the real fabric of rural life, enacting a labor pastoral that will reemerge in subsequent narratives as a crucial device for evoking a transformed social existence. Subsequent to the villagers once again agreeing to conduct labor on a unified basis, then: "[The peasants] had rolled their trousers up to above their knees, and were standing in the river water which lapped against their calves, and everywhere in the gully there were those caressing their hoes, and their hoe tips were making a striking metal sound as their struck against the rocks, forming a great ensemble across the village."[61]

This set of narrative images presents the peasants as having been unified on a common temporal basis, that is, according to a new rhythm, that is also the site of a concrete futurity, one no longer disconnected from the present. Within the ideological grammar of the novel, then, the resolution is a pleasing one. Yet the utterly tendentious means by which the novel first imparts narrative dynamism, and then brings about the resolution of its newly visible conflicts, in both cases relying on an external force, also demands its own diagnosis, which is to say that these formal weaknesses of the novel are at the same time indicative of problems of social form, namely whether the transformation of the countryside can take place solely on the basis of imminent forces at the village level. Yet, so too does the formal reliance on an "outside" device have as its complement, the problem of the "inside," which is to say how the domestic and its related practices of reproductive labor are dealt with. The novel begins, as we have seen, with a double instance of temporal disjuncture in which Wang Kejian returning home late to the midday meal is one part. Thereafter, the problem of domestic and familial labor periodically reemerges, not least in Wang Kejian's reliance on his extended family to rupture with the collective planting schedule of the village, and yet its persistence as a problem is evacuated by the end of the novel, within the terms of narrative resolution. At the level of content and form, the legibility of domestic labor would remain a challenge for socialist culture after this point, as well as the task of remaking "life."

To this extent, Liu Qing's text marks the difficulty and the possibility of remaking the novel as literary form adequate to a set of social demands that resisted the more familiar conventions of psychological narration and an individual protagonist. It is suggestive as a failed attempt to produce a narrative totality—failed, because achieving the collective forms of agriculture to which the novel aspires relies on an external device at one remove from the social world of the characters. Yet others would turn not toward totalization, but to the intimacies of the everyday in their attempts to address the transformation of social relations, and especially gendered dimensions of labor.

Her double life

The operationalization of Mao's Talks through the dispatch of writers to "enter into life," was, as Liu Qing's texts demonstrate, an experimental process, one bound up with a search for new narrative practices that were adequate to the task of intervening in the conditions of life that also served as the basis for the transformation of intellectuals. The irreducibility of Maoist cultural politics lay ultimately in the porousness of the very category of life itself, the exact scope of which was the site of ongoing elaboration. Not the least of these was how or whether "life" could encompass life-making in its relation to gendered forms of reproductive labor and the everyday, which is to say, the embodied substratum of the reproduction of the immediate conditions of life.

In this setting, there was no more attentive critic of the gendered tensions of the emergent revolutionary project than Ding Ling, who, in Yan'an and after, occupied an institutional locus directly opposed to that of Zhou Yang, with whom Ding Ling also experienced antagonistic personal relations. She did so, however, as a critic who inhabited the possibilities of the Maoist cultural vision. In the conjuncture immediately prior to the Talks, Ding Ling was already attentive to the complex entanglements between writing, labor and friendship as a political idiom, above all in a remarkable literary essay published in the journal *Spring Rain* as part of the same issue in which Liu Qing's short story had appeared, entitled "Remembering Xiao Hong Amidst Wind and Rain" (1942), which commemorated the death of Ding Ling's fellow writer and confidante. The larger part of this essay is given over to excavating the problem of "friendship," but here examined specifically in the form of the encounter between Ding Ling and Xiao Hong. Yet the introduction of this subject matter is itself preceded by a series of sustained interrogations of writing itself. With Xiao Hong having passed in January 1942, the text predates Mao's Talks, yet Ding Ling markedly anticipates much of the Maoist cultural project in the way she poses the problem of writing as a solipsistic condition that threatens to divorce the writer from conditions of sociality, at the same time as it imposes physical privations on the writer. She does so through a renewed emphasis on the physicality of writing, such that, being faced with a transformation in the "era," Ding Ling finds that "I set about writing, during the day, during the night, such that these arthritic arms of mine came to ache after having been placed on my table for too long, just as my trachoma-infected eyes became blurry after having written under a faint light."[62]

The physical pain of writing is here counterpoised to the force generated by revolutionary possibility, a force that becomes embodied through a new compulsion to write despite the physical difficulties of doing so: "I feel that within my body there is something colliding; it sustains me in my tiredness, it enables me to envisage the future, it makes me leap over the present, and it offers me peace, it encompasses truth and intelligence, it is the force within my life 生命, it is more beloved than the unworried youth of my younger years!"[63] The possibility of a renewed horizon of the future—"it enables me to envisage the future"—marks the close relation between Ding Ling's text and the formation of new temporal horizons of revolutionary cultural practice, and which enables the writer to persist despite the profoundly lonely dimensions of writing. The unstable relations between writing and revolutionary commitment emerge in Ding Ling's essay through her commemoration and memorialization of the previous revolutionary generation of the 1930s, emblematized by the great theorist of cultural popularization, Qu Qiubai 瞿秋白: "Yesterday I bitterly thought of [Qu] Qiubai, who spent so long amidst political life 政治生活, and yet was ultimately unable to thoroughly transform himself. His mode of double life 二重的生活 meant that, even at the moment of death, he could not avoid a certain complaint. I often rebuked him for his 'superfluousness,' and yet when I came to dwell on his history of internal struggles, I could not help but be moved, even if this was only a small part of the whole."[64]

The intrusion of the past into the present in a temporal doubling effect, narrated in the form of an almost involuntary memory on the part of the Ding Ling, has its own echo within her memory of Qu Qiubai through her extraordinary formulation of "double life." This formulation marks the difficulty of reconciling the different modes of life that impinge on the culture worker, namely, between political and creative life, or the collective life of the party versus the individuating effects of writing as a mode of life, for which Qu Qiubai's own favored trope of "superfluousness" marks a gap between these different modes of life. It may be surmised that Ding Ling's formulation of a "double life" was itself an adaptation of a formulation that Qu had himself deployed in his extended personal essay *Superfluous Words*, in which he diagnosed his condition as a "bifurcated personality" 两元化的人格 denoting his tragic incapacity to overcome the unevenness separating the life of writing and the life of revolutionary praxis. In this sense, between Qu Qiubai, Ding Ling, and Zhou Yang's observed distinction between the time of life and the time of writing, there pass a consistent set of concerns over how the time of writing comes to differentiate itself from the life of the collective, albeit, crucially, posed by Ding Ling through the distinct cultural form of the commemorative essay. Within its narrative logic, then, her commemoration of Qu Qiubai passes over into the subject matter of the essay proper, namely, the memorialization of Xiao Hong, the essay therefore being a double commemoration. To no less an extent than her treatment of Qu Qiubai, Ding Ling's evocation of Xiao Hong also bears the marks of the conjuncture of the Talks, namely in her orientation toward the language and political possibilities of friendship.

In terms formally consistent with the demand for intellectuals to embrace friendship with the masses, but here orientated toward the intimacy of friendship between two women, Ding Ling not only recalls the frequent moments of mutual care she enjoyed with Xiao Hong but also does so in terms that explicitly invoke a transgression of the narrow boundaries of the intellectual in favor of a new mode of radical collectivity. The recognition of Xiao Hong's premature death provides the conditions for a radical, gendered practice of friendship, as marking a partial antidote to the loneliness of writing. Ding Ling recalls of her departed friend, then, that "we were truly intimate with one another, from one to the other 彼此 we did not feel any hint of a reclusive character 孤僻的性格."⁶⁵ Her eventual knowledge of Xiao Hong's death and her distance from "female friends" 女性朋友 provides the impetus for an aspired rupture with the isolated conditions of an individual writerly consciousness in the wake of Xiao Hong's own tragic demise amid conditions of profound isolation:

> For anyone who is living in this kind of world, to have an additional true companion means to grow in strength, our responsibility lies not only in opening up the situation, or in pointing out light, but rather in creating light and beauty; if the soul of a human being can only be constrained within the narrow limits of the individual self 个体, then so too will it only ever suffer the infatuation of minor, individual achievements. We must make everyone capable of experiencing the pleasure of the sublime, and to make great sacrifices for this kind of pleasure.⁶⁶

The formulation of a "pleasure of the sublime" 崇高的享受 through an abnegation of the narrow authorial subject provides, here, a counterpoint to the otherwise persistent emphasis on bodily pain that characterizes Ding Ling's earlier treatment of writing. The memory of departed comrades maps onto Ding Ling's earlier invocation of the "force" of the historical present that can serve as a stimulus to the labor of writing in all its painful physicality: "I want to make use of this wind and rain, and tell of it to you, departed and living friends of mine. I want to press out 压榨 that remainder 余剩 of my life 生命 for your comfort and glory." The formulation of pressing out the remainder of life in this context assumes a double significance, being not only an aspiration to commit her writing practice for the sake of a collective project of emancipation supported by the memory of dead friends but also a response to the problem of superfluousness invoked by Qu Qiubai and repeated by Ding Ling, where the intimate force of gendered, revolutionary friendship can also minimize that gap between different modes of life that Qu, a male intellectual, found himself unable to transcend. The end of the essay, then, marks a recognition of female writers as comrades in labor: "Even if I should work solely for you, this is no bad thing, because you are laborers 劳动者 who have endured bitterness, and your ideals are true."⁶⁷

The stream of female friendship that runs throughout this brief but extraordinary essay underscores its links with Ding Ling's earlier, and more critical interventions, such as her famous "Thoughts on March 8." In its content if not its strict phraseology, that earlier essay also invokes the problem of "double life" but does so in a specifically feminist mode, by posing the contradiction between the life of communist militancy and the life of gendered norms demanded of intellectual women in Yan'an. Ding Ling's essay also points toward the different modalities that friendship might assume as a basis on which to overcome the challenge of a double life exemplified by Qu Qiubai. Having been written before Mao's Talks, "Amidst Wind and Rain" nonetheless appeared in the same issue of *Spring Rain* as a later essay dating from June 1942, entitled "My Views on the Problem of Stand." The connections and divergences between the essays therefore underscore Ding Ling's changing conception of her literary practice and the problem of friendship as she moved into the conjuncture brought about by the Talks. The basis of this theoretical text lies in its extension of Mao's understanding of the transition from one class to another to pose transformation that rested on the reworking and transformation of the most fundamental modes of embodied experience. It therefore also marks Ding Ling's departure from the trajectories mapped by both Xiao Hong and Qu Qiubai, who did not undergo the Maoist cultural project. For Ding Ling, drawing on Mao's categories, the concept of "feelings" marked that form of commitment that went beyond a merely theoretical understanding, without which theory could only become abstract and isolated from the social practice of life. In this vein, she argued that, with respect to the ideas that were reflected in literary works, "it is absolutely not possible to rely solely on our understanding 认识 or attempts, but is instead due to our consciousness, it is due to the coherence of theory and feelings 情感." Moreover, she wrote:

> In order to truly understand the feelings and ideas of the masses, if you want to write about the proletariat, it is absolutely necessary to live 生活 together with them; in order to transform yourself, and cast off all your old feelings and consciousness from the root, it is absolutely necessary to undergo a long period of tempering amidst the struggles and lives of the masses.... This is not just a matter of changing our [theoretical] conceptions, but of changing our feelings, to completely transform oneself as a person.[68]

The difficulty and sustained nature of the process Ding Ling described was given a specifically embodied character not only by the distinction between feeling and a purely theoretical knowledge, but also by the striking suggestion that the process of transformation among the masses was, in fact, a violent one, one that left its traces on the body. The intellectual undergoing transformation, Ding Ling said, must be prepared to undergo "hardship" 苦, a hardship that is "not visible, or easily expressible; it is rather a kind of tempering 磨练 that changes a person from one kind of person into another."[69] The exact contents of this tempering were as of yet unspecified except in terms of the general formula of entering into the life of the masses, but Ding Ling's language nonetheless underscores the extent to which the transformation of the intellectual was necessarily an embodied process. This also marks a conception of physicality and pain quite different from that of "Amidst Wind and Rain" insofar as in this later essay pain serves as the necessary condition for the transformation of the writer rather than solely a negative attribute of the lonely condition of writing. The two essays that appeared in the same issue of *Spring Rain*, then, differ from each other in generic characteristics, one being a largely theoretical response to Mao's Talks, the other a lyrical reflection on the death of a female friend, and yet they both orient themselves toward the radically affective dimensions of writing in terms that draw on the possibilities of Mao's cultural politics. In actual fact, the vocabulary of friendship was to remain central to Ding Ling's conception of writing, even in the later years of her life. Recalling the transformations wrought by Mao's Talks in 1982, in her essay "On Writing" she was able to reflect:

> I had never previously imagined that I could have bosom friends [among the masses], because my bosom friends 知己 were all writers, they still consisted of those of us on the mountaintop of the Resistance Association, where, with nothing to do, we would sit together and chat. The scope of our discussions, when I think back now, was very restricted, consisting only of the anguish of intellectuals! Our dissatisfaction with reality! We satirized this, satirized that. I expressed my feelings, you expressed yours, and thus did we derive happiness. But after going through the Forum, and with Chairman Mao's encouragement, I realized that there was no benefit to sticking in the same place. That was when I resolved: I would go to the masses.⁷⁰

In the context of Yan'an, Ding Ling was dispatched to the base significantly later than other intellectuals such as Liu Qing, on account of her extended involvement in the Rectification process as a party member with experience of imprisonment. When in May 1944 she was dispatched to the base, it was initially in order to seek the labor model Wu Manyou, who had achieved renown as part of a conference of labor models held in the direct aftermath of the Talks, in March 1943. Yet, at the insistence of the writer Kong Jue, who had already assumed a role at the base, Ding Ling turned instead to the village of Mata. This village marked the site at which Ding Ling was faced with the transformation of gendered relations of labor, which in turn conditioned her resumption of cultural practice, as Mata was one of the sites that had pursued the expansion of textile production. This was largely to do with the changes that emerged with respect to women's policy in the period after 1943, and the emphasis given to home-based weaving as a strategy for mobilizing women. In particular, February 1943 marked the promulgation of the Decision of the Central Committee of the Chinese Communist Party Concerning the Present Direction of Women's Work in Anti-Japanese Base Areas.

The resolution criticized the previous direction of women's work as lacking a "mass perspective," and for having failed to "grasp that the mobilization of women to take part in production is the most central link in protecting women's own interests."[71] In these terms, the resolution called for a reevaluation of women's work on the basis of their participation in production, and the formation of new, collective spaces beyond the individual household: "[Cadres] must pursue organization on the basis of the needs of the women masses, and correct our previous methods of organization that were merely formal and without substance, such that we should organize women by means of cooperative production and different kinds of methods of production (such as small weaving groups and so on). These kinds of organizations should become the base organizations of the Women's Association or the Salvation Association, rather than being some empty bodies or apparatuses that have the name without the substance."[72]

The journalistic accounts that emerged in this context stressed how the expansion of weaving in particular would also enable the effective mobilization of women (and female labor power). This was true in the way women's textile labor shifted from being for the purpose of immediate use to being part of an emergent commodity economy. In a reportage text entitled "A Page in the History of Weaving Women" and published at the same time as the February 1943 policy announcement, reporter Mo Ai reported that the advantage of weaving was that it could preserve the home-based structure of women's textile weaving and at the same time draw women into a system of market exchange based on the selling of their yarn, that is, production of exchange values, whereas previously spinning might have been solely for immediate and personal use, that is, use value. In these terms, the exchange relations in which women became engaged amounted to a mediated wage-relation, which therefore marked a transformation in the status of labor power. Mo Ai described as one of several "typical" instances of women weavers, the case of the wife of one Zhao Wanshan, of whom, it is reported:

> In the depths of the night, in [the village of] Collapsed Autumn Tree, when all is quiet and the lamps have been extinguished, there is only one home from which a feeble light still shines, and inside there is a woman of more than twenty years old. She is the wife of the almost semi-crippled often-sick Zhao Wanshan, her husband and child of seven years old are all sound asleep, but she, sitting alone besides her wheel, is spinning away the long night. Having learned for just a month, her skill is exceptional. Every month she spins seven *jin*, and in the second half of last year she spun more than forty *jin*, so that not only did she assist the eating expenses of the whole family, last year she also remade their home by using the 1,200 *kuai* she had accumulated from her remaining ten *jin*.[73]

The incorporation of female labor into circuits of exchange value extended, moreover, to the reorganization of women's labor time, insofar as hitherto "frivolous" uses of time became available for production. With reference to the period before the introduction of household spinning, Mo Ai said, with more than a little misogyny, that "more than half of the free time of the women was wasted away on 'calling on friends' or 'gossip.'"[74] In a separate report entitled "The Experience of Developing Women's Weaving in Yan'an Southern District," Lu Zhi similarly commented with reference to the second township of the district that "as for the women, apart from taking care of household tasks and sending food to their menfolk during the busy agricultural season, and drawing water and so on, they do not have any other forms of work."[75] It is because of the economic benefits that households can derive from spinning labor, Mo Ai said, that "the vast majority of women in the district, whether they be old, young women or small children, all use every second of their free time to take part in the textile battle front." In the larger part of the year, "for those women who generally do not take part in agrarian primary labor, apart from cooking, collecting water, other daily tasks, and some needlework, the rest of their time can all be used for spinning."[76]

At issue here is the way that these and other reports acknowledge the pressures of domestic labor, only to pass over these tasks by failing to grapple with them as meaningful labor, positing women as having reserves of free time that can be invested in production. The disparagement of peasant women's domestic labor as, at best, secondary, generated as its corollary the notion of women as a body of surplus labor that could be drawn into production as part of the process of surplus accumulation. In other words, the mobilization of female labor posed the question of how to theorize "life" with respect to forms of activity not easily recognizable within the frame of collective production outside the home.

In this context of this policy reorientation, Ding Ling's "Assorted Recollections Over Three Days" (1945) marked her resumption of writing practice as a result of being dispatched to Mata, as well as an attempt to intervene amid the problems presented by women's labor, and the neglect of women's reproductive time in broader debates.[77] In formal terms, Ding Ling's text marks a direct contrast with Liu Qing's response to the post-talks conjuncture. Whereas the reconfiguration of Liu Qing's writing took the form of an abnegation of the I-narrator in favor of a drive toward totality, Ding Ling's reportage takes advantage of the position afforded by an I-narrator, ostensibly equal to Ding Ling herself, to investigate the recalibration of affective relations with the masses. The text is devoted to the three days spent by Ding Ling and other culture workers at Mata. As distinct from her other more famous reportage texts from this period, such as "Tian Baolin," concerned with an eponymous labor hero, "Assorted Recollections" does not focus on a singular figure but rather seeks to convey the social changes underway in a remote settlement and the new, affective relations that emerge between Ding Ling as the assumed narrator and the women of this village community. In this respect, this text offers a complex relation with Ding Ling's earlier recollection of Xiao Hong, in that it seeks to expand the bounds of gendered friendship beyond the immediate relation between two intellectuals, and does so crucially, on the basis of labor, consisting above all of the images of weaving labor that also formed a key part of the transformation of social relations in Yan'an following the Talks.

The point of entry for this expanded conception of friendship therefore lies in Ding Ling taking up residence in the house of the village head. Throughout this opening segment, and much of the narrative that follows, the village head functions as the crucial mediator for Ding Ling's introduction to other figures within the village. This is, for example, true of the unnamed wife of the village head, who is described in moving terms as she and Ding Ling share a room. When a fellow villager comes early in the morning to rouse her husband to labor, her response and intimate bodily presence are described as follows: "'Don't bother calling, he got up some time ago, we have a comrade staying with us.' The wife of the village head who slept by my side raised her head out of the coverlet, and I felt that her shape was like that of a small child."[78] Ding Ling continues:

> I could not see her, but could hear her voice, so I could imagine that she was certainly wearing a bashful smile. I felt sorry for this crippled old lady, so I began to talk with her about certain family matters. It turned out that she was lame, but I didn't know whether she had caught some illness and become wizened as a result, or whether she had been this way since she was young. None of her four limbs were straight, and her joint bones protruded on her slim arms, fingers and legs, like the joints in a willow tree. Her hair was yellow, dry and sparse, but this wasn't on account of her age, it had always been so. She wasn't lively in her movements, only being able to toil with great difficulty, so instead she sat alone the whole day mending shoes, spinning thread, with people only very rarely coming to chat with her.[79]

The transition from an initially aural mode of encounter with this figure to a description of her physical attributes produces a vision of a laborer in the home that is sharply distinguished not only from the homosocial narrative dimensions of Liu Qing's work, but also from the figure of the able-bodied peasant that emerges in Chernyshevsky's aesthetic discourse. Moreover, the time spent in a gendered communal space emerges in this context as precisely not the frivolous use of time that writers such as Lu Zhi and Mo Ai viewed as available for integration into productive labor, but rather as a gendered form of time that enables a reparative form of emotional labor, based on the construction of new bonds of sociality between Ding Ling and the village women.[80] The stated desire for sociality, moreover, underscores the significance of the intimacy that emerges between Ding Ling as I-narrator and the wife, an intimacy that is strengthened by the revelation that lying close by is the daughter-in-law, wedded to their adopted son. This daughter-in-law provides, in turn, the site of mediation for the introduction of a yet larger community of women in the following section, which revolves around a practice of weaving quite different from that of any solitary, isolated mode of labor. The section dealing with the daughter-in-law marks the withdrawal of a purposive I-narrator in favor of the sequential portrayal of young women and girls weaving in common with each other, a shift in narrative perspective that is announced through the change in focalization and use of psycho-narration in the opening sentence: "The daughter-in-law heard the sound of footsteps outside their dwelling, and understood who it was, so she began to busy herself by moving her spinning wheel. A young girl with braids wearing a big red cotton jacket came to stand at the threshold; she placed her fingers in her mouth and gazed with her head askew at the crippled old lady. 'Let's go! Landao! Let's go to your place.' The daughter-in-law placed her spinning wheel on her back and walked out, knowingly smiling at the young girl."[81]

Between these two sections—that dealing with the wife of the village head, and that marking the collectivity of younger women—there intervenes an unspecified amount of time, though with the understanding that the following events take place on the same day as Ding Ling waking up next to the wife of the village head. The congregation of varied village women to engage in weaving marks a suggestive contrast with the isolated character of weaving on the part of the wife of the village head, whereby the household—that of Landao—here takes on the role of a site of collective sociality in the practice of weaving. The sustained recounting of the involvement of various village women in weaving yields in the next section to an analepsis concerning how weaving came to be introduced in the village, with the village head having sourced the first spinning wheel from the cooperative of the southern district to give to his wife, before inviting the sole woman in the village capable of weaving to give a demonstration in his home, after which "a whole chain of people went off to spin thread, and an enthusiasm for spinning took off." In a return to the narrative present, Ding Ling comes to recognize that the quality of weaving remains insufficient, not least on account of the poor state of the spinning wheels themselves, as a result of which they, the culture workers, assist the villagers in repairing the machines and organizing a spinning competition before their departure. This competition takes the form of an expanded congregation of women, whereby "after eating lunch, the various married women on the mountainside came down, clutching their willow baskets. Their spinning wheels were born by their kids or by their husbands who had stayed at home, and it was like a temple fair, with so much laughter and excitement."[82]

Most significant, in this context, is that this formation of a new, expansive setting of gendered labor comes to encompass even those women who will not themselves engage in weaving, including the wife of the village head, who marked Ding Ling's introduction to the village community: "The older women also came to look at the proceedings, clutching their thread twisting hammers. The wife of the village head, who had not left her courtyard in more than a year, also came out on this day, holding her hammer. She had no intention of taking part in the competition, and gave her wheel over to the daughter-in-law, each of them sharing the same wheel." The incorporation of the otherwise disabled wife of the village head into an enthusiastic, carnivalesque community of laboring women crucially passes over into Ding Ling and the other assembled culture workers, and does so via the medium of writing, where they assist the village head in recording the results of the competition, at the same time as they assist in the competition: "the village head and the cultural director were truly busy, clarifying the number of people present, writing down names and lighting incense [to keep track of time]. We helped them write on the one hand, and on the other we helped the women repair their machines, rolling their cotton, and explaining what to do."[83] The competition eventually takes on the narrative form of an aesthetics of collective labor, one which is given in combined sonic and visual modes of description: "The sound of the turning wheels cohered into a single sound, and on all sides people were talking in excited terms, the youngsters dancing and running around, shouting for their mothers, laughing loudly, and becoming a mass of excited children. When the incense had burned down halfway, everyone showed greater enthusiasm! Look, Wang Shengting had spun the fastest, as her spindle carried the most thread."[84]

The narrative injunction at the end of this passage to "look" establishes a direct relation with the reader so as to underscore the radical contemporaneity of this scene of collective labor, one in which the reader herself is enjoined to become part of the collective crowd that witnesses the achievements of the village women. Their participation is, moreover, one that suspends the hierarchical and differential ordering of different women in terms of household and generational difference. The effect in relation to the wife of the village head in particular is to mark the site of collective labor as one of care, one that suspends the distinction between the able-bodied and disabled through participation in spinning. In addition to the progressive incorporation of this community to encompass all the women of the village, as well as the assumed reader of the passage, must be added here the group of culture workers of whom Ding Ling as narrator is herself a part. The end of this section articulates the ways that the frenzy of the spinning competition also creates the possibility of a new mode of friendship, one that relates to that between Ding Ling and Xiao Hong even as it ceases to be confined to intellectuals:

> Everyone fought among themselves to get us to come to their homes to eat, they wanted us to help them repair their spinning wheels and roll up their strips of cotton. From the afternoon to the evening of this day, we became the good friends of the women in the village, without a moment of rest. They took us as people who were bosom friends 知己, and wanted us to stay until the next day before leaving, asking us when we would next return. In spite of ourselves, we came to regret our departure even more, and in our hearts thought that we should surely come visit a second time.[85]

Here, as elsewhere throughout the text, the "we" primarily identifies the group of culture workers, yet this passage, with which the long section on the weaving competition closes, is distinguished by the fact that the penultimate reference to "we," referring to the agonizing prospect of departure, takes on a more ambiguous role in the way it can potentially establish a shared "we" between the culture workers and the weaving women of the village, formed and articulated through the shared experience of gendered labor, having become bosom friends. This is, in the same terms, also an emergent "we" that is no longer strictly mediated by the male village head. In these ways, this reportage text undertakes a series of nuanced formal shifts that stage an expansion of relations of intimacy among women. Ding Ling herself, even while she remains present as an I-narrator, is progressively sublimated into this set of social relationships. The weaving wheel emerges as an emblem of collective labor that cuts across distinctions between women, and which also offers the possibility for a transformation of Ding Ling, as a female culture worker, in the form of a radical expansion of friendship beyond the ranks of intellectuals.[86]

Even while reproductive labor in its most familiar sense does not explicitly appear in the narrative economy of Ding Ling's text, there is an orientation toward the emotional labor of building new bonds of sociality. There is, contained here, then, the optimistic, naïve hope of a reconciliation of that "double life" that Ding Ling articulated in her earlier essay in 1942, as well as a feminist extension of the Maoist concept of "life" to encompass gendered forms of sociability and intimacy.

Out of the fields, into the factory

The central place of Mao's Talks in the Chinese socialist project was formalized in 1944 through the publication of *Marxism and Literature*, which collected extracts from a range of theoretical sources from the Marxist classics, as well as Mao's own Talks, thereby placing Mao within a genealogy of Marxist thinking on the problem of writing under socialism. None other than Zhou Yang wrote the preface, which was also published as an independent article in *Liberation Daily*. Zhou left the classical status of Mao's work beyond doubt, asserting that "from this book, we can see that Comrade Mao Zedong's Talks in one respect effectively demonstrate the literary thought of Marx, Engels, Lenin and others, and in another respect their literary thought precisely demonstrates the correctness of Comrade Mao Zedong's own theories of literature." Yet even this moment of confidence bespoke some of the emergent contradictions around writing under socialism. Zhou Yang also paraphrased literary theorists such as Maxim Gorky to the effect that the separation of mental and manual labor, or the formation of the writer as a professional agent of culture, was a historical process bound up with the emergence of class society, such that the future communist society would in turn reunite mental and manual labor on a new basis. Zhou therefore stated with reference to Marx and the terminology of *The German Ideology*, "He predicted that in the communist society, every person will be released from the constraints of professional occupation 职业上的限制 and reliance on the division of labor, so that, at that time, 'there are no painters, but men who among other things do painting.' "[87]

Zhou Yang's intervention was then a summation of the major lessons of Mao's Talks, but in charting the supersession of the individual writer as key to the business of communist transition, it also introduced a tension, namely by registering the culture worker as herself a figure of transition, being, on the one hand, the site of an ideological reconstruction of the practice of writing through the injunction to "enter into life" and reject literary modes tied to the solipsistic practices of bourgeois writing, and yet writing itself remained the practice of an individual producer, whose works appeared under the name of an author. This was a contradiction that was to persist and that came to generate increasingly more radical attempts to change the material configuration of writing in order that the figure of the culture worker would be eventually superseded. These were not the only contradictions that the Yan'an period left unresolved. As the victory of the revolution approached in 1949, the problem of how to organize rural labor in the base area was brought into sharp contrast with the problem of how to organize labor in an industrial, urban setting, and how these two zones, the rural and urban, were to be synchronized with one another according to their respective modes of labor. The peasantry was already a problem in Yan'an, but in the 1950s the disorganized character of peasant labor would be deepened in the ideological register of the new government, as revolutionaries grappled with the problem of how to turn peasants into workers.

In this new context, so too did culture workers shift from the countryside to the cities. Yet when they did so they would become professional writers under the aegis of the post-1949 socialist state. For a revolutionary project that sought to abolish the writer as a narrow professional occupation as part of a critique of the division between mental and manual labor, this would generate challenges that were to last until the end of the revolutionary process.

CHAPTER 2

LAZY PEASANTS, PRODUCTIVE PROLETARIANS

The Developmental Logic of Cultural Labor and Uneven Development

If an institution of literary creation or a culture worker does not produce any works over a period of one or two years, or writes works that are not of any use, then this shows that he has not completed his production tasks, and as far as labor discipline is concerned, this is impermissible

—Zhou Yang 周扬

The creation of the People's Republic in 1949 marked the formalization and extension of the project of producing the culture worker as a figure of socialist culture. The formalization of the culture worker took place amid increasing challenges for the new socialist state and led theoretician of cultural labor Zhou Yang to demand, in his speech "Rectify Ideas of Art and Literature, Enhance Leadership Work," the reorganization of cultural production according to a new model of temporal discipline. That he did so was due in large part to the changed configuration of social relations from 1949 onward. In place of the rural environs of the Yan'an period, the nationwide conquest of power confronted the revolution with a national social landscape characterized by radical forms of uneven development between the countryside, with its reserves of peasant labor, and the cities, which were posed as the primary sites for factory labor and industrialization during this period. The task, in this setting, was to support a process of urban-based industrialization, including through the production of the working class itself. During this period, the model of socialist industrialization followed the example of the Soviet Union, whereby the locus of industrialization would be in the cities and thus structured the relationship between city and countryside in ways that compelled a constant transfer of value from the latter to the former. To this end, cultural production was invested with the power and responsibility to aid the process of industrialization. To no less an extent than the mechanisms of industrialization, the reorganization of cultural labor also took inspiration from the example of the Soviet Union, emblematized by the convening on July 2 of the All-China Congress of Literary and Arts Workers (First Cultural Congress) and the ensuing creation of the All-China Federation of Literary and Arts Circles, followed in turn by the formation of the Literature Workers Association (later renamed in 1953 as the Writers Association), as that body that would assume responsibility for literary culture workers as laborers of socialism—or, in Soviet parlance, as engineers of the human soul.

Yet this process was no smooth march to victory, but one of emergent crisis. In the face of a nationwide process of industrialization, writers were faced with the ideological and narrative challenge of the relations between proletariat and peasant labor. As such, the predominant narrative image of the peasant in cultural production of the 1950s was no longer that of a revolutionary class, nor even that of a class that can be effectively integrated into new kinds of social relations, as in Yan'an. Instead, the construction of the working class through cultural production and the transformation of cultural labor itself according to the demand for a proletarian labor discipline were dependent on a constant assertion of difference between the working class and the peasantry, as part of which the negative attributes of the peasants provided the counterpoint to the relationship between workers and their envisaged social environment of collective, mechanized production. The logic of a sharp demarcation between factory and peasant labor resulted in the frequent marginalization and denigration of the peasant, and above all, the peasant in the factory, as a source of indiscipline, laziness, and a fundamental incompatibility with the requirements of the modern factory workplace. This uneven treatment of the factory worker and the peasant continued, even while it was the peasantry that provided the base for the expansion of the working class in the factories, and even while cultural production also assumed responsibility for transforming peasants into workers. At the heart of the negative portrayal of the peasant were the discordant temporalities of peasant and proletarian labor. As a matter of fact, the problem of the temporality of peasant and proletarian labor posed, as its third term, the temporality of cultural labor itself, consisting of how to integrate the particular requirements of cultural production with a tempo of accumulation very different from that of the rural base areas. The problem of writing at the beginning of the People's Republic was therefore felt at different levels and rendered the cultural production of the working class an unstable, contingent process, and one that fed into an eventual crisis of the new socialist cultural system from 1957 onward.

Socialist writing, socialist state

The convening of the First Cultural Congress in July 1949 marked the integration of different kinds of cultural producers into a state-led system of cultural production based around the All-China Federation of Literary and Arts Circles, which functioned as the umbrella body for different kinds of specialized bodies. The hosting of the First Congress was rapidly followed, in the same month, by the First Congress of the China Federation of Literature Workers (Literature Association), which marked the formal inauguration of a process by which writing would be increasingly institutionalized under the state. In the years following, the Literature Association would exhibit an increasing expansion of its organizational capacities, tending toward the replication of the Soviet literary system and eventually emerging as a decisive Ideological State Apparatus (ISA).[1] With respect to the influence of the Soviet model, its prestige owed much to the personal contacts between Chinese writers and their Soviet counterparts, above all Alexander Fadeev, chairman of the Union of Soviet Writers. In a highly explicit adulatory mode, as part of a 1946–1947 trip in which he met Fadeev, Mao Dun 茅盾 connected the remuneration of Soviet writers with the Stalinist category of the "engineer of the human soul," noting in particular that the Union of Soviet Writers would provide for the costs of writers so that they might "go to a calm and beautiful scenic environment in order to write in peace." So too did he note that "in the Soviet Union, writers occupy a high position, but they do so not because so many of them are parliamentarians in the Supreme Soviet, but rather because they are 'engineers of the human soul.'"[2] These contacts between Chinese writers and their Soviet counterparts, especially Fadeev, in the Soviet Union itself were reciprocated as early as October 1949, as part of an extensive delegation to China in which Fadeev participated, accompanied by the systematic translation of contemporary essays, not least Fadeev's essay "The Labor of the Writer" in which he enumerated the Soviet conception of the writer as engineer.[3]

The effect of these encounters was to encourage the restructuring of the post-1949 Literature Association on the Soviet model, through an enhancement of its capacity to organize the cultural practice of writers. The envisaged future of the literary system lay in what critics and literary officials understood to be the "professionalization of writers," signifying not a position of *political* autonomy, but rather the creation of material conditions in which writers would be able to devote themselves entirely to writing without other administrative responsibilities. Mao Dun then declaimed in 1950:

> We must have a large contingent of professional writers 职业作家. In our literary circles, we must hold professional writers in high regard. As far as such "professional writers" are concerned, in society there exist some mistaken views to a greater or lesser extent. Yet in actual fact, in modern literary history, around 90 or 80 percent of great writers have precisely been professional writers—that is, they had writing as their sole occupation. In the socialist Soviet Union, the great majority of writers have been professional writers. We must do our utmost to ensure that our writers (or those that are willing to become professional writers) should not have to perform administrative work, or undergo interference.[4]

The strengthening of the capacity of the Literature Association on the basis of the aim of "professionalization" was given additional force by the critiques concerning the inadequate labor discipline of culture workers in the post-Liberation period, above all in the quote from Zhou Yang with which this chapter began. There thus emerged in the period 1951–1952 a rectification campaign orientated toward the problem, in Zhou Yang's terms, of inadequate labor discipline, one that emerged, in his account, from the fact that "culture workers are relatively used to a work method based on individual inspiration."[5] This rectification was rapidly followed by a period of intense study in the theoretical basis of Soviet socialist realism. The documents selected as part of the rectification campaign included not only Mao's Talks—which marked their extension to those writers who had not been part of the experience of the Yan'an base areas—but also two key sets of Soviet documents, namely "Four Resolutions of the Central Committee of the Communist Party of the Soviet Union (Bolshevik) on Matters of Art and Literature and a Report of Zhdanov" and Stalin's "A Letter to Comrade Demyan Bedny." This initial program of study came to expand, so that, from late 1952 onward it encompassed not only documents from the Nineteenth Congress of the Communist Party of the Soviet Union held in that same year but also Stalin's *Economic Problems of Socialism in the USSR*, preparing culture workers for their incorporation into socialist industrialization.[6] These periods of study were accompanied by the formal dispatch of writers to the base, which, for the first time, included industrial sites as well as the countryside. Yet so too did a series of administrative decisions seek to enhance the organizational capacities of the literary system. A resolution passed at the Fifth Expanded Meeting of the Standing Committee of the Literature Association in August 1952 under the title "A Work Plan for Adjusting the Organization and Improving Work" committed the

Literature Association to carrying out regular supervision of the activities of its members.⁷

A further resolution was passed on March 24, 1953, introduced under the auspices of the Sixth Standing Committee Meeting of the Literature Association with the title "Concerning a Work Plan for the Revision of the Nationwide Literature Workers Association and the Strengthening of Leadership Over Literary Creation." It marked an explicit commitment to hosting a Second Congress and discussing formal changes to the structure of the Association. Crucially, the second resolution, that of March 1953, followed the comments of Mao Dun and Zhou Yang closely in calling for the professionalization of writers, combined with a pointed critique of the Literature Association up to this point:

> There are still many writers who possess considerable creative ability and experience who have to assume administrative tasks and therefore do not exclusively engage in creative work; or they are dispersed among various literary units, and as such do not regularly undergo strong leadership. This condition seriously undermines the development of our creative forces ... thus, the Literature Association must diligently assume the task of leading the study, criticism and creative activities of writers and at the same time also guide popularization.⁸

These tendencies point toward the ongoing crafting of an Ideological State Apparatus (ISA) adequate to the task of coordinating cultural production with the early socialist project on the basis of "professionalization," not least in ensuring that culture workers were not encumbered with excessive administrative duties. Conceiving of the post-1949 system of literary institutions as an ISA in the Althusserian sense underscores its crucial role in the ideological and social reproduction of socialist social relations themselves, relations that were equally the product of the labor of cultural production. Yet the possibility of this capacity was itself dependent on the reproduction of the very forces of cultural production that comprised the emergent state literary system. This process itself had both a material and an ideological/organizational component, the first of these consisting largely of the problem of remuneration, the second relating to ideological education and binding culture workers to the temporalities of socialist industrialization. These tasks fell to two committees that were organized under the Literature Workers Association as a result of the March 24 meeting, the Literature Fund Management Committee and the Creation Committee.

The first of these assumed responsibility for the material support of writers by organizing the payment of manuscript fees 稿费. The system of manuscript fees had already begun to be adopted over the period 1949–1953, which witnessed the steady adoption of those practices of remuneration that had, for Mao Dun, elevated Soviet writers to such a privileged position. In this regard, in reflecting on her conversation with Fadeev during her own visit to the Soviet Union, Ding Ling noted that: "Writers rely on manuscript fees to live. Fadeev told me: writers receive a large income, equivalent to four engineers. In the Soviet Union, engineers are the best-paid, but I imagine this is not true of every writer. The payment of manuscript fees is divided into many ranks, determined by the quality of the manuscript."[9]

This system as it operated in the Soviet Union came to be adopted in China, with various radical shifts. In both contexts, payment was not made according to consumer purchases but according to a shifting combination of the character of the work, length, and the number of printings.[10] As a consequence, individual writers in China over the 1950s accrued significant income. In close parallel to the formation of the fund management committee, the creation committee assumed a decisive role in the process of ideological reproduction, as the official body that would conduct concrete guidance over literary creation activities. The creation committee assumed responsibility for organizing and planning the process by which resident writers were dispatched to the base to "enter into life." In this process, the same organization also undertook responsibility for liaising with writers who had been dispatched to the base, resolving problems that arose in the course of their work with the masses, and organizing discussion meetings among writers concerning their works in progress.[11] In close conjunction, the committee assumed editorial responsibility for an internal circulation journal, *Writers Dispatch*, which carried information on the creative activities of writers. Central to this process was the official support given to the crafting of "plans" by writers whereby they would commit themselves to a temporality of writing over the forthcoming year.[12] *Writers Dispatch* provided the platform for the publication of these plans. Of no less importance in these terms was the role of the creation committee in further enhancing the ideological authority of the Soviet Union in the Chinese literary sphere. To this end, from April to June 1953, following the formation of the creation committee itself as well as the study campaign that had been introduced at the end of 1952, the committee organized Beijing-based writers and critics to conduct a two-month study session on the theory of socialist realism, encompassing familiar Soviet theoretical questions such as the problem of typicality, the partisan character of literature, and so on, with senior writers giving lectures and guiding discussion sessions.[13] These varied programs of study under the creation committee aimed at the validation of the Soviet literary canon, not only at an organizational level but also with respect to narrative form. These markers informed a process that eventually gave way to the formal redesignation of the Literature Association as the

Writers Association 作家协会 in September 1953 at the Second Congress of the Literature Association, convened simultaneously with the Second Congress of the All-China Federation of Literary and Arts Circles.[14]

This body marked the effective stabilization of the literary ISA under early Chinese socialism. The Writers Association as it emerged after 1953, then, was truly a national body, in which the national-level organization of functions was replicated down to lower levels.[15] So too was the formation of the Writers Association followed by the further intensification of those tendencies toward organizing the material and ideological reproduction of writers that had already taken hold after 1949. In the following year, 1954, then, further commitments were made to the material support of writers through the passing of the "Temporary Measures Introduced by the Chinese Writers Association For Loans and Allowances," which made provisions for providing financial support to writers in the interests of their further "professionalization" 职业化, including nonrepayable allowances.[16] In similar terms, the creation committee continued to assume new capacities in the process of ideological reproduction. In 1954, it organized two extended education guides, published in November 1954, the first consisting of a "Directory Index Concerning Theses on Soviet Literature" and containing theoretical works that had been published across Chinese periodicals since 1949, and the second consisting of a similar index listing introductions of Soviet literary works. The tendency of the ongoing organization of writing at a material and ideological level was toward the production of a social relation of writing, summed up in the appellation of the "resident writer" 驻会作家 or "professional writer" 专业作家 as Mao Dun had anticipated in 1950.[17] This was a formal category that referred to writers who were attached to the national Writers Association and its local affiliates, without further responsibilities in the form of administrative tasks or editing literary journals.[18]

The transformation of cultural production along these lines sought to resolve the failures of discipline that Zhou Yang had identified in 1951, by remaking writers in the image of the Soviet-derived "engineer of the human soul." If, in 1951, in the speech with which the chapter began, Zhou Yang decried that "culture workers are relatively used to a work method based on individual inspiration," by 1954, in his speech heralding the creation of the Writers Association under the title "We Must Struggle," Zhou Yang located the creation of heroic protagonists as the basis on which writers would fulfil their function as engineers of the human soul: "The Second Congress of Literary and Art Circles posed that the creation of images of positive, advanced characters, and of personalities that can be emulated by the masses is the most important task for present-day artistic creation. In doing so, the function of literature as an active way of transforming society and of writers as 'engineers of the human soul' can be developed to the greatest extent."[19]

In a yet more enthusiastic elaboration the same year delivered at the Second Congress of the Soviet Writers Union, Zhou Yang paid credence to the Soviet elaboration of the "engineer of the human soul" as a sufficient definition of the writer under socialism. Having acclaimed a number of recent Soviet literary works, including Fadeev's *The Young Guard*, Zhou Yang asserted: "In these words, [readers] can see totally new characters of a kind unprecedented in human history, a kind of character possessed of the highest communist spirit and moral qualities. In their work in creating typical images of positive characters according to the conditions of actual life, beloved Soviet writers have completed their most glorious task of serving as 'engineers of the human soul.'"[20]

The implication of the structuring of writing by the Writers Association marks this period as one of profound contradiction. The formal, professional status of writers as "engineers of the human soul" was part of a project to bind them to the task of national industrialization, whereby writing would be synchronized with industrial development, yet this mode of synchronization at the level of national policy depended on and formalized a bifurcation of writers from the conditions of the masses, above all with respect to the ways that the temporal division between the time of writing and the time of labor under the aegis of "entering into life" became institutionalized.[21] For this reason, the problem of the professional writer (and, later, the question of the professionalization of amateur writers) would quickly assume a radical importance in the Chinese Revolution. Yet, lest it be assumed that the consolidation of the Soviet-derived literary ISA brooked no dissent in the early 1950s, the very year 1953 also provided the opportunity for a reexamination of those categories and practices from Yan'an, above all by those writers who had passed through the Rectification process in Yan'an.

In this regard, Ding Ling's interventions were of crucial importance. This was true above all of two essays, both written in 1953, namely "Go Among the Masses" and "Writers Must Cultivate Feelings Toward the Masses." In the first of these, given as her speech at the 1953 Writers Congress, Ding Ling located the culture worker within the formal institutions of the socialist literary system as a restricted form of existence: "While the world itself is broad, the scope our activity is extremely narrow; while life itself is thriving, rich and dazzling, our own everyday life 日常生活 is exceptionally impoverished."[22]

In the same terms, Ding Ling stressed that the commonplace, increasingly formulaic vocabulary of "experiencing life" 体验生活 embodied a distortion and limitation of the practices that had first emerged in Yan'an insofar as it had come to designate purely instrumental visits among the masses for the purpose of collecting materials for literary creation, comprising, therefore, a kind of "way of life" 生活方式 rather than the radical transformation of the social organization of writing embodied by a true process of "entering into life." Ding Ling, then, explicitly counterpoised an insufficient practice of "experiencing life" to a Maoist practice orientated toward the abnegation of intellectual subjectivity, insisting that to truly enter life means that "he participates in the life of the masses, strides forward with them while forgetting the self 忘我, and fights with them against all old forces, and all old persons, ideas and institutions that prevent the development of new forces. He is not a bystander."[23] Ding Ling's powerful interventions in these terms took on a further logic in her second text, where she insisted that the life of the culture worker under the socialist literary system was a "lonely" 孤僻 one, in which "those who come visit us in our homes are those who write, and those people with whom we are familiar in our daily lives are not those we write about, as those we write about are in fact distant from our everyday life 日常生活."[24] She further stressed: "A true writer cannot lead a double life 两重生活, that is, one kind of life conducted within the restricted circle of writers, and one kind led among those that he seeks to write about. We should eternally live together with the masses.... We must seek out familial relations among the masses, seek out cousins, seek out bosom friends. We must establish relations with them such that when they experience joy or bitterness, they will come searching for you."[25]

Ding Ling's deployment in this context of the formulation of a "double life" marks a striking point of intersection with her critique advanced in Yan'an more than ten years earlier, as does her explicit invocation of a language of friendship. In that context, Ding Ling had advanced this formulation in reference to Qu Qiubai's inability to resolve the contradiction between his political and cultural life under the conditions of underground struggle in Shanghai and the Soviet base areas, that is, prior to the formulation of the Maoist cultural project. Ding Ling's renewed invocation of this same figure of critique marked an understanding that the formal socialist literary system as it had emerged after Yan'an deepened the bifurcation attending the professional status of writing, and had done so through those very literary institutions that were supposed to organize writing around the tasks of socialist construction.[26] The division between these two modes of life as articulated by Ding Ling ultimately emerges as a temporal bifurcation, incumbent in the structural alteration between short-term exposure to life among the masses and the isolated process of cultural production, but where the understanding of the intellectual life as a "lonely" one is counterpoised to an expanded conception of friendship premised on the abnegation of the intellectual. These visions were otherwise negated by Zhou Yang's adoption of the "engineer of the human soul" and the structuring of writing under the Writers Association.

Yet the eruption of these bifurcations with respect to the temporality of writing were, as we shall see, also homologous with the internal contradictions of the political economy of early socialism, which in turn made their way into the narrative texts of this period. The attempted incorporation of writing into the march of early socialist industrialization not only encompassed its own antimonies through the figure of the "professional writer," but so too did texts render visible the ways in which the Soviet-derived model of early socialist industrialization tended toward the production of other temporal disjunctures.

Peasant time, proletarian time

In his further polemical article entitled "Socialist Realism: The Path of Advance for Chinese Literature," Zhou left little doubt as to the expectations for culture workers. In addition to reprising his familiar emphasis on socialist literature operating from the perspective of the working class, Zhou demanded that literature tackle the incompatibility between "the requirements of national industrialization and the presence of masses of dispersed small producers 小生产者; the incompatibility between continued existence of old ideas and habits in the life and consciousness of the people, such as the self-serving and conservative beliefs among the peasants, and the task of raising the political consciousness of the people on a daily basis."[27] In these terms, 1953 marked the moment at which the peasant, and more specifically the temporal relations between workers and peasants, emerged as the site at which cultural laborers would be enjoined to intervene in order to reorganize these otherwise discordant temporalities of labor along the lines of a new synchronicity, geared toward the interests of rapid accumulation. The problem that Zhou Yang identified, that of the peasant as small producer, was here coded as the problem of the peasant as internal to the working class. This reconfiguration emerged amid a larger discursive background of political economy in which ideas of peasant "backwardness" were intensified as peasants joined the working class in the guise of "new workers" 新工人. The extent to which peasants newly incorporated into the working class were projected as a problem became radically visible with the initiation of the First Five-Year Plan in 1953. It did so in conjunction with the incorporation of a Soviet model of industrialization as the basis of early Chinese socialism, premised on an ongoing transfer of surplus from the countryside to the city as the basis for an urban-centered pattern of industrialization. The adoption of the Soviet model in textual terms consisted of the canonization of Stalin's 1952 *Economic Problems of Socialism in the USSR*, followed by the first edition of the *Political Economy: A Textbook*, in 1954. These theoretical documents were discussed and serialized across Chinese periodicals and introduced a Marxist vocabulary of public and collective ownership, the function of the law of value under socialism, and, as we shall see, the formula of remuneration according to labor.[28]

So too, as noted, did Stalin's text form a part of the ideological reproduction of professional writers under the aegis of the new literary ISA. From 1953 onward, therefore, increasing weight was placed on the entry of writers into industrial sites. The editors of *Writers Dispatch* noted in 1953, then, that "the state requires that more authors describe industrial construction, yet from the conditions of the second contingent of authors to enter into life we see that those who have gone to the factories and mines are still few in number, the majority still going to the countryside."[29] The release of the "Directive on Strengthening Cultural and Artistic Work in Mines, Worksites and Enterprises" in June 1954 similarly identified the trade unions as responsible not only for organizing cultural activity in different worksites, but also for assisting writers and artists as they themselves conducted actual work in these workspaces.[30] At a formal level, the attempted incorporation of cultural production into urban-centered socialist industrialization resolved itself into a theoretical discourse around the problem of "character" 人物, specifically the incorporation of wayward peasant characters into a regularized industrial temporality. The veteran novelist Zhou Libo's reflections are of particular relevance here, due to the way he explicitly foregrounds the problem of divergent temporalities:

> Workers have their common characteristics, for example, they hold the collective in high regard, observe discipline, and love science. When writing a certain literary work, I gave it to the party secretary of a steel factory to have a look, and he gave me his feedback, saying that in this work I had used the formulation of "high noon," but this was a rural expression, whereas everywhere in the factory there are watches, clocks, as well as the factory siren, so that when the time comes, someone will sound the siren, time therefore being calculated in hours and minutes. This was different from the countryside, where people told the time by constellations in the sky and could often be off by one or two hours, without it mattering very much.[31]

The literary work to which Zhou refers in this suggestive anecdote was his early industrial novel *Rivulets of Steel* (1955), which marks an attempt to devise narrative strategies adequate to the conditions of the First Five-Year Plan, being therefore distinct from the agrarian novels of the Yan'an period. This work had comprised Zhou's primary object of cultural labor in the post-Liberation period, consisting of multiple periods of writing and entering into life. In response to a formal request that he and other writers submit their creation plans for 1953, then, he wrote, "in January of 1953, I plan to go to a steel factory in Shijingshan, where I will continue to enrich my understanding of life. I plan to work as the head of a small group in a workshop department or with the trade union, to better understand the workers. In February of 1952

I had already written up a novel entitled *Rivulets of Steel* reflecting the lives and struggles of workers, and so on this occasion of entering into life I plan to spend half a year carrying out edits."[32]

The historical setting of the novel lies in the early days of Liberation, therefore taking the form of a historical prologue relative to the conditions in which the novel itself was written. It takes the form of the depiction of the rejuvenation of a derelict steel factory, subsequent to the defeat of the Japanese occupation and the entry of the People's Liberation Army. The novel is distinguished, in formal terms, by its strictly linear temporality, being altogether devoid of the significant use of prolepsis and analepsis, a fact whose relevance will become clear shortly via comparison with other industrial narratives of this period. The rejuvenation of the steel factory is, furthermore, largely narrated through the progress and development of an individual worker, Li Dagui, who figures early in the narrative and undergoes a sequential political development throughout the larger part of the novel. To this extent, the novel marks the formal adoption of many of the classical strategies of socialist realism, not least in the form of the transition from spontaneity to consciousness that Katerina Clark has located as the structure of the socialist realist novel.[33]

The pedagogical process that Li Dagui undergoes is marked early on by the flexible use of focalization, whereby, even while it is largely narrated from the focalized position of Li himself, the novel strategically moves to focalize around other figures, not least the initial party members who arrive with the People's Liberation Army, or with zero focalization, to depict Li's political development. The strategic deployment of focalization may be seen from the first chapter, in which, just subsequent to his appearance, Li takes on the role of a narrative focalizer who bears witness to the arrival of the People's Liberation Army, as follows: "Li Dagui did not reply, but merely looked in front, where three soldiers of the Liberation Army had run close. He could already clearly see the steaming perspiration on their faces, and how, on their facial hair and eyebrows, there lay tiny, shining shards of frost."[34]

In this same narrative context, separated only by a fragment of dialogue, the focalization shifts to that of the collective group of workers at the factory, rendered as: "the workers stood still. This was the first time that they had seen their own army, and wanted to draw close, and yet did not yet dare to do so, so they stood at some distance, looking at how these soldiers held their carbines, how they had hand grenades at their waists, their heroic postures, and so too did they hear their questions, with even Li Dagui struck dumb for a moment unable to reply, and those at the rear also wanted to duck out."[35] This transitory moment of collective focalization quickly yields in turn to that of one of the soldiers, with Li Dagui himself becoming the object of a similar pattern of visual focalization: "The tall soldier used the corner of his jacket to wipe the sweat and sleet from his brow, and looked this fellow up and down, taking in his bushy brow and big eyes. He saw the scuffed cap on his head, and the dark, patched cotton jacket he was wearing, as well as the grass cord around his waist, his clothes and face covered with oil, and his large stubby fingers, and he knew that before him, this was a true worker."[36]

The swift and well-regulated movement of focalization across these different moments—suggestive of a shot/countershot set of transitions in film—not only establishes much of the formal construction of the narrative that follows, whereby periodical movements in focalization enact Li Dagui's development as a political subject in tandem with the restoration of the industrial site, but in turn also establish a radically homosocial, masculinized relationship between the workers and the soldiers, with each bearing the visible signs of proletarian and martial masculinity respectively. The novel in its formal devices, then, enacts a kind of pact in the way that shifts of focalization are used to stage an alliance between the incipient conscious worker, Li Dagui, and the soldiers who initially function as the agents of his political pedagogy. The forging of collective bonds through a masculinized register becomes a trope during the early chapters of the novel, and one that comes to assume a sexual dimension in the way that a shared experience of heterosexual intercourse and accompanying bawdy jokes provides the stuff out of which the affective bonds of a male proletarian subject are fashioned. When in the absence of production workers are found to be fishing in the reservoirs of the factory, Li Dagui himself jokes in relation to a worker, who has yet to hook a catch:

> "If the fish aren't biting your hook, how can you blame me? I bet you got it on with your wife last night, didn't you? The fish can smell it, you know, their noses are quite sensitive." Yu Yonghe laughed: "that's the first time I've heard of fish having noses." "Not just their noses, you know, their eyes are pretty impressive as well. They can see your hook, and they'll think to themselves: that's the hook of the worker Old Yu, the skinny fellow likes his wife, not us. It won't do, we can't nibble his hook. So, you see, if you do it with your wife, the fish won't come to you."[37]

Even as bawdy episodes of this kind fashion a shared male proletarian set of bonds, however, they also enact the danger that arises from the defunct character of the industrial site, consisting of the reabsorption of the workers into the peasantry, with the ensuing danger to the formation of a collective, disciplined working class adequate to the demands of a socialist state. In the same chapter as that in which the workers exchange sexualized jokes, therefore, as Li leads the new military administration around the factory, and as the political director inquires as to when they might restore power, there emerges a sustained passage of psycho-narration from the perspective of Li himself:

At this moment, there emerged in Li Dagui's mind a scene of dissolution: of the electric cables and lines in the factory, around half were broken, some of the electric columns had been knocked clean over and so too was the electric generator. He was a machine fitter, and so not entirely familiar with the electrical side of things. Yet he understood that, with the workers seeing the factory in such a disordered state, they would be uneasy, and some of them would consider going home to till the land.[38]

The depiction here of a disordered factory site through the perspective of Li Dagui emerges as the inverse of any aesthetic depiction of labor, either rural or industrial, and one of which Li is himself fully aware. Seen in these terms, the position of Li in the larger formal organization and political subtext of the novel is a multivalent, even contradictory one, as a character that introduces the soldiers to the industrial site and is conscious of the dangers posed by the absence of industrial production, especially posed via the specter of the peasantry, yet who must himself undergo a process of proletarian development. The guarantee of Li's own formation as a conscious proletarian emerges through a distinct and contained narrative episode that takes up a struggle session against a former yellow union boss, Hu Dianwen. With Li Dagui having been selected as one of the workers due to articulate their experience of suffering, the meeting quickly transforms into an angry set of denunciations that almost result in the death of Hu, with Li departing from his prepared script, until the intervention of the political director. The adoption, in this context, of a struggle session that threatens to overspill any set of boundaries would emerge as a problem within the formal construction of the narrative were it to imperil the development of Li as a conscious proletarian subject, and yet his spontaneous anger is itself quickly folded into his capacity to function as a powerful emblem of proletarian masculinity, and one that is rendered in formal terms through a cacophony of proletarian voices, none of which are assigned to any explicit narrative figure: "'Old Li is really quite something!' 'Were it not for him, that meeting would have come to nothing.' 'He was a little rough in the way he spoke.' 'Why should that matter? If you speak the truth coarsely then it's not coarse after all.' 'With one blast he demolished an entire fortress.' 'He's a big gun, for sure.'"[39]

The yet greater significance of this narrative episode, however, with respect to Li's development as protagonist, and recalling the shifting focalization of the novel, is its end, whereby Li, riding away from the scene of the meeting, is the victim of an assassination attempt from the agents of Hu, recorded as follows: "Just as he was passing by the willow trees, from a shady place by a building next to the second furnace there rang out a clear shot—ba!—causing him to cry out and release his two hands from the handlebars of the bike, causing the vehicle to crash to the ground as it veered southwards, Li himself falling into a pond by the side of the road that was covered in ice. Those far and near had all been given a shock by the gunshot."[40]

The significance of this episode, occurring as it does at the end of the chapter covering the struggle meeting, is that it produces a wholesale withdrawal of focalization from Li, not only as hitherto, whereby the immediate scene of narrative comes to be depicted through another character within the same space, but through a spatial withdrawal that leaves Li's fate in a state of suspense, being perhaps the only episode in the whole novel which aims for suspense in the specific sense of leaving a decisive narrative episode unresolved. In doing so, it brings into question how the remainder of the narrative might organize itself, in the absence of Li as the key protagonist. The quick resolution of this suspense around Li's supposed death on the first page of the following chapter, then, when it is revealed that he has survived this attack, takes on a key formal significance within the novel as a whole, insofar as it provides the guarantee of Li's capacity to serve as the organizing protagonist for the narrative, and at the same time marks a moment of transition, in which the immediate context of the takeover of the factory and the defeat of class enemies recedes in favor of the more anodyne task of restoring production. The clearest emblem of Li's political development emerges, in turn, through his introduction into the party, though not without some obstacles. The episode of the attempted assassination is ironically recapitulated toward the end of the novel when he succeeds in preventing a sabotage attempt and is injured in the process, though without any accompanying narrative suspense suggesting his possible demise. The transition to the second half of the novel is accompanied by the receding of any prospective danger of a reabsorption into the peasantry, a shift enacted by the emergence of a different set of aesthetic devices and modes of description that eulogize industrial labor, being therefore the obverse of the psycho-narrated scenes of industrial desolation that emerge earlier in the novel:

> The organization for the repair work having been settled, the technical workers appointed to provide support from beyond the factory also arrived. More than a thousand workers at the site busied themselves day and night. A cacophony of sounds of motors, vehicles, the drumming of steel hammers, mixed with work songs, formed a single stream of sound above and beyond the furnaces... in the evening, things were just as busy at the worksite. The electric lights atop the furnaces shone like stars, beaming down from above. The intense sapphire light of the electric and gas welders faded in and out of visibility above and below the furnaces, dazzling the eyes of the workers.[41]

Even with this change in narrative emphasis and descriptive language, however, the problem posed by a spatial and social "outside" to that of the immediate site of factory labor persists. It does so, in the second half of the narrative, however, not strictly in the form of the peasantry, but rather in the way that the temporal relations between industrial labor and the household process of social reproduction comes to mark a possible narrative problem. Yet, to a much greater extent than the recurrent anxiety around the problem of the peasantry, this problem is easily resolved in the formal context of the novel in the way that the household is effectively subsumed into the factory site, thereby allowing the narrative to maintain its spatial focus around industrial production. The wife of Li Dagui, Li Ersao, is, suggestively, only rarely the subject of narrative focalization in the novel, with the exception of a closing scene in which she witnesses Li Dagui following his injury at the hands of a saboteur. The terms of resolution for domestic labor emerge in the chapter immediately after that quoted above, in which the novel advances an aestheticization of the scene of industrial labor, when it is simply stated that "because of the intensity of the repair work, Li Dagui could not return home to eat at noon. Each day, Li Ersao prepared an aluminum loin-shaped two-tiered lunchbox, and sent it to him at work."[42] The two problems of the outside to industrial production as they emerge in the novel, then, consisting of the rural on the one hand and the domestic site of social reproduction on the other, are both folded into or synchronized with the immediate site of the factory with varying degrees of ease.

In this same context, the further maturation of Li Dagui as a political subject also encompasses an expansion of his role to become an arbiter of social relations and affective ties in the factory more generally, a role especially marked through his function as an arbiter of marriage. This narrative trajectory first emerges when, subsequent to his admission to the party, Li Dagui undertakes a study course, marking one of the few instances across the narrative during which he departs from the space of the factory. His encounter with another young party member, Fan Yuhua, produces a brief flirtation, one which Li seeks to curtail by encouraging marriage with his own apprentice, Niu Fushan, which succeeds in incorporating Fan herself into the factory with responsibility for family dependents. This trajectory occupies a minor position within the narrative, and yet it reemerges in the final chapter, coinciding with another marriage scene, this time on the part of an engineer in the factory, which is conveyed with a clear focalization around Li Dagui:

> He looked in through the window and saw Fang Junlan. This pure newly wedded bride was wearing a wide silk shirt with a red flower embroidered on her breast, and below a flower-cloth skirt. To her right side there fell a braid upon which there was tied a pink silken butterfly knot. She seemed embarrassed and sat with her head lowered to the right of the window. Yu Song was wearing a new uniform and sat to her right. Many others were laughing and bustling around them. Li Dagui was still feeling weak, so he did not enter. But he did recall that today was also the day on which Niu Fushan and Fan Yuhua

would celebrate their marriage. At that moment, they too would surely be conducting their ceremony, in the cultural club, so he resolved that he would send them a congratulatory note when he returned to the hospital.[43]

The use of marriage as a device of narrative closure in this final chapter in conjunction with the restoration of industrial production marks a key instance of homology in which the formation of a disciplined working class is marked not only through the success of labor at the immediate site of production but also through the stabilization of sexuality and social reproduction around the form of the nuclear family. It marks, to this extent, the sublimation and incorporation of those bawdy forms of sexual humor that provided the initial bases for a homosocial proletariat closer to the beginning of the novel, as enacted, crucially, through the role of Li Dagui as an arbiter of social relations, a capacity enacted through his role as the site of focalization in this final segment. Just as the novel secures the political development of workers in such a way as to distinguish the proletariat from the peasantry, so too, then, does the family emerge as functional to the demands of industrial production, secured by the promise of a heterosexual union as the point of culmination for a resolutely linear pattern of narrative.

It is, in fact, precisely these facets of Zhou's industrial fiction that would be opened up by other novels of the First Five-Year Plan, which, even while they also envisage the formation of a disciplined proletariat adequate to the tasks of industrialization, do so in formal ways quite distinct from those of *Rivulets of Steel*. Symptomatic in these terms is the novel *For a Happy Tomorrow* (1953), which, at a level of greater formal sophistication than *Rivulets*, critically intervenes in the theoretical construction of peasant and proletarian labor, and the way that both relate to the gendering of the laboring subject. Written by the veteran socialist feminist author Bai Lang, it was initially serialized over 1951 in the periodical *Women of New China* before then being revised and published as a standalone volume in 1953. Read solely at the level of story, the novel seems to closely cohere with the narrative form of peasant-worker transition as articulated in other literary texts from this period. It takes up the life story of a young woman worker, Yumei, who at the cusp of liberation comes to be employed at an armaments factory producing shells for the war against the Nationalists. Being an adopted child of rural origin, the novella stages a process of development in terms of the transition from the countryside to the city, or from rural forms of agricultural labor to the modern factory environment.

At the level of form, however, the novel is significant for its effective use of prolepsis, in that the beginning of the text consists not strictly of Yumei's childhood, but rather with an event that will later emerge as the dramatic climax of the narrative, consisting of an industrial accident that Yumei incurs as a laborer at the site of industrial production. In contrast to the linear temporal trajectory of Zhou Libo's text, then, this novel allows for a disjuncture of story and plot. The accident arises from Yumei dropping dangerous substances due to her state of exhaustion, with the accident itself causing the loss of an arm. The novel therefore begins in medias res, not by introducing its narrative protagonists as might be expected of a more conventional narrative mode, but rather through a scene of workers retiring from their shifts, which is suddenly interrupted by the sound of a loud explosion, which is later revealed to have been the cause of Yumei's injuries:

> Boom! There was suddenly a deafening noise, which sounded both like dynamite and like a shell, it was too heavy, even causing the buildings to shake a little; the workers who were entirely occupied with eating were shocked to attention by this sudden sound, and so they all stopped their gobbling, and, as if by common agreement, raised their shocked eyes to look outside. Because the sound had come from nearby, as if it had taken place right next to them, they thought there was something odd going on, and had a premonition that an accident might have taken place.[44]

The sudden invasion of this moment of industrial violence marks a dramatic departure from the more conventional narrative tropes such as might be observed in texts such as *Rivulets*, as well as the breakdown in the development of production and the relationship between the proletarian body and their instruments of labor. This also marks a delayed exposition with respect to Yumei as the protagonist. Before Yumei has been named as the victim of the accident and the protagonist of the novel, she emerges in the form of a mangled and bruised body. The description embodies a visual force that is, again, in sharp contrast to the aestheticized images of industrial production and the proletarian body that emerge from other texts of this period: "Under a cloud of thick smoke, just outside the window of the mixing room, there was a large accumulation of fresh blood, and amid the pool of blood there lay a person 人 of indistinguishable flesh and blood, and whose face was unclear, it wasn't even clear if they were a man or woman, their face was just as muddled as their blood."[45]

The explicit reference to the sexual ambiguity of the subject anticipates the larger part of the narrative that is to follow, in which forms of gendered longing and their transgression form an important part. Throughout this opening scene, Yumei is, as one might expect, largely speechless, lying inert and her chances of survival as of yet unclear, such that it is her brother, Shaoren, who assumes the role of the focalized narrative subject, not least in his anxieties around his failure to take better care of his sister. With Yumei's fate being as of yet left unclear, and the reader being aware in advance that a disaster will eventually occur, the narrative switches to a more conventional pattern that more closely mimics the protocols of other narratives of proletarian development, namely in a biographical mode that begins with childhood, encompassing the movement of Yumei and her family from countryside to city, and her eventual entry into factory labor. The larger part of the novel therefore consists of narrating the events that will eventually climax in the scene of disaster, of which the reader is already aware, such that this opening scene assumes the function of an anticipatory prolepsis in relation to the events that comprise the larger part of the narrative. Significantly, throughout the childhood biography that narrates her experience of abuse at the hands of her adopted mother, Yumei is altogether absent as a direct subject of speech. When she appears as a narrative subject, it is in the form of internal direct discourse, that is, in the form of the quotation of Yumei's thoughts, and psycho-narration. The most persistent trope of discourse that is ascribed to Yumei is highly gendered, consisting of a rejection of her gendered status as a young woman. In the midst of her unhappy childhood, then: "She hated the fact that she was not a boy. She thought to herself: were I a boy, wouldn't I just be able to run off every time my mother hit and cursed me? From that point onward, she set a small desire for herself, that when she grew up, she would absolutely become a woman like a man 男人一样的女人!"[46]

The precise expression of wanting to be "a woman like a man" recurs again in the narrative when, following the liberation of their city, Yumei's brothers have either joined the People's Liberation Army or already begun to work at the very armaments factory where she will eventually become herself a worker. In this later case, however, the desire to be like a man is explicitly posed in terms of avoiding restriction to the domestic sphere:

> She wanted to be a woman like a man. Would it ever do to spend the rest of her life by the stove? So, she even dreamed about studying and going to work in her dreams. She wished that there would be a day when her older brother would find a wife, so that she would be able to relinquish the burden of housework. Yumei's hopes were not in vain and came to fruition the following year. [Her older brother] Shaoren hadn't even been working at the six-one factory for a year when his life conditions underwent a great improvement, such that he gained the ability to get married. As soon as his wife entered their home, Yumei immediately passed on the housework and very quickly began working in a private match factory.[47]

The preservation in the second sentence of an oral pattern of speech in the form of a question, marks an instance of free indirect style, in which the position of the narrator fuses with that of Yumei herself, granting authority to her discourse. The summary that follows is in the style of a narrative report—also containing an ellipsis, via the statement "in the following year"—and is significant for the fact that the possibility of Yumei's entry into the match factory is explicitly presented as dependent on the marriage of her brother, whereby domestic labor is displaced onto another woman. As it happens, she is rapidly rendered unemployed from this factory when it goes bankrupt, compelling a retreat back into the domestic realm. There is nothing in the presentation of these events to problematize this dynamic, and it is in fact lent legitimacy when Yumei receives a letter from her brother in the PLA, in which the brother urges her that "everyone has a responsibility to serve the country, and in this era women also need to do their bit for the people, so I hope you will be a useful woman 有用的女人."[48] The formulation of a "useful woman" in this context demarcates an implicit contrast with a housebound woman whose labor is therefore discarded as not useful. The subject-position of a "useful woman," into which Yumei is interpellated by her brother's letter, is, in these terms, closely related to Yumei's own desire to be a "woman like a man," and both combine to compel her to enter the armaments factory where her brother is already at work. It is in these terms that the gendering of proletarian labor as implicitly masculine, even (or especially) in the case of women workers, sets up Yumei's actual movement into the factory. Across the first part of the text, from the beginning of the narrative account of her childhood up to her entry into the factory, there is an accelerated tempo of narrative, in which only specific events receive attention, the narrative otherwise making uses of summary and ellipses. It is only with her emergence as a proletarian that the rhythm slows down so as to devote more attention to specific episodes.

The hopes that attend Yumei's entry into the factory coincide with what might otherwise be seen as a positive shift toward her maturation as a proletarian subject, that is, a "useful woman." Yet these hopes are strikingly contrasted with a process of disillusionment, in which Yumei finds in the factory not any straightforward notion of liberation, but instead a gendered structure of power that calls her own masculinized desires into direct question. She frequently encounters the bullying behavior of varied male workshop officials, who unfairly reward different women workers with different positions. The disciplinary structure of the factory manifests itself, moreover, in the form of a language of "culture," in which Yumei is projected as being of inferior cultural level, a fact that causes her no end of distress, despite her desperate efforts to acquire advanced literacy. To these male officials and the pressures of factory life, however, there are counterpoised moments of intimacy and friendship between Yumei and other female workers, above all in the context of the factory dormitory For example, when driven to despair by her alleged lack of cultural development, Yumei's crying awakens her roommate in the factory dormitory, Xiaoyu, which provides the impetus for a touching moment of contact between the two women in which Xiaoyu "peeled the coverlet aside and stretched out her hand to stroke [Yumei's] face, who, not having time to withdraw, felt Xiaoyu touch her tears." The moment of intimacy between the two provides the impetus for the narrative to record other such moments between Yumei and Xiaoyu, as well as between Yumei and another woman worker, Wang Ying, from whom Yumei seeks to learn the names of the chemicals that go into the manufacture of explosives in order that she herself will eventually be able to enter into the most dangerous parts of the production process. In order to do so they must overcome the bureaucratic objections of Group Leader Liu, who as a male factory official comes to prioritize another woman for promotion to the chemicals section, one described as having "a sense of the intellectual about her."[49] Wang Ying and Yumei eventually devise an arrangement in which "after work, provided that there was no meeting to be held, Yumei learned the skills and common knowledge about mixing chemicals from Wang Ying. During the day, whenever there was an opportunity, Yumei would lean against the window of the chemicals room in order to watch Wang Ying mix the chemicals, and she often got up early or went to bed late in order to study."[50]

The emergence of regular, repeated mutual relations of study and labor between these women, in conjunction with the suggestive relations of intimacy and support that emerge in the setting of the factory dormitory, calls into further question the extent to which the aspiration of being "a woman like a man" is adequate as a vision of gendered emancipation through labor. In other words, the expectations that are set up by the narrative and which are central to Yumei's own subjectivity come to later be challenged, insofar as relations such as those between Yumei and Wang Ying indicate instead that the unequal relations of power between male cadres and women workers in the factory requires new relations and subjectivities that are specific to women and that will activate new possibilities, possibilities that in turn register a set of profound contradictions and tensions with those very imaginaries of masculinized labor that otherwise inform the first part of the narrative. To this extent, the novel poses the narrative protocols of a certain process of proletarian development only to call them into question when Yumei's experience of the factory proves to encompass its own forms of masculinized power.

This incipient critique is, however, necessarily overshadowed by the advance knowledge of the accident that is to befall Yumei, of which the reader is aware as a result of the formal prolepsis with which the text begins. The tragedy of this event is all the more significant for the fact that, unlike later texts, it is not devolved onto a specific agent in the form of a "saboteur" but emerges as the consequences of an overaccelerated tempo of industrial production. In view of the political requirements that devolved on writing in the period, the closure of the novel is naturally one that seeks to preserve the possibility of a worker who has suffered bodily injury still playing an important role in the socialist industrialization project, with Yumei being selected as a model worker. Her own fate is anticipated in these terms by that of the party secretary, Li Qiang, who has suffered the loss of a leg due to his service as a soldier, and yet otherwise serves as the archetype of a loyal party secretary. Here again, however, there are signs of a deferral of narrative expectations that are strongly gendered in nature, as, despite indications that Li Qiang will marry Yumei in a marriage of those who have suffered injury at the site of production, Li Qiang eventually comes to marry Wang Ying, situating Yumei outside of any conventional image of a stable proletarian family. While undergoing hospital care, and having undergone a painful adjustment in the positioning of her arm at the hands of the Soviet doctor, she eventually resolves, in spoken dialogue with Wang Ying, as follows: "'Does it hurt very much?' 'It's all right, I can bear it. Comrade Gastev has been able to leave me with one hand, and wants to help me become a useful person 有用的人, but had I cried out in pain, would he still have been willing to help me?'"[51]

The adjustment in this context of the formulation of being a "useful person" marks its recalibration, and not only through the displacement of the gendered signifier of "woman" in favor of the generalized "person." Whereas previously it derived from an opposition between factory labor and domestic work, here it takes on a radically different significance, one that in fact displaces the hegemony of able-bodied productive labor over the category of "use," and in doing so also intersects with the shifting role of the aspiration to be a "woman like a man" that also surfaces in the text. The ultimate form of "use" of which Yumei proves capable is an educative and affective one, in the way that she herself assumes a role of care in relation to other workers who have suffered bodily injury. There are, then, multiple ways in which this novella works through the tensions within the narrative paradigm of a smooth transformation into a disciplined proletarian, consisting of the striking prolepsis with which the novel begins, but also by the critique it introduces of those very forms of gendered desire that account for Yumei's initial movement into the factory, and finally, of the way it poses the problem of "useful" labor. At its most radical, Bai Lang's novel poses powerful questions about the gendered status of labor under socialism and the status of the socialist factory, subverting narrative protocols that otherwise naturalized the privileging of industrial over urban spaces, and masculinized over female labor. It may be said that the novel works against its own discursive subtext at the level of narrative form.

The moments of tension that surface in both narratives were, however, not merely narrative in nature, but corresponded to real antimonies in the political economy of Chinese socialism, not least the systematic reproduction of those very sites of temporal unevenness between rural and urban spaces that the First Five-Year Plan was supposed to overcome. In this light, in 1954, even several years after Zhou Yang called on culture workers to align their writing with the temporal demands of industrialization, there was a further meeting called jointly under the aegis of the Writers Association and the Trade Union Federation on the subject of "how literary and artistic creation should express the problems of national industrial construction," at which Bai Lang herself was present, together with Li Fuchun, the latter speaking in his capacity as vice premier and head of the State Planning Commission.[52] Li reprised the familiar critique of the prevalence of the ideas of the small producers among the industrial working class and called on writers to commit themselves to exposing these problems through literature, suggesting that, with respect to its incorporation into industrial production and suitability for the tasks of socialist modernization, the Chinese working class remained several generations behind that of the Soviet Union. In addressing the problem of how culture workers should go down to the factory, Li emphasized that writers should enter the factories as "participants in actual work," whether in a cultural or other kind of capacity. Moreover, they should so according to a formal regulation of their time: "Before engaging in work, [culture workers] should put forward a plan, to determine first of all which workshop we should go to, what questions we should seek to understand, how much time we should use, and then afterward the places we should return to, the problems we should seek to understand."[53]

The proposal of a plan to inform writers during their time in the factory marks a further demand for the whole process of cultural production to be aligned to a temporal process of industrial labor and modernization. The dialectic of ever-increasing demands on both writers and workers came to intensify over the mid-1950s, whereby the regularized production schedule of the factory came to provide the image for writing itself. In his 1955 article "Culture Workers, Busy Yourselves," Lao She not only reiterated the paramount importance of writing plans but further demanded that "we enlarge our plans somewhat, so that we can better enable ourselves to automatically enhance labor discipline, and consciously work to complete our plans. As such, those who have not already drawn up plans should do so quickly, in order to eliminate any blank spaces 消灭空白."[54]

These demands gave way in turn to a direct comparison between the tasks of writing and the schedule of factory production, so that Lao She further called on writers to "draw up plans for increasing production in the manner of the workers in mines and factories."[55] In this way, an image of a disciplined working class was deployed to spur on writing in order to help produce that very class through the power of cultural production. There was, in this sense, a contradiction at the heart of these constantly increasing dynamics, whereby a socialist working class was both immediately present, and invoked as a model for cultural labor, and yet the very urgency of cultural labor lay in the need to eliminate the remaining peasant habits of work at the site of industrial production. The peasant assumed a haunting role that could never be fully abolished, and it is partly in these terms that we may understand the repeated injunctions to execute and enhance plans, which tended toward a constant intensification of the demands on culture workers. There subsequently emerged intimations of the limits of the totalizing organization of writing, including in the directives to plan writing according to the temporalities of factory production. Even as early as April 1954, a report in *Writers Dispatch* stressed that "creation is a specific kind of labor, a highly complicated and detailed form of labor, and these specific features in turn determine that creation plans must differ from production plans. Creation plans cannot have ready-made and unified quotas, and nor can they have precise targets and figures. Therefore the creation plan is indeed the most difficult of all plans to settle." The basis of this difficulty lay not only in the differences between cultural and other forms of production, but also in the distinction between writing and other forms of culture: "in the case of production departments such as film, plans to establish film content in accordance with objective requirements and the subjective capacities for creation are entirely necessary, and so too it is necessary to work to guarantee the completion of an annual production plan for films. Yet, generally speaking, leading departments of literature and art should understand the specific features of literary and artistic production and the specific laws that govern creation."[56]

These lines of critique re-emerged in February 1956 at the second expanded meeting of the Council of the Writers Association, which reposed the question of the specificity and temporality of writing. In his address, Ba Jin directed himself to the question of the collaborative contents of writing and chose his formulations carefully: "I would not deny that creation is a collective enterprise 集体的事业 quite the contrary, I emphasize that creation is indeed a collective enterprise and is absolutely not the enterprise of the writer as an individual. Yet creation is [also] a form of individual labor, and the literary work has an individual character."[57]

The collective character of creation, for Ba Jin, lay in the fact that the writer is necessarily located in a broader system of social relations, and yet so too did the individual character of writerly labor—"intense labor" 强度的劳动, in fact—resolve itself into an explicit demand for time, and time not only for the immediate practice of writing but also for the uneven and irregular character of the work of literary creation. He articulated this as follows: "Allow those of us who engage in creation to have sufficient time, at the minimum, allow us to have the time to raise the pen in order to write to a certain degree, and time, too, for the purpose of fermentation and consideration before we turn to the actual business of writing."[58]

Ba Jin further emphasized the ways in which the specific temporality of writing took forms that might not be legible in terms of standard conceptions of productivity, noting, then, that "there are many who, when they are interrupted, simply cannot immediately return to the protagonist of their novel. Negligence is also no method of success. We simply have to look at the manuscripts of Tolstoy to understand the kind of labor that creation is."⁵⁹ The practice of writing, as understood here, comprised an irregular mode of repetition, consisting of the constant movement between the immediate business of writing and periods of mental accumulation, as well as the revision of literary works themselves. The reinvocation of the autonomy of writing called into question the more extravagant demands for the planning of cultural production, as well as the proliferation of demands made on culture workers. So too did it pose the further question of how to understand writing as a truly collaborative enterprise. Yet if nothing else, it indicated the exhaustion of the professional culture workers, and the need to forge new writers—from the working class.

Proletarian writing in and beyond the factory

The accumulation of demands placed on culture workers drawn from the pre-1949 cultural system over the first half of the 1950s provided the conditions for an expansion in the ranks of writers, an imperative made explicit at the same second expanded meeting of the Council of the Writers Association at which Ba Jin had spoken. In his speech to the meeting, entitled "Cultivate New Forces, Expand the Literary Ranks," Mao Dun called direct attention to the insufficient numbers of culture workers able to assume the manifold tasks that writers were called upon to assume. The practical corollary of this set of problems was for a dramatic shift in emphasis to the cultivation of new writers from among the working class.⁶⁰ In the "1956–67 Work Program" agreed on at the meeting, which marked the further extension of the organizational role of the Writers Association, there was included an explicit commitment to support the cultivation of new writers.⁶¹ In actual fact, this demand was hardly limited to the immediate problem of the limited numbers of writers. It also related to the political task of developing new writers from among the working class, as distinct from the writers of petty-bourgeois origin that had passed through the Yan'an period. Already, in 1938, Mao had anticipated the formation of worker-peasant intellectuals as a parallel to the ideological transformation of petty-bourgeois intellectuals, noting, then, that "worker and peasant cadres will at the same time become intellectuals, while the intellectuals will at the same time become workers and peasants 工农群众化."⁶² For this reason there had already emerged, over the first half of the 1950s, programs aimed at encouraging workers to write, especially in Shanghai and Tianjin, of which the most famous was the Literary Lecture Institute, founded in 1950 under Ding Ling.⁶³

In Shanghai, from which the most famous worker-writers emerged, the cultivation of these writers was largely indebted to mass publications which created training programs giving writers from the working class who showed promise in writing opportunities for training. The Shanghai-based *Liberation Daily*, for example, organized a training class for worker-correspondents, in which professional culture workers served as sources of guidance, including such famous authors as Ke Lan, Hu Feng, and Ru Zhijuan.[64] Shanghai ultimately produced the most successful and well-known worker writers, among them Hu Wanchun, Tang Kexin, and Fei Liwen.[65] Yet, as we have seen from Mao Dun's remarks and the direction of cultural policy, the emphasis at this juncture was on the primary role of professional culture workers in meeting the demands of workers as consumers of culture. In this context, the 1956 meeting reckoned with the alleged failure of culture workers to commit themselves to the cultivation of new writers. From 1956 onward, those worker-writers who had already published in periodicals in the early 1950s gained a new, national visibility. This process was not without its own contradictions. Subsequent reflections on the part of worker-writers themselves, written for the purpose of narrating their self-incorporation into the cultural apparatuses of the socialist state, demonstrate that the desire of such writers to undertake their literary craft tended to overspill the expectations of narratives about their immediate industrial environments or matters of production. Zhang Ying, part of the Shanghai-based nexus of writers, wrote in 1958 with reference to his trajectory of writing that, having initially failed to get submissions accepted by literary periodicals, and showing distaste for stories based solely on "industrial themes" 工业题材: "I began to follow the trend of writing romance novels, so that while others wrote about love triangles 三角恋爱, I wrote about affairs involving five people 五角恋爱, making my stories very complex indeed. Yet my drafts were still rejected, with the editor comrade writing in his rejection letter that I carried petty-bourgeois sentiment. Upon reading such letters I felt aggrieved, thinking: I'm a worker writer, so how could I have petty-bourgeois sentiment?"[66]

The hilarity of this anecdote should not conceal the importance of the point at hand, which is that the problem of the unruliness of workers at the point of production and the continued difficulty of organizing the writing of the professional culture workers extended to worker-writers as well, insofar as their desire to write about subject matter beyond the purview of their immediate sphere of "life," that is, beyond the sphere of production, marks its own form of unruliness, and one that could not easily be contained. The status of worker-writers therefore posed crucial questions around the contents of cultural labor. These debates were to persist throughout the socialist period, focusing specifically on the problem of temporality, namely, the relationship between the temporality of writing versus that of the site of collective labor from which working-class writers arose. The practical permutation of this problem was whether workers who showed interest or promise in writing should ultimately be transformed into professional writers, or how else, if these writers remained "amateur" cultural producers, sufficient time should be allocated for writing. This marked, then, the intensification of that very problem that had already arisen with respect to professional writers, who, in the 1950s, had to reconcile diverse demands made on their time, but who could nonetheless expect to have time away from the immediate site of production to conduct writing. Within the immediate context of the 1950s, new worker-writers were, however, seen to embody the democratic cultural aspirations of the new socialist state, namely in those writings that—as against Zhang Ying's desire to write about romance—do take the industrial as their appropriate subject matter. In this context, Tang Kexin's early writings, emerging from his experience in a textile factory, possess a special significance.

His landmark story, "Gu Xiaoju and Her Sisters," having first been published in *Liberation Daily* in 1954 and then republished in Tang's 1956 collection *Spring in the Workshop*, offers a further elaboration of the images of proletarian sisterhood introduced by Bai Lang. The decisive feature of this narrative in its spatial arrangements as compared to the other narratives of proletarian development examined in this chapter is the radical spatial restriction to the urban in place of the complicated spatial and temporal relations between city and countryside that emerge from other texts, through the figure of the "new worker." The larger content of the narrative consists of the shifting relations between different female workers in a textile factory as they seek to uncover the potential for the rationalization of production. "Gu Xiaoju and Her Sisters" tells of a rift between Gu Xiaoju and her close friend, Wang Yufang. Wang initially rebuffs Gu's interest in rationalizing their methods of inserting yarn in the cloth workshop, only to later emerge as the originator of a yet more effective work method that allows workers to attend to a larger number of textile machines on a more efficient basis. The narrative construction of these two workers and their relations enacts a separation from the countryside that allows the narrative to be self-contained in its orientation toward the immediate site of the factory, which thereby emerges as a totalizing setting both for the narrative world and for the life experiences of the workers themselves. In the introductory sequence that recounts their life histories,

> The women yarn insertion workers all knew that Xiaoju and Yufang were young sisters who got on very well with each other. Since a young age Xiaoju had no mother or father, nor any brothers or sisters of her own, and instead she had grown up with her uncle until the age of fourteen whereupon she had

entered the factory to serve as an apprentice. As for Yufang, her family were in the countryside, and she worked in the factory on a solitary basis. As a result, both of them lived in the singles factory dormitory.[67]

The positing of these narrative figures allows for a focus around a specifically urban site of production in such a way that the narrative can both avoid the problems of the rural/urban relationship as actualized in the kinds of narrative figures that inform other texts from this period and the pressing problem of the role of the family in the reproduction of labor. The site of factory production functions as a surrogate family to which the functions of the production of labor power have been devolved, including through factory-based forms of collective culture. The narrative, then, makes frequent references to the kinds of cultural activities that define the factory space as not only a site of production but as a totalizing space for the organization of life. The opening scene of the narrative, prior to the introduction of its protagonists, immediately concerns cultural production, narrated as part of the regular life of the factory, so that "every Sunday, in the garden club of the factory, there was always a weekly evening show, where, while the items on the program were not all particularly magnificent, they were varied in number, and so there were always many participants, of whom the majority were young people."[68]

The point of departure for the narrative proper lies in a trip undertaken to a neighboring factory where Xiaoju witnesses a new work method whereby insertion workers handle yarn "one by one," which allows for the avoidance of wasted material. This visit, through which Xiaoju meets a worker from the sister factory named Lingling, marks a broadening of the spatial parameters of the narrative to encompass another factory. This moment of spatial movement also provides for a dispute between Xiaoju and Yufang over the validity of this work method which tests the extent of sisterhood between the women, in which the basis of Yufang's opposition focuses around the allegedly slower speed of inserting yarn this way, framed in terms that draw attention to the precise features of factory labor. Yufang insists that "our direction of development is mechanization and automation, not this kind of "handicraft work" method" 手工业 and argues that the only method that would truly make for efficiency gains is one that would parallel the Hao Jianxiu method, referring to a work method introduced in textile factories based on the regularized bodily movements of workers on the shop floor, and widely promoted throughout China in the 1950s.[69]

Yufang's rude objection to Xiaoju's own interest in adopting the work method of their sister factory inspires teasing and mockery on the part of other shop floor workers, including the petty Guiying. As a result, Xiaoju is forced to reconsider the limits of her immediate bounds of sisterhood. In an extended soliloquy, delivered through unquoted rhetorical questions that infer free indirect style, Xiaoju's own understanding of sisterhood shifts from her immediate companionship to a political sisterhood that identifies sisterhood with the politically advanced workers at the factory:

> She felt herself to be terribly isolated, like a flag pole standing all alone; but as she thought about it, she realized that this was not absolutely true, she felt that she did indeed still have a family, she did still have many brothers and sisters, she thought of Lingling; how good it would be if Lingling were with her! If there were two or three others, their strength would be yet greater, and there would be more ways of doing things. At this moment, all the different characters in her workshop appeared before her, surely there were at least some who were like Lingling? Had not Cailan of the third row always refused to speak cruel words to her? She thought also of the first shift, and of the branch secretary of the youth brigade Hu Jinxiu, who had already become a party member.[70]

This passage, combining psycho-narration with the use of free indirect style, ends with the realization, directly quoted as Xiaoju's murmur to herself, that in fact "aren't the party and young organization my own, most warm family!" The invocation of the party as family here marks a family that is twice removed from the absent biological family, in that this political family is itself a certain replacement for the immediate bonds of sisterhood between Xiaoju and Yufang that have been frayed due to their disagreements over the introduction of new work methods. There is, here, then, a difference between this text and Bai Lang's novel, insofar as the latter sought to ground visions of proletarian sisterhood as an incipient critique of the disciplinary structure of the factory and its gendered forms of authority. In Tang Kexin's text, on the other hand, it is precisely the site of industrial production that informs the content of sisterhood, and more specifically by the progressive integration of workers into the temporalities of the factory shop floor. Through her new relationships with Lingling and others, Xiaoju finally arrives at a new work method that will allow for a regularized pattern of bodily movement on the shop floor, parallel to the Hao Jianxiu method, one in which, in the words of a worker from Lingling's factory, "in the past I ran wildly this way and that, going horizontally and vertically, but if I ran vertically would we not be able to save time?"[71] In the event, the introduction of a regularized movement pattern allows for Xiaoju to take care of a new record of forty-eight machine stations on the shop floor within a compressed period of time. The semicomic denouement of the narrative comes when Yufang is not only convinced of the attempts to transform the pattern of labor as pioneered by Xiaoju and her sisters but, it is revealed, has also herself developed a method through which workers will be able to supervise fifty-four machine stations, which Xiaoju pledges to introduce to Lingling and other workers at the sister factory. In the end, their shared participation in developing new methods of production is the occasion for the renewal of sisterhood between Xiaoju and Yufang.

The fact that this sisterhood is renewed on the basis of an acceleration in shop floor temporalities underscores the contradictions in the narrative, and its divergence form the more critical narrative arrangements of Bai Lang. One the one hand, the narrative emphasizes the intimate contours of a female proletarian sisterhood together with the agency of female workers to intervene in the production process. On the other, the narrative lays bare the inevitability of the woman workers' self-incorporation into a factory temporality that tends toward the incorporation of leisure as well as production at the factory site and pursues a constant rationalization of the movement of the proletarian body on the shop floor. The total character of the factory temporality is rendered legible by the spatial contours of the narrative, which exclude the characters from any relations with the countryside and focus on the immediate site of production.[72] In this context, those sites of temporal irreducibility within the narrative loom more important. This is true especially of Guiying, one of those workers who teases and mocks Xiaoju. When, having been convinced of the merits of Xiaoju's method, Yufang seeks to discuss the matter with Guiying, her reply is perturbing:

> "Even if you were to succeed in doing that, I would not do it myself."
> "If you don't do it, and then the rest of them were to supervise forty-eight machine stations, then surely you wouldn't just sit there and keep supervising only thirty-six?"
> "Well, why not? If that's not acceptable then they can just reassign me to do some other form of work, who do they think they can frighten? I, Lu Guiying, am not some kind of person without backbone."[73]

Guiying's refusal to adhere to a prospective acceleration in workshop temporality reenacts the problem of the remainder that reemerges across narratives from this period and which is elsewhere narrativized in the form of the peasant, but which here persists even within a narrative context without explicit references to the peasantry and the countryside. As such, Guiying gestures toward the ways in which the production of the socialist working class in the image of a disciplined class that is always already reorganized around the temporal demands of factory life and socialist industrialization was always a project that remained incapable of completion, just as the organization of accumulation around the extraction of rural surplus also served to reproduce the spatial and temporal antinomies between the city and the countryside. The temporal irreducibility of a minor diegetic figure on the grounds of their backwardness within Tang's texts also gestures beyond the narrative toward the temporality of writing as embodied by worker-writers such as Tang himself, which would reopen the most fundamental questions around cultural production.

The republication of this short story in 1956 coincided with not only the announcement of the completion of the basic tasks of socialist transformation but also the initial publication of the journal *Sprouts*, designed to showcase the work of new writers, as well as the important Nationwide Youth Literature Creator Meeting held in March 1956 in order to survey the achievements of worker-writers since 1949, in which Tang Kexin, Hu Wanchun, and Fei Liwen served as members of the Shanghai delegation. The central point of theoretical consideration of the speeches and discussions around the conference, largely derived from long-standing professional culture workers, lay in the problem of the temporality of writing as a feature of the professional culture worker. In the vocabulary of the discussions, this problem resolved itself into the distinction between professional and amateur practices of writing, and more specifically still, whether worker-writers should undergo professionalization whereby they would cease to be located in their initial contexts of factory labor and instead become members of the Writers Association. To work as an amateur writer, by contrast, meant to write while retaining a status as a worker at the point of production, rather than draw material support from the Writers Association. The meeting witnessed a key intervention from Zhou Yang around these problems. He argued that we "should not make [amateur worker-writers] leave their site of work" but that they should nonetheless be allocated definite periods of leave for the purpose of writing. Moreover: "In the case of those people who have spent long periods of time working, who have talent in creation, and who already have a rich basis of life experience 生活经验, consideration should be given to such people being transferred to being professional writers."[74]

In these respects, Zhou followed closely in the steps of Liu Shaoqi, who also argued that writers should maintain their amateur status at the point of production. In addressing the formally separate problem of the relationship between professional writers and life, Liu argued that experiencing life demanded that writers participate in "actual work" but that, provided this work was relevant to their literary task, "even a short period of time is also suitable."[75] The problem of a permanent location at the point of "life," in the sense of the experience of production versus periodic experiences as a preparation for writing, was here cast as a temporal one that underpinned the distinction between amateur and professional models of cultural production. Lao She indicated the complexity of this problem at the 1956 meeting. He emphasized that the location of amateur writers at the point of production meant that their encounter with life was limited to their immediate environment but also reliable, so that "to experience life in this way is more reliable than occasionally going down to the countryside for three months or spending half a year in the factory." In the same terms, he pointed out that: "If, after having issued forth one or two texts, we then leave the location of work and go become a professional writer, then success is not guaranteed. To leave the location of work is also to depart from the base for experiencing life."[76]

Problems of this order became increasingly intense over the duration of the entire socialist period. The moments of uncertainty and hesitancy that emerged from these early debates marked both the dangers of a premature professionalization of writers and the value of an ongoing encounter with "life" in its Maoist permutation. At the same time, and recalling Ba Jin's remarks on the complex temporality of writing, these moments marked an understanding of the limitations of amateur practice, insofar as writing was understood to maintain its own specific temporality that could not be posed simply as an appendage to regular employment at the point of production or relegated to something to be done in leisure time. The most prescient articulation of these problems came from the worker-writers themselves. Fei Liwen recounted in his 1956 article "We Must be Masters of Time" that, upon encountering a failure of writing in 1953, he ascribed this failure to a lack of time: "If only I could go and be a professional writer then it would all be alright, the twenty four hours of a day would all be under my own control, and I could safely spend all my time and energy solely on creation, and so too could I constantly carry out visits, and carry out improvements, to ensure that I could better carry out [cultural] production as compared to the present, and so too would my creation be ten times stronger."[77]

The upshot of Fei's aspiration is that, separating himself from the conditions of production, he found that his problems of writing were not resolved, and was eventually forced to recognize that the solution lay not in his becoming a professional writer but rather in the more effective organization of his leisure time through a literal timetable, so that he began to methodically organize his time: "The time for study, the time for writing, the time for mass work, the time for watching films and leisure activities and so on, all of these I strictly stipulated, and on my timetable I wrote: 'In order to be a good writer, one must first of all be someone who respects the system.'"[78]

Fei also insisted that "an amateur writer must, in order to be able to use leisure time to write, organize this time just as one would conduct a production task, and, over the long term, to strenuously make use of every moment of free time, and then it is possible to write many drafts."[79] Fei's emphasis on the scientific organization of time as central to the successful practice of the amateur writer, whereby the temporality of factory production came to structure writing itself, seeks to provide a counterpoint to his expressed desire to become a professional writer, and yet the fact that many amateur writers did become professional writers provided the point of departure for a series of struggles that were to prove central to the problem of cultural labor. This latter state informed Tang Kexin's 1957 intervention, published in *Sprouts* as part of a series of reflections from worker-writers on their experiences of creation. Tang reflected on his changed social situation as a result firstly of having withdrawn from the shop floor to engage in trade union work, and then having become a professional writer under the aegis of the Writers Association, as well as being part of the editorial staff of *Sprouts*. Tang's emphasis is on the detrimental effect of withdrawing from immediate contact with life, hence the title of his short article "Let Me Once Again Return to the Factory!" Tang argued that his capacity to understand "life" has been rendered more complex since his separation from production: "The sole condition [for creation] was: I lived among the masses, and moreover I was one of them, so there was no matter we did not discuss, and so it was not necessary to pay special attention to them, whenever I wrote things, the first thing to leap to my mind was the colleagues with whom I was most familiar, and when I wrote of these people, it was not necessary to exert any great effort to express the details of their characters because I was familiar with each gesture of these people."[80] By contrast, Tang's professionalization had produced a separation from the conditions of life due to the separation between the time of writing and the time of labor which can only be resolved by his renewed contact with the immediate conditions of social life at the point of production. Tang's intervention along these lines as combined with Fei Liwen and others showed the emergent contestation of the culture worker as the professional organizer of social relations under early socialism. This contestation grew from the specific conditions of the worker-writers but would quickly assume a wider significance, especially over the period 1957–1958. The question of whether amateur writers should undergo professionalization, while seemingly practical, was also the site of fundamental theoretical questions about the temporality of writing and that of labor and whether the figure of the "professional writer" as the assumed figure of transition under socialism did not also reproduce a division between mental and manual labor.[81] The contested figure of the professional writer and the related distinction between professional and amateur forms of writing process therefore marked a premonition of crises to come.

A year of consequence

The discussions around the problem of worker-writers in 1956 beckoned a larger transformation in the social relations of labor that would, in turn, generate crucial problems for the duration of the Chinese Revolution. The completion of the nationalization of industry in 1956 and the formation of advanced producer cooperatives in the agricultural sector in the same year allowed for a thoroughgoing transformation in the content of the wage, manifested in the introduction of a unified payment system in that year, across both industrial and agricultural settings. In an early 1956 speech that presaged the formal introduction of the wage reform in June 1956, Li Fuchun insisted that "the wage under the socialist system is fundamentally different from the wage under the capitalist system." Whereas under capitalism labor power functions as a commodity, under socialism "labor power is no longer a commodity, and instead its wage reflects the laborer's relation between serving society and serving the self." The practical import of the reform as executed in industry was to institute a nationwide eight-rank wage scale based on the principle of "from each according to their ability, to each according to their labor" which Li argued "was the socialist principle." He cautioned that "in the area of wage remuneration it is necessary to oppose egalitarianism, by making sure that, between skilled and unskilled labor, and onerous manual labor and light manual labor, and between mental and manual labor, there exists a certain difference" with respect to the wage.[82] In these terms, socialist transformation was said to have abolished wage labor as a capitalist social relation and to have rendered labor directly social in character.

Whereas in the industrial sector a comprehensive system of state ownership enabled the introduction of a nationwide scale, in the countryside the adoption of a system of collective ownership under the advanced cooperatives necessitated a more complex remuneration system. The standard for rural remuneration was stipulated in the "Model Regulations for an Advanced Producers Cooperative" issued in late 1955, which called for cooperative cadres to stipulate quotas commensurate with different kinds of agricultural labor, under a work points system based on the calculation of labor days, with work points being paid on the basis of the household, to the family head.[83] The adoption of these wage systems supposedly marked the transcendence of the capitalist wage, but so too did it institutionalize the division between rural and urban spaces and their attendant temporalities. Yet most important for present purposes is that these wage reforms also extended directly to the culture workers themselves, in their capacity as formal employees of the state. The regulations issued in 1955 on the payment of state employees under the title "Order Concerning the Universal Implementation of a Wage System and the Reform of the Monetary Wage System Among State Employees" replaced the "supply system" of open provision that had provided the material needs of culture workers in Yan'an in the early 1950s.[84] Culture workers were henceforth paid a formal, monetary wage according to a nationwide scale that distinguished between different culture workers according to seniority, as well as receiving income from manuscript payments.

Between urban and rural spaces, therefore, as well as with respect to cultural labor, the year 1956 marked the codification and institutionalization of a set of differences under Chinese socialism, premised on the understanding that labor power had ceased to be a commodity. The very next year, however, this system would be thrown into crisis, beginning with the cultural sphere, and leading radicals to argue that ostensibly socialist labor remained linked to capitalist logics.

CHAPTER 3

TIME FOR COMMUNISM

Mass Writing, Revolutionary Form, and "Bourgeois Right"

This surely demonstrates: my pen cannot keep pace with the speed of production.

—Guo Moruo 郭沫若

Guo Moruo's 郭沫若 comment on the inadequacy of his writing, reflective and triumphant in equal measure, was a response to the extraordinary increases in production reported by the People's Communes over the course of 1958. Having written a celebratory poem under the title of "Mounting a Rocket" in August on the production achievements of Macheng, Guo was forced to acknowledge that, previous targets having been surpassed, he would henceforth have to change an entire stanza of his poem. Its humorous contents notwithstanding, Guo's remarks also spoke to a set of fundamental issues concerning the politics of writing amid a period of incredible transformations in the social relations of labor. The Great Leap marked the moment at which the Chinese Revolution posed anew the problem of transition. In the same terms, this chapter also marks the central moment of transition within the book, as the Great Leap provided at least a formal definition of what communist labor would entail. In April 1958 the countryside witnessed the founding of the first commune and the beginning the commune movement, which sought to create communes as new modes of social organization that would take advantage of the vast reserves of rural labor power, not only for reservoir construction but also for the formation of new rural industries, marking, therefore, a rejection of the urban-centered pattern of industrialization that had dominated the earlier period. The Leap was, if nothing else, an attempt to forge a new set of relations of labor that would overcome the temporal imbalances between city and countryside that China had inherited from the prerevolutionary period and which had been systematically reproduced throughout the early 1950s. Yet the changes wrought by the Leap also extended, in the cities and countryside, to the partial socialization of reproductive labor in the form of collective housework, childcare, and above all by the collective canteens that were formed across the countryside over the latter half of 1958. The collective canteens were distinguished by the free or partially free distribution of foodstuffs, a system that was designed not only to release larger bodies of women's labor for mobilization in agricultural and other kinds of production but also fed into key discussions around the wage as an arbiter of socialist social relations. The Great Leap therefore sought to forge a new set of egalitarian social relations, especially in the countryside, as well as a drive to maintain a high rate of accumulation by ratcheting up the intensity and duration of labor, in ways that ultimately had horrific consequences, above all for China's peasants.

The theoretical conclusions that emerged from these attempts and failures were to have far-reaching consequences for the problem of labor in China's revolution. The scale and speed of this process was also, however, intimately connected to the problem of the writer. Guo Moruo's lament in September 1958 therefore reflects a crisis of precisely that model of the professional writer that had been produced by the cultural institutions of the post-1949 period. The aspiration behind the culture worker, as an intellectual who had undergone transformation and so become adequate to the production of a new socialist culture orientated toward the masses and the transformation of social relations, came to appear inadequate by virtue of the way that the location of writing in an individual author produced and reproduced the division between mental and manual labor. But so too, and in the more practical vein indicated by Guo Moruo's lament, was an individual practice or rhythm of writing deemed inappropriate to the temporal demands of the Great Leap, that is, the demand to develop practices of writing that could respond to and embody the extent of social revolution, especially with respect to speed. The demands that were put on the problem of cultural production during the Great Leap were therefore indicative of the contradictions of the Great Leap more generally, consisting both of a critique of the professional author from the perspective of challenging the division between mental and manual labor, and accelerating cultural production in order to engender a total acceleration in the conditions of labor and accumulation. The demand in the Great Leap, then, was above all to write quickly, in order that pens would, in Guo's words, be able to keep pace with the speed of production.

A factory of literature?

The emergent critique of the modes of cultural organization that had emerged in the first decade of socialism was rendered possible by a wide-ranging crisis centered on the problem that had already become evident in 1956, namely, whether amateur writers drawn from the working class should undergo professionalization via incorporation into the Writers Association. This apparently technical issue posed wider questions for the problem of writing under socialism, namely the ways in which the retention of writing as the practice of an individual author, and especially one whose social function as a writer was formally validated by an institution such as the Writers Association, would systematically reproduce the division between mental and manual labor and render culture inadequate to the task of supporting the ongoing project of social transformation. The theoretical contents of this critique, moreover, introduced the conceptual categories which also aided a larger critique of the Soviet model of socialist development as it had emerged from the 1950s, namely, the category of "bourgeois right" 资产阶级法权, which assumed a wide-ranging significance from the Great Leap onward. The cadre responsible for opening the theoretical problem of the inadequacy of the culture worker was Lu Dingyi 陆定一, and it was amid the tumults of the Anti-Rightist Movement of 1957 that these problems emerged in a theoretically explicit way, by posing the question of how to theorize the reproduction of the capitalist intellectual under socialist conditions. The answer, Lu suggested, was a complex one. It lay not only in the continued influence of ideas from the old society, but also in the way that, under socialism: "'Bourgeois right' still exists in the distribution of the means of consumption, it is still not possible to distribute according to need, but rather only according to labor, whereby we distribute means of consumption according to the principle of equal exchange in commodity production."[1]

The theoretical significance of this category was, at this juncture, left unexplained, and yet, in a further elaboration of the economic reproduction of a privileged class of writers, Lu explicitly extended his critique to the problem of manuscript fees. There are some such writers, he said, "who have a large income from manuscript fees, live in the cities, do not go down among the laboring masses, such that their life becomes corrupt and degenerate, and in political terms they degenerate into capitalist rightists."[2] Perhaps most important within this critique, however, was the suggestion that the very conditions of an individualized practice of writing generate an ongoing tendency toward ideological degeneration and the reproduction of a division between mental and manual labor, as "the means of work of writers are a mode of handicraft production 手工业, which very easily gives rise to ideas of individualism and liberalism." The cruel irony was that the occasion for Lu's intervention was the campaign against, among others, Ding Ling, for her alleged rightist tendencies, even while Lu implicitly drew on the grammar of Ding Ling's own concerns about the problem of a "double life" under the post-1949 literary system. Echoing Ding Ling even while she was cast out of the ranks of writers, Lu's speech provided a materialist account of the author as a social relation of cultural production drawn into socialist society, and the attendant problem of the ongoing reproduction of that relation under socialist conditions. If this was true of the culture worker who had been drawn from the pre-1949 period, Lu argued, then so was it also true of the worker-writers who had been cultivated under the socialist system itself, precisely via their transformation into professional authors embodied in formal literary institutions. Lu argued that these writers "live among the masses for a few years, write a few relatively good works, and then become placed in the 'creation groups' that are divorced from the masses, such that they excessively early become so-called 'professional writers,' whereupon they are divorced from life, live in the big cities, only occasionally go down to the countryside to 'experience life,' and so gradually become separated from the sole source of creation."[3]

The emergence of the worker-writer as a site of anxiety concerning the professionalization of writing under socialism would reemerge during the Cultural Revolution, and yet the content of this criticism could hardly be limited to those new writers alone, but rather also extended to professional writers drawn from the prerevolutionary period. Thus, the major editorial "We Must Have a Great Cultural Detachment of the Working Class" drew upon Lu Dingyi's intervention but did so with specific reference to the recurrent problem of "experiencing life," arguing that this practice, foundational to the post-1949 institutionalization of the culture worker in the 1950s, suffered from an internal temporal disjuncture between the time of labor and the time of writing. The limitations of "experiencing life," it was argued, is that it is "only temporary, the kind of thing one only does once in a while and is done solely in order to collect materials for creation. This is to say, that authors do not become one with masses, they do not live with them, and share their pleasures and joys, but rather only go and serve as a guest among them on an occasional basis."[4] At the theoretical heart of this mode of critique, then, is the understanding that the withdrawal of amateur worker-writers from their immediate site of production coexisted with the periodic dispatch of professional writers to the base in the temporal production of a division between mental and manual labor.

The anxiety around the professional culture worker resolved itself, by the end of 1957, into a renewed Rectification marked by the dispatch of writers to the countryside, with the "Report on the Problem of Writers Going Down to the Countryside and Down to the Factories" setting out detailed conditions for which categories of culture workers would be dispatched to the base, and demanding that such writers be distributed widely in order that they might support cultural practice in their localities. This same report also emphasized, in responding to earlier critiques of the premature disengagement of worker-writers from conditions of collective labor, that such writers: "should not undergo professionalization. These young writers should, without exception, participate in actual work and productive labor, and should constantly be among the masses, and should not be permitted to undergo premature professionalization, and in fact do not necessarily need professionalization [at all]."[5]

The anxieties expressed by these early critiques were confounded as the Great Leap got underway by the understanding that a practice of writing located in the individual writer could be resistant to the demands for acceleration embodied in the utopian frenzy of the Leap. Yet this did not negate attempts to reinforce the demands for the planning of literary production that had already been central to cultural work from the early 1950s onward. In March, a special conference of the Writers Association drew up a series of "thirty-two articles" on the role of literature in the Great Leap. The resulting open letter, published under the title "Authors! Leaps, Great Leaps!" in *People's Daily* called on authors to draw up quotas and schedules for the production of new literary works, noting that "in the Great Leap, individual [cultural] labor 个体的劳动 must have collective supervision, only in this way can everyone work quickly and effectively."[6] Among the concrete demands that this public letter embodied was the revision of existing literary plans, including an orientation toward new forms that could be adequate to the demands of the Leap:

> [Writers should] revise and fill out their existing plans, should change from doing what is within our means and taking it easy, to going all out, so that we rush surge forward and make our plans a "vanguard" plan among the writers. Each plan must be supplemented with several short and concise works that reflect and inspire the current Great Leap Forward. When writers have committed to writing novels, they must be executed according to the plan, being fast and good, and of high quality. At the same time, writers must write some short works and publish them at any time. In addition to long spears, we also need short clubs. No matter how long or short it is, we must create works.[7]

The injunction here that writers should intensify their literary creation within the framework of the creation plan, as one of the administrative measures that had informed the emergence of the cultural ISA in the early 1950s, underscores the tensions within the Great Leap. On the one hand, it marked the intensification of the demands put on professional authors and the state cultural system with which they were associated. Yet the incapacity of this system to fully accommodate these demands, together with the critique of the professionalization of writing that had emerged in 1957, also meant a search for new, amateur models of writing that surpassed and came to challenge the established ISA. The most ambitious of the practices associated with amateur culture was the new folk song movement, which, unfolding from mid-1958 onward, involved the active compilation of folk songs from rural and urban environments. The poems included in the major compendium *Red Flag Ballads*, a famous collection edited by Guo Moruo and Zhou Yang, were, crucially, published on an anonymous basis, allowing the circumstances of their authorship to be subsumed within the production of a new, mass writer, which the editors greeted as the sprouts of "communist art and literature."[8] The anonymization of these amateur poets and their inclusion within a single compendium pointed toward a search for alternatives to the model of writing as "handicraft production" that Lu Dingyi had condemned. The significance of this anonymization and the development of collections that escaped any singular author marks a radical vision of cultural production that surpassed the transitional figure of the culture worker, insofar as it offered an imminently collectivist form of writing. These two paths of approaching writing, namely the deindividuation of writing through communist projects such as the new folk songs on the one hand and the ongoing transformation of the culture workers themselves became, from this point onward, two lines of cultural transformation whose relations with one another were profoundly complex. In close relation to the anonymization of poetry was a renewed turn toward "collective creation" 集体创作. The practice of collective writing as it had emerged during the Leap had its pre-Liberation antecedents, but under post-1949 conditions a return to such practices offered a path for superseding the culture worker as the professional writer. In the editorial "Art and Literature Have Released Satellites," Hua Fu announced that "the creations of the worker and peasant masses since the Great Leap Forward, such as the new folk songs, already mark the widespread appearance of sprouts of communist literature."[9] Yu Heiding was no less enthusiastic when he wrote that "in thoroughly implementing the mass line in creation, it is necessary to comprehensively eliminate superstition, to destroy the idea of the special character of the author, and to destroy the mystical character of cultural creation."[10]

The works accommodated by this method of creation varied from single publications compiling many works written by individual amateur writers from among the peasants, such as the large collections of reportage collections that appeared during this period, but so too did it include dramatic texts that had been written and revised by amateur writers at a single workplace in concert with one another.[11] It was ultimately in the case of drama that these methods attracted the greatest enthusiasm, in large part because they could be linked with experiments during the Yan'an period, and also presented as adequate to the enhanced temporal demands of the Great Leap. In one of the first articles to appear on the subject in *Art and Literary Gazette*, Chen Baichen acknowledged the benefits of collective creation and did so with specific reference to the capacity of collectively written drama productions to reflect contemporary events, such that collective writing was invested with a capacity for simultaneity that differentiated it from the extended temporality of the professional writer. In Chen's words, then, "Chinese spoken word drama has a good tradition, which is to reflect reality in time with real events, and to be closely appropriate to present political tasks. Moreover, this good tradition is closely related to collective creation. The reason is simple: in order to be aligned with the present, it is necessary to write quickly, and in these terms collective creation can generally resolve such challenges."[12] The framing of collective drama in terms of the legacies of Yan'an suggestively allowed for a critique of the practices of cultural labor that had emerged earlier in the 1950s. The article "Collective Creation Is a Varied, Quick, Economical and Good Method of Creation" therefore stressed that:

> Since entering the cities, there has come about a wind of opposition to collective creation, though from where is unclear. The general sense seems to be: creation is an affair of the individual, and cannot be developed on a collective basis; each person has different perspectives on life, which makes it very difficult to devise a work together; artistic style must also acknowledge the style of each individual, which cannot be made identical with one another[13]

As dramatic as these ambitions were, however, only rarely did theorists of collective creation hint at an expansion to encompass all cultural forms. Hua Fu suggested, then, in his article "The Benefits of Collective Creation Are Many" that so too might collective creation be "applied when it comes to relatively long works of fiction." Hua Fu further stressed, however, that collective creation could not be allowed to entirely supplant the individual culture worker, noting that "the promotion of collective creation is not equivalent to rejecting individual writing, but is rather the "simultaneous development" of both methods. At the same time, collective creation is a creative form of artistic labor, and the amalgamation of the two can only give rise to positive results when it is a voluntary amalgamation."[14] Moreover, the same Chen Baichen who had celebrated the capacities of collective creation in drama noted that "literary creation is fundamentally an individual mode of labor, and in the future there will not appear any such factories of literature 文学工厂, and nor will collective creation acquire the leading position in creation."[15]

When collective creation did expand beyond drama, it was in the context of new prose forms that had emerged during the Great Leap itself. These included, for example, the "collective histories" that had first been promulgated by Maxim Gorky in the 1930s Soviet Union, and were introduced in China during this period as a basis on which workers, peasants and soldiers might write collective histories of factories, communes, and army units.[16] It is a matter of no little significance that this form began to circulate in China when it had ceased to exist in the Soviet Union itself, a fact of which Chinese theorists were themselves aware.[17] The opening of new forms of writing such as factory histories registered the ways in which the problem of writing engendered, in turn, a search for new literary forms. Yet the problem of form in the Great Leap ultimately drew its logic from those accelerated tempos of labor that also impelled a shift in the material organization of writing. There thus emerged from early 1958 onward a vocabulary of "short forms" that, being distinct from the extended temporalities of reading and writing that characterized the long-form novel, would be capable of intervening in the transformation of social relations. An expression of the theoretical rationale for new, short forms emerged through an editorial published in the *People's Daily* in April under the title "We Must Create More Literary Works in Short Forms," which stressed that "the enthusiasm of the masses for production and construction is so great, the situation developing so rapidly, and the demands of the masses so urgent, that those authors who commit themselves to serving the masses cannot take such a long time to write those kinds of works that only appear after eight or ten years."[18]

The "short" dimensions of these texts were themselves varied, extending not only to their length as texts, or the time required for creation, but also, as we shall see, the rapidity of their narrative rhythms. The demand for new, short-form texts gained support from many quarters. The theorist Zhang Chunqiao 张春桥, who will reappear at the end of this chapter, writing in his article "The Style of the Great Leap Forward," insisted that an uncritical valorization of long forms served to reproduce an atomized practice of cultural labor rooted in an extended temporality of writing. As against this, he asserted "the actual facts have already told us: although people do enjoy reading long works that describe history, yet even more so do people like those short works that reflect our reality of struggle in good time."[19] The occasion for Zhang's article was the upsurge in new folk songs. Yet, with respect to prose fiction, there was no short form more experimental than that of the "short short story" 小小说, which enjoyed an intense period of popularity over the course of the Leap, being a key site of theorization around the problem of form, but also a site of struggle over different modes of writing.

Writing on speed

The proliferation of the short short story was centered on key national literary journals, especially those hosting the work of worker-peasant writers, such as *Sprouts*, *New Harbor*, *Changjiang Art and Literature*, and *Liberation Army Art and Literature*, all of which made a decisive turn toward the short story as a primary focus of their publishing efforts over the Great Leap. There had, over the first half of the 1950s, already existed a theoretical discourse around the problem of short form. Hu Wanchun, for example, found it necessary to emphasize in 1957, writing in *Sprouts*, that amateur writers should not seek to privilege the novel as the point of departure for their writing practice, but should instead take smaller literary forms such as the short story as their initial base of writing, before moving into more extended forms such as the novel.[20] Yet the short short story of the Great Leap designated a practice quite different from that of its ostensible progenitors in other contexts, in that, in the Great Leap, the short short story was understood not only as a site of pedagogy in the manner of the early 1950s, but rather explicated in terms of how its temporalities of writing and reading provided the adequate rhythm of cultural labor for the demands of the historical moment. In these terms, literary theorists sought to finely distinguish the short short story and its practices of writing not only from the novel, but also from the short story itself. In an often-cited definition of the short short story, then, Mao Dun, writing in 1958, sought to argue that the short short story comprised texts not exceeding two thousand characters and stated that such a new literary form condensed the characteristics of the "sketch" on the one hand and the existing fictional short story on the other, so that, in his own summation, the short short story "is not only short and concise, but also, because they combine the specific features of the sketch (if we acknowledge that the sketch is concerned mainly with taking real people and real affairs as its object of description) and the short story (if we do not deny that the short short story also takes summation as its fundamental method) so has the short short story already emerged as a new form with its own individual character."[21]

Yet more important still for Mao Dun and others was the relationship between the short short story as textual form and its immediate historical present, such that the short short story was able to relate to immediate events and developments in such a way as to call into question the absolute status of its fictionality and even its relation to narrativity as such. The theorization of the short short story with respect to temporal simultaneity and the absolute force of the contemporary produced comparisons with visual media, typified by Mao Dun's comment:

First of all, the narratives of short short stories are very simple, often to the point of not having a narrative, consisting solely of the episodic actions of a character within a definite context. In the second place, this kind of "camera shot" 镜头 sketches out the bearing and spiritual world of this character. In terms of the narratives of short short stories being not entirely fictional, they are different from the creation process of short stories; but in terms of the fact that their portrayed characters are not real-world people but are rather more summary than the depiction of real people, they are also different from "sketches."[22]

The orientation toward a visual aesthetics carried over into other important theoretical articles surrounding the short short story, typified by that of Hu Qingpo, who therefore stated in terms strikingly suggestive of Mao Dun's initial article that "writers have a responsibility to extract their topics from life, and rapidly and intensely reflect such topics. There are certain characters and affairs within life, that we might say are common occurrences, but if they are expressed in a concentrated way, like a "close-up" camera lens in a film, so that they become prominent and are enlarged, then the audience will see more clearly, and the significance will become clearer."[23] The intense interest in visuality marked the ways in which the short short story as literary form was privileged for its relationship to immediacy, consisting not only of the temporal immediacy of the historical present but also the social immediacy of amateur writers in contexts of social labor. Yet more remarkable still is that the short short story also offered a new vision of reading, so to speak, one in which reading would no longer be bifurcated from labor as leisure or located in an individual reader but rather temporally and spatially synchronized with the site of labor. Song Shuang wrote in 1959: "Because they are short and lively, and generally consist of works concerning the newest and most beautiful life, feelings and thoughts, they can also be appreciated by the laboring masses even outside and during the process of strenuous labor, and in doing so rapidly and directly become a force of agitation and propaganda. It can be said without exaggeration that the short short story is a 'new genre with its own specific character' that accompanies labor."[24]

The emphasis on the short short story as offering a new temporality of reading as well as writing, and the combination of both reading and writing with the time of labor, underlines that the short short story was not simply one among many of the new forms that emerged during the Great Leap but rather denoted a new, recursive relationship between cultural production and manual labor, one in which amateur writers would undertake to write short short stories on the basis of their own, immediate experience of labor in order that these texts would provide the conditions for a collective experience of reading at the site of production, one that would, in turn, stimulate a new commitment to extended and intensified temporalities of production during the Great Leap. Yet this recursive dynamic within the form did not merely enhance an already existing set of narrative conventions, as so too did the short short story form also intervene in the very contents of socialist labor by drawing attention to new sites and practice of labor that had been largely absent from the narrative conventions of the preceding period, or not recognized as socially productive labor.[25] These capacities relied on a transformed relation to language as such. A veteran culture worker no less famous than Lao She, therefore, came to argue that the short short form demanded a new economy of language, and in fact a totalizing change in the material relations between writing and language. Concerns of this order emerged through Lao She's article "We Must Write More Short Short Stories," published in the combined February/March 1958 issue of the journal *New Harbor*. Lao She's emphasis in this text and throughout much of the theoretical discourse around short short stories during the Great Leap was that long-form texts do not in and of themselves embody greater literary value, and that they can, instead, lend themselves to a proliferation and excess of language:

> Writing with economy has its advantages. First, with respect to writers, there are some people who believe that the longer a literary work the better it is, and so they can easily push out a work of several tens of thousands of characters. But the actual facts demonstrate that the value of a work is not determined by its length. Within these tens of thousands of characters there may well be much superfluous language 废话.[26]

The more intense demands generated by an orientation toward short forms from the perspective of professional writers emerged as a problem to which Lao She would repeatedly return. In a separate article published in *People's Literature* under the suggestive title "The Shorter, the More Difficult," which offered a further rebuke to the conceit of "the longer the work the better it is," Lao She stated that "with respect to structure, a literary work must have an orderly structure and cannot resemble a sheet of loose sand. Yet, because the novel is after all long, even if it has some places in which it is not tightly structured, this can be tolerated. As for short texts, they are only a few thousand characters in length, so it is impermissible for there to be some places where the language is too extended, others where it is too brief or altogether insufficiently focused, balanced or composed."[27] These repeated interventions marked the most sophisticated critique concerning the problem of form as it emerged during the Leap, insofar as Lao She called into question the hierarchy of literary forms and their associated conditions of cultural labor that arose from the bourgeois heritage centered on the novel. There were further intimations of this line of critique from other radical theorists during the Great Leap, which therefore resonated with the critiques of reified notions of authorial creativity. Xu Ming, writing in 1959 stressed, therefore,

> If we believe that the short short story is only a transitional method of training the masses in creation, then this would demean its significance. When experienced writers instruct beginners, they often say: "writing should best begin from short stories, rather than with novellas and novels." This is beneficial encouragement and comes from experience. But people should not therefore assume that the short story can only be seen as a transitional method toward the novel, and so too does the short short story have its own significance[28]

In these terms, the problem of form as it emerged during the Great Leap exceeded the contingent circumstances that were said to render short forms necessary and posed the question of form in its relation to the totalizing transformation of writing and culture as a component part of the transition toward communism. The emphasis, in other words, on the fact that the short short story should not be seen simply as a transitional or pedagogical form had the effect of opening the possibility of literary and cultural forms that were proper to communism, holding out the possibility of a displacement of the novel. If the forging of a communist literary practice emerged here as a site of theoretical exploration, then more remarkable still are the ways that the most sophisticated short short stories pointed toward their own conditions of production as textual forms through the capacities of narrative. Suggestive in these terms is a contribution from Ba Jin, published under the title "Little Sister Compiles a Song" (1958) in the *People's Daily*, and translated in full as follows:

> Little Sister returned home, and excitedly told her Mother: "Mother, tomorrow I'm going to take to the streets to propagate the general line."
> Mother laughed and said: "You're also going to engage in propaganda work, are you? Will you be able to speak clearly?"
> Little Sister raised her head and proclaimed: "Mother, how could you forget, I'm twelve years old already! Our teacher wants us to devise a song to sing in the street."
> Mother laughed again: "You're really composing songs?" But in actual fact, Mother was very happy indeed.
> After dinner, little Sister spread out her paper on the dining table and wrote the three characters "the general line" as her heading, whereupon she began to hum the tune "Waltz of the Youth," with which she was already familiar, considering lyrics that she might compile to accompany this tune.

She hummed it through two, three times, and then thought over the instructions the teacher had given to the students on that day.

"The general line is like the sun.... shining..." she hummed, gradually raising her head to look at the electric light. It was as if she was gazing at a large, red sun, emitting golden rays, and everywhere illuminated.... the brilliance before her was so beautiful. She raised her pen but did not move, simply intoning to herself: "wonderful, truly wonderful." She lay down her pen and rested her chin in both hands, imagining a beautiful scene under the sun, and as she did so, the happier she became, thinking of all the best things she could imagine. She, alone, laughed at the electric light.

Her Mother called little Sister upstairs to sleep, whereupon she was startled, and gazed at the paper and pen before her, saying to herself: My uncle the worker is creating new products, going several days and nights without sleep, so how could I, who have not yet composed even a song, go to sleep?"

She stood up and, smiling, closed the door.

Her Mother finally came down stairs, and found the door tightly closed, but heard the happy song of young sister coming from within. Little Sister sang the song over, leaving her Mother at the door spell-bound.[29]

The extreme brevity of this text nonetheless encompasses a sophistication of composition insofar as the text narrates that very problem of writing to which the short short story form was itself a response, namely the integration of cultural production with the demands of an accelerated tempo of labor. Of particular importance is the way that cultural production becomes linked to moments of fantasy, first signaled by the paragraph encompassing the soliloquy of the young writer when she considers the immanent future of the Great Leap as one full of light and beauty, a paragraph that contains intimations of an internal stream of consciousness comprising a series of images, and then, again, at the end of the story when, having heard her daughter's composition, the mother is herself draw into a moment of fantasy, the contents of which are left to the imagination of the reader. This exchange is underwritten by a carefully wrought shift in focalization from daughter to mother with the final moment of the story being the mother overhearing the daughter. There emerges, then, a reciprocal set of relationships between fantasy and cultural production, in which the immanent possibilities of the Great Leap enable and necessitate short-form practices of cultural production, which then serve the function of drawing further collectivities and individuals into an emergent community of shared communist commitment. That this expansion of a community of fantasy occurs here at the site of the household, and between two women, also marks a shift away from the narrative conventions of the preceding period in which household labor served primarily as narrative foils for the elucidation of those modes of labor located outside the home. If in this respect

Ba Jin's own attempt at the form provides a self-reflective confirmation of the short short form itself, other short short story texts are ironically significant for the way they stage modes of writing that inhabited a more traditional conception of cultural practice, specifically with respect to their temporal duration, as well as the requirements of writerly craft. This is true above all of Lao She's text "Phone Call" (1958), which was published in the journal *New Harbor*, otherwise dedicated to the work of new, amateur writers:

> Wang Erleng was quite a character indeed. Even when making a telephone call, he did it his own way: first he would light a cigarette, and before the cigarette had been entirely finished, already the cigarette would be hanging down from the corner of his mouth; even with ash falling all over his shirt and trousers he didn't give a damn; sometimes his clothes even got burned, but he still didn't care, that was his way. When puffing away, his mouth was twisted, so his speech was far from clear. Well, who gives a damn! Wang Erleng has the freedom to spit out words unclearly, doesn't he?
>
> His way of making phone calls was also quite something. He didn't use his fingers but rather a stubby pencil. He absolutely believed in the sensation of his pencil, as flexible and reliable as a finger. He trusted the pencil so much that even when dialing a number he would often be staring at an illustrated calendar or some other object. Not only did he look elsewhere, but he would also chat with his mates, so that he would often assuredly dial the wrong number. He would dial wrongly only to be wrong again, and then he would quarrel with whoever answered the phone. Ah, look how busy he is, dialing phone calls to no end!
>
> Having dialed wrongly eight times, Wang Erleng became even more of a character: he pushed his hat back and straightened his chest, at which point the cigarette ash also fell from his chest. Resolving himself, he wouldn't look at "you," but would look to see if he had gotten through or not. He wouldn't look at the illustrated calendar, but rather at the ceiling.
>
> "Heya, Old Wu? Mate! . . . what? I'm looking for Old Wu! . . . he's not there? Fuck! What? What are you talking about? Stop talking crap! Are you saying I can't even make a phone call? Who am I? Where? Don't worry about that!" He slammed down the receiver and added—"how rude!"
>
> "You . . . what? What? The ninth detachment of the fire brigade? We don't have a fire here!"
>
> "Wang, the file!" called out a colleague.
>
> "Where is it? Where? Hey, ninth detachment, wait! Wait a second . . . ah, here!" Wang both asked the fire brigade to wait a moment, and also scuttled around for a file on his desk—which was burned by a cigarette end dropping from his mouth. "Hey, hey! No problems! There's no huge fire, there's only a hole in the file, nothing to worry about!" Wang was very satisfied, and

confidently instructed his colleagues: "Look, it's not such a bad thing to dial the wrong number! If there should be a fire, then at least the fire brigade will get here straight away, ha!"

Wang lit another cigarette and threw the match into the trash. "Hey, Old Wu? You... where is he? Find Old Wu! What, you again? How weird! Speak politely! With socialist morality you have to help others, don't you know! Humph!"

As soon as Wang put his pencil back into the hole of the telephone dial, a comrade said: "Wang, I'm going to write a big-character poster about you!"

"What are you criticizing me for, again?"

"Think about it yourself! How much time do you waste every day, and how often do you interfere with other people's work? You're sitting on the line of the fire brigade, who probably have to get to places where a fire has broken out, and if they're a second late it causes a lot of damage! You might also dial through to a writer..."

"What a coincidence!"

"Do you think people are only here to fool around with you, wait on you?"

"Hey, Old Wu?" Wang had once again gotten through on the phone. "... it's not you? You're a writer? I've interrupted your chain of thought, so you probably won't be able to resume for a while.... Well then you should hang up! What are you waiting for?" Wang thought it was very funny. He said to the comrade who wanted to write a big-character poster: "What a coincidence, that I should really get through to a writer..."

"It's smoking again!" someone shouted. "The waste basket!" "Wang, call the fire brigade!"

"I don't remember the number, it was a coincidence just now!" Wang rummaged around in the waste basket, with great panache.[30]

The exceptional quality of this short story lies in the fact that the central role of the phone call and the humorous content of the buffoonish character of Wang allows for precisely those forms of narrative economy that Lao She himself theorized as being necessary for a new practice of writing during the Great Leap. The brevity of the text encompasses suggestive moments of the ironic use of free indirect, as in the opening statement as follows: "Well, who gives a damn! Wang Erleng has the freedom to spit out words unclearly, doesn't he?" These exclamations are clearly based on the voice and the position of Wang himself, and yet far from giving authority or credibility to Wang they provide the conditions for an ironic mockery of his poor discipline. The injunction, "Ah, look how busy he is, dialing phone calls to no end!" on the other hand, more clearly belongs to the voice of a colloquial narrator alone in the way it is clearly directed at the assumed reader of the text. The skill of this short text lies in the consistent deployment of external focalization, in that the reader is never granted direct access to the phone conversations in which Wang is engaged. Yet, altogether, the fact that the story only narrates one side of the phone conversation, as if the reader were positioned among those colleagues who were party to Wang's lack of concern for the values of socialist discipline, does not in any way preclude an understanding of the humor and absurdity of these encounters, or require a "filling-in" of the other side of the conversation, such as would result in a considerable lengthening of the story, because the reader can quite easily imagine the responses on the other end from the brief interjections of Wang himself. The character of Old Wu, then, is left entirely unexplained in the narrative, and yet this character—their background, relation to Wang, and where, ultimately, they might be found—requires no further narrative information or context in order for the story to work its intended functions as a disclosure of the deleterious and occasionally hilarious effects of an undisciplined, unconscientious worker like Wang. There is, moreover, a productive and carefully arranged tension within the narrative between, on the one hand, the aural content, based around its reliance on dialogue and the capacity of the reader to "overhear" Wang's side of his misplaced phone conversations, and, on the other, its visual dimensions, consisting of the brilliantly wrought description of Wang that constitutes the opening of the story, and then the threat of a big-character poster to expose Wang's negligence. In structural terms, the story demonstrates the extent to which the short short story as form lent itself to the narrative pattern of a joke and relies on humor as a way of disclosing social contradictions, whereby the final line constitutes the inevitable punchline, presenting Wang in a foolish but by no means unsympathetic light.

Yet the previous elements of the narrative do themselves comprise other, smaller jokes, often relying on a singular comic image, as when Wang manages to burn a hole in the file, for example, while having wrongly phoned the fire brigade, or Wang's own, "lame" jokes, as when he is heard to comment that "If there should be a fire, then at least the fire brigade will get here straight away, ha!" In view of the recursive set of relations between writing, reading and labor to which the short short story was said to be orientated, then, humor here emerges as the impetus for an accelerated set of temporalities. The persistence of humor throughout the narrative also underscores a more troubling dimension, however, which is the appearance toward the end of the narrative of the figure of the writer, whose train of thought is interrupted by Wang's repeated phone calls. The appearance of this figure marks the emergence in the story of the problem of cultural labor, but in a very different mode to that of Ba Jin's earlier story, insofar as the tropes of writing that are summoned with reference to this writing figure, namely the interruption of their train of thought, demarcates precisely that mode of extended cultural labor for which the short short form was ostensibly intended to provide a critical response.

This passing moment within the narrative may therefore be said to direct attention back to a dimension of the short short story that Lao She himself identified, namely that the economy of language necessitated by the form did itself demand a command of literary craft, precisely because this requirement was more difficult than the allowances for superfluous labor that a longer form such as the novel might generate. Yet it was this very expectation of craft that wrenched the form apart from its most democratizing ambitions, in that, even with amateur writers being prominent among the authors of short short story texts, there emerged a certain irony with respect to their conditions of production, which is that the most lauded practitioners of this form were the professional culture workers themselves. There therefore emerges a reabsorption of this experimental form back into precisely those modes of cultural practice to which the figure of the amateur or collective writer had been opposed, such that this experimental form came to generate its own critique. In the midst of an experiment around literary form, then, the question of craft and of the specificity of writerly practice reposed itself, which accounts for the reabsorption of the short short story form back into the practice of the professional writers.

The emergence of this kind of autocritique even within the narrative logic of a short short story put pressure on whether this form was adequate either to overcoming the professional figure of the culture worker or to the accelerated tempos of writing that the Great Leap was said to demand. Even as writers threw themselves into the pursuit of experimental forms, therefore, so too did they make use of more canonical forms to reimagine the very definition of socialism during the Great Leap, above all in relation to the restructuring of reproductive labor.

Wage form, literary form

It is no coincidence that the most enthusiastic experiments in short forms belonged to the early, utopian months of the Great Leap. From late 1958 onward there emerged a shift on the part of culture workers back to longer forms such as the novella. Yet even as they did so, their work also demonstrates an attempt to rework or even displace some of the narrative conventions that had emerged over the preceding period, including above all the narratives of proletarian development examined in the previous chapter. The return to these longer forms, even accompanied by an attempted search new narrative devices and rhythms, however, also entailed a return to a temporal practice of writing that had more in common with the professional culture worker than the amateur writer who was called on to combine their writing with the demands of daily labor. It is in these terms that the Great Leap registers a set of contradictions that would become increasingly difficult during the Chinese Revolution, namely how to address the increasingly more complex contradictions of socialism without in turn necessitating those modalities of cultural labor that restored the division between mental and manual labor.

Among the longer form texts that were published during the Great Leap and also take that period as their narrative object, the possibilities and challenges opened up by a return to long forms are rendered starkly visible by the texts of Li Zhun 李准. Li Zhun's 1958 story "A Chain of Keys" (1959) is not among Li's classical works, but it fully demonstrates the coexistence of different approaches to literary form as well as the intersection between the transformations of the Great Leap and the problem of women's labor. The story itself maintains the comic devices characteristic of the short short stories examined here and shares with "Telephone" the fact that an older male worker serves as the object of humor, which in turn becomes capable of engendering further processes of social transformation. In the case of "A Chain of Keys," the basis of the narrative lies in the strained relations of a family, whose overbearing patriarchal head, Bai Jufeng, insists on the right to collect the earnings of his family members even under the conditions of the Great Leap, as well as the right to decide on their allocation to labor even in contravention of the formal decisions of the commune. The point of departure and putative narrative subject of the story is the arrival of the deputy commune head, Lin Genli, at a local work team, whereupon he overhears a discussion between two women concerning the merits of their respective marital fathers. It rapidly emerges that one of these women, Fang Qiaofang, has ample grounds for dissatisfaction, insofar as Bai Jufeng continues to impose demands on the women of his household by refusing to take advantage of the new, collective dining halls. When Qiaofang discovers that Genli has overheard their conversation, this provides the basis for the ensuing narrative development. Qiaofang neatly explains the situation to Genli as follows:

> Yesterday the commune dispatched wages, didn't it? In our family we have a total of thirteen people who earn wages, but once again, he went off to collect the whole lot himself. In the past, with the cooperatives, you know of course that when they "distributed the proceeds" 分红, he also went to collect the money all by himself, and we three sisters in law don't even know how much he gets in a year. But now with the People's Communes, people can eat in the dining halls, and yet he still takes all the money for himself. Our wages are based on everyone assessing our labor, but he takes it and doesn't give it to any of us, would you say that's fair?[31]

Qiaofang's recounting of this situation produces a plan for a family meeting at which these contradictions will be worked through, but the following section of the story takes the form of an analepsis, and one that is no longer narrated according to the focalized position of Genli with which the narrative began, but rather in terms of a humorous recounting of how Bai Jufeng came to acquire his nickname, of "mental labor" 脑力劳动. It transpires that Jufeng's insistence on drawing the collected wages of his family member is the last remnant of a broader structure of patriarchal authority that has been progressively disassembled with the development of the collectives and most recently the transition to the commune system. This "mental labor" is the work that Jufeng undertakes in the patriarchal management of his household, and which provides his alibi for refusing to engage in labor outside the home, even when ordered to do so by the local cadres. Here is an ironic recalibration of the figure of the household laborer that previously emerged in narrative texts of the 1950s, whereby it is the younger, female members of Jufeng's family who work outside the home, whereas Jufeng himself asserts control of household management in a patriarchal mode, while remaining the object of mockery for his aversion to labor. In a moment of reflexivity, the narrator, which here offers an omnipotent and sweeping overview of the development of Jufeng's village community, observes:

> Speaking of a few years prior, Bu Jufeng's "mental labor" had, in fact, some degree of fact about it. This kind of labor could be seen from the chain of keys that he wore at his arse, on his belt. There were ten of the keys altogether, and they used to chime as he walked. There was a key for the grass room, the fodder room, the animal pen, the grain storage room, the oil and salt drawer, and the box containing the land deeds, the drawer containing money and the cooperative work points accounts. He held on to all these keys.[32]

Yet, "since his family had entered the cooperative the year before last, a good half of Bai Jufeng's keys had ceased to have any point." The humorous image of these keys, therefore, provides a compelling instance of the relationship between patriarchal control in the family and the precollective state of the rural economy, as well as the diminishing of patriarchal control as new sets of rural social relations emerge, culminating in the events of the Great Leap itself which serves as the narrative present for the story, by which point the keys have become a symbol of total redundancy, no more than an ideological alibi for the maintenance of patriarchal power, such that "Bai Jufeng's 'mental labor' in the home was like two legs being thrust into a single trouser leg—it couldn't be kicked off." The narration of the progression of social change in the village up to this point also brings the story up to the narrative present, and in doing so ends the analepsis that has been narrated from a perspective without any specific diegetic focalization, restoring focalization instead to Genli in the manner of the first segment of the narrative. The climax of the narrative lies in the family meeting announced at the beginning, which emerges as a cacophony of voices from the various members of the family, including Qiaofeng, who insists, in the face of Jufeng's obstinate insistence on the legitimacy of his patriarchal authority: "Dad, you're stuck in the old ways, now women don't rely on men to eat, or for clothes to wear. Everyone has their work to do, everyone labors, so the days in which men might seek to control women are never coming back!"[33]

The upshot of this extended narrative sequence, as summarized by Genli, is that "the women are more advanced than you! All that people want is to know how much they've labored in a year, but with you wanting to control things, and doing it badly to boot, it has a negative effect on everyone's activism."[34] The relinquishing of patriarchal authority is rendered visible by Jufeng finally discarding his last remaining key, followed by the final section of the narrative, which once again withdraws from any specific narrative focalization and provides instead a report of the changed and more harmonious conditions in the family. The use of images of family harmony persisted as a characteristic device of narrative closure in longer-form texts from the Great Leap. Yet the most conspicuous element of this text is the way it is constructed around the problem of the wage, and where it is the failure to achieve a full individuation of labor through the form of the wage that generates a situation of family discord and the maintenance of patriarchal authority. By contrast, the possibility of specifying each individual's labor and the devolving of wage payments to the individual laborer rather than the mediating role of the family head carries a liberation from patriarchal authority while also reorganizing the family itself on a more egalitarian basis, together with the liberating effects brought by a shift toward new forms of production.

The dense connections between the wage and the formation of new sets of social relations, together with the gendered constitution of labor in "A Chain of Keys" anticipates subsequent developments in Li Zhun's own literary practice. Li Zhun's story "Two Generations" (1959) differs significantly from "A Chain of Keys" with respect to its temporal framing. The point of departure for the story lies in the news that one of its protagonists, Gao Xiuzhen, has been appointed to the new position of leading an alcohol factory at the height of the Great Leap, having received the news at an expanded meeting of the Zhaohua People's Commune, in place of her previous position as district director of the women's association. While Gao waits for the news, the opening paragraphs of the text significantly stage a moment of writing in a topos that will return at a significant, later moment: "Having arrived at the party committee of the commune, their meeting was in fact still in session. Gao Xiuzhen therefore found a cool place to sit down beneath the eaves of the western building, and she took out her own notebook, carefully looking over the summary report of the meeting that she had recorded, and then adding in some characters that she had missed earlier."³⁵ Having staged the moment of writing on the part of this peasant woman protagonist, the true point of departure for the narrative emerges when the party secretary, Secretary Xu, not only informs Gao that she will take on new responsibilities as a factory head, but also notes that her current position will be filled by none other than her own daughter, recorded in jovial dialogue as follows:

> Secretary Xu explained to her the prospects of the alcohol factory, and set down the conditions, whereupon Gao Xiuzhen excitedly accepted this task. Yet she was not willing to simply give up her work among the women of the Wenxi village management district, and so she asked Secretary Xu: "Once I've left, who is going to take up women's work in the district?" Secretary Xu asked her in amusement: "well, who do you guess?" At this moment, Gao Xiuzhen suddenly understood. She hit Secretary Xu in laughter, exclaiming: "Ah, you're going to make me and my daughter a laughing stock again! Including this time, that means I'll have passed on 交代 my work to her four times. That daughter of mine doesn't fool around!"³⁶

The introduction of the daughter, Zhu Zhu, as a further protagonist and the suggestion of a considerable backstory via the intimation of previous instances of Gao having passed her work to her daughter provides the conditions for the opening of a sustained analepsis and one that comprises the larger part of the text, in which the first decade of socialist construction is narrated through the periodic exchange of labor between mother and daughter. The impetus for this analepsis, arising early in the second part of the narrative, lies in Gao Xiuzhen witnessing the visible signs of the momentous transformations of the Great Leap as she takes the road leading from the commune headquarters in the township to her own village, producing a memory of her repeated journeys along the same road:

> She had run back and forth along this road for a full ten years. She had come to attend meetings, to make reports, to buy their first donkey from the cooperative, to help the masses in midwifery, to celebrate international women's day ... altogether, then, she had run along this road quite a number of times over those ten years, but each time she had done so, she had always felt a sense of excitement.³⁷

The paragraph immediately following announces an act of memory on the part of Gao Xiuzhen: "she could still remember the first time she had come to the township, which now appeared quite silly to her." The analepsis that follows, then, is wholly subjective, deriving from Xiuzhen's specific position, such that the narrative stages at a formal level the possibility of narrating the history of the socialist present in terms of women's labor, situated in the countryside, and actualized through the events that prompt Gao's spatial movement between the village and township. Consistent with this narrative having arisen from Gao's own act of memory, the analepsis that follows is heavily focalized around her perspective and consists, as indicated by Gao's earlier conversation with Secretary Xu, of the repeated instances in which she and her daughter came to exchange their tasks with one another. The first of these lies in the early postliberation period, when Gao seeks to attend a meeting for women, only to be rebuffed by her husband, Yang Zhengxiang, who imagines that she will not return, and asks, who, in her absence, will prepare food. Zhu Zhu's response is recorded as follows: "Gao Xiuzhen burst into tears, such was her upset, but at this moment Zhu Zhu came over. She was then still a young girl of only twelve years old, with her feet bare, her hair a mess. But she said: 'Mum! Go and attend your meeting, I'll do the food for you these three days!' "38

While her mother initially questions whether she can take on this responsibility, when Zhu Zhu indicates that she can in fact take on these responsibilities, the initial transfer of work takes on the form of an act of pedagogy between the women: "[Gao] was so happy her eyes were moist, and she said 'Zhu Zhu, come, I'll teach 教教 you right now.' She took Zhu Zhu to the kitchen, and pointed to the chopping board and coal stove, handing over 'work' for the first time." The pairing, here, of the transfer of work with a practice of shared pedagogy in the tasks of household labor is, crucially, here, not the incorporation of Zhu Zhu into a fixed, patriarchal division of labor that is maintained through the generations, but is, rather, a form of mutual enablement by which Gao becomes capable of taking on an expanded social role. The maintenance of focalization around Gao herself across this recounting is underlined through the fact that Zhu Zhu's experience of household work is not given directly by the narrator, but only made visible after the fact, when Zhu Zhu recounts her success to Gao upon the latter's return. An ensuing ellipsis (within the analepsis) is followed by the second occasion on which a transfer of labor occurs, whereby Zhu Zhu becomes the director of women's work in the village in order that her mother can study new childbearing techniques, followed, in quick succession, by her mother becoming the district head of women's work, whereupon her daughter, in turn, studies childbearing, marking their assumption of those roles which they also hold in the narrative present, at the time of the Great Leap. Zhu Zhu's proximity to the business of sexual reproduction in her role as a childbearing expert produces, however, a potential crisis of social relations, insofar as her prospective father-in-law is understood to object to Gao Xiuzhen that "when the kids have grown up, it would be better if she did some other form of work."39

No sooner has this crisis has emerged, however, it becomes clear that the repeated transactions between mother and daughter, having, on the first occasion, served to enable Gao's entry into political mobilization, have also taken on a reciprocal dimension in the way that Zhu Zhu is able to insist to her father-in-law that she is proud of her role: "I'm talking about my work. There's nothing shameful about childbearing work. You can't look at these things with old eyes."[40] In an instance of obvious narrative artifice, aimed at maintaining a controlled pattern of focalization, these events are delivered as overheard by Gao Xiuzhen. Gao's response, delivered as psycho-narration, is:

> [Zhu Zhu]'s remarks were both reasonable, and full of feeling. [Gao] felt an intense feeling of admiration. She thought of how the young girls of today were truly happy, how they could go anywhere, say anything. She thought of how, during her own time as a child bride, she had spent thirteen years in the Yang family, without ever having spoken a single word to Yang Zhengxiang, so that she resembled a mute every day. Thinking of these matters, she truly felt that Zhu Zhu had grown up at the right time.[41]

This passage of psycho-narration has a formal significance in the way that it marks a further instance of subjective analepsis on the part of Gao within the larger context of the second part of the narrative, which is itself an analepsis. It also underscores, however, how the passage of labor and pedagogy between Gao and her daughter has engendered a more generalized transformation of their capacities of women in the village, each being able to stake out more egalitarian and indeed reciprocal relations with husband and father-in-law respectively. The significance of these repeated acts of exchange, not least in their capacity to support new forms of gendered equality at the level of affective relations between men and women, then, demonstrates how they actualize an incipient logic of social relations in which labor itself functions as immediate and fully social for the women themselves. This marks a considerable shift from Li Zhun's earlier narrative, in which it is precisely the universalization of the wage-form that enables a greater degree of equality within the family. The expansive capacity of the reciprocal relations between mother and daughter assumes a further dimension in the third, final section of the story, which also marks a closure of the analepsis via a return to the narrative present, marked by the opening sentence of "it already having grown dark, Gao Xiuzhen returned to Wenxi village."[42] It thereupon emerges that Zhu Zhu was the original impetus for her mother having been given new responsibilities, due to her desire to participate in the radical transformations in village life during the Great Leap, as opposed to remaining in the township with responsibility for delivering births. Hilarity ensues, but more important still is that Gao's announcement that she will henceforth transfer her skills to her daughter generates a scene of writing, one that recalls the topos of writing at the beginning of the narrative, but this time posed as writing that both gestures, in terms of content, toward the ongoing socialization of labor across the communes, but also writing that, in its imminent features and objectives, is geared toward the formation of new, communist relations between women, across the village as a whole as well as in the immediate context between mother and daughter:

> Mother and daughter sat in the courtyard together, each holding their pen and notebook, and began to exchange their work. Gao Xiuzhen explained to her daughter how many nurseries there were in the district, how many canteens, how many sewing groups, who the heads of the teams of women were, who were party members, who were members of the communist youth league, what the conditions of work were like, she explained all of this in great detail, and so too did Zhu Zhu copy it down with great seriousness, such that mother and daughter exchanged continuously for the larger part of the day[43]

The repeated posing of mother and daughter in this context, the two having been spatially separated from one another in the first part of the narrative, that which also takes place within the historical present, takes on a final, comedic significance at the end of the narrative, when Zhu Zhu gives her mother a haircut befitting her incipient role as a factory head. The final line, as delivered by her husband as bystander—"Look, look, you've grown younger by at least ten years!"[44]—suggests, however, a leveling even of the generational difference between mother and daughter such as to further extend the intimations of equality between these two narrative actors.

The exploration across this text of the formation of communist relations, achieved formally through the recapitulation of the history of the present through a process of labor exchange between women, one that finally becomes visible through a shared practice of writing, would take on a yet further extension, not least in temporal scope, through Li Zhun's most famous text from this period, *A Minor Biography of Li Shuangshuang* (1960). It encompasses the transformation in the marital relationship between the title character Li Shuangshuang, a peasant woman, and her wayward husband, Xiwang, above all in relation to questions of domestic labor and the commune movement. While the plot of the novella is simple enough, the generic expectations established by the fact of it being named as a biography nonetheless sit alongside a series of formal shifts throughout the narrative, shifts that render the text significantly more interesting and which draw attention to the possibilities opened up by its greater length as compared to short form texts, or even the relative economy of "A Chain of Keys." These are especially true of the shifts in narrative focalization that emerge across the novella, the pacing of narrative rhythm, and its intersection with the key questions of political economy that emerged during the Great Leap. The novella therefore begins with a literal brief biography of Li Shuangshuang herself in the manner of a narrative report, in which the emphasis is on the relatively subordinate position of Li Shuangshuang in her village community before the changes introduced by the Leap. This report is marked as coming from a temporal and epistemological position after the totalizing transformation in the social relations of the village, denoted in the second sentence by the formulation: "before the establishment of the Commune and the Great Leap Forward, there were very few in the village who knew her name was Shuangshuang," being instead referred to only in relation to her husband, Xiwang. This absence of any independent term of address that does not make Shuangshuang dependent on the extended family system is also explained in relation to the modes of remuneration operative in the early-stage agricultural cooperatives. In these terms, "she was rarely able to head out to the fields to do any work" such that even such work points as she gained from harvesting work were "entered on Xiwang's work record."[45]

Through this opening report, then, the emphasis is on Shuangshuang's exclusion from those forms of labor outside the home, underpinned by the structure of political economy and remuneration that prevailed in the countryside under the collective system that emerged in the 1950s, and which also forms the narrative concern of "A Chain of Keys" whereby the allocation of work points as the basis of income in collective units took place on a familial basis. The temporal framing of this opening, moreover, denoted by the *before*, implies not only a narrator who speaks from a position of future knowledge, but also mode of anticipatory prolepsis, whereby the reader understands from the outset that Shuangshuang *will* have eventually become well-known as Shuangshuang as a result of certain as of yet unspecified transformations. In this sense, the temporal framing of the narrative at its opening may be understood in terms of Tani Barlow's formulation of the future perfect as central to the formation of feminist consciousness in modern China, premised on a vision of what the gendered agent of liberation *will have become*.[46] The effect of this slender opening summary is therefore to mark the gap between a past situation and a transformed future from which the narrative takes place, such that the content of the narrative in its mode as biography must address how this transformation comes to pass, a task marked by the self-reflective comment on the part of the narrator: "Yet it is necessary to take a step back. The first time that her name truly appeared was after the Spring Planting in the year 1958, in the form of a big-character poster posted in a meeting for the airing of views at Sun Village. It is here also that our story must begin."[47]

The beginning of narrative time proper takes place in near medias res, namely in the form of this big-character poster authored by Li Shuangshuang herself in order to demand that the commune undertake the formation of a collective canteen so that she and other women be able to undertake reservoir mobilization work. This big-character provides, in turn, the point of departure for the developments that comprise the narrative, including the eventual transformation in the familial dynamics between Li Shuangshuang and Xiwang and social life for the commune inhabitants. The narrative records an encounter with the big-character poster on the part of the township secretary Luo Shulin and the commune party secretary Uncle Leap. The narration of this encounter also further establishes the ignorance of male diegetic figures, as, for Luo and Uncle Leap, the author of the poster, that is, the identity of "Li Shuangshuang," remains ambiguous, yet is naturally known to the reader on account of the opening introduction. The narrative relays the poster from the perspective of a bystander:

> The characters on this poster were oversized, and the handwriting was rather crooked, but the content was exceptionally novel:
> "Household chores are such a drag! We have the will but not yet the means! If we're chained to the stove the whole day, then how can we achieve a Great Leap? If only there were a canteen, 'women would hold up half the sky.'"
> At the bottom there was signed "Li Shuangshuang."[48]

The decision to begin real narrative time with a scene of writing, and one that is explicitly ascribed to Li Shuangshuang herself on the basis of term of self-reference, marks an investment in the transformative capacities of writing as a practice. It is, then, all the more significant that this initial scene of writing does not immediately yield to Li Shuangshuang becoming the focalized center of the narrative, but rather gives way to a further encounter with the big-character poster on the part of Xiwang, Li Shuangshuang's husband. Xiwang's uneasy recollections of a fight between himself and Li Shuangshuang provides the conditions for an analepsis in the form of an extended history of their relationship. This analepsis contains elements of Xiwang's indirect discourse on the one hand, as well as, on the other, the fragmentary use of free indirect style: "Xiwang was actually fond of Shuangshuang. He liked her fiery personality, and he liked the way she had turned into someone with a forthright nature, always daring to talk and laugh. Shuangshuang was good-looking, skilled with a needle, and quick and neat about her work."[49]

The final sentence of this extract, following on from multiple statements of indirect discourse, suggests a register and a position that is particular to Xiwang, even though it is formally given through the voice of the narrator. The privileging of Li Shuangshuang's physical appearance and her capacity to conduct those forms of domestic labor and household production associated with rural women marks a delimitation of Li Shuangshuang's agency as a model of labor, even with the grudging acknowledgment of her "fiery personality." The narrative then shifts into an extended description of the fight between Xiwang and Shuangshuang that occurred several days before the posting of the big-character poster, which in turn also marks the first appearance of Li Shuangshuang as an actual diegetic figure who is possessed of speech, as distinct from the opening narrative report, or her projection through the perspective of Xiwang. This fight is said to have arisen from Xiwang's initial refusal to allow Shuangshuang to participate in labor at a reservoir, and thereafter his unwillingness to get involved in household labor. The extended description of this fight still remains within an analepsis relative to the posting of the big-character poster, and yet it also marks a progressive focalization around the figure of Shuangshuang herself, including access to her internal thoughts, culminating in a visual and aural encounter with the mobilization of labor during the Great Leap:

> Shuangshuang peered eastward through the window, knowing it was the night shift on the Red Rock River irrigation project. Lanterns were strung out in a row, like a fiery dragon; the lanterns lit up a long line of dark figures, their pickaxes and shovels in constant motion as they rose and fell. The pounding of stone sledgehammers beat out a rhythm, while the clear voices of young men and women singing work songs flowed like a tide that swept through the window into Shuangshuang's home.[50]

The visual and aural dimensions of this passage mark a penetration of the domestic space in ways that open the possibility for new modes of collectivity on the part of Shuangshuang, and so too does the opening reference—"Shuangshuang peered"—establish her as the center of narrative focalization, in the most familiar sense of "who sees." It is no coincidence, then, that the scene of labor as encountered by Li Shuangshuang is almost immediately followed by the dramatic scene of writing with which the narrative began. These two moments are mediated only by Li Shuangshuang's encounter with two other women in the community, of whom one, Auntie Leap, the wife of the party secretary, provides the direct inspiration for writing the big-character poster. The emergence of Li Shuangshuang as capable of writing is therefore enabled in large part through a momentary collectivity of women, which brings the narrative up to the initial scene, and in doing so opens into a horizon of the transformation of social relations. This in turn marks the closure of the analepsis with the moment of the big-character poster, though not as of yet the moment marked by the anticipatory prolepsis with which the narrative begins. More important still, however, is that, from this point onward, in narratological terms, the narrative is almost entirely focalized around Li Shuangshuang. In these terms, the diegetic scene of writing within the text has a doubling function, whereby it also provides the moment for a reorganization of the narrative itself around Li Shuangshuang, and so produces the narrative possibility of the biography as a textual form determined by the biographical object herself. The events that follow the scene of writing include the formation of a collective canteen under the leadership of the party cadres, which is accompanied by not only the reorganization of domestic labor but also a reversal in which Xiwang becomes head chef so that Li Shuangshuang can participate in raising pigs.

This reversal marks an ironic reconfiguration of the kinds of narrative tropes that emerged through the literature of the early 1950s, in which the possibility of women taking part in factory labor forced a series of displacements of domestic labor onto other women. Here, however, that displacement takes place onto a man, and in the form not of a continued pattern of social reproduction inside the home but rather the formation of a new, collectivized system of reproduction based on the canteen as a new mode of communal space. It is precisely the scene of collective reproduction that comprises the site of social encounters throughout this part of the narrative, such that Shuangshuang's involvement in reservoir construction is assumed, but is not directly part of the narrative content. The narrative economy therefore remains focused on the site of reproduction throughout. The accumulated transformations based around the socialization of housework mark the progression of the narrative up to the temporal position from which the narrator had announced the need to "take a step back," and in doing so largely completes the process by which Shuangshuang becomes the model of labor that, as the narrative introduction promises, she will have been, such that the progress of the narrative joins up with the moment promised by the anticipatory prolepsis. There then follows a narrative summary, the details of which are provided by the narrator with a degree of omnipotence and sweep similar to that of the opening with which the novella begins, in the manner of a summary: "After the move to communes 公社化以后, the masses' enthusiasm was greater than ever, and the forces of the commune flourished. In the mountain, the commune built a number of ranches, forestry stations, and agricultural experiment stations. In the environs of the Lu Ban temple to the west of Sun village, the brigade also built a pig breeding station, where Shuangshuang came to work."[51]

The extent and fantastical character of these changes and their compression within a brief comment on the part of the narrator establishes a temporal break between the events surrounding the immediate aftermath of the socialization of reproduction and an unspecified point in the future, such that the exact duration of the diegetic time marked by this summary is therefore never stated. The shift into this moment in the future is also the inauguration of a new temporality, crucially, one that exceeds or traverses the temporal moment with which the text began. If in other words the text begins with an anticipatory framing premised on a "before," we are at this moment offered a vision of a temporality inaugurated by an "after." This produces a dividing line within the text in relation to its formal status as a biography, insofar as the temporal arrangement of the biography (and especially the autobiography) in its standard mode consists of a progressive closure of the gap between the assumed temporal and experiential position of the reader and the position of the narrated subject. In the case of Li Shuangshuang, however, she surpasses that very position of knowledge (and contemporaneity in relation to the reader) with which the narrative begins. It becomes possible, then, to speak of a new, communist temporality—that of the *after*—one that exceeds the boundaries of the contemporary moment, such that the later parts of the narrative present events lying in the future relative to the Great Leap, and so too can we understand the time of narration as also coming from the future relative to the assumed reader. In this future, communist temporality there remain contradictions of different kinds, as the narrative from this point onward revolves largely around the exposure of Xiwang's poor performance on the job as chef as well as the political misdeeds of various minor characters who seek to extract private advantage from the collective canteen. Xiwang's unwillingness to continue in his position lest he be compromised results in Li Shuangshuang herself becoming a worker in the canteen. She eventually secures membership of the party, providing an appropriate moment of culmination for her biography, whereupon she cooperates with other women in resolving any recalcitrant individuals who doubt the capacity of the communes. She does so at the same time as devising fantastic technical innovations in order to meet the food needs of the other commune members.

It is through a narrative register of the fantastical that this communist temporality and its corresponding narrative episodes emerge, so that Li Shuangshuang eventually succeeds in completely mechanizing the food system of the commune and devises new varieties of noodles to meet the demands of her fellow commune members. She does so, moreover, in close cooperation with Xiwang, who himself undergoes a transformation via the example of Shuangshuang:

> After this conversation [with Shuangshuang], it was as if Xiwang became a different person. The next day he devoted all his attention to the pancake stove. He wanted to create a method of shifting pancakes at utmost speed. He put his mind to it the whole night, and suddenly thought of the furnace they had used to boil tea when he had worked as an apprentice at a restaurant. This tea furnace had quite a number of fire spouts, making it possible to warm several pots at once. He thereupon decided over a single night to create a "multi-vent pancake stove," which could support six plates at once, allowing a single person to cook enough pancakes for more than a hundred people in a single hour.[52]

The incredible speed of producing foodstuffs in combination with the resolution of marital conflicts between the two poses a utopian imagination in the interstices of everyday life, one withdrawn from the pressures of scarcity, yet still organized around an accelerated tempo of production. The end of the narrative is therefore a fitting conclusion insofar as it marks the extension of Li Shuangshuang's labor into the construction of new kinds of social relations, from her intimate relations with her marital partner to her capacity for invention in the commune. It is moreover imagined by Li Shuangshuang as a moment in which the relations between different kinds of labor have become legible in effect within a single totality, whereby she is said to realize that "the beads of sweat that poured off the canteen workers were flowing along with the spring water into the rich, flourishing high-yield fields, turning into wheat and rice."[53] The extension of the temporality of the text into a future that carries marks of the fantastical, in tandem with its organization of narrative economy whereby problems of social reproduction take precedence over industrial production, marks *Li Shuangshuang* in particular as offering a formal departure from those texts of the early 1950s that stage the synchronization of peasants with the demands of industrial labor.

The same is true of those aspects of the text that are rendered absent as the narrative progresses, above all that problem of remuneration that is registered at the beginning of the narrative but thereafter never reappears, namely whether the changes in the rural community remain within the limits of Shuangshuang's labor being remunerated independently of that of her husband. The becoming-absent of this problem points toward the construction of a relation of labor that is no longer contingent on the individuated wage form.

Marx at Beidaihe, Lenin in Shanghai

The problems of remuneration that resurface in the longer works of the Great Leap point toward the most far-reaching theoretical problematics that emerged from the Great Leap, namely, that of "bourgeois right." This category was, so to speak, ready to hand even before the Great Leap, having emerged, in its earliest manifestation in the hands of Lu Dingyi. Yet the expansion of this vocabulary to encompass problems to do with the social organization of labor proceeded via its own autonomous trajectory, one that was in fact led by Mao himself but was later rearticulated in relation to the problem of writing. Throughout this process, and as works readily demonstrate, the problematics associated with bourgeois right demanded to be passed into narrative in order that they might be legible, and yet this very process itself also necessitated the specific cultural labor of the culture worker. There emerged from this point, then, a profound and haunting contradiction, which is that the very complexity of problems of the political economy of labor to which Chinese theorists addressed themselves, and the assumed bases for overcoming those problems, necessitated a certain specialization of intellectual labor, including cultural labor, even while the very logic of the conceptual vocabulary of bourgeois right from Lu Dingyi onward was to identify the reproduction of the difference between mental and manual labor as one of the problems to be overcome under socialism. In the early days of the Great Leap, however, such profound contradictions remained in the future. The vocabulary of bourgeois right emerged out of a series of theoretical attempts to excavate the limitations of the Soviet-derived model that had informed the early 1950s. This was a process in which, subsequent to Lu Dingyi's early invocation of bourgeois right as a problem of cultural labor, Mao himself had a central role.

Mao's interventions over the course of key meetings held from early 1958 onward reveal a process of theoretical development in which Mao sought to locate a vocabulary to think the ways in which formal transformations in the status of ownership do not exhaust the problems of social relations under socialism, and how, therefore, to attend to the constant production and reproduction of sites of inequality in the lived fabric of social relations. This was at the same time a project of locating new theoretical categories that would not be dependent on the edifice of Soviet political economy as had been introduced in the early 1950s. This was a process in development, insofar as Mao initially sought to break new theoretical ground within Stalin's vocabulary of the different components of socialist political economy. He did so via Stalin's definition of political economy in his 1952 text, where he had declared the object of the study of political economy to consist of the forms of ownership of the means of production, "the status of the various social groups in production and the mutual relations that follow from these forms," and the accompanying forms of distribution. The formulation of the "mutual relations" in this context provided the initial basis for Mao's understanding of the noncoincidence between the formal status of socialist ownership and the equality of social relations, such that he came to argue, at the Chengdu Meeting held in March, for example, that, despite a change in the system of ownership, "workers and peasants do not yet feel that they enjoy relations of equality with us." Mao added that "the system of ownership and distribution have transformed," but "the mutual relations have not yet been changed."[54] These initial interventions marked a stretching of the theoretical categories of the Soviet edifice of political economy, namely via a new emphasis on the noncontemporaneity of different dimensions of the social totality, but so too did this generate a need for a theoretical vocabulary that was autonomous from the Soviet experience. This was also the opportunity for a return to Marx. The Marx to which Chinese theorists returned was not the early Marx whose language of alienation motivated critiques of the Soviet socialist model in other contexts (and which, in the 1980s, also legitimized the hollowing-out of the socialist project in China itself) but rather the late Marx of "bourgeois right," which Mao introduced for the first time at Beidaihe in August: "We must smash the ideology of bourgeois right, for example, the competing for position, the competing over ranks, seeking bonuses, the fact that mental laborers earn higher wages, and manual laborers lower wages, all of these are manifestations of bourgeois right."[55]

In view of its fundamental importance to emergent problems of labor in the Great Leap, it is necessary at this point to excavate the position of bourgeois right as a point of intervention in Marx's textual corpus. The formula of bourgeois right—which, being derived from the German *bürgerliche Recht*, is therefore only ever used in the specific singular, not as "bourgeois legal rights"—had as its major textual locus Marx's 1875 "Critique of the Gotha Program" while also making passing appearances in multiple volumes of *Capital*. The "Critique" itself was only published after Marx's death. It grew out of the strained political conjunctures of German social democracy at the end of the nineteenth century and consists of Marx's sustained argument against the programmatic proposals of Ferdinand Lassalle as part of an attempt at unity among the different wings of the German socialist movement. That part of the text in which Marx introduces the theoretical rubric of bourgeois right consists of an attack on the idea that, in a society after capitalism, remuneration would proceed according to norms of a "fair distribution" of the proceeds of labor. Marx argues that on no account will any given worker simply receive, in the form of rights to consumption, their own contribution to the total social product because of the deductions that will have to be made in order to support those unable to labor as well as for the purposes of accumulation. Yet so too does Marx attack the conceptual imprecision of terms such as the "proceeds of labor," and therefore he seeks to historically delimit the problems he is addressing in terms of a society that has already undergone a radical transformation in its social organization, that is, a society in which "the producers do not exchange their products; just as little does the labor employed on the products appear here as the *value* of these products, as a material quality possessed by them, since now, in contrast to capitalist society, individual labor no longer exists in an indirect fashion but directly as a component part of total labor."[56]

This is a society, in other words, that can no longer be understood in terms of the categories of value and commodity production. Yet even a society of this kind, radically removed from capitalism, Marx argues, is not yet the communist society regulated according to the principle of "from each according to his abilities, to each according to his needs," because, having emerged from the cultural and ideological conditions of capitalism, it is "still stamped with the birthmarks of the old society from whose womb it emerges." For this reason the adequate mode of distribution in this society is one of "equal right," or more precisely "bourgeois right," meaning a mode of distribution that remains premised on the exchange of equivalents, where "the individual producer receives back from society—after the deductions have been made—exactly what he gives to it. What he has given to it is his individual quantum of labor."[57] As Marx acknowledges, in a statement that caused endless consternation for subsequent theorists, with the exchange of equivalents in the sphere of labor, "the same principle prevails as that which regulates the exchange of commodities" in capitalist society, namely the conduct of remuneration according to an abstract norm of universal exchangeability, that is, remuneration according to labor done, that does not account for the particularity of different individuals. It is this same observation that emerged from Lu Dingyi's invocation of bourgeois right in his discussion on the reemergence of bourgeois thought under socialism. Insofar as remuneration according to a universal norm of labor contribution fails to take account of differing needs and abilities, it "is, therefore, a right of inequality, in its content, like every right." The transcendence of this horizon of right as an abstract norm that reproduces inequality is precisely the business of transition, which has, as its aim, a communist society. This "higher phase of communist society," is one where

> After the enslaving subordination of the individual to the division of labor, and therewith also the antithesis between mental and physical labor, has vanished; after labor has become not only a means of life but life's prime want; after the productive forces have also increased with the all-around development of the individual, and all the springs of cooperative wealth flow more abundantly—only then can the narrow horizon of bourgeois right be crossed in its entirety and society inscribe on its banners: From each according to his ability, to each according to his needs![58]

The radical content of Marx's critique, then, was that it offered Chinese theorists a new theoretical terrain for thinking the problem of socialist transition. The key theorist who stepped into the theoretical space opened up by Mao, following Marx, was Zhang Chunqiao, whose article "Smash the Ideology of Bourgeois Right" gained prominence when, having initially been published in the Shanghai theoretical journal *Liberation*, it was republished at Mao's personal intervention in the *People's Daily* in October 1958. This article was a response to Mao's introduction of the terminology of bourgeois right at the Beidaihe Conference. Zhang's pivotal article followed its own specific narrative logic, namely through its recovery of the supply system as a part of the experience of the revolutionary war period that could be retheorized and developed as part of a sustained transition to communism. He cited the egalitarian ethos of the Red Army in the 1930s, which were said to encompass "communist mutual relations" not only within the army but also between the army and the masses, one that offered an alternative to the regulation and incentivization according to the logic of the wage, so that, in Zhang's terms, "When comrades used to live under the supply system they did not envy wage labor, and people liked this kind of expression of a living institution of relations of equality. Before long, however, this kind of system was attacked by the ideology of bourgeois right. The core of the ideology of bourgeois right is the wage system."[59]

The rejection of the wage system effected a rupture with the model of socialist development that had been drawn from the Soviet Union in the early 1950s, in which remuneration according to labor 按劳分配 was said to be distinct from the capitalist wage relation. It is a fact of great significance that here and throughout the text Zhang refers to his opponents, or those who privilege the continued use of material incentives, as "the economists," which allows his own intervention to be posed on the terrain of politics, and therefore autonomous from the discourse of formal, Soviet-derived political economy or a rationality of material incentive constituted as the "economic," of which "the economists" were presumably the main proponents. The contemporary parallel to the supply system of the 1930s were the canteens, which were here also theorized as the basis on which to rupture with bourgeois right by superseding distribution according to labor in favor of distribution according to need, whereby access to basic goods would cease to be linked to any notion of labor contribution. Zhang's article therefore identified the canteens as a return to the revolutionary supply system, which was in turn formulated in terms of the specificity of politics vis-à-vis the Soviet-derived discourse of political economy, in which the principle of distribution according to labor had been consecrated as the socialist relation of distribution. Zhang's critique of the "economists" and emphasis on the specificity of the political was fundamental for the trajectory of the conceptual vocabulary of bourgeois right, both in terms of its capacity to critique the Soviet discourse on political economy, but also in terms of the stretching involved in relation to Marx's intervention in his "Critique."

From his article a series of intense theoretical debates emerged over the remainder of 1958.[60] Significant in these terms is that the discussions around bourgeois right emerged contemporaneously with discussions among academic economists around problems such as the law of value and commodity production. Yet the theoretical discourse on bourgeois right remained autonomous from the discussions on the categories of Soviet-derived political economy. That this was so may be understood not as an "oversight" but rather the result of a certain political logic whereby, in order to take up a critical stance in relation to the Soviet-derived model of socialist development, it was necessary to locate a point of theoretical intervention that was conceptually autonomous and specifically political, even at the cost of short-circuiting a complex set of problems. Only at a later juncture, that of the Cultural Revolution, did these same theorists begin to think through how to incorporate the problem of bourgeois right into a revised political economy that would take the Chinese socialist experience as its point of departure. Yet, at the juncture of the Great Leap, the language of bourgeois right may be better understood from the perspective of a critique of political economy in the sense of remaining autonomous from a discourse whose disciplinary logic remained part of the Soviet model of socialism, and the posing of politics as a distinct field of relations sharply demarcated from the logic of the economic. While, consistent with Marx's own emphasis, the problem of the wage necessarily loomed central to the Maoist conception of bourgeois right, it is important that this term, in close connection with its theoretical predecessor of mutual relations, demarcated a wider set of problems not simply reducible to that of the wage. In particular, and of utmost importance, bourgeois right was also understood to encompass acts of superiority and bureaucracy on the part of cadres and officials, who were as a result compelled to present themselves as "common laborers" in their relations with the masses, as well as the problem of an over-entrenched division of labor in factories.

To this extent, the critique of bourgeois right was at this moment also about exposing and correcting bureaucracy and hierarchy at the level of the state.[61] Yet more complex still is how the problematic of bourgeois right meshed with the complex system of remuneration in the countryside, including the family-based systems of payment that had informed the cooperatives. It becomes in these terms possible to understand Mao's saying in October 1958: "Only if the People's Communes are run well is there a thorough road for women's liberation. The People's Communes are carrying out a wage system and a supply system under which wages are paid to each individual, not to the family head. This makes women and young people happy, and it's a way of smashing the patriarchal system, and the ideology of bourgeois right."[62]

The accumulation of references in Mao's brief statement marks an intervention of great complexity, and yet his insistence that individual wage payments might both break patriarchy and diminish bourgeois right underlines a demand for a dialectic movement, in which laborers first enter into the individuated wage-relation as the basis on which to eventually supersede that wage-relation. For Mao, then, the wage remained a site of great contradiction under socialism. It is possible to this extent to detect a certain divergence between Mao and Zhang Chunqiao, in that Zhang's deployment of the vocabulary of bourgeois right as both an expansive conception of social relations drawn into capitalism and a mode of "thought" gestured toward an increasingly complex conception of consciousness and the problem of how to create the ideological conditions for the supersession of bourgeois right in the form of the wage, rather than the dialectical treatment of the wage that informed Mao's interventions. In his original formulation Marx had posed a condition in which labor had become "life's prime want" as necessary for transgressing the historical horizon of bourgeois right, whereas Chinese theorists such as Zhang sought to locate the ways in which bourgeois right *reproduced* the atomization of labor and so inhibited the growth of a new set of communist social relations. Yet, for Zhang and others, the problem remained a temporal one, and one of temporal unevenness, no longer between city and countryside strictly speaking but rather between the transformation of the relations of ownership and the persistent "temporal lag" with respect to consciousness in the form of a capitalist logic of labor, a lag that was itself reproduced by the maintenance of the wage relation.

Zhang interpreted the reproduction of an atomized relationship between laborers on the basis of the wage relation to amount to a "system of ranks" 等级制度.[63] The political content of Zhang's intervention, then, emphasized the primacy of politics as the basis on which to overcome this modality of unevenness. To the persistence of a capitalist logic of labor, they counterposed a communist consciousness of labor.[64] In these terms, a summary of debates around bourgeois right argued that "it cannot be denied that definite economic relations always give rise to corresponding forms of consciousness, and that with distribution also being a kind of economic relationship, the remnants of inequality in distribution will also generate bourgeois consciousness."[65]

The communist consciousness of labor, by contrast, was characterized as labor "gratis," meaning labor without remuneration. These divergent modes of consciousness were in turn characterized in terms of the distribution of desire and consciousness between the self 私 and society 公. In more practical and immediate terms, enthusiasts for a new communist consciousness of labor cited everyday practices of labor that were characterized, once again, by a new temporality, that is, durations of labor that were not regulated in advance by the compulsive power of either material remuneration or the state. In explicating the content of such a consciousness, the radicals who agreed with Zhang also made recourse to the early, utopian days of the Soviet Union. It was noted, then, that "Lenin had already taken great efforts to support 'communist subbotniks' in the early days of the Soviet Union, because from this he could see 'communist things,' he could see the sprouts of communism."[66] These subbotniks were days of labor in which, Lenin noted in his 1920 "From the Destruction of the Old Social System to the Creation of the New," labor is performed on a voluntary basis, or "labor performed gratis for the benefit of society." The supersession of bourgeois right, therefore, would mean the wholesale reconstruction of consciousness and social relations so that all labor becomes, in effect, "for the benefit of society," meaning *unwaged*. The invocation of Lenin here and from this point onward in discussions of bourgeois right marks the ways in which, as well a return to Marx, this theoretical trajectory also involved a leaping-over of the Stalin period in the Soviet Union.

In these terms, even as a strictly nonnarrative text, Zhang's intervention also embodied a distinctive temporal logic, different from both the figuring of the short short stories in their relation to the historical present, and long-form texts enacting a vision of the future. Zhang's text used a series of detours via the past—the Chinese revolutionary wars, the early Soviet Union, and a rereading of Marx's textual corpus—to break new theoretical ground. The prospective abolition of bourgeois right provided a theoretical matrix for many of the practical transformations of the Great Leap. This was true above all of the collective canteens, which He Wei explicated: "[The canteens have] fundamentally ruptured with the wage form 工资的形式 as everyone, regardless of whether they have the capacity to labor or not, collectively enjoy the supply system that belongs to the whole people. At present, this is a supply system focused [solely] on foodstuffs, but it has the character of 'from each according to their needs.' "[67]

He Wei's projection of the canteens in these terms shared with the larger theoretical language of bourgeois right an expectation of an imminent traversal of capitalist social forms. Yet it ironically also shared with other interventions the effect of introducing certain tensions and silences into this moment of enthusiasm, silences partly revealed by literary texts such as Li Zhun's novella. By far the most troubling silence within the discourse opened up by Zhang's article, and the desire to break with the wage form, lay in those forms of labor that were always already unwaged, and which, with the exception of the partial socialization of reproductive labor, remained as such during the Leap, namely the problem of housework. The very utopianism of the critical discourse marked by bourgeois right therefore short-circuited a whole series of problems that are better registered by the long-form narrative texts of Li Zhun, as well as the complex texture of Mao's interventions, where the incorporation of women into the wage emerges as a necessary moment of transition on the road to a further transformation of social relations. The inability to reckon with the nonwaged character of reproduction as itself a kind of social relation, no less derivative of capitalism as the wage relation itself, emerges, then, as an oversight at what was otherwise a highly dynamic theoretical moment.

This neglect, moreover, was manifested in the way that the critique of bourgeois right licensed the often highly coercive hypermobilization of labor power, the totalizing extension of the working day, and the withholding of remuneration as instances of communist labor, above all through the state-led mobilization of vast amounts of peasant labor. The most enthusiastic proponents of overcoming bourgeois right were able, then, however perversely, to locate a utopian possibility in the total extension of the working day. An article published in *Liberation* greeting a new attitude of labor celebrated that workers, by extending their hours of labor and rejecting piece rate payments, had "broken with the eight-hour day."⁶⁸ In ways that these theorists did not themselves fully appreciate, the embrace of extended hours of labor reposed the problem of how to overcome a capitalist organization of production with respect to time itself, and the ever-greater reduction of the wage as a proportion of the working day as the basis for an increased production of surplus. The imagined surpassing of a capitalist logic of labor, in other words, could easily fall into its opposite, in the reinforcement of just that logic. The point of contact that these Maoist theorists did enact, however, between the theoretical vocabulary of bourgeois right and the larger problems of socialist social relations was that of the culture worker itself, which pointed back toward Lu Dingyi's initial remarks in 1957. The figure who most directly connected bourgeois right with the problem of the culture worker was fellow radical Yao Wenyuan 姚文元, who in his article "On Manuscript Fees" argued:

> The manuscript system is fundamentally a kind of remnant of the system of bourgeois right. It incorporates traces of the opposition between mental and manual labor in capitalist society. In the communist society of "from each according to his abilities, to each according to his needs," cultural creation will have become a need of the cultural life of the mass of laborers, and, like all productive labor, will be conscious and without cost, it will have become the source of life's joy, having broken relations with all notions of fame and profit.⁶⁹

Yao's powerful intervention occurred amid a context in which professional culture workers were voluntarily submitting to a reduction of manuscript fee payments, and yet it pointed to more fundamental issues, namely an understanding of the professional author as itself a kind of social relation, for which the manuscript system served as a site of ongoing reproduction.⁷⁰ In other words, the apparently parochial issue of manuscript payments drew Yao's attention because it marked one of the structural practices through which the culture worker was reproduced as a professional author demarcated from amateur cultural work, thereby maintaining the culture worker even in their position as a supposed figure of transition, freezing that figure in *place as a social relation*. The logic of this argument, then, was to underline that the experiments to overcome the professional writer that had arisen during the Great Leap were no mere expedient but themselves a necessary part of the remaking of social relations. Yet Yao's explicit linking of amateur cultural production to all other productive labor also demonstrated that the amateur writer was, then, not merely the image in which all cultural production should be transformed, including, if possible, in the form of collective practices of writing, but did themselves embody that vision of communist labor—labor performed gratis, or independent of the wage relation—that would mark the supersession of the wage relation more generally, at the same time as such cultural labor assisted in the generalized transformation of consciousness.

Hence, amid the Great Leap there emerged a dense and complex set of relations that pointed toward the overcoming of the professional writer and the supersession of the wage as decisive parts of a revolutionary process. Yet already, during the Great Leap, there were indications of the difficulty of this process, namely the reincorporation even of avant-garde amateur forms such as the short short stories back into the practice of the professional writer and the continued necessity of long-form texts with their associated rhythms of cultural labor. The intense difficulty of overcoming the author as social relation would, to no less extent than generating the conditions for superseding the wage, render no easy answers after the Great Leap.

From triumph to disaster—and beyond

The experimental phase of the Great Leap posed both a practical and theoretical challenge to the Soviet-derived model of development. Whereas the adoption of this model in the early 1950s had reproduced the temporal and spatial bifurcation of the countryside, the People's Communes sought to overcome this site of difference through the industrialization of the countryside and the mobilization of peasant labor. Whereas the Soviet program had codified remuneration according to labor as the basic method of distribution under socialism, the reintroduction of the supply system sought to instantiate the basis of communist norms of distribution. These and other transformations produced theoretical attempts to critique the Soviet model, which, in the case of bourgeois right, staked out the terrain of politics in opposition to the reified logic of even socialist economics. Taken together, these transformations, in tandem with the Rectification Campaign of 1957–1958, and a general acceleration in the pattern of accumulation also led to forms of cultural practice that sought at least partially to supersede the individual figure of the culture worker, based on collective methods of cultural creation that would be able to keep time with the social changes underway. Already, in late 1958, however, the internal tensions of the Great Leap, consisting of an extension of the temporality of labor on the one hand and the attempt to forge a new, egalitarian pattern of social relations on the other, began to come undone. The eventual, tragic consequences are already known to historians. Mao's own response was to urge caution. He did so particularly with reference to heady expectations of an imminent supersession of the wage by arguing, at the Wuchang Conference: "It is only possible to eliminate one part of bourgeois right, such as bureaucratic airs, excessive privileges, masterly attitudes, old relations, these must definitely be destroyed the more thoroughly the better. But the other part, such as the wage system, relations between upper and lower levels, and the definite compulsion of the state, cannot be done away with."

He went on in even more striking terms to say that "there is a part of bourgeois right that is still of use under socialism, and which must be preserved and made to serve socialism." The ambiguity of these formulations would become matters of vital debates in the Cultural Revolution. Mao's call for moderation extended further, to a proposal that his comrades busy themselves with a renewed study of Soviet political economy, embodied in the textbook and Stalin's treatise. Yet here, there was also an intimation of the way that "bourgeois right" would become central to a critique of Stalinism. Stalin, Mao said in his comments on Stalin's text at the Zhengzhou Conference in November, "only discusses economic relations, never politics in command." Nor, Mao said, did he "discuss the ideology of bourgeois right, he does not carry out an analysis of bourgeois right, he does not discuss what should be eliminated, how to eliminate, what should be restricted, and how to restrict it."[71] All true. The matter of how to prepare the conditions for abolishing bourgeois right would from this point onward comprise the most innovative theoretical terrain for the Chinese Revolution and was cojoined to the problem of the culture worker.

CHAPTER 4

REPRODUCING REVOLUTION

*Cultural Reconstruction and the Aesthetics
of Communist Heroism*

Artistic creation is indeed labor, and moreover it is a form of labor that is relatively close to handicrafts, it is a form of mental labor, one that requires a great amount of technical training, and is therefore similar to handicrafts.

—Zhou Yang 周扬

These remarks of Zhou Yang were introduced in June 1961 at a Nationwide Art and Literature Work Forum, held in the aftermath of the tragic collapse of the Great Leap in order to calibrate a reorganization of cultural work. The tenor of these remarks marks a totalizing retreat from the experiments around the configuration of writing that had been thrown up by the Great Leap. Even during the Great Leap itself, there had been intimations of these shifts. In his 1959 speech titled "Concerning the Problem of Walking on Two Legs in Art and Literature Work," Premier Zhou Enlai had distanced himself from the heightened tempo of cultural and other modes of labor during the Leap period by arguing that artistic labor could not be compelled according to the same rhythm as industrial production but required a degree of autonomy on the part of artists and writers so that they be able to produce works of sufficient aesthetic quality. More important still, in anticipation of future developments, Zhou Enlai took up the problem of collective labor as the basis for the ongoing transformation of the culture worker, arguing, therefore, that authors should not be compelled to submit themselves to a single model of transformation through labor, as "tempering through labor should not have to conform to a single model, and the old and infirm should have not have to labor."[1] It was the destructive consequences of the Great Leap, however, that brought a prospective restructuring of the literary system to the forefront. The aim of this restructuring was to draw up a series of explicit protocols that would define the tasks and practices of cultural work. These protocols made their appearance in the form of a preliminary draft of the Ten Points on Art and Literary Work at that Nationwide Art and Literature Work Forum, which provided the opportunity for Zhou Yang to insist on writing as a form of handicraft labor in the terms just quoted.

The points that emerged out of these discussions gave direct credence to the problem of time as necessary for the restructuring of writing. Under the second of the points, "Encourage Greater Diversification in Style and Subject Matter," the draft document codified the view that "the specific feature of literary creation is that it is an individual mode of labor 个体劳动, literature must be based on individual creation."[2] So too, under point five, entitled "Strengthen Artistic Practice, Ensure Time for Creation," did the document call for sufficient time for creation among authors. These shifts in the temporality of writing bore the support not only of Zhou Yang but also of nationwide leaders, including those who were not directly concerned with cultural work. The Nationwide Art and Literature Work Forum at which Zhou Yang spoke in June was held contemporaneously with a Nationwide Meeting on Feature Film Creation. Zhou Enlai gave a joint address to both meetings in late June, in which he explicitly emphasized that "art and literature are forms of spiritual production, they are products of the mind, and therefore carry great complexity, and are hard to grasp."[3] More prosaically, but hewing closely to the problem of temporality, he further emphasized for writers to be allocated more "time for writing" 写作时间. The explicit protocols drawn up in this period—the Ten Points—were, in fact, never adopted as formal policy for cultural work. They were rapidly superseded, from 1962 onward, by a different set of protocols, the Eight Points, and a crisis surrounding the practice of writing as well as the revolutionary process more generally. The extraordinary complexity of this brief period of interregnum resists easy conceptualization, and yet, with respect to cultural work, the problem of the reproduction of the revolutionary process resolved itself into the problem of everyday life. The everyday as it emerged during this period consistently indicated a concern with repetitive structures of temporality over and against the anticipation of a fantastical leap into communism that accounts for many of the texts of the Great Leap. In place of the expectations of fantasy there emerged the problem of how, amid the repetitive, regularized rhythms of everyday labor, to manage reproduction with respect to labor power and the revolution itself. This period ultimately emerges as one of the *total crisis* of reproduction.

The obstetrics of revolution

The final year of the Great Leap saw the publication of Ru Zhijuan's short story "All Quiet in the Maternity Clinic" (1960). The story was republished in a collection of the same name in 1962 and rapidly became a site of critical attention, including in the form of a lengthy review in the magazine *Women of China*. That this story, having appeared during the Great Leap, should come to reemerge in the critical discourse of the post-Leap period designates the complex temporal rhythms of the text itself as well as its afterlives. The short story is, as its title suggests, based in a spatial environment and set of practices that are largely absent from other narratives of labor in the socialist period, namely a commune maternity clinic. The point of departure for the short story is the arrival at the clinic of a new nurse, Sister He, who has undergone training at a nearby city to become a midwife, with Auntie Tan already being present at the clinic upon her arrival. The narrative momentum of the short story lies largely in the sets of tensions and disagreements that emerge between the two women as a result of their divergent positions with regard to their experience of the old and new societies, with Auntie Tan's consciousness of women's embodied experience in pre-Liberation China informing her skepticism of Sister He's enthusiasm for new, modern technologies of childbirth.

The short story is largely narrated from the focalized perspective of Auntie Tan herself, which allows for an interrogation of gendered experience and the effective use of a sophisticated range of narrative strategies. Above all, the choice of an older woman as the site of subjectivity and the narrative center through which the short story is focalized mark the persistence of certain narrative conventions of the Great Leap, especially in the fiction of Li Zhun. In the case of Ru's narrative, the focalization of the text through an older woman provides the conditions for a gendered experience of labor that resists the narratives of total mobilization that otherwise informed literary production in the Great Leap, insofar as Ru's texts demonstrate an attempt to accommodate plural temporalities of labor, including those that mark the irreducibility of the biological body. In diegetic terms, the short story covers a short period of time, beginning with the arrival of Sister He at the maternity clinic and ending with the successful delivery of a child. The importance of Auntie Tan in these terms lies not only in the general significance of having an older woman as the narrative protagonist of the text but more specifically in the way that, in temporal terms, Auntie Tan is situated as an intermediary or even liminal figure, whose capacity to function as the experienced midwife of her village is itself the result of the possibilities opened up by socialist modernization. Auntie Tan experiences the temporal anxiety marked by the arrival of Sister He as a new figure whose enthusiasm and knowledge calls into question Auntie Tan's own monopoly over midwifery in the village, thereby introducing the gendered relation between the two as one of complexity and conflict, but without Auntie Tan being reduced to a narrative foil, as a character who is inadequate to an accelerated tempo of labor. The short story begins, then, with Auntie Tan awaiting the arrival of Sister He, which opens up into a series of extended soliloquies on her own experience as a midwife worker who acquired knowledge of modern techniques of childbirth through training in the local township, and who, as a result of the formation of the rural communes, has gained a new status in her community, with the assignment of a maternity ward.

The narrative device of the soliloquy—that is, the subjective analepsis—constantly occurs across the entire short story and may therefore be seen as central to the narrative arrangement of the text, marking the ways in which the pressures of the past constantly intrude and force themselves into the temporality of the present, as mediated through the subjectivity of Auntie Tan herself. At the beginning of the narrative, then, prior to Sister He's appearance, Auntie Tan's recollections of the day on which the commune assigned a maternity ward mark her personal history of self-fashioning as a socialist laborer:

> "Wasn't this much the same as a hospital?" Auntie Tan was so excited [on that day] that she couldn't even get to sleep, she thought of how women had once had to give birth sitting on a footstool and while biting their hair, and then thought of that new bed that was as high as her entire leg; she thought of how, becoming a widow at the age of thirty-nine, she was now coming into this maternity ward to work as.... to work as what, exactly? She thought about it and could not think of an adequate term to describe her job, but finally, she could only, and with hesitation, describe herself as an "obstetrics doctor." The following day she got up early and cut off her braids so that her hair was short, with there being some gray strands of hair behind her ears, which lent her a serious and lively air. When everyone saw her, they conveyed a respect that she had not felt before, and yet they still warmly called her Auntie Tan.[4]

Auntie Tan's self-fashioning as a socialist subject is marked through adjustments and conduct at the level of personal experience but it also contains a certain crisis of language, in which there is no readily available set of categories with which to mark Auntie Tan's location in a rural community that is undergoing vast transformations at the level of social relations. Her account of her self-fashioning therefore leaves unresolved a certain tension between her embrace of being termed an "obstetrics doctor" and the newfound respect that she gains in her rural community as the custodian of new, scientific methods of childbirth, and, on the one hand, her continued situation in a rural community that occupies unequal temporal relations with the urban centers from which Auntie Tan has gained her knowledge, marked, in this brief account, by the insistence on the part of the villagers that she be addressed as Auntie Tan. The problem of language therefore already marks the liminal character of Auntie Tan, whose claim on and access to the protocols of modern scientific knowledge both marks her distance from accepted practices of midwifery in the village but also sets up the narrative tensions between her and Sister He, who instantly emerges in the narrative as a younger, more enthusiastic advocate for scientific advancement than Auntie Tan herself, as Sister He is said to have undergone training not only in the township but, in fact, in the city.

Sister He's enthusiasm is expressed through her mania for introducing further improvements to the maternity clinic, including the installation of an automatic water system, and the introduction of calisthenics to prepare expectant mothers for childbirth, to which Auntie Tan responds by invoking her own, gendered experience of the conditions of childbirth in the pre-Liberation society, marking a horizon of experience to which Sister He has no personal access, as well as reminding Sister He that conditions in rural communities cannot be judged by urban standards. In one further internal soliloquy, therefore, which Auntie Tan invokes on the night of Sister He's arrival, she marks the radical divergences between her own experience and that of Sister He: "These young people, from as soon as they can remember anything they've had white rice to eat, as far as they're concerned, having land and food is the natural way of things, and so too is being able to go so school, they take for granted that we have maternity clinics, electric lighting, tractors, when have they understood bitterness, how could they ever understand what true suffering is like!"[5]

The invocation of the younger generation as lacking access to a body of experience of the pre-Liberation society in this context foreshadows the problem of revolutionary succession that would emerge as central to political and cultural struggles several years after the publication of Ru's text, and yet more important within the immediate narrative context is the way that Sister He's arrival and perceived failure to appreciate the limitations of doing midwifery in a rural setting provides the conditions for a resurgence of the past into the present, in the form of a set of embodied, gendered experiences that cannot simply be done away with through the implementation of a set of scientific forms of knowledge, of which Sister He styles herself as the main custodian. The text, in these terms, enacts a constant process of remembrance on the part of Auntie Tan that complicates its temporalities. The tensions between Auntie Tan and Sister He are therefore formally generational, but they also emerge as

Reproducing Revolution   141

related to different claims of knowledge, which in the case of Auntie Tan includes scientific training but also extends to an irreducible form of embodied knowledge based on the suffering of women in the old society. The conflictual relationship between the two is, however, further complexified by the recurrent emergence of a third term, namely that of Grannie Pan, who in temporal and generational terms occupies the same relation to Auntie Tan as Auntie Tan does to Sister He, being, in other words, the practitioner of midwifery in the old society, whose folk knowledge Auntie Tan sought to supplant. Whereas the tensions between Sister He and Auntie Tan comprise the main narrative axis of the story, Grannie Pan makes periodic appearances, both as remembered through the internal soliloquies of Auntie Tan but also in the real, diegetic time of the narrative itself. In recounting the difficulty of convincing peasants of the value of new midwifery practices, then, Auntie Tan recalls that

> There was one time when a woman was experiencing difficulty in childbirth, and Auntie Tan was careless, sending the woman to the hospital rather late, so that the child was lost. This caused an enormous uproar. An old midwife called Grannie Pan was stuck in the middle of it all and said that Auntie Tan had been responsible for the loss of the child, so there was a huge ruckus in the family of the mother. The more Auntie Tan thought about it the angrier she got, there had been so many children lost on account of those old midwives, but people never voiced a word of complaint, but rather they said that it was the way of the world, but when she herself had an error in her work, it was as if people wanted to swallow her up.[6]

When, having been confronted with Sister He's mania for technical improvements, Auntie Tan excuses herself from the maternity clinic to collect some eggs for the expectant mother, she happens upon the same Grannie Pan, who, it emerges, is now responsible for raising chickens in the commune. This, in turn, prompts a further soliloquy based on Grannie Pan's changed position as compared to her previous work as a midwife in the old society, so that "Auntie Tan looked upon her wizened, smiling face which appeared both good-natured and clever, and she felt bemused, thinking that as people's ideas change, so too do their appearances change. She remembered that when Grannie Pan had worked as an old midwife, her face had been both thin and pinched. When Auntie Tan had introduced new methods of childbirth, Grannie Pan had been absolutely livid, she was constantly coming to swear at Auntie Tan, and on occasion even started some fights."[7] The apparent successful conversion of Grannie Pan into a new model of the socialist laborer is therefore unsettled by the understanding that the supplanting of dangerous practice of midwifery under the guise of a new system of scientific knowledge is at the same time the supplanting of an individual woman and her claims to folk knowledge within a village community, and it is this same anxiety that in turn comes to inform Auntie Tan's anxiety in relation to Sister He. This anxiety becomes legible through the invocation of an accelerated temporality that threatens to outstrip and surpass Auntie Tan, and one whose quotidian manifestations take the form of technological advances that Sister He advances in the maternity clinic. The singular point of condensation for this anxiety of being outstripped lies in the repeated invocation on the part of Sister He of the problem of "backwardness," which instantly forces Auntie Tan to reckon with her own discursive complicity in this language based on her own previous role as a proponent of the eradication of "backward" midwifery practices.

In response to Sister He posing the problem of the backward character of midwifery in the rural areas, then, Auntie Tan recalls that "she herself had said such a thing, three years ago, when they were promoting new childbirth, she herself had said to so many people that they ought to be "both hygienic and scientific," she had said it to women, as well as to the husbands of those women, to grannies, to mothers, and above all to Grannie Pan." In yet more explicit terms, which perhaps mark a moment of excessive intervention on the part of the author, Auntie Tan realizes that she "suddenly clearly understood Grannie Pan's state of mind three years prior, and why, at that time, Grannie Pan had been hopping mad, why she had spoken of bitterness to her, and why she had sometimes had a scary face, at other times a bitter face, and so Auntie Tan now understood, that it was because she was afraid, and that she was also unwilling to fall behind the times 落在时代后面.[8]

It may be seen, then, that the narrative function of Sister He from the perspective of Auntie Tan is to exert a temporal pressure that is at the same time also a structure of return, in which Auntie Tan comes to recognize her relationship with Sister He as one that is formally analogous with her own historical role in the supplanting of Grannie Pan in her village, specifically in the invocation of a discourse of overcoming backwardness. The repeated eruption of memory into the narrative is, therefore, both a marker of the anxiety of being temporally supplanted, but for this reason also renders the socialist present out of joint by drawing attention to the complexities of knowledge over the act of childbirth in the rural setting. To the extent that there is a force that compels resolution to these complex strands, it comes in the form of the imminent arrival of a new child and a turn for the worse in the weather, which requires that all the transport machinery of the commune be used to prevent the crops from being spoiled. When the birth experiences complications due to the exhaustion of the mother, Auntie Tan rushes to phone the nearest hospital, in spite of the necessary operation being simple and one that she and Sister He could perform themselves. In the event, Sister He proves adequate to the task, with Auntie Tan insisting on learning from Sister He's command of surgical methods, but not without Sister He herself being made conscious of the gendered experience that informs Auntie Tan's position. Her realization is significant in narrative terms because it also marks a point at which Auntie Tan ceases to be the sole point of focalization for the narrative. Instead, the narrative gains access to Sister He's thoughts and anxieties via a shift in focalization and the subject of psycho-narration, as well as the moment at which the intergenerational gap between her and Auntie Tan is bridged: "Sister He raised her head, and saw that Auntie Tan stood before her, with fear, courage and determination. At that precise moment, it was as if she understood the entire history of the maternity clinic, and the entire course of the history of the struggle to introduce new midwifery methods. She thought of how Auntie Tan had, in the middle of the night, sat on the back of a bike to receive a new birth, and how she had proudly cherished turning off the electric light."[9]

The narrative denouement, in these terms, is a traversal of the generational gap that otherwise defines the major content of the narrative, and one in which Sister He comes to share in Auntie Tan's embodied experience of the prehistory of the present and its modern possibilities, consisting of the difficult labor of introducing childbearing methods into a village community. It is in this sense, then, that Ru's text marks an attempt to sustain different temporalities and practices of labor. These consist first of the enactment of a constant process of remembrance within the text itself and the tensions that produces with respect to the future-oriented temporality embodied by Sister He, but also the irreducible biological temporality of the process of childbirth, which here emerges as the basic form of biological reproduction whose temporality is fundamentally irreducible to any demands for acceleration. It is also in this sense that the temporal location of the text as event signifies an emergent consciousness of the post-Leap conjuncture, one that became rapidly clear as the text became a central object of critical discourse over 1961. The central concern of this discourse lay in nothing less than the familiar conceptual problem of "life" itself. In particular, Hou Jinjing's article "Creative Individuality and Artistic Uniqueness" set out a defense of Ru's work and marked the problem of literary style 风格.

Hou's central argument draws closely on the theoretical language surrounding the Ten Points and the interventions of Zhou Yang not only in emphasizing that socialist literature should admit a wide range of subject matter, including narratives that emphasize the texture of everyday and family life, but that this diversity may be understood in terms of the variability of authorial style as the ultimate grounds of cultural production. In Hou's observation, therefore, the imperative to allow a diversity of style and form in literature is underpinned not only by the requirements of different kinds of literary subject matter nor the diverse cultural demands of the masses but also differences among authors themselves: "This and that author who are both taking the path of serving the workers, peasants and soldiers, that is, authors who are the same with respect to life experience, political and cultural cultivation, and experience in writing, may, in dealing with the same subject matter, come to produce different literary works. Certain differences between authors, such as differences in individual character 个性 or talent 才能 artistic taste and so on, will certainly give rise to divergences in artistic method and artistic character 艺术风格."[10]

The seemingly prosaic problem of style at this juncture marks an important moment in the history of literary criticism in the post-1949 period, and more specifically during the post-Leap interregnum, whereby the acknowledgment of divergences in the treatment of subject matter between authors amounted to a reindividuation of the cultural subject, but in ways that also redirected the attention of writers to the complex relations of the everyday, in place of the mobilization narratives of the Great Leap. With these interventions having been generated by Ru Zhijuan's work, the conceptual vocabulary of "style" was also profoundly gendered, such that an implicit position of "woman author" was here offered to Ru Zhijuan by a male critic, as a reflection of her sensitive treatment of women's experience, in ways that underscore the potential investments in the author as subject-position from the perspective of female writers. These discussions were accompanied by emergent theoretical interventions around the kinds of subject matter that would be admissible to literary creation. The problem of subject matter received explicit attention through an editorial published in the March edition of the *Art and Literary Gazette* under the title "The Problem of Subject Matter," which provided a theoretical articulation of the problem of the everyday by calling for an expanded conception of "life" as the subject matter and grounds of cultural creation, arguing, therefore, that:

> Life is an indivisible totality, a unity of opposites that incorporates different kinds of social relations, class relations and relations between human beings. The author faces the totality of life and expresses the general through the particular. He selects, from the great ocean of life, things with which he is familiar and of which he has a deep understanding, things which he believes to be of value and of interest, and uses them as the object which he refines and processes, and it is precisely this that is subject matter.[11]

The cycles of literary reorganization of which Ru Zhijuan's short story was an important indication could not but have implications for further experiments in writing. Further literary texts also came to anticipate the problems that were to emerge over the remainder of this interregnum period, above all with respect to the problematic of the everyday and reproduction. This is true above all in that the development in narrative concerns over the period of 1960–1962 marks the shift from the problem of biological reproduction as a dimension of gendered labor to the generational reproduction of the revolution. Indicative of this process is Ru's short story "Ah Shu" (1961), itself part of a two-part series, with the second story, "The Second Step," published later in the same year. "Ah Shu" maintains the problem of generational misalignment that emerges in "All Quiet in the Maternity Clinic" but is formally distinct by virtue of being narrated through an I-narrator, consisting, in this case, of a figure whose identity is never strictly disclosed, but who has come to a rural commune in an official capacity. The use of an I-narrator in this context has the effect of constructing the narrative around a process of discovery for both the narrator and the reader. The narrative opens: "The birds had not begun to squawk, and nor were the hens yet chirping. The sky was still inky-black, but I was already awake, simply waiting for the voice that would come to awake me. The old secretary was to blame for this. If he would only tell me, then all would be good, but for some unfathomable reason he had set up a mystery for me."[12]

With the following line—beginning "last night, when I had arrived at these three small teams, it was already late" - it is revealed that the temporal point from which the text begins is, naturally, the morning after the arrival of the I-protagonist. The narrator reports that on the previous evening a young girl, her identity not yet being known the morning after, had helped the narrator fix a wholesome meal despite having arrived late, but that the old secretary had as of yet refused to reveal their identity simply announcing to the I-protagonist that "you'll know early on tomorrow, whoever comes to wake you up, it's her." The framing of the initial narrative in these terms provides yet a further mark of formal distinction for this narrative, namely that, from the "morning" onwards, the narrative is delivered according to a temporal perspective that is simultaneous with the events described—that is, simultaneous narration—divulging an active process of discovery, rather than with the authority that might devolve on a narrator at a distance from the events described. There is, in other words, no suggestion of a knowledge of the eventual outcome of the narrative. On the morning on which the narrator awakes in a state of puzzlement, the girl in question is quickly revealed to be the titular character of Ah Shu. Through the practice of simultaneous narration, the motivating force for the narrative that follows is the incompatibility between Ah Shu's youthful enthusiasm and idealism on the one hand and the less glamorous, sustained tasks of rural production on the other. The frequent rebuke from Ah Shu's mother when faced with what she deems to be frivolous attempts to contribute to the commune is "she knows nothing of adult matters, no worries in the world!" This contradiction becomes visible through an episode that relates directly to the problem of narrative itself, when Ah Shu demands of the I-narrator that they tell her a story: "'Will it be bitter or not? I don't want to hear bitter stories.' 'Well, what do you want to hear, then?' 'Something interesting, fun.' She didn't want to hear about anything bitter, rather, she wanted comedy, happy reunions, whereas I felt that what she truly needed was precisely not this kind of 'interesting' story."[13]

Ah Shu's apparent resistance to stories of "bitterness" here marks the problem of the narration of the revolutionary past and the old society in its relation to the present, as well as Ah Shu's blindness to the bitterness of the present-day challenges facing the commune. The decisive moment of transition in the narrative comes when Ah Shu and the I-narrator attend a meeting of the commune production brigades, at which the party secretary recognizes the failure of the work team to which Ah Shu belongs to meet their desired production outputs, which the secretary explains in terms of their dependence on the resources of the state, and of other production brigades:

"There are many who have said that our rice paddies aren't bad, but when it comes to our production output for the whole year, we're still eating and wearing what others produce, we..." the old secretary spoke up to this point, at which point the hands holding his tobacco pipe began to shake. I was looking at Ah Shu, and she was sitting in complete stillness, her two hands grabbing the butterfly knot that she had put together with such care in her mouth, swallowing the threads of the silk band.[14]

The impact of the old secretary's speech is to add a spatial dimension to the problem of the bitterness of the past that is enacted in the I-narrator's skepticism about "interesting" stories, in that the old secretary draws attention to the relations of political economy that link the circumscribed production team to which Ah Shu belongs with other teams in the same commune. To Ah Shu's youthful enthusiasm, then, is counterposed an expanded spatial and temporal vision that takes account of the needs of the whole commune, even when that labor proves, like the stories that the I-narrator seeks to tell Ah Shu, to be "uninteresting" or otherwise lacking in glamor. Yet, when Ah Shu and her friends seek out a boat in order to be able to contribute toward the urgent task of gathering river mud for fertilizer, they find themselves rebuffed by, among others, the old secretary, recounted by Ah Shu herself as follows:

"I did ask him. But all he said was 'you've only just graduated from elementary school, and still rather delicate, so better that you do some minor tasks, no need for you to worry about agricultural production.'" Ah Shu paused, and then said "no need for us to worry! If we just rely on other people for food and clothes, won't we end up becoming the kinds of bugs that Granddad Tiangen talked about? What kind of interest could this life possible have."[15]

The problem, the I-narrator remarks, of "what kind of life is interesting" is, indeed "a serious problem." The ultimate response on the part of Ah Shu and her friends is to insist on their own initiative by wading into the river to gather water lilies. This in turn forces a recognition on the part of her mother, who, faced with the joyful state of her daughter and other young women as they engage in voluntary labor, is drawn into the example of their youthful spontaneity. The narrative ends in turn with a spontaneous labor competition led by the old secretary. The denouement of the narrative in these terms marks a successful sublimation of enthusiasm on the basis of demanding acts of labor, and in this respect Ru Zhijuan's text anticipates the key narrative tropes that will proliferate in the years following. Yet equally important is that this sublimation takes place in a reciprocal process, in terms that restage the closing scene of "All Quiet in the Maternity Clinic," in which the older generation also undergo a process of transformation. It is also, here, that the formal significance of the use of simultaneous narration emerges. The coeval temporal situation that unites the I-narrator and Ah Shu herself precludes the use of techniques such as analepsis and prolepsis that might establish the narrator as occupying a temporal position of distance from the events. This temporal simultaneity is also the basis, then, for an egalitarianism and reciprocity in the way the text handles the problem of Ah Shu herself. The question—"what kind of life is interesting"—would, from 1962 onward, become the central question to which other texts would address themselves as part of a concern with the reproduction of the revolution. Yet, as distinct from Ru Zhijuan, they would do so in overwhelmingly masculinist terms, where the binding of the youth to the demands of bitter labor could only be conceived of in terms premised on the enhancement of the male-dominated family as the primary unit of reproduction under socialism.

Family arguments

Beginning in 1963, the problem of cultural labor and its relation to the transformation of social relations took a quite different turn, namely in the form of an incipient crisis of ideological and political reproduction. It was problems of this order that likely occupied Mao when in 1962 he demanded at the Tenth Plenum that revolutionaries "never forget class struggle," based on an emergent analysis of the perceived failure of the revolutionary process in the Soviet Union.

This intervention provided the conditions for a series of important shifts and adjustments in the contents of cultural labor, of which the most immediately visible was the revision of the Ten Points draw up by Zhou Yang into the Eight Points, which, while continuing to embody a retreat from the ambitions of the Great Leap, nonetheless reemphasized the need for the transformation of culture workers. With respect to culture, the ultimately more influential line of combat lay in a meeting called for April 1963 to discuss the problems of cultural work generated by Mao's 1962 injunction. This meeting witnessed a series of intersecting interventions on the prospects for cultural work, consisting in the first place of the demand, associated with Jiang Qing and Ke Qingshi, that socialist art and literature focus on the contemporary, meaning events since the founding of socialist China, or, in the formulation of Ke Qingshi, "the thirteen years," which gained the support of Zhang Chunqiao.[16] At the same meeting Lin Mohan teased out the divergences between the Chinese and Soviet practices of cultural work, specifically that of ideological transformation: "on the question of the intellectuals, the Soviet Union never put forward or at least never seriously put forward the slogan of the transformation 改造 of the intellectual." Moreover, "in another respect, that of creation, they put forward the following position: that provided that authors wrote about reality 真实, they would naturally tend toward Marxism. Today we can see that this is wrong, or at least overly partial."[17] The absence of any revolutionary politics of transformation combined with the false thesis of class struggle having effectively ceased meant, Lin argued, that the Soviets were unable to resolve the problem of the worldview 世界观 of writers:

> Having failed to insist on thought transformation, [the Soviets] undertook excessive use of material incentives and excessive praise toward authors and artists, such that they enjoy a high salary, and are overly praised as engineers of the human soul, people's performers, and recipients of the Stalin Prize [etc.]. In both material and spiritual terms they have come to depart from the masses on a daily basis, and rather than being common laborers, they are a privileged caste, an aristocracy. This is one of the primary reasons behind the degeneration of the cultural sphere in the Soviet Union.[18]

The implicit contrast between overreliance on material incentives and the elevation of writers in the Soviet Union and the transformation of consciousness in Chinese socialism marked not only a historical account, but also a certain restaging of the logic that underpinned the emergence of the vocabulary of bourgeois right during the Great Leap, whereby what initially began as a cultural critique eventually assumed a wider valence as a category of political economy. In its immediate context, however, Lin Mohan's intervention was part of an increasing critique of the Soviet Union across a range of theoretical fronts, in which the question of culture and the cultural subject was of great importance.[19] The cultural shifts associated with the emergent anti-revisionist critique included, for example, the formation in 1963 under the Propaganda Department of the Art and Literature Anti-Revisionism Writing Group, which was headed by Lin Mohan but whose leading members also included important cultural critics such as Zhang Guangnian, Li Xifan, and Li Zhi. The task of the group was to prepare materials and publish articles and translations that would assist in the campaign against revisionism in art and literature. Mao's contribution to these highly public broadsides was, however, more situated as a mode of intervention, insofar as he aimed his ire at the very system of ISAs that accounted for the reproduction of socialist culture. At the end of the year, and in responding to a published speech by Ke Qingshi, Mao put forward the first of two crucial commentaries 批示 on the question of culture:

> Among the different artistic forms—theater, local operas, music, fine arts, dance, film, poetry, literature, and so on—there are many problems, and for many people and many departments the effects of socialist transformation have been slight. Many departments are still controlled by the "dead." We cannot underestimate the achievements in film, new poetry, folk songs, fine arts and literature, but so too are there many problems. The socialist base has already been transformed, and yet there continue to exist many problems in the artistic departments that form part of the superstructure that serves this base[20]

The problem of the "lag" that Mao identified here between the role of the cultural ISA and the demands of socialist constriction identified that ISA as the "weakest link" in the ongoing revolutionization of social relations, whereby the literary ISA, far from reproducing the conditions for socialism, had come instead to reproduce the division between mental and manual labor. This crisis mirrored that of the immediate pre-Leap period in that the famous amateur writers of the 1950s who had been incorporated into the Writers Association—Tang Kexin, Hu Wanchun, and others—were again cited as evidence of the failure of ideological reproduction. The crisis of ideological reproduction as it related to the literary ISA, however, was itself part of a much larger crisis around the cultivation of "revolutionary successors," or the ideological reproduction of the younger generation. It was also, ironically, these same writers, and Hu Wanchun in particular, whose works provide the clearest insight into the broader problem of reproduction that emerged in this period, through the narrative topos of the despondent youth. The problem of reproduction as it emerged in Hu's texts marks no longer the biological reproduction of the laboring body as such, but rather the reproduction of the revolutionary process, based on the challenges posed by a new generation of laborers, which is to say *reproduction as subjectification*. Yet the narration of this set of problems could hardly avoid a more familiar set of problems surrounding the gendered reproduction of labor power, in ways that produced an intersection of problems and narrative conventions.

The complexity of these problems might be judged from a short story, "A Family Affair" (1963), by Hu Wanchun. The story revolves around the return home of a young worker, Fumin, after graduating from a technical training college and the ensuing conflicts with his father, Master Du. These conflicts revolve around Fumin's resistance to manual labor and the cultivation of desire around access to material goods. The strong focalization of the short story through the figure of the father provides the conditions for a series of visual encounters that mark Master Du's distaste for his son's habits of consumption. Fumin rapidly emerges as a figure whose experience of formal training has engendered an aversion to shop floor labor and an embrace of the division between mental and manual labor, which is at the same time a source of familial conflict, between Fumin and his father, as well as between father and wife. The traumatic scene of encounter, when Master Du encounters Fumin for the first time after his return from higher education, is narrated in strikingly visual terms, with a radically clear site of focalization: "This young fellow was so finely-attired from head to toe that he was a bit threatening. His finely-cut youthful hair was shiny and smooth. He was wearing a plush lapel jacket and brown suit trousers, clutching a large paper bag in his hand, with a smile adorning his long face. He took a few steps forward and called out with affection, but Master Du felt odd."[21]

The clear focalization contained within this extract is marked by the shift from the moment of visual encounter to the psycho-narration of Master Du's unease. The spatial context in which this encounter takes place is that of the household, which emerges across the narrative in a tense relationship with the shop floor, insofar as the home and its associated practices of reproductive labor are presented as both a necessary appendage to the factory, but also as a site of danger, embodied in the form of consumption, whose seductions threaten the ideological reproduction of the revolution itself. The problem of ideological reproduction marked by "A Family Affair" sits alongside other texts from this period, of which the most famous are the plays *Never Forget* and *The Young Generation* as narrative interrogations of the emergent conflicts of socialist reproduction and the task of forging a socialist everyday.[22] In this context, however, "A Family Affair" has a special significance that has hitherto gone unnoticed, not only because it was among the first texts to introduce the problems of revolutionary succession, but also because it underwent a process of cinematic adaptation, with Hu Wanchun himself writing the screenplay. The cinematic version (1964), to an even greater extent than the literary Ur-text, allows for the conscious construction of the narrative rhythm around the cojoined spaces of the home and shop floor, whereby those crises sparked by displays of consumption inside the home become the basis for Fumin's enforced dispatch to shop floor labor under the tutelage of none other than his own father. The conflicts that emerge on the shop floor itself are, within the discursive grammar of these texts, not the result of problems imminent to socialist relations of production themselves but are rather an extension of the uncontrollable forces of consumption and desire for consumption goods to which manual labor provides the assumed response.

4.1 Fumin retrieves objects of household use.

Source: Film still from 《家庭问题》 (*A Family Affair*), directed by Fu Chaowu 傅超武, screenplay by Hu Wanchun, 1964.

At multiple levels, then, this genre of texts marks a sharp departure from the distinctive narrative economy of texts from the Great Leap, oriented as they were to the reorganization of social reproduction in primarily rural contexts. In addition to texts of the 1960s being marked by a return to the urban, there is a reorganization of authority within narratives, whereby the source of crises is displaced onto the domestic space, no longer as the site at which women laborers such as Li Shuangshuang contest male figures of power, but rather as that site which is called upon both to assume responsibility for the reproduction of labor power, and also emerges as a site of danger in its relation to consumption and leisure. This process is naturally a gendered one, with often misogynistic consequences, as demonstrated by the opening scene, when Fumin has returned home from university, and his initial source of encounters with his mother are shown to be mediated by the exchange of objects. In figures 4.1 and 4.2, Fumin is shown handing over certain objects to his mother, and then eventually receiving tokens to be able to buy a new coat and scarf:

The constitution of the social relations between mother and son according to a logic of consumption in this scene is due not only to the object-mediated interactions between the narrative protagonists, but also due to the careful arrangement of the mise-en-scene, whereby, through a series of close takes

4.2 Fumin's mother provides consumption coupons.

Source: Film still from 《家庭问题》 (*A Family Affair*), directed by Fu Chaowu 傅超武, screenplay by Hu Wanchun, 1964.

delivered from different angles inside the apartment, it is revealed to comprise a world of objects, including, for example, the multiple layers of objects that emerge from figure one, ranging from the porcelain bowl in the foreground to the varied objects in the background. The mise-en-scene arrangement of this opening scene directs attention to the ways that the film also preserves the narrative pacing and spatial arrangements of the other famous texts from this period—*Never Forget* being the foremost among them—that staged the crisis of the domestic through dramatic performance. This is true at a structural level in the way that the film alternates between scenes on the shop floor and the domestic interior, but it is also true of the domestic arrangement shown above, which, to a greater extent than the shop floor, approximates the aesthetic of dramatic performance through the use of a demarcated spatial environment and the use of medium close-up shots that incorporate the multiple protagonists who are present in any given domestic scene and situates them within the domestic mise-en-scene comprising objects of consumption. The association between the domestic space and the problems of consumption from the opening scene of the film onwards, and above all the gendering of consumption, is subsequently strengthened by the visceral reaction of the mother to the decision of Fumin's father to dispatch him to the shop floor to work on his own team before he is able to take up his position as a qualified technician.

With Fumin's mother consistently demanding that Fumin be allowed to enjoy the material and professional privileges proper to him as a qualified technician, she emerges altogether as an object of mockery in the film who is herself in need of ideological education. When, for example, halfway through the film, she implores her husband to reconsider his treatment of Fumin, he agrees that she should go and talk to the factory head for that purpose. He provides her with a note explaining the situation, only for the camera to reveal that the letter the father has prepared in advance calls on the factory head to correct his wife's ideological errors, the implication being that Fumin's mother is illiterate. The joke enjoyed between the father, the factory head, and the audience posits Fumin's mother as the object of mockery. Whereas, in the scenes dealing with the domestic interior, the film mimics the visual techniques of a domestic drama, in the shop floor scenes, by contrast, the film more closely preserves the visual techniques specific to cinema, such as wide-angle shots of the inside and outside of the factory, as well as tracking shots that take in the factory as a site of labor. The social logic of the factory floor is regulated according to a radically gendered form of labor, in the form of homosocial bonds among overwhelmingly male workers, based on the familial bonds that connect Fumin, his brother Fuxin, and their father. The familial nature of these bonds is made visible in one of the first scenes of the film, before Fumin has returned home, when his mother calls to the factory from home in order to tell the father of the imminent return of their son, only for his older brother to mistakenly come to the phone, believing that the call for Master Du is referring to him, "small Master Du," rather than his father, "elder Master Du." In the subsequent scenes dealing with Fumin's experience on the factory floor, the homosocial social relations that comprise the factory are made visible through the problem of the body, whereby Fumin's body is initially revealed to be inadequate to that of the working class and forced to readjust itself to the tempo of factory labor. Most striking of all, however, is that when Fumin first arrives home, his father looks with evident distaste on his carefully combed hair, which has been styled as a quiff, shown in figure 4.3. This shot is unmistakably a cinematic adaptation of the prose extract examined at the beginning of this section. The highly focalized literary prose naturally lends itself to the use of a subjective point-of-view shot, in which the visual gaze of the father supplies the grounds for castigating Fumin as inadequate to the demands of manual labor. In a further visual gesture, human hands emerge as a powerful visual trope of working-class masculinity or lack thereof. When Fumin is preparing to undertake shop floor labor for the first time, his father inspects his hands, shown in figure 4.4.

Having felt that his son's hands are not those of a worker in a masculine mold, his father comments that, with labor, his hands will become "sturdy and

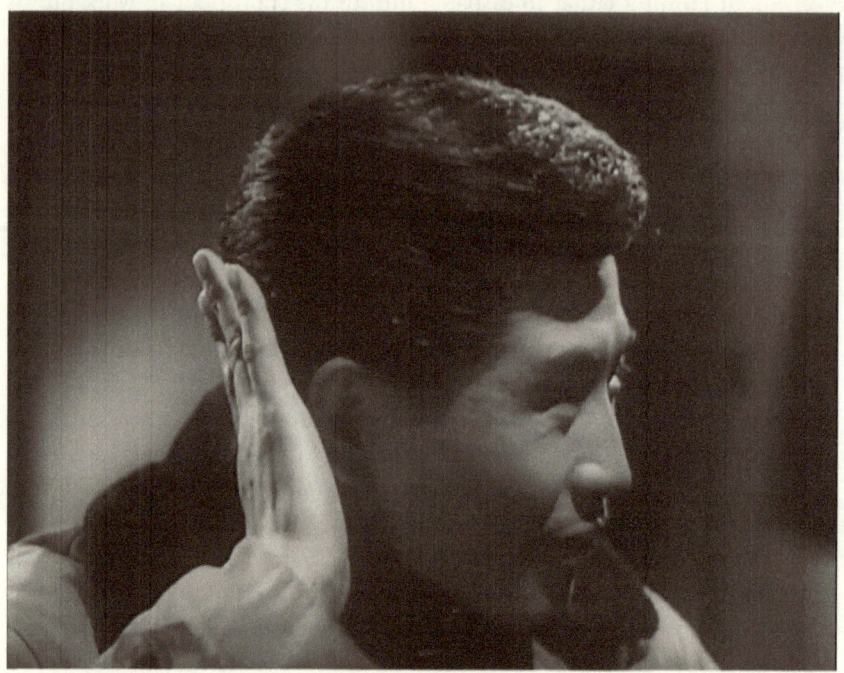

4.3 Fumin greases his hair, as seen from the perspective of his father.

Source: Film still from 《家庭问题》 (*A Family Affair*), directed by Fu Chaowu 傅超武, screenplay by Hu Wanchun, 1964.

good-looking."[23] In the remainder of the film there are further narrative events that position Fumin in a negative light due to his failure to embody the tropes of working-class masculinity, including, for example, not being able to drink liquor. To this extent, not only are the relations of labor that comprise the social in the factory characterized as masculine, in contrast to the gendered domestic sphere and its relations, but Fumin's problematic character is narrativized partly in terms of his failure to embody the image of the male worker provided by his father and brother. He is to that extent also himself part of the ensemble of feminine characters who provide the negative foil in the film, and who must therefore be reintegrated into the masculine world of the factory. The construction of the cinematic narrative according to a rhythmic alternation between the shop floor and the domestic is not without its tensions, however. The constant depiction of the household even as a site of danger has the unintended effect of making the labor of social reproduction visible in a way that threatens to upset the projection of the domestic only through the lens of dangerous consumption, as the master narrative of the film intends. The narrative moment that most radically foregrounds the domestic space as one of

Figure 4.4 Fumin's father inspects the hands of his son.

Source: Film still from 《家庭问题》 (*A Family Affair*), directed by Fu Chaowu 傅超武, screenplay by Hu Wanchun, 1964.

reproductive *labor* comes when Master Du and his wife first quarrel about the matter of Fumin. The wife storms out, leaving Master Du to make noodles. There follows a dissolve, eventually revealing Fumin putting on his gloves in preparation for work, shown in figures 4.5 and 4.6, potentially juxtaposing the hands of Master Du versus his son, the former demonstrating the visible signs of labor—albeit in a domestic context—the other putting on gloves as a way of resisting contact with the factory environment:

The momentary refusal of the wife to undertake her assumed tasks of domestic reproduction marks a crisis within the filmic narrative, embodying as it does an unexpected withdrawal of labor. This crisis is resolved by the decision of Master Du to step into the breach, and yet the following dissolve nonetheless marks a moment of powerful ambiguity in the way the visual trope of hands suggests a moment of encounter between the domestic interior and the shop floor that is not delineated along the binary of consumption and manual labor. It also enacts one of several moments of alliance between the mother and Fumin as the younger and consistently feminized son. Yet this moment of crisis is itself recuperated at the end of the film, as in so many other narrative texts, by the restoration of a stable familial order in which Fumin

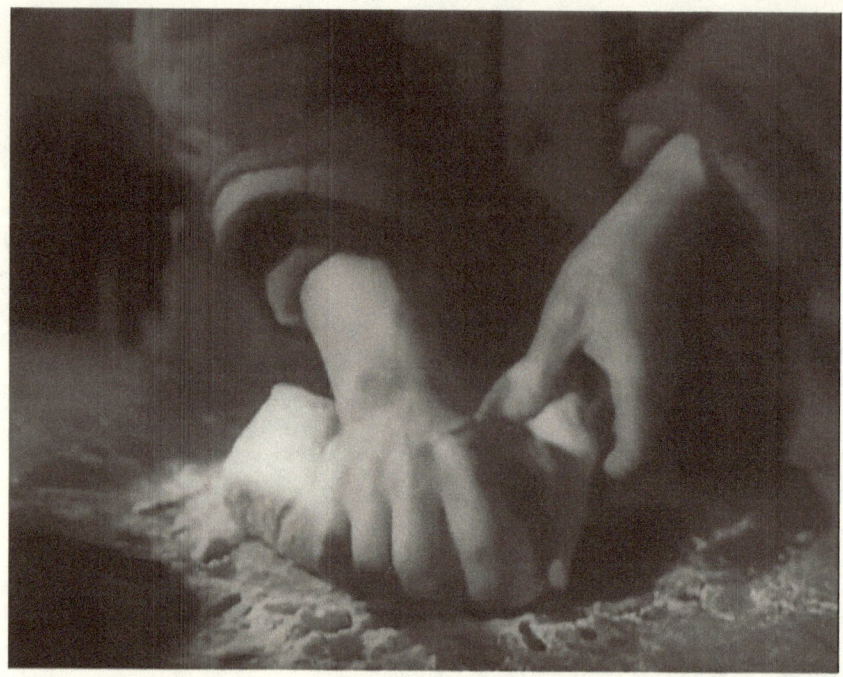

4.5 Fumin's father takes up domestic labor from his wife.

Source: Film still from 《家庭问题》 (*A Family Affair*), directed by Fu Chaowu 傅超武, screenplay by Hu Wanchun, 1964.

has been reconciled to the demands of the factory floor. It is the father, Master Du, who is central to this multilayered process, in which the incorporation of Fumin into the demands of shop floor labor is also the enabling condition for the resolution of family conflicts and the restoration, therefore, of a smooth model of social reproduction, which also ensures that Fumin is able to guard against the seductions of inappropriate uses of leisure and income in the form of material objects. The family, then, altogether emerges in the film as both a necessary and naturalized site of the reproduction of labor power *and*, through the relationship between feminized subjects and consumption, a potential threat to the ideological reproduction of socialism, requiring the patriarchal authority of the father embodied by Master Du.

Just as the film is organized around the spatial relationship between shop floor and the domestic, this relation was itself closely implicated in the temporal relation between the time of production and the time of leisure. The problem of what young workers would do with their leisure time, or how, in other words to produce a practice of socialist everyday life became a source of political and moral crisis after the release of the film and similar texts, marked by a

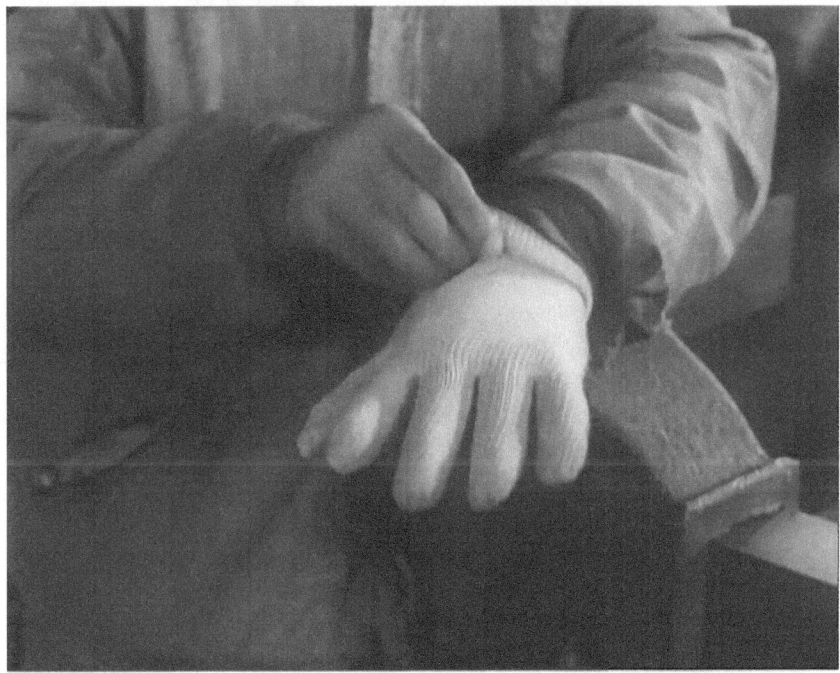

4.6 A dissolve yields to the gloved hands of Fumin on the shop floor.

Source: Film still from 《家庭问题》 (*A Family Affair*), directed by Fu Chaowu 傅超武, screenplay by Hu Wanchun, 1964.

series of discussions in *China Youth* on problems of leisure, with commentators seeking to disclose the integration of leisure and labor time. In one such instance, entitled "It is Necessary to Treasure Leisure Time," the author Xie Qipei invoked the vocabulary of the self 私 and society 公 to argue against those who would disaggregate the time of leisure and labor: "I have never imagined that [the eight-hour working system] is a sharp dividing line between the time belonging to 'society' and the time belonging to the 'self,' and still less have I ever imagined that leisure time is solely for the purpose of having fun."[24]

In this discourse, the conceptual binary of self/society that had been invoked to articulate the task of transcending the wage form during the Great Leap was restructured according to a moral wariness around the inappropriate use of leisure time. Interventions of this order reveal, in fact, a profound ambiguity around the problem of time, and more specifically the working day, in that Xie simultaneously invokes the division between the time of labor and the time of leisure, while also seeking to avoid any sharp delimitation between those two temporal spheres whereby one might become the preserve of "private life." At issue here, then, is a variation on the problem of the "double life," yet no longer given in terms of the disjuncture between the time of writing and the time of labor, but rather the division of the everyday into the time of leisure and the time of production. These concerns persist in other narrative texts. If, in the case of "A Family Affair," it is Fumin's tendencies toward wayward consumption that designate his narrative function as a problematic youth, different problems emerge in Hu Wanchun's novella from the same period, entitled "Generations" (1963). This text also takes the topos of the return of youth as its point of narrative departure. Here the subject of return is Liang Haisheng, a worker who, like Fumin, returns to the factory of his apprenticeship after undergoing technical education. The text therefore revolves around the temporal difference between moment of his return, that is, 1963, and the previous moment of his apprenticeship, 1956, together with the transformation of the factory itself as well as various narrative figures in the intervening temporal gap.

The opening pages of the story construct the quasi-familial relationship between Haisheng and other members of the factory, provoked by his witnessing the visual changes that the factory site has undergone in his absence: "at this moment he only had to close his eyes, and he could imagine the different scenarios in the workshop. There, he would find his own master, Meng Xingchang, and his own two female apprentices—Yanqian and Hong Mei."[25] The anticipation of a recognizable factory community into which Haisheng might easily reintegrate himself, with its familiar chains of familial authority, is embodied through Haisheng's remembering of iterative narrative events that foreground the recurrent temporality of factory production itself, as in the instance of the security guard, Old Xu, whose exchanges of greeting comprise a powerful synecdoche for the temporality of the everyday:

> He thought of the doorkeeper Old Xu. Seven years prior, when he went to work each morning, he would always greet Old Xu as he passed through the factory gate, and so too would Old Xu always reply in laughter: "Liang! You've turned up early!" In the evening, when he got off work, he would also say to Old Xu: "See you tomorrow!" and Old Xu would likewise laughingly reply "See you tomorrow!" Over so many years, they had said these two phases two each other almost every single day, and never had they experienced any sense of vexation.[26]

This anticipated structure of easy, straightforward recognition, whereby Liang's experience of the factory as a returning technical expert might itself replicate the pattern of recurrence that comprises the remembered factory of his youth, is, however, upset and frustrated when it transpires that, at the moment of his return, Old Xu does not, in fact, recognize Liang. When Liang encounters his old Master, Meng, a more affirmative moment of recognition

Reproducing Revolution 159

emerges, between Liang, and the head of the personnel department, Old Zhu, and Meng himself. The terms in which Old Zhu reintroduces Liang to Meng mark, significantly, an explicitly gendered and familial turn of phrase: "'he's returned to his parental home' 娘家 said Old Zhu, blinking, 'don't you think so, engineer?'" The positing of the factory as Liang's parental home, and Liang himself, by extension, as a feminine figure who has married out, would, when read in light of the narrative pattern of a contemporaneous text like "A Family Affair," set Liang himself up as the object of critique in the text, as he who must be reintegrated into the patterns of the factory life and the corresponding modes of working-class masculinity. In their ensuing conversation, Meng mentions that Hong Mei—already introduced through Liang's own recollection as one of his apprentices at the time of his departure from the factory—has become the deputy factory head. This provides the impetus for a further act of remembrance on the part of Liang and Meng, introduced in the form of a further visual image: "There immediately arose before his eyes the image of a young and proud girl. Thereupon, as master and apprentice walked and talked, events of seven years prior once again emerged in their minds."[27]

The suggestion of a pattern of remembrance common to both yields, in turn, to a sustained description of prior events involving Hong Mei, which takes up the entire second and third part of the narrative. While, in technical terms, this comprises a subjective analepsis, it nonetheless incorporates a marked shift in focalization away from Liang (or Meng) and toward Hong Mei herself. With this analepsis and shift in focalization, it also becomes clear that the primary site of contradiction across the whole text lies not, ultimately, with Liang as the technical worker returning to the factory in the narrative present, but rather Hong Mei's prior history of integration into the rhythms of factory production. The emergence of Hong Mei as the primary site of contradiction is enacted above all through the strategic use of free indirect style. While this entire section lies in a subjective analepsis on the part of Liang and Meng, the voice which participates in free indirect style within the analepsis is that of Hong Mei in the narrative past, as her younger, less disciplined self. The spur for these instances of free indirect style lies in Hong Mei's disappointment upon entering the factory as apprentice at how the scenes of industrial production with which she is confronted when she is first introduced to the factory under the aegis of Meng and Liang fall short of her envisaged ideals of the romance of labor. For example:

> Hong Mei looked toward the planing machine, aiyah! What kind of machine was this? Some dark and swarthy thing, ugly and small, like some kind of dark dog crouching on the ground, with two horns on the top. This was really too far away from her ideal 理想. Surely she would not be expected to work at this small machine for the rest of her life? The more she thought about it the

sadder she got, so that her face came to alternate between furious red and deathly white, and she looked quite pathetic indeed.[28]

The replication of internal patterns of speech in the form of rhetorical questions in the voice of Hong Mei herself is here accompanied by an explicit articulation of the problems that motivate the narrative, namely the frustration of romantic ideals around the factory and the expectation that she will have to accommodate herself to the repetitive, extended rhythms of factory labor for the rest of her life. The problem of "ideals" thereafter emerges as a recurrent topos, and one that signifies the desire for individual achievement and the excitement of daring occupations. In a suggestive overlap with the characterization of Fumin, Hong Mei's resistance to the demands of factory labor is registered at the level of the body and clothing, especially via the trope of hands that do not bear the signs of labor. When, for example, Hong Mei is unable to pick up a fallen nut, a contingent shift in focalization to Liang reveals the reason: "Liang Haisheng took a glance at her hands and saw that she was wearing three sets of gloves, so that her hands were twice as thick as before. How would she have been able to pick up a small nut in that state? Liang Haisheng could not, at that moment, restrain himself, and said: 'Hong Mei! Are you afraid your hands will catch a cold?' "[29]

This same narrative context also introduces a foil to the repeated demands for a bodily transformation on the part of Hong Mei, in the form of the other female apprentice, Yanqian, who exclaims: "haven't you seen Hong Mei's two hands? How white and slender they are, really, there's something poetic about them!"[30] The trope of hands thereby becomes a veritable site of aesthetic struggle in the narrative, one enacted on the body of Hong Mei as she faces a prospective sublimation to the decidedly unromantic demands of labor under the aegis of Liang, counterpoised to the admiring gaze of Yanqian. Yet these demands encounter a more rigorous affront in the scene immediately following, when Yanqian, returning from a liaison outside the factory, and finding Hong Mei in a state of great upset, approaches her from a perspective of care, albeit in terms that also gave insight into her own supposed ideological failings:

> Yanqian wildly leapt out of her own bed and snuck into Hong Mei's coverlet. She grasped Hong Mei's two hands, and said "it's already spring, but still so cold! I'll rub your hands, it's ever so cold!" She saw that Hong Mei did not make a sound, and said in pity: "Oh you, you worry too much...ah! I'll tell you something...I was walking on the road just now and saw a woman wearing a pair of pumps! What a pair of shoes!" As she talked and talked, they finally fell asleep.[31]

The suggestion of intimacy in this mode provides a suggestive echo of Bai Lang's 1950s text, in the form of an alliance of female workers, albeit rendered more contradictory moments later when Yanqian quotes her mother: "as women, if you don't marry a man, all you can expect is a lifetime of suffering!" The framing of Yanqian as a woman orientated toward affairs of consumption and self-insertion into the domestic sphere via marriage sets up the conditions for Hong Mei's own incorporation into the demands of the factory and its masculine structures of authority. When Liang subsequently departs to take up his training as a technician, he does so with words of advice to Hong Mei and Yanqian to incorporate themselves into factory labor, advice that is revealed to embody a patriarchal line of descent within the factory insofar as "the words he spoke were the same words that Master Meng had said to him when he passed over the planing machine." There ensues the end of the analepsis and a return to the narrative present of the 1960s, which is inaugurated by the renewed meeting of Hong Mei and Liang, a meeting that is announced through Liang's focalized perspective in terms of Hong Mei's radical transformation: "Liang Haisheng looked at Hong Mei closely and was struck dumb. She was already completely different from the Hong Mei that he had held in his mind. No longer was she that young, arrogant Hong Mei of the past, she had, rather, become a healthy, sturdy young woman."[32]

The introduction in this same narrative context of Hong Mei's own apprentice allows Liang to exclaim, in yet another familial image, that "we are now 'four generations under one roof 四世同堂.'" In this same context, however, Hong Mei also reveals that Yanqian has already been married for three years, no longer working on the factory floor. The ensuing tour of the newly mechanized and modernized factory under Hong Mei, as witnessed by Liang, provides a partial ironic reversal of that opening segment of the analepsis, in which Hong's introduction to the factory under Liang provided the conditions for her initial disillusionment. Liang's gentle mocking of Hong's transformation into a factory laborer as compared to her initial disillusionment and haughtiness provides, here, the grounds for a recounting of the process of Hong Mei's transformation, which is said to have arisen from the events of one particular year: "since Liang had left the factory, he did not know much about Hong Mei's circumstances. Thereupon, Hong Mei began to tell him about what had happened that year." As compared to the earlier transition, between the first and second sections of the narrative, the suggestion here is of an intradiegetic oral narrative on the part of Hong Mei, rather than a shared subjective analepsis, as previously, yet the effect is the same insofar as the following section, the fifth, takes the form of an extended recounting of events later in time (that is, closer to the narrative present) as compared to the first analepsis. The upshot of this intradiegetic narrative as delivered by Hong Mei is that

Hong Mei's pursuit of romantic ideals of individual achievement combined with Yanqian's literal pursuit of romance caused damage to the planing machine of the factory, earning an angry rebuke from Master Meng: "Hong Mei! You must remember, to take your own desires as ideals is the most selfish thing of all. We only have one ideal, which is communism. As an ideal, it depends on our ordinary labor 平凡的劳动 and our capacity to achieve it with our own two hands."[33]

The invocation of ordinary labor here marks a specific temporality, and one that provides the compelling demand for a sublimation to the unglamorous and repetitive labor of collective production. Hong Mei's subsequent angst over the damage posed to the factory and to Meng's health provides for a radical divergence between herself and Yanqian, and the eventual end of this intradiegetic narrative, followed by a resumption of events in the narrative present as the final section of the text. The repetitive structure of analepses, albeit ostensibly emerging in the form of either a personal remembrance, or an oral account followed by a return to the narrative present thereby emerges as homologous to the repetitive, cyclical pattern that Liang identifies with factory labor itself, and to which Hong Mei is expected to modulate her youthful temperament. The final return to the narrative present, in section six of the text, is inaugurated by a fragment of description that underscores the extent to which the foregoing analepsis is ostensibly to be read as the discursive property of Liang and Hong: "as Liang Haisheng and Hong Mei spoke to each other, without realizing it they had already walked out of the seventh side door of the factory." In this final section, however, there is a marked return to Liang as the sole site of focalization, announced explicitly via the formulation, "Liang Haisheng opened his eyes, and saw before him the residential blocks of five or three stories arrayed neatly on both sides of the road." This, then, further establishes a formal symmetry across the narrative, in which Liang is granted the power of narrative focalization in those sections comprising the narrative present, as distinct from the focalization through Hong Mei in those sections dealing with her own troubled assimilation to the rhythms of factory production in the 1950s. The function of the final narrative segment, then, is to indicate that Yanqian has also fulfilled her aspiration of an incorporation within the nuclear family as a housewife, a fact that emerges, for both Liang and Hong Mei, as the site of contradiction, even danger, leading them to agree on their shared responsibility to incorporate her into factory life: "On the road, Liang Haisheng wanted to hear some views from Hong Mei, and so asked: 'Hong Mei! What do you think of our Yanqian?' 'I think her mind is getting narrower,' Hong Mei said with great solemnity. Liang Haisheng glanced at Hong Mei with shock, and then also nodded his head."[34]

The careful temporal arrangement of the narrative, then, consisting of its staged invocations of the past, is to record Hong Mei's integration to the temporalities of the shop floor at the same time as it marks Yanqian's retreat to the domestic realm. In the playful vocabulary of the story itself, then, both Liang and Hong Mei come to be incorporated within the factory as a "paternal home" in which the structured lines of hierarchy between different masters and apprentices comprise "four generations under one roof." If, in these terms, the factory itself emerges as a kind of family, it is one that is also founded on patriarchal lines of descent, and the prioritization of the aesthetic signifiers of repetitive manual labor. The family as a private site of kinship remains given, yet it is given primarily as a negative threat to the revolutionary process, emblematized in "Generations" by Yanqian's suspect decision to become a housewife. The recurrence of this trope across Hu Wanchun's text of the 1960s marks the constant attempt to think the problem of the household, but so too does there emerge the same sticking point. Hu's texts gesture toward the family as part of the social basis for reproduction of bourgeois ideology and the private status of labor power, yet they do not understand the family as a site of production or envisage the conditions under which its reproductive functions might be altogether transformed. The household and its gendered forms of labor came to comprise a double bind, as the accepted site of social reproduction of labor *as well as* a threat vis a vis the reproduction of the revolutionary process.

The tentative reconsolidation of accumulation after the experiments of the Great Leap, then, as well as the response to the emergent problem of revolutionary succession, took a patriarchal form, one that relied on the further retrenchment of the division between waged and masculinized labor on the one hand, characterized by its industrial setting, and unwaged, feminized labor in the home on the other, the latter bearing responsibility for the reproduction of labor power. Hu Wanchun's texts demonstrate how the problem of ideological reproduction in the 1960s could receive its imaginary resolution only in patriarchal and masculinist terms, in which recalcitrant elements were called upon to resubmit themselves to the authority of the literal and figurative father, with little to no room for the socialization of reproductive labor imagined during the Great Leap. This mode of reconsolidation suggests a set of limits that would need to be transcended, surrounding the conditions of the reproduction of labor power. To the reproduction of labor power, there emerged, as a corollary, the problem of the socialist ideological reproduction in the form of the ISA, which is to say, the superstructure, forming a *total crisis of reproduction* at this conjuncture. The problems of the superstructure that Mao had enumerated through his first commentaries in December 1963 had not been resolved, as Hu Wanchun's texts attest. The figure of the professional culture worker would, from this point onwards, emerge as itself part of the system of contradictions to be surmounted.

Modeling communist labor

Mao's continued dissatisfaction toward the state of cultural work did not go unnoticed. Subsequent to his first commentary, and while texts such as "A Family Affair" were seeking to narrate the emergent crises of socialism, Zhou Yang and other cultural leaders set about examining the shortcomings of cultural work. The result was a "minor rectification" in March 1964 and an associated report under the title "Report on Rectification Conditions in the National and Local Writers Associations," whose authors identified that cultural institutions had "ignored the necessity of writers and artists entering into life and amalgamating with the workers and peasants; they have ignored the long term character of the intellectual transformation of the culture workers, and they have not emphasized the work of cultivating new forces."[35] The period following this "minor rectification" marked, then, an emergent return to the figure of the amateur writer, marked by the relaunching of the magazine *Sprouts* in 1964 and the eventual All-China Meeting of Youth Amateur Literary Creation Activists held in 1965. Yet even amid this turn toward a revitalization of amateur work, Mao made his second crucial intervention. He stated in June 1964 as a commentary on a draft version of the report that:

> The vast majority of these associations and the periodicals that they run (reportedly there are a minority that are good) have, over fifteen years, fundamentally (it is not, however, everyone) failed to implement the policy of the party, they have become haughty officials, have failed to get close to the masses, they have not reflected socialist revolution and construction. In recent years, they have come to the margins of revisionism. If they do not seriously undergo transformation, then there will certainly come a day when they will become a group like the Petofi Club in Hungary.[36]

There followed, beginning in August of that year and continuing through to April 1965, a more sustained rectification movement, later condemned during the Cultural Revolution as a "fake rectification."[37] The thrust of Mao's critique recapitulated those basic lines of argument that had already been posed by Lin Mohan in 1963, namely that the institutions of socialist cultural production tended to reproduce the division between mental and manual labor and so tend toward the ideological degeneration of writers. Yet an indication of the increasing urgency of this set of problems was that they also generated the reemergence of the theoretical language of bourgeois right. The resurgence of this conceptual vocabulary was posed amid increasingly intense polemics against the Soviet Union, reportedly authored by Mao himself. The fiery polemic "On Khrushchev's Phony Communism and its Historical Lessons for the World" released in *Red Flag* in July 1964, threw down the gauntlet: "The influence of the remaining bourgeois right and the force of habit of the old society all constantly breed political degenerates in the ranks of the working class and Party and government organizations, new bourgeois elements and embezzlers and grafters in state enterprises owned by the whole people and new bourgeois intellectuals in the cultural and educational institutions and intellectual circles."[38]

The theoretical depth of this critique lies in the understanding that the reproduction of the bourgeois intellectual under socialism is no mere aberration but rather reflects the maintenance of a whole system of social relations and forms that are here categorized under the name of bourgeois right. The understanding, in other words, of the author as itself a kind of social relation, and one bound up with the wage relation as a site of the persistence of capitalism within a socialist society, gave new weight to the search for an alternative, insurgent cultural ISA beyond the formal structure of the Writers Association. Such an alternative locus emerged in the form of the People's Liberation Army. The "Directive on Cultural Work in Army Units" released in May 1964, that is, just prior to Mao's second commentary, envisaged a militarization of literary creation according to the formula of the "three amalgamations" 三结合 in which cultural work would be organized around the guiding role of political leaders, professional cultural producers, and the masses. The aim would be for "creation can be like fighting a battle, with the central authorities having an effective command over creative personnel and assigning specific tasks." To the formula of the three amalgamations was added the formula of the "three masteries" 三过硬, encompassing mastery of Mao's works, entering into life, and in basic skills.[39] The emergence of the PLA as the institutional locus for a renewed enhancement for the transformation of culture workers assumed wider significance for the problems of labor as such, whereby the PLA served as the conduit for the reemergence of the theoretical language of bourgeois right. The 1964 proposal released by the Central Military Commission on the abolition of ranks, put into practice the following year, therefore explicitly stated that the system of ranks imported from the Soviet Union was inappropriate for a revolutionary army like the PLA: "Practice demonstrates that this system is not in accord with the glorious traditions of our army, it is an expression of hierarchy and of bourgeois right 资产阶级法权, which encourages the formation of individualist attitudes and a sense of inequality, being therefore disadvantageous to the revolutionary construction of our army, as well as to unity between comrades, levels and army detachments."[40]

The visibility of the PLA as the locus of a struggle against bourgeois right provided the conditions for the promotion of selfless militarized discipline as a model for the transformation of the consciousness of labor, as well as being a model for the transformation of writing. Already in early 1964, then, the editorial "The Whole Country Must Study the People's Liberation Army" published in *People's Daily* explicated the universal significance of the PLA in terms of the renewed problem of the reconfiguration of desire as the basis for the supersession of bourgeois right, whereby the soldiers of the PLA were promoted as exemplars on the grounds that "they are full of public spirit and reject narrow interest 大公无私, and they selflessly strive for the public and disregard themselves, they work solely for others rather than for themselves, and even devote their youth and lives to socialism."[41] The political significance of the PLA as a basis for the cultivation of a new communist morality was articulated explicitly in terms of the ideological transformation of everyday life. A subsequent *People's Daily* article, "Disseminate the Three-Eight Work Style Throughout the Country," therefore enjoined, "to disseminate the three-eight work style throughout the country requires political thought work, it requires cultivation and tempering amid labor and everyday life 日常生活."[42]

The invocation of daily life in this context therefore designates the problem of how to combine selflessness, as embodied in acts of heroism, with the daily, repetitive experience of labor, marking, therefore, the problem of how to mediate between different temporalities. The intended transformation of everyday life according to the model of the PLA was underpinned by a consistent emphasis on the overriding significance of consciousness as compared to the technical dimensions of production and warfare, via the formulation that "man is the foremost factor among such factors as productive forces." The elaboration of the transformative powers of consciousness therefore marked the importance of the reconfiguration of individual desire as a way of overcoming the continued effects of capitalist social relations, theorized in terms of the ideology of bourgeois right, and the task of generating a communist consciousness of labor. The effectivity of literature would be to mediate between the communist virtues of the PLA and the repetitive experience of everyday life in order to effect a transformation in consciousness. It is no coincidence, then, that in tandem with the turn toward the PLA as an alternative ISA and model of communist labor, the period 1964–1966 also encompassed a renewed turn to the theoretical problem of aesthetics as the basis for the overcoming of bourgeois right. Central to this turn, and related to the PLA as the alternative ISA, is the *Diary of Lei Feng*, which, having first been published in 1963, gives explicit recognition to the problem of an aesthetics of labor in terms that borrow from the visual iconography of hands in Hu Wanchun's text:

The faded and patched yellow uniforms of the soldiers are beautiful, the oil-stained blue overalls of the workers are beautiful, the sturdy, calloused hands of the peasants are beautiful, the tanned faces of the laboring people are beautiful, rough and majestic labor chants and the souls of those who work tirelessly for socialist construction are the most beautiful. All this constitutes the beauty of our era 时代的美. Whoever thinks this is not beautiful does not understand our era.[43]

The articulation here of a communist vision of beauty under the name of Lei Feng as a solution to the problem of ideological reproduction had a double valence insofar as it mapped on to those texts of Hu Wanchun dealing with revolutionary succession, and so too was it rapidly applied to ideological reproduction in the literary sphere, in that the propensity of culture workers to undergo ideological degeneration was explicated in terms of the persistence of a bourgeois worldview that was itself aesthetic in character. In these terms, the period immediately prior to the Cultural Revolution, as well as the Cultural Revolution itself, was characterized by a radicalized vocabulary in which the improper treatment of apparently progressive or "new" subject matter on the part of professional writers came to be explained in terms of the persistent influence of a bourgeois aesthetic horizon. None other than Hu Wanchun therefore stressed in his densely theoretical article "We Must Rupture with the Old World" in 1965 that even as writers took the new society and new humans as their subject matter, their practice of writing continued to be determined by "old ideas and feelings, old artistic tastes, and an old conception of beauty 审美观." The contradiction that Hu identified between the choice of subject matter and the execution of writing demanded a totalizing process of transformation in which, he said in yet more dramatic vocabulary, it becomes possible to "transform the standpoint, perspective and methods of Marxism-Leninism and Mao Zedong Thought into flesh and blood."[44] Yet by far the most radical dimension of Hu's text lay in his critique of any reified notion of "artistic technique" as something withdrawn from the exigencies of aesthetic practices that were themselves determined by diverging class horizons. The question, in this context, of how to work up material into literature became explicated through a vocabulary of class struggle raised to the level of aesthetics. He argued:

> Artistic technique 艺术技巧 is certainly not a [simple] matter of skill 技术, but fundamentally is a reflection of the conception of beauty of the author—there is a unitary relationship between technique and the worldview of the author. The kind of works that an author writes is determined by their conception of beauty. The requirements of our era compel us to transform our conceptions

of beauty. There are two kinds of conceptions of beauty, the proletarian and the bourgeois. Therefore, our authors face a struggle between these two conceptions of beauty. Only if we can undertake a transformation of our own conceptions of beauty can we establish our own, proletarian conception of beauty, and serve the creation of proletarian literary works.[45]

The explication of artistic critique in these terms marked a further critique of the reification of writing as a specialized practice, as well as of any reified notion of artistic "craft." The emergent recourse to the aesthetic here in the guise of "conceptions of beauty" was joined in Hu Wanchun's text to a series of repeated invocations of the problematic of bourgeois right, in terms that reflected the influence of polemics against the Soviet Union and its failure to insist on the transformation of writers, such that the need for writers to undergo frequent cycles of transformation to combat the influence of bourgeois conceptions of beauty arose, for Hu, from the persistence of class struggle throughout socialism: "with the continued existence of bourgeois right, and the continued influence of old moral ideas, we naturally should not require that all authors will be able to write works without any blemishes whatsoever."[46] The totalizing prioritization of a proletarian aesthetic passed over from the problem of the culture workers into the envisaged tasks of cultural works themselves, whose function came to lie in the promulgation of concrete models, specifically in the form of the creation of "heroic characters," which, following the archetype of Lei Feng, promised to provide the conditions for an aesthetic education along the lines imagined by Hu and others. Rebecca Karl has therefore noted, with reference to an earlier moment, but in terms that also speak closely to the problems of the mid-1960s, that the figure of the individual model designated a "a process of abstraction" in which "his particularities came to be dissolved into a universal type" in such a way as to stage a new set of social relations through a "play of temporalities," which may here be understood as the play between the exceptional moments of heroism and the repetitive experience of everyday life.[47] A discussion along these lines closely approximates the theoretical discourse that arose as part of discussions around the literary creation of heroic characters in this period. The theorist Zhang Jiong therefore argued that "the ideal content of the hero is the respect in which the hero differs from nonheroic [characters], which is also the respect in which the hero functions as a model 榜样 and banner for everyone, and is able to perform an important function in communist aesthetic education."[48]

The understanding of the specifically aesthetic dimensions of heroic or model characters designate both the capacities for moral transformation that were invested in these literary and artistic figures, but so too does it immediately demarcate some of the emergent tensions of this paradigm of cultural production, namely in the way that the "aesthetic" provided the common grounds for the transformation of professional culture workers and the transformative capacities of cultural works themselves, as well as in the relationship between abstraction and particularity marked by Karl, that, is the problem of how exactly models were to mediate between the exceptional time of heroism versus that of the everyday experience of labor. It is, as ever, through the literary texts themselves that these tensions most radically emerge. The publication of *The Song of Ou Yanghai* (1965) by author Jin Jingmai 金敬迈 marks one such text, received to enormous acclaim in the short period between 1965 and the eruption of the Cultural Revolution.[49] The novel is based on the story of a real individual, and takes the form of a biographical novel charting Ou Yanghai's trajectory from birth in the old society, and his eventual success as a soldier in the PLA. The novel begins with Ou Yanghai's destitute family in their village before liberation, but its larger part is concerned with Yanghai's military life. Despite its purportedly military subject matter, however, the novel is noteworthy for its absence of any military action. This fact is central to the novel and its relation to the problem of making a communist spirit of labor imminent within the temporal experience of everyday life, because the novel itself is based on a narrative temporality of deferral, and more specifically the deferral of desire, in which Ou Yanghai's constant pursuit of singular acts of heroism are deferred onto the repetitive labor of everyday life. Already, in fact, when Yanghai remains a child, he is forced to wait a period of time until he can pursue his desire to join the PLA. This process of deferral is at the same time a deferral of readerly expectations cultivated by the military subject matter of the novel, insofar as the novel contains no scenes of combat with the enemy.

Significantly, the cultivation of Ou Yanghai's desire for combat is dependent to a larger extent on cultural texts, including those centered on individual heroes, which constitute a textual genre of hero biographies, of which the novel *The Song of Ou Yanghai* is itself a part. This is true above all of the biography *The Story of Dong Cunrui*, which, having first been published in 1954 as the biography of a heroic soldier, accompanies Yanghai's person throughout the novel and comprises a frequent point of reference for Yanghai's own reflections on his conduct. Yet a more specific and suggestive point of contact lies in Yanghai's viewing of a film in the first third of the novel when he has already joined the PLA and is undergoing training, and more specifically a documentary feature on the socialist transformation of Tibet that precedes the Korean War film *Triangle Hill*. The scene is worth quoting in full:

> As with previous occasions, they were showing two films: before the main showing of Triangle Hill, they had added a documentary film showing the uprising of the million serfs. Having heard that the film Triangle Hill was a story about the struggle against American imperialism, Ou Yanghai was

excited. Even if he himself couldn't go off to fight the American imperialists, and the reactionaries, to be able to watch a film about the struggle against imperialism was no bad thing.

There was a white sheet hung between two poles, which served as the screen. The soldiers were sitting down in rows with bursts of song following one another.

The film began, and on the screen there emerged white snow-covered mountains and fast-flowing rivers, dark primeval forests and boundless grasslands. The somber voice of the narrator rang in Ou Yanghai's ears:

". . . . on the southwestern border of our motherland, there is a Tibetan plateau that is called the "roof of the world," which is the southwestern boundary of our great nation."[50]

This brief extract reveals the competing forces of desire that constitute the novel. Having already been disappointed in his expectations that he and his fellow recruits will be able to enter into combat straight away, the snippet of free indirect style embodied by the formulation "to be able to watch a film about the struggle against imperialism as no bad thing" reveals the ways in which the cinematic experience offered to Ou Yanghai functions as a surrogate for his desire for combat, in which a cinematic project offers the vicarious opportunity to participate in real combat. The more radical moment of encounter, however, lies not in the main feature but in the preceding documentary film, whose depictions of peasant suffering are experienced by Ou Yanghai in terms of his own village community and the depredations suffered by his peasants at the hands of landlords, in ways that foster his desire to be able to go to Tibet and fight against feudal oppression. The moment of climactic encounter: "Ou Yanghai saw and heard clearly, and it was if he felt that the tall soldier who was striding at the head of the detachment sent to repress the reactionary rebels was none other than Dong Cunrui. It was as if Dong Cunrui was turning his head back from the screen, and, with enlarged eyes and in anger, was shouting to him: 'Quick, Ou Yanghai! What are you waiting for? Charge forward with me, my brother!' "[51]

The viewing of the documentary therefore provides the conditions for an interaction between different modes of media, namely between the cinematic depiction of socialist transformation in Tibet and the literary form of Dong Cunrui's story, which take on a fantastical, real-world form which is seen to directly address—or more specifically interpellate—Yanghai and call on him to throw himself into a military expedition. The excitement of desire for military combat in these terms is also the evocation of a specific temporal experience that is part of the heroic desire for a singular moment of combat. The excitement of desire results in repeated pleas from Yanghai to his commanding officers that he be immediately dispatched to Tibet. It should be noted that the depiction of this excitement of desire is radically focalized on Yanghai himself, in such a way that the depiction of the encounter with the documentary, in which one of the soldiers is imagined as Dong Cunru directly speaking to Yanghai as the specific object of his address, also provides a staged encounter for the reader, and which, to this extent, generates a set of readerly expectations and desires for combat. The responsibility of deferring Yanghai's desire therefore falls to his commanding officers, which in turn necessitates a shift in narrative focalization and voice, from Yanghai's immature demand for heroism to the experienced voice of his superiors, as follows:

> For three days, as soon as Ou Yanghai finished work he would run to the company command to request the results of his "report." The secretariat and the correspondents were rather annoyed with him: they didn't come across this kind of soldier very often, and it was a total dead end. But Guan Yingkui and Zeng Wujin arrived at the opposite conclusion: good! A soldier actively wanted to participate in combat, and they were of such enthusiasm, signified that he was not the kind of person who was warm one moment and cold the next. Now, the responsibility of these leaders was to conduct thought work in good order, to make him understand that revolution also has a division of labor, so that they would not undermine his revolutionary enthusiasm, but would rather carry out an education in organization and discipline. Provided that he might take his elementary class feelings 感情 of wanting to kill the enemy and transfer 转移 it to national defense construction, then, that would develop a tremendous force![52]

The stated desire on the part of these commanding officers to use the mechanism of thought work in order to enable a transfer in feeling to a practice of labor designates the narrative problem that informs the entire novel, that is, the problem of transferring or sublimating a desire for the singular moment of combat into the repetitive demands of daily labor. The absence of maturation on the part of Ou Yanghai at this point is rendered visible in formal terms by the fact that the series of statements beginning with the exclamation "good!" registers a confluence of the authoritative voice of Ou Yanghai's army superiors and the narrative voice, such that Ou Yanghai has not yet himself been entrusted with the capacity for narrative, at a formal level. Within this contained narrative episode, the process of political education exercises its effects: "'I won't go to Tibet!' Ou Yanghai said with conviction, 'I may not be able to distinguish myself in battle at the moment, but I can distinguish myself for the people in the battle for industry, and in labor and daily training.'"[53] The process of maturation in which Ou Yanghai engages across the novel takes this deferral of desire as its basic model, comprising the process by which the desire for combat and its associated temporalities becomes automatic on the basis of Yanghai's own subjectivity, forming a self-supporting process in which the deferral of desire no longer requires the political pedagogy of his superiors, and where there is, as a result, a constant play of temporalities between the desire for combat and the everyday practice of labor. Everyday labor comes to provide the conditions for a quotidian heroism premised on communist consciousness. When, therefore, his comrades are dispatched in preparation for an imminent conflict with the Nationalists, Yanghai brooks no resistance at being kept behind to labor. The consequence is that Yanghai becomes the concretization of a new set of social relations or the play of temporalities that Karl recognizes as central to the Maoist conception of the model.

Yanghai's function as a site of pedagogy becomes visible during an extended narrative episode in which he returns back to his narrative village, which marks the only segment across the entire narrative, with the exception of its opening during Yanghai's childhood, in which he is spatially dislocated from his military unit. The narrative function of such a return is to estrange the social conditions of the village and to enable the hero protagonist to function as a site for the elaboration of new social relations, a function that depends on their leaps forward in political consciousness gained through experience outside of the village, and on the temporal gap that separates their childhood from their moment of return as an adult. In the case of Ou Yanghai, the moment of return, which takes up the larger part of chapter seven, also marks the capacity of Yanghai to make his consciousness of labor effective in the temporal fabric of everyday life in his village community. This includes, for example, dissuading his elder brother from engaging in forms of petty commerce that damage the commune. Yet more significant, within the terms of the problem of desire as central to the novel, are Yanghai's dealings with another character who also follows a trajectory of return, namely the educated youth, Chunzhi, a young woman who returns to the village to assist in rural development. It emerges that Chunzhi's father, with whom Yanghai's brother has been engaging in petty commerce, has chosen to restrict her to the home so that she can sew clothes for sale rather than allowing her to participate in agriculture and industry. When Yanghai's family repeatedly urge Yanghai to meet with Chunzhi, it becomes apparent that his relatives intend a courtship between the two, which Chunzhi's father seeks to monetize through an expensive dowry, by requesting that Yanghai's mother secure the marriage between the two youths by buying him a new sewing machine. Having overheard the negotiations between Chunzhi's father and his mother, the terms in which Yanghai marks his resistance are highly suggestive:

> Mother! This machine that he's demanding isn't only to earn money, it's also so he can bind the hands and feet of Chunzhi, and not allow her to participate

in collective labor. If you agree to this marriage arrangement, isn't that of great harm to Chunzhi? Mother, Chunzhi is a member of the youth league, she is an educated youth who has returned to the countryside to participate in collective production and labor, so how can we allow her father to keep her inside their home the whole day?[54]

The terms in which Yanghai asserts his opposition to this marital arrangement and the treatment of Chunzhi restage the familiar binary between external production and the conditions of labor that is restricted to the home, which also marks the difference between labor that is organized on a collective basis in the service of rural transformation, and labor that follows a temporal logic of market exchange. Yet more important still are the terms in which Yanghai marks his refusal to pursue a hasty engagement with Chunzhi, explaining to his mother that "you don't need to worry on my behalf. I have no intention of being a monk, and in any case a temple would hardly accept a soldier! Wait for five, seven years, and I will bring back a girl with big hands and feet and who loves labor as my wife for you."[55] In view of this, Yanghai's insistence that his mother should continue to wait for him to bring back a girl to his parental home assumes in advance a series of rural protocols of gender and marriage which, unlike the exposed dowry negotiations, are not criticized for being part of a feudal social logic. But this sequence is also important in view of the analysis above because the temporal deferral of desire assumes a literal significance, insofar as Yanghai defers any suggestion of romantic or sexual desire, be it in relation to Chunzhi, who in fact makes no actual appearance during this entire narrative sequence, or any other woman. If in this respect sexual desire demands temporal deferral according to the same logic as the desire for combat, this dimension of the narrative nonetheless indicates in advance some of the instabilities around the figure of the hero, namely that they are called upon to both condense a new set of social relations and to assist in the formation of new social relations of labor, and yet, being removed from quotidian demands, threaten to be deprived of any concrete social dimension. These tensions would, in fact, be pushed further under the Cultural Revolution.

The logic of the temporal deferral of desire in the service of the everyday experience of labor across the novel results in a novel with a military setting that has no scenes in combat. When, toward the end of the novel, children enjoin Yanghai to give them stories of his military velour, he flatly admits, "I have never participated in battle, really!" The consequence of this constant logic of deferral, however, is to generate a largely episodic organization in the novel, especially after Yanghai has assumed the autonomous capacity to displace his desire for combat onto the everyday labor. For this reason, the shocking conclusion to the novel has a significance which far exceeds its factual relation to the actual circumstances of the actual death of the historical figure of Ou Yanghai. Yanghai is crushed to death by a speeding train when trying to save a horse, a death that bears close similarities with the deaths of other famous heroes from the PLA in this period, including Dong Cunrui, whose exploits serve to excite Yanghai's desire over much of the novel. At the moment that precedes his sacrifice, the pressure of time presents itself: "The time of four seconds did not permit any consideration, the event that was about to take place did not permit any hesitation. This was the key moment 关键时刻! At exactly that moment Ou Yanghai was like an arrow leaving a bow, a bullet leaving a rifle chamber, he rushed before the train, toward the house, welcoming danger."[56]

The gruesome events of this death risk obscuring its narratological significance, which is that, with the novel up to this moment having been organized around a play of temporalities in which the desire for combat is constantly deferred onto regular, daily labor, its conclusion can only emerge through the reemergence and ultimate fulfillment of that singular moment of temporality marked by the "key moment" of individual heroism. In its conclusion, the novel casts doubt on that very process of deferral that, up to that point, had seemed to guarantee the possibility of making a communist attitude of labor imminent in everyday life. The play of temporalities threatens to become sundered precisely in the attempt to envisage a communist hero in narrative practice, whereby the hero risks falling into a hyperaesthetic image of heroic subjectivity, visible through the singularity of the sacrificial moment, but withdrawn from the extended temporalities of the everyday as the site for the process of communist subjectification.

Foreshadowings

The quest to reforge cultural production and the transformative functions of culture itself reached an uncertain conclusion in the form of the 1965 All-China Meeting of Youth Amateur Literary Creation Activists. The amateur writers who were present at the meeting and were designated as worker-peasant-soldier amateur writers included, for the first time, many writers drawn from the PLA itself, underscoring the militarization of cultural work at this juncture. As one of the speakers at the conference, Zhou Yang underscores that the amateur writer was envisaged not only as an adjunct to professional writers but as the basic model of writing as such, in which these writers would never undergo professionalization but would always remain at the site of labor, allowing the time of labor and the time of writing to be organized into a coherent totality. It was in these terms that Zhou Yang insisted to the assembled writers that "the great majority among you will never leave your positions of production and work at the base, you will labor and create in tandem and it is in this respect that you are fundamentally different from the old generation of authors."[57]

Only on this basis, he argued, would a new generation of amateur writers be able to ensure the overcoming of the gap between mental and manual labor. Zhou Yang's formulations of the future of amateur writing were explicitly posed in the terms derived from the 1964 directives on cultural work issued by the PLA, specifically, the notion of a three-way amalgamation between leaders, professional writers and the masses. Zhou therefore enjoyed that "the leaders must provide a clear direction to writers, they must put forward tasks, and in the course of writing they must provide help and writers with respect to ideology." The consequence, Zhou observed, would be that "politics shall take command over art and literature, there will be a unification of individual and collective intelligence, and creation shall no longer be a purely individual mode of practice 单纯的个人的事业, rather, it will truly become part of the practice of the party, part of the revolutionary practice of the people and the masses."[58] He went on:

> Our amateur literary creators should on no account seek professionalization. Our literary detachments encompass both professionals and amateurs, of which amateurs are the majority, and the professionals the minority. With future developments, the amateurs will increase in number. When we get to communism, it is possible that there will only be amateurs. Marx said that "in a communist society, there are no painters, but men who among other things do painting." At such a time, everyone will engage in both manual and mental labor.[59]

In these terms, then, the conclusion of the debates around cultural production that emerged in the post-Leap period was an envisaged transcendence of the individual writer, for which the amateur writer and the militarization of cultural production provided the key coordinates. At this moment officials envisaged the abolition of the culture worker as a professional writer as a future if not imminent possibility. Yet the very utopian horizon that Zhou cited from Marx concerning the abolition of the "painter" as a professional cultural producer had, in fact, already figured as part of his comments in 1944, in his preface to *Marxism and Literature*. As such, Zhou's repetition of this aspiration in 1965 registered the extent to which the problem of the division between mental and manual labor remained unresolved. The persistence of a professional relation of writing may be understood as one of the conditions for a more radical set of cultural shifts that followed. In February 1966, Jiang Qing 江青, who had been excluded from cultural activism since the founding of the People's Republic, convened the secret Military Arts & Literature Work Conference in conjunction with Lin Biao. The conference offered a paradigm of cultural critique that far exceeded the amateur writers meeting convened the previous year. It narrated the history of socialist culture in terms of a class struggle between reactionary and proletarian lines, arguing that the overwhelming majority of writers had been unable to resist the ideological influence of the bourgeoisie, and in those terms called for a total reorganization of the literary ranks. Such a total reorganization did in fact occur. In 1966, for several years, culture workers ceased to write to any rhythm whatsoever as a result of that unprecedented, revolutionary process, the Cultural Revolution. The key moment had arrived.

CHAPTER 5

IN AND OUT OF PETERSBURG

Soul and Writing Under Late Maoism

After the establishment of proletarian dictatorship, "the bourgeoisie does not give up the aim of restoration, they do not give up attempts to restore their own rule." Let us recall that after the October Revolution there was a reactionary bourgeois intellectual who said through gritted teeth: "there is one field where we do not grow frail, on the contrary, the longer we survive, the more we grow in strength and experience." This field is the field of art and literature. Thus, they unwaveringly and painstakingly maintain this form of bourgeois dictatorship under the dictatorship of the proletariat, by creating a vast assortment of "little Petersburgs."

—Ren Du 任犊.

The publication of the late Cultural Revolution polemic "Get Out of Petersburg!" marked the near-conclusion of a decade-long process which had launched an uncompromising assault on the whole socialist ISA as it had emerged after 1949. At the heart of this assault had been the suspension of the Writers Association, and the total cessation of all cultural activity over the period 1966–1969. The authors of this polemic extended the lines of critique as they had emerged before 1966 by locating in the Writers Association a site for the persistence of bourgeois dictatorship, in the form of capitalist relations of cultural production and the reproduction of bourgeois hegemony in the sphere of ideology. This was to a considerable extent a recognition of defeat with respect to the attempted transformation of intellectuals since 1949. The organized systems of intellectuals "entering into life" and even the support for amateur producers had not, in this account, engendered an ISA consistent with the demands of building a communist society but had instead threatened the revolutionary process in exactly the way that Althusser had anticipated, whereby bourgeois culture had come to "survive, reproduce itself, and spawn a terribly dangerous effect—insinuating itself for good and all into one or another weak spot in the relations of production or the political relations of the socialist state." The socialist ISA had turned out to be a bourgeois dictatorship in disguise. The Petersburg polemic was the repudiation of much of the post-1949 cultural legacy.

It was necessary, then, to start again, to safeguard the revolution. The recognition of defeat embodied by "Petersburg" was also the endpoint of efforts to establish a new practice of cultural production during the Cultural Revolution, together with a transformed conception of communist labor. From 1972 onward, there emerged an attempt to reactivate cultural production in the absence of an ISA that had tended to reproduce the divisions between mental and manual labor.[1] The reemergence of cultural production on this transformed basis emerged in tandem with a reconsideration of the problems of political economy, chiefly through a reactivation of the theoretical language of bourgeois right. The task of Cultural Revolution culture was to provide the conditions for a definitive surmounting of bourgeois right, beginning from the transformation of consciousness, expressed in the injunction that all laborers should conduct a revolution in the "depths of the soul" 灵魂深处. The result, and ultimately the central contradiction of this period, was that cultural production was invested with demands and hopes for social transformation that far exceeded any preceding period of the Chinese Revolution, in the way that the forging of a communist attitude of labor would, it was hoped, provide the ideological conditions for the supersession of bourgeois right. Yet, just as the reforging of labor and the transformative capacities of consciousness were invested with greater significance than ever before, when the transformation to communism did not emerge, the figure of the writer became the site of intense hostility and critique, to the extent that the possibility of an effective transformation of the professional writer was denied. So too, at the level of narrative, did the demand to conduct a totalizing subjective transformation resolve itself into features of cultural texts themselves, namely in the supplanting of the temporal capacities of narrative in favor of hyperaestheticized characters bound to a model of heroic subjectivity. This ultimately marked a wholesale abnegation of the Maoist concept of "life" that had held out the possibility of intellectuals undergoing a change "from one class to another" and provided the rich foundation for cultural production.

The cost, in other words, of the repudiation of so much of the socialist cultural legacy was also the rejection of its most transformative and egalitarian theoretical vocabulary.

The Cultural Revolution was therefore simultaneously a project in which the most sophisticated categories of Maoist cultural production were emptied out, and itself a period of great theoretical production in attempts to excavate the problem of socialist social relations.

Laboring the soul

The resumption of organized writing in 1972 was accompanied by the formalization of the aesthetic criteria derived from the model works, namely, the "three prominences" 三突出, whereby texts were called upon to exhibit the struggle between revolutionary and reactionary forces in a stark, dichotomized mode which would afford viewers and readers the capacity to instantly recognize the moral, political and social struggles that informed these works. The transposition of these categories was accompanied by their explication in terms of a proletarian aesthetics that would assume responsibility for transforming consciousness on the basis of a communist attitude of labor. The privileging of the large-scale choreographed performances of the model works conditioned the formal choices in the area of prose narrative. Whereas in the Great Leap writers had searched for new, operative cultural forms adequate to the task of transforming social relations, the Cultural Revolution was characterized by the prevalence of the long-form novel as the privileged literary form. Within this category, the sent-down-youth novel, concerned with the contemporary experiences of sent-down youth in the countryside, looms central as a set of narrative topoi. As distinct from the industrial and cooperative settings of pre-1966 texts, and consistent with the militarization of cultural production immediately before the Cultural Revolution, these texts enact the experiences of sent-down youth in remote or liminal settings. As well as the examples of this novel form by sent-down youth themselves—Zhang Kangkang's *Dividing Line* (1975) among them—the sent-down-youth novel as genre also encompassed writers with pre-1966 histories of writing. Their relation to aesthetics lies in the way their protagonists overcome the debilitating conditions of the countryside to exhibit a communist consciousness of labor through exemplary acts of heroism.

Yet among the large body of texts that fall into this category, Zhang Changgong's 张长弓 *Youth* (1973) has a special significance for the fact of being almost wholly in the form of a diary, and as such demonstrates a novel attempt to envisage the self-production of the communist practice of labor through writing. At the level of form, therefore, the novel deploys the diary form *not* in order to reproduce a bourgeois mode of subjectivity and interiority or the sovereignty of the subject, but rather in order to excavate the conditions for that transformation of the "soul" that the language of the Cultural Revolution held as necessary, in and through the repetitive time of the everyday.² The content of the novel is simple enough, consisting of the experiences of its protagonist, Miaomiao, in a sent-down military brigade organized in Inner Mongolia. Its interest lies in the way that the diary as it emerges in the novel is structured within collective, citational modes of writing, first of all in the way that the novel begins through a frame narrative, marked explicitly in the form of a "prologue" in which an ostensible narrator records his encounter with a heroic sent-down youth, Miaomiao herself, on a boat traversing the Yellow River. It emerges that the narrator has himself worked as part of a border construction brigade and so recognizes the protagonist as an old comrade. In the midst of recalling certain common acquaintances from the brigade, however, disaster strikes, with the boat suddenly facing collision with a block of ice in the river. The as of yet unnamed narrative protagonist with whom the author of the frame narrative has been conversing displays a sudden heroism by organizing other travelers on the boat before herself leaping into the raging waves in order to clear the way for the boat and avoid disaster. In this opening narrative gesture, therefore, the novel already introduces many of the tropes that are recognizable from other instances of the Cultural Revolution novel, and which indeed reappear in the main narrative body of *Youth*, namely the demonstration of selfless qualities through an encounter with nature, which is in turn presented as a source of danger that must be defeated in order to secure the revolutionary process. More important still, however, is that with the dispatch of the heroic youth, who introduces herself as He Miaomiao, the diary emerges as the purpose of the frame narrative and as the ostensible origin of the text that follows. The author of the frame narrative describes it as follows:

> I stood for quite some time on the bank and only then did I return to the ship to pick up my own things. At that time I found that next to my net basket, at the place where He Miaomiao had lain down her army coat, there lay a diary with a red binding. This was the diary of that warrior of the production and construction brigade, in which there were recorded their 他们的 life of struggle, their history of hardship, the joy of their battles, and the ecstasy of their victories.³

The frame-narrator accounts for what follows in terms of a process of editing, in which they report that they read through the contents of the diary and then decided that, before returning the diary to its owner or to another responsible person, they would take the liberty of transcribing down the important matters. If possible, I would also prepare some chapter titles, in order that worker-peasant-soldier readers 工农兵读者 would be able to take a look, and see the youth of our era, and the strength, courage, intelligence, forbearance they have demonstrated in the great wilderness of the northern border region, under the cultivation of the Chinese Communist Party, and Mao Zedong thought, and how they have actively surged forward, with their heroic postures![4]

The beginning of the novel therefore embodies a series of formal tensions that anticipate what follows. The recovery of the diary through the frame narrative provides the opportunity for a text that might narrate the self-conscious emergence and production of a communist laborer through a practice of writing, and yet the whole point of the frame narrative also consists of the separation of the physical, fictional artifact that is the diary from its purported author, as a result of a singular act of heroism. The frame narrative thereafter gives way to the contents of the diary proper, which, consistent with the information of the prologue, is ordered both according to the temporality of the diary itself, that is, according to a succession of days that are narrated according to the direct experience of a specific I-narrator, but with these days also being organized according to a set of thematic chapter headings that delineate the different stages and events of the protagonist in the northern border regions. So too is the reader given to understand that certain content has been excised from an assumed originary diary that would be lengthy and more varied than the actual text presented, though naturally this originary diary is a theoretical object that exists only in the narrative world of the novel.

The organization of the main narrative body in terms of a frame narrative and the positing of an ostensible process of editing mark the novel with a formal importance that is directly relevant to the excavation of a new collective practice of writing as labor, beyond the limitations of any individual subject. This is in fact already registered even in the account that the frame-story narrator gives of their reasons for wanting to transcribe, edit, and publish the diary, in that they invest it with a significance and value that radically exceeds the particular experience of its immediate author, noting specifically through the use of the plural possessive "their" that it can express the experiences of a generation of the educated youth. The larger part of the diary text that follows recounts how Miaomiao joins her classmates in a marsh clearance project in the borderlands, only to be reassigned to the rear support role of preparing food, meeting the cultural needs of her comrades, and engaging in pig farming. The assignment of the protagonist to a quotidian form of labor to which they must sublimate their heroic desires recalls elements of texts from the early 1960s. Miaomiao initially rejects this reassignment on the basis that her purpose for joining the sent-down youth at this marginal location was to embrace the most arduous conditions of labor, or, as she puts it, the "frontline." Yet the guidance officer appointed to oversee the activities of the brigade insists that meeting the basic needs of the other sent-down youth is a task of vital importance:

> Miaomiao, haven't you realized, our warriors are all little tigers who as soon as they begin think they can raise mountains on their shoulders. Each and every one of them wants to triumph over the salt marshes, and even in their dreams they think of giving their all, and experiencing bitterness; and yet we, as cadres, what do we have to consider? We have to think about how to cherish these warriors, how to protect their activism. If our warriors don't eat well, if they don't have enough to drink, if they eat neither meat nor vegetables, then I can't imagine how we would ever be able to talk about them standing firmly or putting down roots!⁵

In these terms, Miaomiao is called upon to commit herself to quotidian forms of labor whose repetitive and even banal character compliments the temporal structure of the diary, which, in its formal structure, embodies the regular passing of time in the form of the daily experience of labor. She shares this fate with Cai Hong, who occupies the conventional position of an ideologically vulnerable character who demands the pedagogy of Miaomiao. Yet for Miaomiao herself, and her formal role as the heroic protagonist notwithstanding, the practice of diary writing also comes to stage a process of auto-pedagogy. The pedagogical function of the writing process is incumbent partly in the particular nature of the narrating instance that emerges from the fictional diary, namely an interpolated practice of narration, in which the events described in each entry are ostensibly written immediately afterward. Yet perhaps more important is the way that Miaomiao's practice of writing tends toward the incorporation of other texts, most notably other diaries in the form of the famous diaries of Lei Feng and Wang Jie. Among the first appearances of this form of citational practice, for example, is when Miaomiao has first been allocated to the rear guard but has not yet realized the importance of this ultimately unglamorous form of labor. The citation of other diary texts, in this context, brings Miaomiao's self-production as communist laborer into moments of contact with other laborers, with whom Miaomiao shares a common temporality of a constant, routinized inspection of her own practice of labor. Following the successful development of a way of feeding pigs on the reeds that populate the marshland, for example, the opening segment of an entry from Miaomiao's diary is as follows:

> The advanced soldiers of the proletariat all have revolutionary tenacity. Comrade Lei Feng praised the spirit of the screw, showing that in order to ram a

nail into a board of wood, you need to rely on squeezing and drilling. Considering "squeezing" in terms of the problem of time: whenever there is the slightest free moment, it is necessary to occupy it with revolutionary content. Considering "drilling" in terms of one's effort in work: any given matter requires repeated grinding, and constant initiative.[6]

The pedagogical significance of this extract within Miaomiao's narrative world lies in the injunction to fill every moment of time with a self-directed process of revolutionary transformation, and ones that allows for a recognition of the revolutionary importance of what might otherwise be seen as fundamentally banal forms of labor. The text, in these terms, comes to emerge as the site of multiple sites of copying and transcription, consisting of Miaomiao's copying of the freely circulating diaries of Lei Feng and Wang Jie within her own diary, all encompassed by the frame story, which posits the text as itself having been copied by the frame narrator. The narrativization of a regularized process of inspecting the self and constructing the subject of communist labor is, then, at the same time, a staging of a mode of writing that displaces any fixed notion of authorship through a revolutionary practice of copying and citation. The abnegation of a monopoly on authorship and action in the novel on the part of Miaomiao reaches its most intriguing level in a distinct narrative episode focused on the arrival of Miaomiao's mother, insofar as this episode also opens up a process of pedagogy that, against the conventions of the Cultural Revolution novel, situates Miaomiao in a receptive position. The arrival of Miaomiao's mother comprises an initial moment of misunderstanding between Miaomiao and her mother, in that the mother's concern over Miaomiao's state of health causes Miaomiao to write, "Yet, there were some respects in which mother was wrong. She was, after all, a housewife, with not much in the way of learning. She shouldn't speak in such unprincipled terms. What was there to be done. This place was dangerous, wasn't it? This place was bitter, wasn't it? Thus, I had grown thin and become sick. Ah, she still wanted to pull me back! She still wanted to pull me back to the city to be by her side, didn't she?"[7]

This moment of misunderstanding marks the internalization and repetition through writing of the trope of the backward housewife that occurred in different narrative contexts across the socialist period, yet the conditions for overcoming his prejudice also emerge when Miaomiao's mother delivers a report on their experience in the old society, including her experience of being raised by a Mongolian foster mother. Significantly, within the specific diary entry in which the mother is said to have given this report, Miaomiao declares a sudden failure of writing, noting, then, that "I wanted to completely write down everything that mother had said, and yet . . . I could not write, how excited I was!" Yet the significance of this report nonetheless emerges through a reconciliation between Miaomiao and her mother, one that compels Miaomiao to reflect that "I, I who had undergone such a long period of education at the production construction brigade, how could I still have regarded my mother with old eyes!"[8] In the following entry, at the compulsion of the brigade political adviser, Miaomiao sets to transcribing her mother's narrative in full, which also appears in the diary entry itself, marking a further mode of textual citation, through the extended transcription of an intradiegetic narrative. It transpires that Miaomiao's mother benefited from the care of a Mongolian foster mother during her infancy. To be sure, the inclusion of the report itself in the diary serves an obvious narrative artifice in allowing the reader to also become aware of the class background and struggles of Miaomiao's mother. Yet, considered in terms of the way that the novel handles practices of writing within the larger framework of the diary form, the transcription of this narrative constitutes a further way that the diary opens itself up and provides the conditions for a mutual penetration of different texts in such a way as to challenge the notion of singular creative authorship. Within the narrative sequence of mother's visit, Miaomiao's self-critique of her projection of her mother "merely" as a housewife also produces a moment of mutual reproduction between mother and daughter, centered on the shared preparation of food in a way that displaces any fixed positionalities of guest and host. Following their reconciliation, then, Miaomiao writes, "Mother smiled and used her chopsticks to point to the pan of vegetables, encouraging me to eat some, as if I were the guest and she had become the host 主人. But thinking about it more closely, Mother had just come to our detachment, and yet she was helping our leaders carry out the work of thought education. Now that, in all respects, was the attitude of a master 主人."[9]

The fleeting image of a conviviality in mutual care, constructed around the mother-daughter relationship, emerges within the novel as a moment of communist labor that is not subject to the otherwise exacting demands of harsh labor in the countryside. The staging of these intersecting practices of collective writing, from the frame story through to the citational practices of the diary itself, mark the radically reflective dimensions of the novel. Yet they are to a considerable extent counterpoised to the other, more formally conservative dimensions of the Cultural Revolution novel, namely the way that the heroic character—in this case Miaomiao—encounters the narrative world as one that has been designed for their heroic action. It is, ironically, also the role of Miaomiao's mother that tends toward this distinct formal feature of the Cultural Revolution novel, namely those elements of predestination which tend toward the production of the protagonist as a site of a singular, heroic subjectivity. The operation of predestination comes about through those narrative elements in which it is revealed that the setting in which the protagonist (in this case, Miaomiao) finds themselves is one to which they have some form of (often familial) connection, one that becomes knowable to the reader and the protagonist through discovered coincidences in the novel itself. In the case of *Youth*, it transpires that the Mongolian foster mother of whom Miaomiao's mother speaks in her narrative is none other than an older woman living on the grasslands with whom Miaomiao herself shares a warm relationship.

It is, in fact, coincidence itself, understood in literal terms as the crossing over of two events or narrative processes in time, that comprises one of the major temporal characteristics of Cultural Revolution fiction, being determined by the pedagogical ambitions of the text, and consisting of a penetration of the past into the present in the form of unexpected encounters. So too does coincidence via predestination underscore the temporal contradictions of these novels, namely in the fact that, opposed to happy revolutionary coincidences that secure moments of revolutionary intimacy, such novels also rely on *disruptive* interventions of the past into the present, in the form of the exposure of reactionary figures in accordance with the totalizing demands of the aesthetic protocols drawn from the model works, which also provide the conditions for narrative closure. In *Youth* this negative form of predestination emerges through the struggle against a narrative figure, Group Leader Fan, who, during earlier moments of the narrative, is connected to Cai Hong as the reputed friend of her father but has sought to entice Cai Hong to leave the countryside to become a professional stage performer. The effect of these elements of predestination is to undermine any semblance of contingency in the text. If in the case of the heroic protagonist their predestined relationship to the spatiotemporal setting of the narrative provides a guarantee of their heroism and even of authenticity, the negative dimension of predestination marks the site of anxiety whereby the past comes to make a set of conservative threats to the revolutionary present and possible future. The effect of predestination is to demand a totalizing extension of a heroic subjectivity on the part of the hero, underscoring how the supposedly radical cultural artifacts of this period also engendered a basic conservatism with respect to form. These instances of heroic subjectivity are dependent on the invocation of forces external to the immediate world of the narrative. In the case of *Youth*, the exposure of Group Leader Fan is reliant on a letter sent by Cai Hong's father articulating the counterrevolutionary history of Fan. The sudden intervention of a moment of textual exposure from outside the immediate spatial conditions of the narrative anticipates the tendentious resolution of the narrative proper, whereby Miaomiao exhibits her capacity for revolutionary heroism through a chase that ends with her suffering bodily injury and recuperating in hospital. The end of the narrative, to this extent, recapitulates the events of the frame narrative with which the novel begins, whereby a situation of danger provides the grounds for exhibiting the scope of a new communist consciousness of labor, albeit with labor itself being absent. Miaomiao intervenes between Cai Hong and Group Leader Fan to prevent Cai Hong being assaulted, and as a result herself suffering bodily injury, recounted as follows: " 'Bastard! Where are you running off to!' Cai Hong shouted with rage and went over to Fan Bin. I saw that Fan Bin's eyes were shining like stars and he suddenly shouted 'go!' and held up a big cudgel. If Cai Hong were to keep walking forward, then she would be in great danger! At that precise moment, how many matters to stir the heart rushed through my mind!"[10]

The temporal imperative indicated by the precise moment restages, to a certain degree, the gruesome end of *The Song of Ou Yanghai*, but with the difference not only that the staging of this moment of communist heroism became the basis for the narrative resolution of a great many works in the literature of the Cultural Revolution, but also that the adoption of this strategy in *Youth* comes to expose the total artifice of the diary form. The chapter in which the events are recounted is purportedly written after the fact, with a subtitle to the chapter heading indicating that the events described were written by the fictional author with their left hand during their convalescence in hospital, and yet the detail with which they are described and the lack of any discernible difference between this moment of resolution and that of other Cultural Revolution novels that do not rely on the purported diary form mark the extent to which this narrative strategy is also a total collapse in the purported temporality of everyday labor and the fashioning of the communist subject to which the diary is formally committed. In these terms this narrative conclusion encompasses the temporal breakdown of the work and the consequent emptying out of narrative time, whereby communist labor becomes expressible only in terms of singular acts of heroism. The fact that in *Youth* this moment of heroism takes the form of the apprehending a villain rather than a scene of labor underlines the depth of this formal problem, namely that labor itself could not supply the narrative grounds for envisioning the subject of communist labor, which instead needs to be rendered visible through an act of struggle against the villain, and the resulting bodily injury to the protagonist. There is in this respect a certain circularity and symmetry between the frame story with which the novel begins and the final events described in the diary, both consisting of that aestheticizaion of the single act and the consequent evisceration of narrative time. The terms of resolution are testament to the problem of envisioning and generating the communist consciousness of labor demanded by the discourse of the Cultural Revolution, whereby the "past" emerges within the novel in the form of a reactionary figure, only to serve as the impetus for a singular moment of struggle by which this past can be transcended, offering an aesthetic metonym for a general solution to the problem of socialist transition and the unevenness in consciousness, in the mode of a fantasy of finality.

This marks the effacement of narrative time in favor of a hyperaesthetic register, which is also the evacuation of "life" as the grounds of cultural production in itself, or else the transmutation of "life" into an apocalyptic mode, rather than as the complex system of social relations that render creation possible. The narrative tropes of the sent-down-youth novel thereby anticipate the formal discourse of political economy during this period. Yet first it is necessary to follow the Maoist theorists of this period as they attempted to rupture with the "Petersburgs" of the pre-1966 literary system, through the renewed figure of the "amateur."

Communist writing

If the long-form narrative works examined above mark a series of attempts to envision a dramatic overcoming of the problems of socialist transition, mediated by the aesthetic image of the hero, then the work of amateur writers reveals a self-reflective orientation toward the material practice of writing itself, including that problem of how to overcome the persistence of an individual practice of writing. This is true above all of the works of Duan Ruixia 段瑞夏, Duan having been one of the amateur writers who came to prominence during the Cultural Revolution.

Duan's works demonstrate a profound concern for the mediations between cultural production and other forms of practice, and how these mediations might in turn inform a revolutionary culture autonomous of the professional writing capacity of culture workers. The work for which he first gained attention, "Not Just One of the Audience" (1973) explores the attempts of a technical engineer to improve a sound system so that a performance of the model work *Taking Tiger Mountain by Strategy* might work its full set of aesthetic effects without being hindered by sonic interference. The heroic protagonist, Ji Changchun, calls for his electronics factory to commit to developing a sound system that will transmit the model opera to its full effect, and in doing so he overcomes the hesitancy of Old Su, who warns that only foreign countries would be able to develop a sound system of sufficient quality. It is revealed that the same performing troupe had earlier asked a research institute to carry out the improvement in their equipment, but that the technician in charge had refused to do so, citing technical difficulties. To no less an extent than the long-form novels of the Cultural Revolution, this short story also relies on the device of coincidence, in which an apparently contingent set of events is revealed to have a connection to one or more of the protagonists in the text. In this instance, the conditions for coincidence are established early on when a junior performer with the performance troupe, Young Zheng, with whom Ji and Su meet, reveals that his inspiration as a performer comes from a story told to him by the master performer, who is currently overseas:

> I'm in Cast B. Comrade Lin Ying [the master performer] who is in Cast A has gone on a foreign performance tour. He is better at singing than I am. On the matter of who taught me, my teachers were the workers, peasants and soldiers. We can't sing well unless we really understand the feelings of heroic characters. And that's why I still can't play the part of a hero well. Lin told me a moving anecdote about this, when coaching me in this passage. But that's a long story.[11]

This initial encounter between the performer Zheng and the technical workers Ji and Su is followed by the departure of the opera from the stage, so to speak, of the narrative, and the invocation instead of the conflicts over whether the factory can meet the tasks of producing new, high-grade sound equipment. The renewed encounter between the factory workers and performers involves Lin Ying having returned from his overseas trip, at which point he reveals that his commitment to embodying and performing the model of the hero, or the story which he is said to have told Young Zheng to spur his own efforts at performance, is precisely the story of Ji himself, whereby Ji is said to have demonstrated commitment to communist heroism by braving danger during a military exercise, as a soldier in the PLA. The setting up of the conditions for this narrative coincidence, albeit one visible to the reader from the beginning of the text onward, is, as we have seen, a conventional device of Cultural Revolution writing, such that, in these terms, Duan's text may be seen as doubly derivative, in the first place at the level of content insofar as it is concerned with the stage-based model works, and in the second place at the level of form insofar as its narrative strategies bear a close link with those of the long-form novels discussed earlier. Lin Ying provides this contextual information through a long extract of reported speech that encompasses the previous encounter between Lin Ying and Ji, recounting a moment at which Ji insists on repairing a radar station during a military exercise:

> "Better turn back," I [Lin Ying] suggested feebly.
> Ji threw me a disapproving glance, then quickly assembled his tools and started out.
> "It's too dangerous!" I tried to stop him.
> "This is war, understand?" Stripped to his vest, he flexed his powerful muscles, and his words rang like metal upon the decks.
> I protested, "No, it's only an exercise."

"An exercise?" His eyes were like daggers. "You're an actor. Can you play the part of the hero well on the stage if all the time you remember you're only performing?" Then he ran to the captain:
"Reporting for duty, Ji Changchun requests to repair the radar."[12]

The significance of this reported account or intradiegetic narrative, other than the fact that it completes the anticipated denouement of the narrative through a coincidence, is that it poses a conception of the relations between cultural production, heroism and other areas of social life that enjoins a constant process of merging performance and lived heroism, whereby even staged activities, whether in the form of a military exercise or an actual stage performance, should engender and stage forms of heroism that can then pass into the totality of social activities, including other forms of labor. This is an autonomous, circulating notion of heroism as culture, and one that emerges in the narrative precisely through the device of Lin Ying's report, understood as a temporal movement that recaptures a previous moment in time. This temporal movement, delivered in the form of an oral narrative situated within the fictional text, thereby provides the key to understanding the positions of the different protagonists, whereby this same narrative has passed from Lin Ying to his junior apprentice only to be reported again to Ji himself, marking, therefore, a circular movement. The coincidental second meeting between Ji and Lin Ying provides the grounds for yet a further coincidence when it is revealed that Old Su is none other than the previous research institute technician who refused the improvement of the audio equipment. Much as with the sent-down-youth novel, then, "coincidence" functions as a narrative device in which otherwise distinct narrative trajectories encounter one another in a moment of pedagogical significance. The story closes with a promise to inscribe Ji's present-day feats in dramatic form, having brought the sound system up to standard:

"The sound was first-rate," exclaimed Zheng. "We have the working class to thank for this."
"We've done no more than our duty," replied Ji. "It's good to see an audience of workers, peasants, and soldiers watching a play about themselves."
"Your singing was incredible," Su told Lin. "Especially that passage 'The More Bravely I Advance.' It's an inspiration for us in our work."
"We must keep learning from the audience and improving our technique," replied Lin. "Art has to be closely linked with real life. We ought to ask our scriptwriters to write an opera about the two of you."[13]

The specification of the model work as being a play watched by the masses "about themselves" establishes the goal of the autonomous and self-supporting process of cultural production that is the ultimate object of this short story, and yet more important still is the closing suggestion of writing an opera about Ji and Su, which shows that their efforts in labor, themselves intimately linked with providing the conditions for the successful performance of the model works, are the basis of a further process of writing, and one that will generate a further practice of performance orientated toward proletarian heroism. While Ji laughingly questions whether his acts are suitable for being turned into an opera, he does, however, suggest that the active role of the working class in resisting bourgeois art might provide suitable material for the factory-based journalist. The final lines of the story are as follows:

> "Yes, and they can write about me as well. Only if intellectuals integrate with the workers, peasants and soldiers, will the path become open for them!" Su said with feeling.
> It was then, dear readers, that I wrote this story.[14]

This closing fragment is liable to cause some degree of surprise on the part of the reader to whom it is addressed, because the narrative up to this point has contained no suggestions whatsoever that the narrator is anything other than a strictly heterodiegetic narrator, and one who refrains from explicit commentary on the events described, and yet the final declaration of the decision to write situates the narrator within the story, in the purported subject position of the factory journalist to whom "I" refers, rendering them closer to a homodiegetic narrator, albeit with a very minor role in the narrative world. The significance of this narrative gesture is explicable in terms of the larger content of the narrative up to this point, which is to say that the possibility of an immanent practice of heroism among the life of the masses allows for a supersession of any extravagant forms of literary artifice and fabulation, such that the task of the writer approaches simply "recording"—in a nonnaturalist sense—those events that comprise their own social existence. It is in this sense, then, that Duan's early story marks an attempt to stage a form of writing that calls its own fictionality into question. The formal sophistication of this short story as compared to others from the Cultural Revolution therefore lies not only in the fact that it stages the conditions of its own production, but also that it does so through a sophisticated play of temporalities, consisting of an interaction between the singular moment of heroism or coincidental meeting, and the suggestion of a cycle of labor and cultural production, in which heroism as labor provides the material for inscription into writing, which then, being performed, inspires further acts of heroism.

Duan Ruixia's story attracted attention as a result of a series of efforts to permanently transform writing as an amateur practice. The institutional locus for these efforts was the Shanghai Writing Group formed in 1971 at the prompting of Zhang Chunqiao. The Shanghai Group was one of several such organizations that emerged during the Cultural Revolution in different locales. The Shanghai Group differed from these other institutions, however, due to its direct links with the radical left in Shanghai and the breadth of its activities. It was therefore under the auspices of the Shanghai Group that, in late 1972, varied professional writers together with individuals with experience of administration and editing in cultural production were called to a meeting on the subject of how to reorganize cultural production and the possibility of forming a new literary journal. That this meeting included important writers and critics such as Ru Zhijuan immediately underscores the contradictory position of professional writers during the Cultural Revolution, namely that such writers were simultaneously the objects of repudiation, and yet the task of reconstructing cultural production on a transformed basis could not ultimately reject the role of these professional writers, in administrative as well as in other capacities.[15] The outcome of this meeting was a series of collections of short stories, plays, essays, and other written works. The organizational structure for soliciting works was consistent with the practice of cultivating new writers before the Cultural Revolution, namely in the form of training classes for aspiring writers, the first held in January 1973.

The works of these writers came to make up the larger part of the first two collections of works published under the series *Shanghai Art and Literature Collection*, the first issue of which appeared in May 1973 under the title *Morning Glow*. It was also in this collection that Duan's "Audience" appeared. Yet the writers whose works figured in this and other collections had already issued works in newspapers or publishing houses in the years immediately prior to the first collections of the *Shanghai Art and Literature Collection*, including Duan Ruixia himself. More striking still was the return under the aegis of these collections of worker-writers from the pre–Cultural Revolution period, who had been returned to their original places of work as part of the dismemberment of the pre-1966 cultural system, including, for example, Hu Wanchun. In the second of the collections published as part of the *Shanghai Art and Literature Collection*, then, entitled *The Long Cry of the Golden Bell*, there was included an essay from Duan on the process of writing that informed "Audience," under the title "Serve as a Recorder of the Life of Struggle of the Great Era." Duan's account makes explicit that the production of "Audience" did not begin with the writing classes organized under the Shanghai Group, but through the cultivation of new writers at the factory level, with Duan only later passing his work through the classes of the Shanghai Group, and altogether undergoing five separate processes of drafting and consultation among other amateur writers. The effect of these collective processes of redrafting, which encompassed changes in the handling of characters, as well as the reduction of lengthy descriptions of the technical processes of production amount, in Duan's analysis, to a radical expansion of the category of writing: "To say that I am the author behind 'Not Just One Of The Audience' is not strictly correct. The true writers are not me, but rather the broad masses of the workers, peasants and soldiers."[16]

This is true, for Duan, not only to the extent that his writing relied on multiple rounds of collective revisions, but also in the way that his writing is posed as an imminent recording of the possibilities for heroism emerging from the Cultural Revolution, such that the daily labor of the masses "educates me every second and every minute, infects me, and makes me feel that Yang Zirong," the heroic protagonist of the model opera *Taking Tiger Mountain by Strategy*, "is in our very factory, so that I have a responsibility to raise my pen, and use literary works to reflect [these heroes]."[17] There is, here, an explicit link to the content of "Audience," in that it is also the force of Ji's example that provides the starting-point for a collective practice of communist labor. The notion of writing in the title of the article—a "recorder of life" 生活的记录员—thereby seeks to excise any notion of singular authorial creativity. Duan used his position in a collective set of social practices to postulate that the work "Audience" is a "cake of a thousand people" whereby:

> The life of struggle of the workers, peasants, and soldiers provided me with the source of creation, the concern of the leaders and the support of the masses gave me the power of creation, and under the collective revision of the amateur writers (the vast majority of whom were not writers in command of the pen) I was able to complete this draft, this is not simply a "cake of a thousand people" 千人糕, it is rather a "draft of ten thousand people!" 万人稿.[18]

This reflective text thereby poses the question of how to locate a porous and collective conception of authorship and writing, and therefore of the cultural subject, that does not, in Duan's own terms, restrict itself to the person in immediate command of the pen.[19] Duan's text therefore amounts to an anxiety around the individuation of writing, and a consequent desire to abnegate his determining role as a professional arbiter of cultural production, a desire that emerges, ironically, through this very text, as the product of a practice of reflective writing on his own craft as an amateur writer. The search for an open practice of writing was to emerge yet further through a collectively written reflection on amateur writing that was published in 1973 in *Study and Criticism*, a journal also published under the aegis of the Shanghai Group that specialized in political theory and historical criticism.[20] Duan and other amateur writers pledged:

> We should liberate ourselves from the notion that creation is simply a form of individual spiritual labor 个体的精神劳动. We should conduct socialist

transformation against this so-called individual kind of spiritual labor and invest it with a new meaning. Look at some actual cases: there was a worker amateur writer who read his first draft among the workers of his factory in order to solicit their opinions. Then, that evening, an old worker, having thought about it for some time, realized that he himself had quite a number of life materials, and that, if these were introduced [to the work], certain passages of the work would have a greater educational significance. On that very night, he rushed straight to the home of the writer.[21]

The repudiation of the reduction of writing to atomized "spiritual labor," combined with the charming anecdote of an old worker offering their experiences for incorporation into the text, offers an idealized form of mediation between the individual writer and their social context of collective labor, in which the text itself becomes the staging ground for collective production, and where the writer need never depart from their immediate conditions of labor. Here, as elsewhere, the aim is one of transcending the limitations of an individual author, whereby the conditions for participation in textual production are radically widened beyond the immediate author of the written word, to encompass oral participation in the ongoing production of the text. In these terms, a critique of the individual figure of the author takes place through a challenge to the bifurcation of orality and writing. So too, in the same terms, does the initial writing of the draft and its being located in a context of collective industrial labor function as an invitation to intervention (that is, the "soliciting" of viewpoints) that is at the same time a contestation of the ideological conception of authorship and writing as an individual mode of spiritual labor. Yet even in the reflections of Duan and his fellow writers on amateur writing, there are intimations of the difficulty involved in trying to forge a practice of writing that would wholly overcome the specific temporality of writing as individuated practice. In a quasi-etymology of the figure of the "amateur," they argued that the relationship between the "work" 业 and "non-work" 余 of the "amateur" 业余 writer should be understood in terms of a positive dialectic whereby the immanent location of the amateur writer at the location of labor provides the condition of possibility for their writing. They nonetheless noted that "in emphasizing 'work' 业, this is not to say that it is then simply not necessary to create some appropriate conditions for their writing 余, such as expanding the life of the author, or concentratedly arranging some time for creation 创作时间."[22]

The issue, then, remained one of time, whereby amateur writers, in their conception of their own craft, needed time to write, time that remained autonomous from shop floor labor. It is anxieties of this order that would comprise the further development of theoretical reflections on the problem of writing. The success of Duan's initial writings and the publications of the Shanghai Art and Literature Series enabled the further expansion of the experiments in writing under the auspices of the Shanghai Group through the initiation of the single most important cultural journal of the late Cultural Revolution, *Morning Glow*, which joined its counterpart, *Study and Criticism*. From this point onward, further volumes of the Shanghai Art and Literature Series were published as part of the Morning Glow Series.[23] The editors associated with the magazine were drawn from the ranks of the amateur writers. These personnel alternated between labor at their original sites of work, and editing work for the periodical in order to prevent the amateur writers from becoming a specialized literary caste.[24] The contents of *Morning Glow* were wide-ranging, encompassing short stories, including further works from Duan, as well as poetry and plays, but by far the most important were the further theoretical interventions centered on the deindividuation of writing. These included the expansion of emergent cultural practices that preceded the Cultural Revolution. In 1975, Zhou Tian argued under the title "A Newborn Thing on the Literary Battle Front" that the Cultural Revolution had generated a cooperative practice of writing through the expansion of the "three amalgamations." While this category had a prior history, Zhou's article insisted that the practices of the Cultural Revolution differed from the past in the ways that cadres across every level of the state had become intimately involved in guiding collective cultural production. The significance of the reconstitution of writing on a collective basis lay in the fact that it ruptured with the location of writing in an individual subject, such that "creation through the three amalgamations creates the conditions for breaking with private ownership over creation and other forms of bourgeois ideology." The bourgeois line in cultural production is said to have "mystified literary creation as being fundamentally a form of individual spiritual labor 个人精神劳动" whereas collective creation has established "new kinds of human relations and a communist spirit of cooperation within creation groups."[25] A final transformation of writing along directly collective lines is therefore said to provide the foundation for a definitive supersession of the author figure and its associated tendencies toward a reversal on the cultural front: "With the three amalgamations, the participation of worker-peasant-soldier amateur writers allows for the incorporation of the proletarian mode of production 生产方式 and their advanced ideas into the creation collective 创作集体. They understand that the work in which they engage is just the same as when they produce any given mechanical component, in that they absolutely do not think that, because this is my individual product, you have to engrave your individual name on that product."[26]

Zhou's insistence that the collective methods of machine production might be transferred to writing poses the possibility of precisely that "factory of literature" that had been raised but negated as a possibility during the Great Leap Forward. More important is his recognition that the attaching of the name of the individual author to the literary work—unthinkable in the factory setting—is itself a profoundly ideological and political gesture, indeed a mode of the author function, and one that contributes toward the ongoing reification and mystification of literary production.

To the extent that Zhou Tian's remarks mark a set of imminent possibilities that were never fully systematized—the vast majority of works were published under the name of a single author—they were, however, offset by a more apocalyptic mode of theorization that aimed criticism at the dangers of capitalist restoration inherent in the pre-1966 literary system. This was true above all of the single most important intervention of the late Cultural Revolution in the cultural sphere, the article "Get Out of 'Petersburg!,'" which appeared in the March 1975 edition under the name Ren Du, one of the pen names for the literary department of the Shanghai Writing Group. As with other past moments of crisis surrounding the cultural subject, the impetus for this crisis lay in the cultivation of the worker-writers of the 1950s and their relation to amateur and professional practices of writing. These writers, such as Hu Wanchun and Tang Kexin, had been returned to their original sites of work during the early years of the Cultural Revolution ostensibly at the personal direction of Zhang Chunqiao, and yet gained new opportunities for writing from 1972 onward, not least on the pages of *Morning Glow* itself. In this context, the article "Petersburg" was prompted by a letter received by the editorial board of *Morning Glow* from Hu Wanchun, on the subject of Lenin's interactions with the Russian proletarian author Maxim Gorky, specifically Lenin's letter to Gorky in 1919 urging him to exit the intellectual circles of "Petersburg" and instead seek to "observe how people are building life anew ... somewhere in the countryside, or in a provincial factory (or at the front). There it is easy, merely by observing, to distinguish the decomposition of the old from the first shoots of the new."[27]

The notion of "Petersburg" here, as posed in Lenin's writing and incorporated by Maoists, provides the conceptual basis for the ultimate theoretical concern of the polemic, which lies in the contradictions created by the success of amateur writers, namely the form of their social and ideological estrangement from the masses as a result of their elevation into formal literary institutions and the professionalization of their role as writers, engendering the conditions for a "double life" premised on the bifurcation between writing and collective labor. The reproduction of the division of mental and manual labor in and through the ISA of socialism itself, then, is what allows the authors to identify the Writers Association as a "form of bourgeois dictatorship under the dictatorship of the proletariat." The authors insist, therefore, in the lines following their extraordinary condemnation of the continuation of bourgeois cultural dictatorship under socialism, that "before the Cultural Revolution, the different kinds of literary institutions controlled by the revisionist black line in art and literature, and especially those varied kinds of 'associations,' are precisely this kind of 'Petersburg.'"[28]

The associations in question consist especially of the Writers Association. This polemic therefore offered an explicit theoretical rationale for the closure of just these institutions on the grounds that they provide the structural grounds for the reproduction of the division of mental and manual labor. The "danger" that Mao had identified in 1964 with respect to the Writers Association turning revisionist was thereby extended back into the whole of the socialist period, such that the persistence of bourgeois ideology and capitalist relations of cultural production was held to mark a form of bourgeois dictatorship within the socialist state, or a sense of ideological unevenness in which culture, organized through the ISA, became legible as the "weakest link" threatening capitalist restoration. This weakest link became visible in the way the organized figure of the professional writer constantly threatened to pull worker-writers out of the ranks of the working class and into the bureaucratic ranks of the Association. In yet more prescient terms, they argued:

> All bad things in the world begin from not taking part in labor. Once you leave your station of labor and depart from the frontline of the three great revolutionary struggles, and if you are not careful, and do not pay attention to thought reform, then, in actual fact, you will already have begun to depart from the social existence of being a worker, and the term "worker" in the formulation "worker-writer" will simply become a merely formal designation, or a kind of historical retrospective. Thus, as far as a writer is concerned, it is not only that, because they depart from the source of creation, it will become difficult to write excellent works that are rooted in revolutionary current life, but also, because existence determines consciousness, their standpoint 立场 and perspective 观点 will inevitably change.[29]

Interventions of this order have more than a polemical significance insofar as they demonstrate gaps that separate the Cultural Revolution from the faith in the possible transformation of the intellectual that informed Chinese socialism in its earlier articulations. For the authors of the "Petersburg" polemic, culture workers were not only a privileged intellectual caste, but also participated in the conditions for the degeneration of worker-writers such as Hu Wanchun, by providing the institutions that wrench such writers apart from the conditions of manual labor. The understanding of the "worker-writer" becoming a historical retrospective here takes on multiple levels of significance. The immediate referent is the way that professionalization results in workers drawn from the working class ceasing to have organic links with the class, such that their relation becomes a merely formal one of class origin: "An individual worker cannot represent the proletariat. If a worker leaves the class ranks, in the manner of a worker-writer such as Gorky, then, regardless of how good their background might be, or how illustrious their past achievements, they will have no way to defeat the bourgeoisie, even no way to resist the corruption and harm exercised by the bourgeoisie against them as individuals."[30]

Yet there is also here a more fundamental problem that stretches beyond the specific problem of worker-writers, which is the positive attempt to actually eliminate the position of the professional writer as part of the process of overcoming the division between mental and manual labor. In a crucial theoretical turn, this problem becomes registered in terms of an individual practice of writing as a manifestation of bourgeois right, as Liu Shaoqi and Zhou Yang are said to have "used the web of bourgeois right to pull workers out of the ranks of their own class."[31] The individualization of writing around the figure of the author, or the temporal bifurcation of writing from labor, is therefore integrated into a vocabulary of political economy, that of bourgeois right, one that made its dramatic reappearance in the late Cultural Revolution. The effect was to theorize the professional writer as themselves a manifestation of capitalist relations of cultural production under socialism, indeed of professional writing as itself a kind of social relation, with the Writers Association itself comprising the continuation of bourgeois dictatorship. The recurrent invocation of the dangers of "Petersburg" in other contexts marked the always present danger of an ideological degeneration of culture workers in terms that were explicated by their allegiance to an individual mode of writing, which in turn generated a tendency toward bourgeois consciousness.

Problems of this order had already been anticipated to a degree in literary works themselves, not least Duan Ruixia's 1973 text "Audience," which imagined a set of cultural practices that were coterminous with material production and avoided the mediating capacities of the professional culture workers. So too does his later fictional work provide a condensation of otherwise impossible theoretical problems. The short story published by Duan Ruixia in *Liberation Daily* under the title "Hammer and Poem" (1975) represents a more sustained engagement with the problems of writing that had arisen in the interim. The short story begins in medias res, with a group of metal workers taking a momentary break from labor in order to write a letter to a recipient called Yu Geng, his identity being, at this point, still unclear. The composition of the letter is, however, revealed to be a collective process, albeit under the guidance of a single metal worker, Hua Weijun. The scene of composition is arresting:

"Those of us who wield the hammer, wish to talk to you about poetry...."

People's eyes followed Hua Weijun's notes, and they made occasional comments, and so too did Hua Weijun's pen make some adjustments in line with people's remarks—but before reading the letter, let us first introduce the recipient and authors, and the origins of this letter.[32]

The personal mode of address from the narrator to the assumed reader—"let us first..."—following this initial scene poses it as an anticipatory prolepsis, such that the narrative as a whole will recapitulate the events leading up to this scene of collective composition. It transpires that Hua Weijun is an amateur poet whose poems on the subject of labor have been repeatedly published and have, as a result, also attracted the attention of a cultural official, Yu Geng, who undertakes a visit to the factory where Hua Weijun works in order to convince him to move into specialized cultural production. It is an indication of Duan's own craft that the scene at which Yu Geng considers the value of recruiting Hua Weijun makes use of a focalized narrative perspective that is of Yu Geng himself, as well as free indirect, a suggestive move in light of the fact that Yu Geng comprises the object of critique in the story. When, for example, Yu Geng first considers Hua's talents and the prospect of inviting him to a poetry reading, the narrator reports that "it would be crucial to make a special invite to such talents 人才 and invite them up onto the podium, so that they might set an example! Yu Geng was as happy as an astronomer who had discovered a new star, and so hurried to the factory."[33] Even without Yu Geng having spoken at this point in the narrative, the preservation of an oral pattern of speech in the sentence beginning "it would be crucial" without the explicit marking of reported speech allows for a contingent meeting of Yu Geng's personal voice and the voice of the narrator in a manner evoking free indirect style. With Yu Geng's actual arrival at the factory, the use of a focalized narrative position is rendered yet clearer, as the worker accompanying him, Old Zhu, is seen "saying a few words in the ear of Old Sha," but without those words being reported, indicating a narrative viewpoint that is temporarily focalized through Yu Geng, who is not familiar with the clamor of the factory.

The encounter that follows between Yu Geng and Hua Weijun sets up yet another conventional coincidence, albeit not as extreme as the examples from other texts, in that it transpires that Yu Geng and Hua Weijun enjoyed a previous meeting at a time in the unspecified pre–Cultural Revolution past, when Yu Geng also enjoined Hua Weijun that "poetry is a beautiful literary genre 文学体裁. You should write beautiful things, but you can't use hammers, chisels, and electric welding flowers throughout." In the context of their second meeting, which still precedes the actual scene of collective letter writing with which the short story begins, Yu Geng's further insistence that Hua Weijun might broaden his understanding of subject matter causes him to confidently reject Yu Geng's entreaties, and there follows a striking intervention concerning the nature of Hua Weijun's poetic craft:

"Sorry, I'm a person who writes poems with a hammer." Little Hua took the poem from Yu Geng's hand, turned and left. A strange fellow! Surely Little Hua didn't write poems only for the sake of publication? Little Hua had never thought about it. In the factory, he used big-character posters to express opinions on major national issues with the workers and masters in the factory, sprinkled sweat on the steel plates, and pointed the criticism at the bourgeoisie. How many slogans and blackboard papers he had written! Sometimes, he felt that simple records were not strong enough, so he gradually learned to summarize and refine powerful and glorious things from many people and many things, so poetry came into being.[34]

The continued use of oral patterns of speech—"a strange fellow!"—in this extract combined with the reference to Hua in the third person mark this passage as also operating in free indirect discourse, but it is with Hua's voice that the narrative has fused, namely in imitation of a possible response to Yu Geng's behavior, rather than that of Yu Geng as previously. Moreover, Hua's conception of his writerly practice marks a radical difference with Yu Geng's demand for an expansion in subject matter and aesthetic repertoire insofar as, here, there is no strict delineation between poetry and other forms of writing, including writing of the most agitational kind. The production of poetry is instead seen as a contingent demand that arises from the collective conditions of class struggle. This is, then, an account of writing wholly opposed to Yu Geng's invocation of poetry as a kind of "literary genre," one that puts pressure on the autonomy of the literary as such and foregrounds the primacy of labor in relation to poetry. The specifically aesthetic dimensions of these contending visions emerge at the end of this episode, when Yu Geng, having insisted on giving Hua Weijun an invitation to a poetry session, leaves Hua Weijun to engage in labor with his fellow workers, an experience recounted from Hua's own perspective: "'Kang-dang! Kang-dang!' The sound of the hammer melted into the chorus of the whole workshop, and he gradually felt the joy of labor. Yu Geng, ah, Yu Geng, why don't you understand? It is such thousands of sledgehammers that create the most beautiful poems in the world!"[35]

This event of dramatic encounter between Yu Geng and Hua Weijun gives rise to an ellipsis of unspecified duration. This ellipsis is followed by the scene of the poetry session which marks the danger of Hua Weijun being withdrawn from the site of collective labor. The events that follow stage a triumphal conquest of the space and time of cultural production by the working class:

Just as the speech was beginning: "Boom! Boom!" A troupe of gongs and drums broke in with no sense of courtesy 无礼貌. Yu Geng recognized that it was Hua Weijun who was beating the drums and Old Sha who was beating the gong. When the team arrived at the stage, the gongs and drums stopped. Little Hua put down the drumsticks and jumped onto the stage. Yu Geng hurriedly gave him the seat of the presidium, but Little Hua walked to the podium and opened his loud voice: "Comrades, dozens of hammer-wielding workers in our workshop will present a poem to today's poem meeting." "Ha! It's a microphone grab!"

This brilliant passage marks a series of skillful shifts in narrative perspective. The judgment of the intrusion as having "no sense of courtesy" marks the position as belonging to Yu Geng, for whom the aesthetic experience of poetry relies on a delineation from the sounds of manual labor, just as the spatial arrangement of the poetry session delineates the presidium from the audience, before the narrative position shifts to that of the collective proletarian subject led by Hua Weijun. This dramatic intervention also fills in the events of the ellipsis that otherwise separate Yu Geng's visit to the factory from this poetry meeting, from a position that is explicitly that of Hua Weijun: "it was as if he saw before him the vibrant scene over the past few days when the comrades had discussed this poem together." The suggestion of a collective scene of poetic authorship naturally recalls the scene of collective letter writing with which the narrative began, and which, in the actual order of the story, occupies a temporal position subsequent to this cultural intervention. The effect of this poetic intervention is to break up the otherwise strict, hierarchized arrangements of the poetry session, resulting in an open-ended exchange of poems—a sort of socialist poetry slam—and one that totally escapes the capacities of Yu Geng, of whom it is said that he "felt hot on his face, and this man who was good at dealing with things suddenly felt that he didn't know how to arrange this scene."[36] The conclusion to the narrative, then, brings the time up to that of the opening scene of letter writing, which becomes explicable as a demand from the workers that Yu Geng surrender his privileged cultural position, and then gestures toward the future:

> Therefore, these bold tailors of steel in this simple work shed decided to write a letter to Yu Geng. The content of the letter can be guessed by readers, and there is no need to repeat it. What needs to be added is that a week later, the leader of the district cultural station agreed to Yu Geng's personal request and asked him to go to the metalworking workshop of this factory to study, stay in place, and grasp the masses' artistic creation. The iron and steel tailors specially gave him a copy of Mao's Yan'an Talks and a sledgehammer.[37]

The self-conscious crafting of a mass practice of cultural production by an amateur writer who, in his theoretical reflections, also emphasized his location in social relations of labor and writing makes this story a particularly rich example of the directions in which the Maoist project was tending at the end of the Cultural Revolution. Yet so too does it underscore a series of limits, not least those contained within the story itself, namely the question of the literary as such, evoked by Yu Geng's insistence on the irreducibility of poetry as a literary mode as compared to other practices of writing. Insofar as the thrust of the text lies in its rejection of the special character of literary production as something set apart from the collective practice of material production, the text itself remains circumscribed by the circumstances of its publication, that is, the fact that the text remained tied to a definite author function, namely by being published under the name of Duan Ruixia himself, introducing, then, a powerful conflict between the narrative intentions of the text and the institutional conditions of its publication and circulation, such that the ideological fetish of the author reemerged even in conjunction with its most sophisticated critiques. In this context, the total repudiation of the name and figure of the author called for by Zhou Tian and others may be seen as a path not taken, or else as a set of emergent possibilities that could not be developed during the final years of the Cultural Revolution before the rightist coup.

Yet the positing, in the midst of the Petersburg polemic, of the problem of "bourgeois right" marks a reminder of the transformation in relations of labor to which Cultural Revolution culture was actually orientated. It was here that the most apocalyptic language and the lapsing into heroic subjectivity—already visible in the sent-down-youth novel—were to emerge with the greatest intensity.

Maoism in command

The figuring of the problem of the professional writer in socialism in terms of the theoretical vocabulary of bourgeois right marks the generalized return of that set of concepts as a way of thinking the problem of socialist transition, not least through the rise of Zhang Chunqiao to become a figure of national political significance. The textual fruits of this project consisted of a program to craft a new textbook on socialist political economy. This project shared with *Morning Glow* the fact of falling under the direct supervision of the Shanghai Writing Group.[38] The concrete process of drawing up the textbook was devolved to a small group drawn from the Institute of Political Economy at Fudan University, but with Zhang Chunqiao providing interventions that shaped the major theoretical categories of the text, of which, over 1971–1976, there were a total of five different drafts, each differing from the others with respect to their understanding of socialism, and their orientation toward the theoretical vocabulary of bourgeois right.[39] The ultimate significance of this project lies in the way that the theorization of political economy shared with the culture of the period a reification of heroic subjectivity, such that the theoretical discourse of political economy became homologous with the narrative forms of the sent-down-youth novel, amounting, ultimately, to an aestheticization of political economy as such.

That these authors undertook the process of writing such a textbook during the late Cultural Revolution and that national-level leaders such as Zhang undertook close supervision of this project demonstrates a shift as compared to Zhang's earlier intervention in 1958. As we saw in chapter three, Zhang's article "Smash the Ideology of Bourgeois Right" relied on a strategic bifurcation between politics and economics, whereby he put the disciplinary apparatus of Soviet-derived political economy at a theoretical distance in order to mount a *critique* of political economy, one that would locate bourgeois right as the problem of how to overcome the ideological effects of the wage form under conditions of socialist transition, and did so by calling for a new, communist consciousness of labor that would transgress the wage. The pursuit, under the conditions of the Cultural Revolution, of a textbook *of* political economy marked an attempt to resolve this strategic bifurcation in favor of a reunified theory but one that would nonetheless differ radically from the Soviet-derived discourse in decisive ways. In particular, Zhang's ambition was to formulate a theory of political economy that would resist any understanding of socialism as a coherent, stable totality of social relations, in favor of an emphasis on socialism as a contradictory ensemble of divergent and conflictual social forms, including those categories drawn into socialism from capitalism. This was to include, crucially, that problem of the wage that had already appeared to Zhang as a major site of contestation in 1958. Moreover, an integrated theory of political economy would also seek to articulate the relations between different sets of categories that had hitherto been rendered separate from each other, namely the political discourse of bourgeois right, and the Soviet-derived categories of the law of value, commodity production, profit, and so on. So too would the revision of political economy assume the form of a mass project in which the masses would assume control of the production of theoretical knowledge over those processes of material production in which they were engaged. The formation of the Shanghai Writing Group therefore coincided with a novel campaign in which the masses were enjoined, in the title of the foremost article announcing this campaign, to "Study Some Political Economy."

This article, released in *Red Flag* and printed under the name Fang Hai, one of the common pen names used by the Shanghai Writing Group, gestured toward the points of departure for a mature Maoist theory of political economy in the mode of a repudiation of revisionism. It argued therefore that the revisionists denied the necessity of a theoretical discourse of political economy under socialism, and did so as a result of their denial of contradictions and class struggle under socialist conditions, including, crucially, contradictions between superstructure and base, whereby socialism was said to consist solely in an increasingly more rational organization of production, the problems of social relations having been basically solved.[40] The emphasis on contradiction in this context establishes the ambition of the Maoist project of political economy as an epistemological break with the Soviet-derived discourse, in which the stability of that discourse would be supplanted by a more dialectical understanding of socialism a riven by contradictory forces and social relations, irreducible to the "laws" that comprised the theoretical solidity of Soviet political economy.

The very ambitions of this project, however, render even more stark the extent to which its articulation required the traversal of old theoretical ground again, which led, in its early stages, to a visible failure to break free from those theoretical and discursive categories that comprised the object of critique, producing, in other words, a circular movement that could not break out of the Soviet categories of political economy. This was true above all of the problem of the wage form under socialism, insofar as early instances of the textbook and the larger discourse of Maoist political economy remained within the terms established in 1956, and therefore preceding Zhang's intervention, in which the problem of the wage under socialism was said to be theoretically and historically distinct from capitalism. In an early study guide published as part of the movement to popularize political economy, also under the title *Study Some Political Economy*, for which Fang Hai's article served as the introduction, a chapter under the title "How Individual Articles of Consumption Are Distributed" stated in explicit terms that, the system of distribution being determined by the system of ownership, remuneration according to labor was self-sufficient as the standard of socialist distribution, and in fact amounted to a "revolution" in the mode of distribution as compared to capitalism. The assertion of a radical distinction between the wage of capitalism and that of socialism continues in the entry on the "wage" given in the same collection as part of a dictionary of terms.[41] This theoretical logic did not differ from the Soviet discourse and is notable precisely for the absence of any serious treatment of contradiction, not only in the a priori assumption of socialism as a radical historical break with capitalism, but also in the understanding of the problem of the wage as simply one of distribution, which is in turn made a mere function of the mode of ownership, rather than being explicated in dialectical terms as itself constitutive of social relations. Nor can the absence of any theoretical break at this moment be reduced to the fact of certain texts being published for popular consumption and discussion, because the same theoretical dependence on an already existing Soviet discourse persisted into the early drafts of the textbook drawn up under the aegis of the writing group.

The first draft was released on a limited circulation basis in September 1972 and maintained the theoretical understanding of socialism as a stable and coherent mode of production, an understanding that passed into the limited remarks on the problem of the wage. The relevant section of this initial textbook acknowledged that remuneration according to labor remained within the limits of bourgeois right, but nonetheless insisted, with the textual support of Marx's "Critique of the Gotha Program," that this limitation "is unavoidable in the socialist phase, it does not in any way depend on human will, because 'right can never be higher than the economic structure of society and its cultural development conditioned thereby,' " such that the problem of the wage was here folded back into a developmentalist account of the "level" of productive development rather than being situated in a dialectical analysis of the persistence and reproduction of capitalist social forms.[42] The theoretical continuity between the first round of textbook drafts and the reductive understanding of the wage and other facets of political economy that served as their purported object of critique provided a self-supporting logic from which further texts were unable to break, at least up to 1975. The invocation of Marxist classics often shed light on the deep conservatism and dogmatism of these early interventions on the plane of political economy, but so too do their defensive theoretical gestures also anticipate the theoretical disquiet that inhabits these same texts.

The 1973 study guide *Two Kinds of Society, Two Kinds of Wage*, then, insisted, in common with other texts, including the first draft of the textbook, that capitalist and socialist wage forms differ from each other in the distinction between the selling of labor power versus remuneration according to labor, but in making this distinction was nonetheless forced to ask the rhetorical question of why the socialist wage continues to be designated a wage. The answer could only be given via a lengthy quotation from Stalin's 1952 *Economic Problems of Socialism in the USSR* that revealed more than it answered, as Stalin insisted, on the problem of how it might be possible to speak in terms of categories of value and commodity production under socialism, that "it is chiefly the form, the outward appearance, of the old categories of capitalism that have remained in our country, but that their essence has radically changed in adaptation to the requirements of the development of the socialist economy."[43] It is precisely this question of form, or the relation of form and substance, however, that had informed the earlier round of discussions around the problem of bourgeois right, namely in Mao's insistence that formal changes with respect to the question of ownership did not exhaust the persistence of inequalities and attitudes of command in the lived experience of social relations. The dogmatic structure and self-validating arguments of these early attempts to popularize political economy in the Cultural Revolution thereby provided the conditions for the personal intervention of Zhang Chunqiao and Yao Wenyuan. Subsequent to the issuing of the first textbook, then, and in the early stages of the campaign to popularize political economy, Zhang and Yao undertook a visit to those directly engaged in the textbook to discuss the theoretical problems that had emerged during its early draft versions. Zhang himself emphasized that the reconstruction of political economy with an orientation toward contradiction necessitated an understanding of the reproduction of capitalist social forms within socialism, and therefore a more dialectical understanding of the tautologies and self-reinforcing logics that had informed political economy before that point.

Yet the total expansion of this emergent theoretical horizon would depend on interventions not simply from Zhang but from Mao himself, for whom the problem of bourgeois right emerged as his central theoretical preoccupation at the end of his life. In 1975, Mao announced two crucial commentaries relating to the subject of political economy, which also announced a new study campaign around the question of proletarian dictatorship:

> In a word, China is a socialist country. Before liberation she was much the same as capitalism. Even now she practices an eight-grade wage system, distribution to each according to his work and exchange by means of money, which are scarcely different from those in the old society. What is different is that the system of ownership has changed.
>
> Our country at present practices a commodity system, and the wage system is unequal too, there being the eight-grade wage system etc. These can only be restricted under the dictatorship of the proletariat. Thus it would be quite easy for people like Lin Piao to push the capitalist system if they came to power. Therefore, we should read some Marxist-Leninist works.[44]

These directives were published across a wide range of platforms in February 1975, above all in the articles "Study Well the Theory of the Dictatorship of the Proletariat" and "Marx, Engels and Lenin on the Dictatorship of the Proletariat," the latter introducing Mao's directives alongside relevant quotes from the Marxist classics. The former of these articles emphasized that those social relations that Mao had enumerated in his directive, namely the persistence of commodity production and the wage, were explicitly formulated as manifestations of "bourgeois right," such that bourgeois right itself "can only be restricted under the dictatorship of the proletariat."[45] The effect of these interventions from Mao, then, was to restate those problems that had hitherto evaded the textbook authors, namely the coherence or otherwise of socialism as a determinate mode of production, or the relation between those social forms that provided the basis of production and distribution under socialism versus their capitalist counterparts. Mao's emphasis on the logic of distribution according to labor as being "scarcely different from those in the old society" marked a rupture with the self-fulfilling logic that had otherwise informed the study of political economy in the Cultural Revolution up to that point, whereby this standard of remuneration had been defended as not only adequate for socialism but also as itself radically distinct from the wage-relation under capitalism. The effect, in these terms, was not only for Mao to insist on the wage as the persistence of a capitalist social relation under socialism, but also, in his second intervention, to argue that the wage and other such relations provided the basis on which the totalizing reinsertion of China and labor back into a capitalist process of accumulation might come to pass, such that the failure to transcend the wage as a social relation central to the organization of labor provided the ready-to-hand means of a reversal in the revolutionary process.

This was, therefore, a political and theoretical intervention that was at the same time the positing of a different temporal logic, namely the incipient temporal logic of a reversal, one in which the drag of the past was omnipresent as a threat to the revolutionary process. It is no coincidence, then, that Mao's interventions along these lines came with a reorientation toward the specificity of politics, one that was revealed by the announcement of a call to study the theory of proletarian dictatorship. The relation between the study campaigns around political economy and proletarian dictatorship was never fully explicated, and yet it may be surmised that Mao sought to delineate the ways that the theoretical discourse of political economy as derived from the Soviet experience was, in the absence of a suitable theory of the state, inadequate to grasping the full set of problems of high socialism. In these ways, the fusing of the theoretical problematics of political economy and proletarian dictatorship resulted in the vocabulary of bourgeois right assuming a totalizing theoretical function. The publication of "Marx, Engels and Lenin on the Dictatorship of the Proletariat" therefore included lengthy extracts from Marx's "Critique of the Gotha Program," but so too, and more radically still, did it draw on Lenin's reflections on the problematic of bourgeois right in *State and Revolution*, including Lenin's startling acknowledgement that bourgeois right "presupposes the existence of the bourgeois state, for right is nothing without an apparatus capable of enforcing the observance of the standards of right. It follows that under Communism there remains for a time not only bourgeois right, but even the bourgeois state—without the bourgeoisie!"[46]

The problem that arose from this and other interventions on the part of Mao was precisely the question of the Chinese state itself, and how to arrive at an adequate theory of the problem of capitalist restoration. In the aftermath of these initial steps within the movement to study proletarian dictatorship, further theoretical interventions established some of those categories that would also inform the final attempt to write a textbook on political economy. In particular, Zhang Chunqiao and Yao Wenyuan published lengthy theoretical interventions under the titles "On Exercising All-Round Dictatorship Over the Bourgeoisie" and "On the Social Basis of the Lin Piao Anti-Party Clique" respectively, both being published in *Red Flag*. These articles were neither homogenous with each other nor with Mao's interventions, and instead they mark autonomous attempts to generate new categories and points of departure that were to feed back into the writing of the textbook on political economy. In particular, Zhang's article marks a renewed attempt to excavate the problem of the wage in terms that allow the wage relation to be thought not simply as a secondary moment within an overall social totality whose determining instance is the status of ownership or the development of the productive forces, but as itself an active social relation and site of struggle, so that, in his own words: "It is incorrect to give no weight to whether the issue of ownership has been resolved merely in form or in actual fact, to the reaction upon the system of ownership exerted by the two other aspects of the relations of production—the relations among people and the form of distribution—and to the reaction upon the economic base exerted by the superstructure; these two aspects and the superstructure may play a decisive role under given conditions."[47]

The running together of the superstructure and the relations of distribution as two moments that may in turn exercise a reciprocal influence on the question of ownership marks not only the autonomous significance of these moments, but also their relation to each other, which is to say that Zhang's article provides a theoretical rationale for the tasks allocated to cultural production in the Cultural Revolution, whereby the production of proletarian heroes would provide the conditions for the supersession of the wage form through a new communist consciousness of labor. Yet in spite of its theoretical radicalism, on the question to which his article was supposedly directed, that of proletarian dictatorship itself, Zhang gives no indication that bourgeois right might be abolished or restricted, except through the enhancement of the state and its apparatuses of coercion. The question, then, of the character of the state itself and the problem of political practices around and even against the state, such as had emerged during the early years of the Cultural Revolution, mark a striking absence in Zhang's text. In this respect, the moment of expansion in the theoretical logic of bourgeois right through the campaign to study proletarian dictatorship was also, and paradoxically, a radical contraction of this same theoretical language as compared to its antibureaucratic dimensions during the Great Leap, in the way it came to feed into the reification of consciousness, being concerned solely with the problem of the wage and its supersession. To this extent, despite its visible attempt to move away from the Stalinist conception of formal ownership as the determining moment in social relations, Zhang also falls back into the Stalinist categories of the division between state and collective ownership as the basis of the continued presence of commodity production under socialism and the accompanying focus on the continued proliferation of petty production and commerce among the peasants. In much the same terms, the logic of his position also remained within the Stalinist categories of the incorporation of the collective agricultural sector into formal state ownership as the effective solution to the persistence of commodity production and other kinds of capitalist social relations.[48]

The reemergence within Zhang's article of a Stalinist and ineffective set of theoretical logics marks the difficulty of overcoming the inherited, Soviet terms for thinking the problems of socialism. As against the uneven theoretical logic of Zhang's article on this problem, Yao's statement marked an attempt to instigate new theoretical lines of inquiry in response to Mao's interventions. It did so through the attempt to provide a theoretical explanation for the danger of capitalist restoration under socialism. To this extent, the problem of the "social basis" announced in his article's title marks an attempt to understand how and why Lin Biao had emerged as the embodiment of a capitalist restoration. Amid the polemic of his article, Yao deployed Marx's formulation from *Capital* that the capitalist is only "capital personified 人格化," arguing that the capitalist roaders in the party were, therefore, ultimately the personification of those social forms or capitalist social relations that provided the material basis for a return to capitalism.[49] The formulation of "personification" would come to pass directly into the final version of the textbook, whose circulation in September 1976 coincided with the definitive end of the revolutionary project. Yet between the launch of the movement to study proletarian dictatorship in early 1975, and this final attempt at envisaging a political economy of socialism, Mao's further interventions on the question of the state were to demarcate a political terrain and set of problems that remained inaccessible even to Zhang Chunqiao. In November 1975 Mao responded directly to Lenin's quotes on the relation between bourgeois right and the state that had been circulated as part of the proletarian dictatorship campaign: "Lenin spoke of building a bourgeois state without the bourgeoisie to safeguard 保障 bourgeois right. We ourselves have built just such a state, not much different from the old society, there are ranks and grades, eight grades of wages, distribution according to work, and exchange of equal values."[50]

This further directive was reprinted and distributed in early 1976 through the collection *Important Directives of Chairman Mao*, together with Mao's other directives concerning problems of politics and political economy under socialism, in tandem with the campaign against Deng Xiaoping's "three instructions."[51] Mao's deployment of the term "safeguard" gestures toward a central contradiction in the politics of the socialist state in the late Cultural Revolution, namely the fact that, on the one hand, it is, following Lenin, the very existence of bourgeois right, and above all the remuneration of labor on the basis of an abstract or formalistic mode of equality, that accounts for the problematic of the state under socialism, and more particularly a bourgeois state charged with safeguarding bourgeois right as its own economic basis, namely through the quantification, supervision and individuation of labor via the mechanism of the wage. Yet, on the other hand, for Zhang Chunqiao and others, it is also this same state that functions as the instrument for suppressing or limiting relations of bourgeois right in order that it might produce the social and political conditions for its own supersession.[52] Mao's intervention therefore gestured toward an impossible bind, and one that attests to the ways in which, subsequent to the early stage of the Cultural Revolution, the problematic of the state reemerged for Mao at a radically expanded level of theoretical sophistication, and one that cast into doubt the possibility of a gradual movement toward communism ending in the eventual abolition of the state itself. Yet it was precisely problems of this order that remained absent from even the most sophisticated analyses contained in the final draft of the textbook on socialist political economy, which did not escape the contraction of bourgeois right around the question of the wage and the attendant reification of consciousness. In other words, Zhang Chunqiao and others could not discern any solution to the complex relations between the state and the restriction of bourgeois right except in the form of a constant enhancement of state power and coercion against social relations and practices that were seen to encompass the reproduction of the bases of capitalist restoration.

This in turn supplied the rationale for constant demands being made on laborers with respect to the overcoming of the wage as the foremost manifestation of bourgeois right in the social organization of labor. In tandem with the enhancement of the state, then, the inability of Cultural Revolution radicals to resolve pressing problems of politics also contributed toward a modification in the theoretical contents of bourgeois right, which lost the porousness and antibureaucratic content it had possessed in the Great Leap and came to refer, in effect, to the problem of how to overcome material incentives. Yet the overwhelming emphasis on the wage was, ironically, also the site of the most radical insights of the final textbook draft, which appeared in September 1976. That is, this draft effected a rupture with the previous drafts and did so on the basis of Mao's 1975 directives, by breaking with the self-fulfilling assumption that socialism and "remuneration according to labor" marked a historical break with their capitalist counterparts, in favor of an understanding of socialism as itself encompassing capitalist social relations that are drawn directly into socialist relations of production. Read in light of the problems of culture, the professional author in their guise as the culture worker marked one of these social forms drawn into socialism from capitalism, hence the inclusion of the author within the category of bourgeois right. In place of the understanding of socialism as a stable mode of production, then, was substituted a sophisticated understanding of socialism as a site of unevenness and as an ensemble of contradictions. The theoretical achievement of the final circulated edition of the textbook therefore lies in disavowing the Stalinist conceptual architecture and instead marking bourgeois right as the point of conceptual departure. The final draft version of the textbook that was released in September 1976 was accompanied by an extended introduction that took the contradictory character of socialism as the starting point, arguing that an expansive conception of bourgeois right accounted for socialism as an ensemble of contradictions and different sets of social relations that were fundamentally uneven with one another, belonging both to the old society as well as containing incipient communist elements. This conception of contradiction and unevenness was also the basis for an account of the emergence of new political forces that threatened to reintroduce the conditions for capitalist accumulation, whereby, bourgeois right, as the site of unevenness and the overlap of different social forms, that is, of the "lag" of transition itself, provides the conditions in which these forces—capitalist roaders—might emerge:

> Bourgeois right is the concentrated expression of the traditions or remnants of the old society amid socialist relations of production, and so too is it the soil for the emergence of capitalism and a bourgeoisie. As soon as bourgeois right is strengthened and expanded, the system of socialist ownership by the whole people will be corrupted and degenerate into ownership by the capitalist owners and the bureaucratic monopoly bourgeoisie. The bourgeoisie inside the party is the personification 人格化 of this system of ownership of the capitalist roaders and the bureaucratic monopoly bourgeoisie.[53]

The invocation of personification in the final available textbook draft—having been introduced by Yao's article, but otherwise absent from preceding drafts—marks a crucial shift in the whole grammar of the textbook, whereby its categories also became legible as persons, or narrative personae, which marked at the same time the wholesale transmutation of problems of social relations into problems of consciousness, including demands for a heroic subjectivity of the kind that had already been posed in the sent-down-youth novel. This is evident in the first place from the framing of the problems of bourgeois right itself. In the long introduction, then, the authors restaged the earlier observation of Zhang Chunqiao in 1958 that bourgeois right is as much a problem of ideology and consciousness as it is one of the structure of social relations, arguing therefore that "the ideology of bourgeois right is the reflection of bourgeois right in conceptual state 概念形态. Its core is the wage system." Yet the possibility of overcoming the structure of bourgeois right was itself dependent on a totalizing transformation in the state of consciousness, namely in the form of a communist consciousness of labor that would make it possible to overcome the wage and its accompanying forms of inequality, so that: "The ideology of bourgeois right, is a reflection of bourgeois right in conceptual state, and serves the preservation of bourgeois right. Therefore, rupturing with the ideology of bourgeois right is also an important premise for restricting bourgeois right. The more thoroughly this rupture takes place, the more effective this restriction will be."[54]

In these terms, the textbook itself staged a contradiction that appeared irreconcilable and insurmountable, whereby the persistence of capitalist relations under socialism in the form of bourgeois right spontaneously produced ideological forces that themselves needed to be surmounted in order to transcend those capitalist relations. The emergent orientation toward the hypertransformative powers of consciousness were accompanied by other theoretical shifts in which the gap between capitalism and socialism was itself progressively reduced. The final textbook thereby came to be characterized by a specific temporality, in which the restoration of capitalism was always imminent within socialist relations of production themselves, above all with respect to the wage: "Socialist relations of distribution, while preserving the external form 外壳 of 'remuneration according to labor,' might change into exploitative relations in which the fruits of the labor of the masses of workers and peasants are controlled by a small privileged caste."[55]

In these terms, the persistence of the wage as category and social relation marks labor under socialism as other than fully or immediately social and offers the ready-to-hand social materials that might enable labor itself to be thrown back into a capitalist process of accumulation and exploitation, even within the framework of a social order whose external form continues to be that of state ownership. The problem of "form" is therefore manifold, marking both the noncoincidence of the formal status of ownership and the real content of social relations, but with social forms also offering the potential for a process of capitalist social relations in which labor can be thrown into a fully capitalist logic. The imminence of restoration is made yet more visible in the section dealing specifically with the wage relation. The fact of this section being folded into a chapter on "distribution" demonstrates the extent to which the formal organization of the textbook continued to encounter the limitations imposed by the Soviet tradition of political economy, insofar as, at least as far as formal organization is concerned, the wage was not fully recognized in the terms given by Zhang Chunqiao, namely as internal rather than secondary to the relations of production.[56] In terms of content, however, the authors attempted to rupture with the self-fulfilling statements that had influenced earlier versions of the textbook and which marked continuity with the Soviet discourse, in that they insisted that the wage under socialism was basically coterminous with the capitalist wage. To the extent that socialism required the use of the wage to stimulate labor, then, this was said to mark a temporal bifurcation within the duration of labor, in which, under socialism, "the labor time of the laborers becomes a part of the total labor days of society or the collectivity, and labor is no longer a commodity. Yet, the labor of the laborers is still divided into two parts: labor conducted for the social fund and labor that is conducted for the fund of individual consumption; the latter portion becomes the yardstick for the distribution of articles of consumption."[57]

The wage was understood to repose a temporal division within the category of labor, between the time that the individual laborer receives in the form of a wage, and that devoted toward the meeting of social needs. Left unstated, but crucial to this observation, is that this temporal division makes a formal parallel with the temporal duration of capitalist wage labor, insofar as capitalist labor is also divided between that part represented as necessary labor, which corresponds to the value of labor power itself, and that part which functions as surplus labor. If, under capitalist social relations, that latter part of the working day marks the site of exploitation, then Zhang and the other textbook authors were faced with the task of extending the labor that is not represented by the wage in order that all labor might come to be for the benefit of society—that is, gratis, or communist labor. The temporal division of socialist labor was therefore itself a site of overlapping contradictions, with the wage altogether, then, being, in the words of the authors, "a problem of great complexity." It is so because the wage itself, even when organized according to the principle "remuneration according to labor" and distinct from the purchase and sale of labor power as a commodity, ultimately remains a remnant of capitalist social relations: "Under the socialist system, while the production relations reflected by the wage are different from the production relations reflected by the wage under the capitalist system, yet the category of the wage and its concrete forms, whether they be time rates or piece rates, are left over from capitalist society."[58]

This intervention marks the single most important theoretical insight on the part of Chinese socialism and establishes a total theoretical distance between China and the Soviet discourse of political economy. The understanding of the wage as itself a social relation and one that comprises a site of bourgeois right and capitalist production within the total ensemble of socialism provides the theoretical foundations for the process of overcoming the wage at a level of sophistication that was absent from Zhang Chunqiao's earliest interventions in 1958. The theoretical category of the "remnant" therefore emerges in the late Cultural Revolution as a way of accounting both for the wage, and as we have seen above, the professional author, whereby both provide the conditions for a restoration of capitalism and whose overcoming is therefore a matter of necessity for the development of the revolutionary process. The wage—in any form—was deemed fundamentally incompatible with the development of a communist society, being instead the possibility for a process of capitalist reversal of the kind that did in fact take place from the late

1970s onward, just as the persistence of the professional author, theorized under the rubric of bourgeois right, also provided the conditions for a capitalist restoration in the cultural sphere. The textbook provided no answer to the question of how to engender the conditions for the transformation of consciousness, which is also to say that late Maoism maintained and exacerbated a debilitating bifurcation between the political and the economic. The quasi-solution to this impasse lay in the imaginary powers of resolution provided by aesthetic categories. If, in other words, the threat of capitalist restoration as the imminence of the past had become materially personified in the figure of the capitalist roader, the possibility of superseding bourgeois right emerged through the equally individuated and personified figure of the hero, endowed with a heroic subjectivity:

> Zhang Side, Lei Feng, Jiao Yulu, Yang Shuicai, Wang Jinxi and other comrades, are the outstanding representatives of proletarian fighters. Their spirit of showing no regard for reputation or advantage, fearing neither hardship nor death, setting one's whole heart on the revolution and the people, unlimited loyalty to the revolution, sparing no effort for the people, eternally exudes the radiance of communism, eternally encourages us to bravely surge forward on the path of continuing the revolution! The establishment of a communist attitude of labor thus requires that we conduct the "most radical rupture with traditional property relations" and "the most radical rupture with traditional ideas," and the most radical rupture with the ideology of bourgeois right.[59]

The radically individuated character of these heroic exemplars is inseparable from the fact that they are also universally masculine, insofar as the masculinized gesture of heroism embodied in the singular act—that is, the temporal moment of "rupture"—provides the paradigm for breaking with bourgeois right, with a consequent effacement of everyday processes of reproduction. The quasi-solution to the challenges posed in this final version of the textbook is, in this sense, homologous with the methods of narrative closure that determine the sent-down-youth novel. More generally, the textbook was ultimately structured around an impossible temporal bifurcation between the omnipresent threat of a lapsing into the past embodied by bourgeois right and the figure of the capitalist roader, and, on the other hand, the overcoming of all problems of transition through the singular act of the hero. This temporal and theoretical impasse yields to an aestheticization of problems of transition, in which the contradictory ensemble of social forms takes on the appearance of an aesthetic and moral conflict between two sets of dramatis personae. The inability to foresee the possibility of overcoming a social form such as the wage except in the form of heroic feats of consciousness, however, and the ensuing myopic focus around waged forms of labor, marks the limits of this particular project, which were at the same time the limits of late Maoism, in ways that remained intimately connected with the problem of culture, whereby, just as political economy became aestheticized in its internal logic, so too did the expected solution to bourgeois right come to devolve onto the powers of cultural production itself. The very impossibility that cultural producers could ever realize these expectations provided, in turn, a basis for the frequent brutalization of culture workers. Returning, then, to the vocabulary of "Petersburg," the persistence of a set of conditions in which professional writers continued to write on an individual basis provided the conditions for the same invocation of the language of "soul" that had motivated demands for the transformation of consciousness. Here, however, the language of soul became an injunction against the culture workers, even while they wrote in service of the ultimately impossible attempt to secure the universalization of a communist consciousness of labor. In an enthusiastic response to the original Petersburg article, then, the author of the text "Destroy the 'Petersburg' in the Depths of the Soul" opined that "if we might say that the various kinds of 'Associations' comprise so many 'Petersburgs' that are visible to the eye, then so too are there many invisible 'Petersburgs,' which Chairman Mao designated in his Yan'an Talks as their 'innermost soul' being 'a kingdom of the petty-bourgeois intelligentsia.'"[60]

The positing of a Petersburg of a soul as being the cause of culture workers failing in their responsibilities to transform social relations provided the justification for the repeated waves of violence against them, not least when the communist consciousness of labor did not emerge in the way that radicals desired, such that labor ceased to be the basis for transformation or utopian possibility. The transmutation of the demands of transition into the problems of consciousness and the turn to aesthetic quasi-solutions had, as its counterpart, the permanent paranoia around the ideological condition of cultural producers themselves and a further lapsing into a language of subjectivity, albeit posed in wholly negative terms. The negation of the definitive transformation of the culture worker marked a central contradiction that Maoism proved unable to resolve, whereby the professional writer, like the wage, could not be abolished as a real social relation, but only put under permanent suspicion, unable to offer evidence of its effective ideological transformation.

The consequence was that when, in late 1976, the Dengist coup against the left came, as it always would, a combination of exhaustion and disillusionment on the part of manual workers and culture workers alike, and the persistence in myriad sectors of capitalist social forms, meant that the reinsertion of China back into a capitalist logic was a rapid process.

The end of (the) Revolution

The unsolved and unsolvable contradictions that emerged during the Cultural Revolution intersect with the theoretical advances and experiments of that period in gesturing toward a set of profound limits, that apply not only to the ten-year period of the Cultural Revolution itself but to the whole Chinese socialist experiment. The projects examined in this book have been posed in terms of a series of wagers, namely, that the individual author could indeed be refunctioned and made adequate to the production of new social relations under the category of the culture worker, and that these culture workers would, operating within the formal institutions of a socialist state, provide the conditions for a process of socialist transition. Faced with these wagers, the Cultural Revolution emerges as a series of radical acts of negation, whereby it became clear that the individual writer was itself, as a relation of cultural production, a capitalist form, and that the Writers Association, as an institution, was not a basis for organizing writing in the service of revolution, but rather the "Petersburg" that provided the institutional and political nexus for reproducing the division of mental and manual labor. Yet part of the tragedy of that sequence lay precisely in the fact that the abolition of the ISA was not sufficient to resolve the problem of the writer at the level of social organization. By 1975 there had returned a vocabulary of crisis that marked the reproduction of the culture worker as an impassable limit of the transformation of culture, emblematized by the "Petersburg" polemic. In a further article, entitled "Deeply Criticize the Ideology of Bourgeois Right in the Cultural Sphere," Fang Yun stressed: "The capitalist class has been overthrown, and yet the capital 资产 of the intellectuals remains. With respect to their mode of production 生产方式, culture workers still carry specific characteristics of the small producers 小生产者 in key respects, and some of them are individual laborers 个体劳动. Moreover, we are still conducting the commodity system, and the principle of commodity exchange constantly seeps into our cultural sphere."[61]

The invocation here of a language of the mode of cultural production and that of bourgeois right marked the problem of the professional culture worker by foregrounding the individual author as itself an element of capitalist social relations that socialism would seek to supersede, yet, coming in 1975, interventions of this order also pointed to the radical difficulty of that process of supersession. The impassable limit in the form of the specific temporality of writing and its corollary of the individual writer was rendered necessary not only by the pre-1966 institutional effects of the Writers Association, but by the increasingly complex contradictions of building socialism itself. The persistence of bourgeois forms at the level of the relations of cultural production even after the dispersal of the ISA, the Writers Association, had as its counterpart the extensive reemergence of the vocabulary of bourgeois right in the theory of political economy. Yet in both of these areas, as well as in the texts of the Cultural Revolution novel itself, these challenges could only be articulated in terms of psychic interiority, either in the form of a heroic subjectivity as the basis for the supersession of the wage form, or in the paranoid projection of writerly subjectivity as always already bound to the logic of capital. This retreat to subjectivity marks the ultimate limits of the theoretical paradigms that were otherwise the source of great inspiration during the Cultural Revolution and portended in turn the defeat of the revolutionary project with Mao's passing in 1976.

THERMIDOR (BY WAY OF CONCLUSION)

I believe that when people engage in common labor it is possible to generate a shared feeling. Labor can break down those barriers erected by human beings and bridge the heart melodies of the self and the other. This was what I desired.

—Ding Ling 丁玲

It was in these terms that Ding Ling recounted her experience of the Cultural Revolution, written in her posthumous 1987 volume *Living Among Wind and Snow*. Having been imprisoned for a significant part of that decade, Ding Ling was finally released in 1975 and permitted to labor among the peasants before then being rehabilitated in the postrevolutionary period. Ding Ling was present at the beginning of this book, and yet she has remained largely absent throughout. Her experience of the socialist period was a complex one. From 1957 onward she was deprived of her position in the socialist literary system and often subject to abrasive, sexist polemics before being dispatched to reform through labor in the Great Northern Wilderness. She was therefore, in the postsocialist period, offered the possibility of interpellating herself into the position of victimhood. She did not take this possibility. Ding Ling refused to follow other intellectuals in negating the aspirations and visions of the Chinese Revolution. Instead, she insisted to the end on the transformative possibilities of labor, above all for intellectuals such as herself, and was, for that reason, a controversial figure amid the developments of the post-Mao period. In reading with Ding Ling, I believe the end of the Cultural Revolution to be the historical moment at which the Chinese Revolution as a whole came to an end as a result of defeats and the weight of its own internal contradictions. The end of the Cultural Revolution marked a moment of totalizing political defeat. There is a general tendency across scholarship to take the 1980s period solely as one in which there emerged new intellectual and cultural possibilities for thinking through different visions of the future and engaging in new forms of cultural production in China. This naive view obscures the ways in which the end of the Maoist period also entailed the closing off of certain possibilities, this closure having been enabled by precisely those elements of the postsocialist theoretical discourse that scholars have seen as radically emancipatory.

The rise of a labor humanist discourse bound to the recalibration of the problem of aesthetics naturally cannot account for all of the intellectual transformations of the reform period or indeed conceptions of culture. The emergence of labor humanism is significant, however, precisely because of its divergences from the conceptual vocabulary of cultural production and labor during the socialist period, in which these problems were specifically not understood according to Marxist humanist tropes of labor as the fundamental attribute (or "species-being") of the human, or unalienated labor as the creative expression of the human essence. The problem of labor and the relations of cultural production during the socialist period were rather understood in terms of the problems of remaking social relations within the sustained historical process of socialist transition, which radical theorists understood in terms of creating the ideological conditions that would enable the supersession of the wage form, theorized through the rubric of "bourgeois right." The advance of a labor humanism in the postsocialist period therefore derived its political logic from the displacement of the very different conceptual vocabulary through which labor had been understood, and social relations transformed, before 1976. To this extent, humanism emerged as the ideology par excellence for a program of capitalist restoration from 1976 onward. In these terms, Dai Jinhua is exactly right to argue that the 1980s saw "a rhetoric of the human [replacing] the discourse of class struggle in the critical discourses of various intellectual communities. The humanism of the young Marx replaced the Marx of political economy."[1] A depoliticized figure of the human lent itself to the withdrawal of problems of aesthetics from the field of class struggle, and, ultimately, the legitimization of the permanent bifurcation between the cultural producer and manual labor.[2]

Labor humanism against revolution

Toward the end of Dai Houying's novel *Humanity, Ah Humanity!* (1980), the figure of the laborer briefly makes an appearance. The larger part of the novel consists of internal soliloquies on the part of various intellectual figures who recount their experiences of suffering during the Cultural Revolution and narrate their divergent responses to a crisis brought about by a prospective publication entitled *Marxism and Humanism*, whose author, He Jingfu, having suffered as a rightist, argues for a reinstatement of the human as a foundational principle of Marxism. The formal organization of the novel informs its validation of the individual conscience as a source of ethical value, structured according to the internal monologues and reflections of various characters at the university where the novel is set, also encompassing the romantic relations between these intellectuals. One such character is Sun Yue, the party secretary of the department to which He Jingfu also belongs, and with whom He Jingfu enjoyed a romantic relationship. In a chapter where Sun Yue expresses her anxieties surrounding the book and its repudiation by more orthodox party members, as well as her feelings toward He Jingfu, she mourns that "over the last years, because of the spread of 'class struggle' into every aspect of life, we had hardly any private life left."[3] As Sun Yue eventually exits the cadre meeting to see He Jingfu, she moves through a garden that has fallen into disrepair because "the gardeners weren't willing to work until their pay had been settled—a question of the 'relations of production.'" Sun Yue reflects: "Were there problems in the relations of production in the realm of thought? If they weren't sorted out, a smooth green lawn could become a tangle of weeds." The gardeners to which Sun refers do not make an appearance, the narrative being focused on the lives of these intellectuals, and neither is this problem of the relations of production expanded upon. The brief suggestion in this context of the lives of laborers and the social relations through which their labor is organized is fleeting, appearing only at the moment where an intellectual crosses from the university to the private home of a fellow intellectual. Even at the moment of its appearance, the problem of the relations of production is rapidly converted into a banal metaphor and enclosed within the "realm of thought," available for the self-pity of the intellectual, performing an act of narrative expropriation, albeit one that gestures toward a larger set of social transformations. The intellectual takes the place of the laborer as the subject of narrative, justified by a universal appeal to the human.

In the late 1970s, before the publication of Dai Houying's novel, Chinese theorists met the young Marx. They did so through the 1979 publication of volume 42 of the *Marx-Engels Collected Works*, which was among the first collections in Chinese to publish a full version of Marx's famous *1844 Economic and Philosophical Manuscripts*. These remain the primary textual locus for humanist Marxism, whereby Marx draws on Hegelian categories of alienation to explicate the effects of the capitalist division of labor and the divorce between subjects and the products of their work. Before the 1970s, the *Manuscripts* had been published in part or in full at various moments during the socialist period. A partial translation by He Sijing and Zong Baihua 宗白华 under the title "Alienated Labor," drawn from the first manuscript, was published in *New Construction* in 1955, followed in 1956 by the first full translation. Among those intellectuals who had engaged with the *Manuscripts* at this earlier juncture, several of them reemerged amid the newfound hegemony of humanist Marxism in the 1980s. Of these, Zhu Guangqian became central to the recodification of the humanist Marx after the Cultural Revolution. Zhu published his own partial translation of the *Manuscripts* concerning communism and unalienated labor in the Shanghai-based journal *Aesthetics* in 1980 as part of the second issue. Yet, the introduction of the *Manuscripts* and circulation of ideas of labor humanism at this juncture possess a political specificity that requires caution against the seductive appeal of a language of a communist society characterized by a plenitude of unalienated labor and a common humanity. The political deployment of these texts in the early postsocialist period marked a shift in the conception of the social relations of writing that was directly opposed to the Maoist program of social transformation.

The discourse of Marxist or socialist humanism as it arose in the late 1970s and early 1980s enabled two interlinked shifts, which, taken together, amounted to the closure of the Maoist program of cultural production based around the transformation of the intellectual. In the first place, humanism enabled a new conception of the aesthetic in which the aesthetic was deprived of the problematic of divergent class horizons in which it had previously been situated, and instead celebrated as transcending class, based on an understanding of labor itself as an aesthetic act, as opposed to the transformative force of the aesthetic as the basis on which to transform social relations.[4] In the second place, the projection of the writer as a practitioner of "spiritual labor" posed the classification of writing as labor as a merely formal problem, whereby labor itself was withdrawn from the concrete problems of social relations and instead reduced to an abstraction that could accommodate writing as labor in and of itself without posing the question and problem of the division between mental and manual labor. In these terms, any critical insights that a return to the early Marx might have generated were ultimately subsumed within a very different set of political priorities. The delinking of problems of aesthetics and the culture worker from class struggle and social transformation were central to Zhu Guangqian's 1979 article "On the Questions of Human Nature, Humanism, Human Sentiment and Universal Beauty," which was among the first texts to take up the discourse of humanism. Zhu's essay takes the form of a call for the opening of several "forbidden areas" to theoretical discussion, all of which are centered on the problem of the capacity for creative labor as the foundation of a universal humanism. As against the Maoist conception of human nature as mediated by social relations in the form of "class nature," Zhu cites Marx's *1844 Economic and Philosophical Manuscripts* as evidence that a universal conception of human nature provides the ethical core of Marxism as a political project: "Marx began from the problem of human nature in order to demonstrate the necessity and inevitability of proletarian revolution, proving that it is necessary to abolish the system of private property in order that human beings be able to develop their fundamental capacities to the greatest extent."[5]

The calls for a renewed embrace of human nature, humanism, and human sentiment provide the basis for Zhu's conception of a universal aesthetic horizon that is rooted in labor, considered transhistorically and without any concern for its concrete forms, itself being an aesthetic act. In this discussion, Zhu again invokes the early Marx in order to argue that "Marx affirmed that, because human beings exercise their fundamental manual and spiritual capacities in the course of carrying out both material and spiritual production, they experience joy," it being this elementary joy arising from the performance of labor as an aesthetic act that is said to account for an experience of aesthetic pleasure constitutive of the human as such.[6] The linking of an aesthetic experience of labor to a transhistorical aesthetic universalism provides the first of theoretical transitions in the finer grain of socialist humanism during this period, namely that it is precisely through the affirmation of labor as a kind of ontological state, one that exceeds the reproduction of material life to become an aesthetic experience, that it becomes possible for Zhu to withdraw the problem of culture and indeed of aesthetics from its relation to the problem of transforming social relations. In this context, his running together of mental and manual labor as equally constitutive of aesthetic beauty further anticipates the depoliticization of culture. This argument emerged more radically in an article published the following year, in Zhu's famous book *Letters on Aesthetics* (1980), in which his 1979 article on human nature was also included under a changed title. The 1980 article was appropriately entitled "Art is a Kind of Productive Labor," which accounts for the central argument of the text, namely, the "equivalency" 一致性 of spiritual and manual labor. Zhu quotes at length from the *Manuscripts* that, unlike animals, humans labor not only in order to satisfy immediate bodily needs but also "in accordance with the laws of beauty." Zhu argues on this basis that Marx demonstrates the equivalency of mental and manual labor: "Human beings transform nature through the practice of labor and create a world of objects 对象世界. This principle can be applied to material production in industry and agriculture, and so too can it be applied in relation to the spiritual production that encompasses art and literature."[7]

The articulation of cultural production as a mode of spiritual production that is equivalent to material production in its realization of the propensities of human beings toward labor here marks a further extension of the rationale embodied in the treatment of joyful labor as the site of a universal aesthetic, whereby it is the very equivalency of mental and manual labor that allows for the problem of the transformation of cultural production, or the gap between mental and manual labor, to be elided. The evasion of this central problem proceeds not via the denial of writing as labor, but rather by a process of formal reduction and abstraction, in which labor itself becomes a merely formal signifier, divorced from any meaningful set of political referents. The formula of writing as "spiritual labor" suspended a whole set of problems and practices that informed cultural production during the socialist period. In this article and that following, entitled "Questions of Aesthetics in Marx's *Economic and Philosophical Manuscripts*," published in *Aesthetics* alongside Zhu's own partial translation of the *Manuscripts*, Zhu displays an admittedly sophisticated knowledge of Marx's account of alienation, finely deploying such concepts as species-being. He also situates Marx's understanding of alienation in relation to theoretical precedents such as Hegel and Feuerbach. But so too does he frequently refer to the problem of how to situate the theoretical problems of alienation and creative labor contained in the *Manuscripts*. It is this problem that in fact marks the most politically salient part of Zhu's work, comprising a practice of reading Marx which was to remain central to subsequent elaborations of socialist humanism in terms that shed close light on that theoretical discourse in its relation to the "late Marxism" of the socialist period. Zhu argued that the ideas of alienation and creative labor embodied in the early Marx of the *1844 Manuscripts* not only did not recede in Marx's mature thought but were rather the key to understanding the conceptual vocabulary of *Capital*, such that problems of surplus value, exploitation, and revolution were effectively reduced to a humanist vocabulary of alienation and alienation substituted for the problematics of class struggle, socialist revolution, and anti-revisionism.[8] This practice of reading amounted to a wholesale reconstitution of Marxism, the political rationale of which lay in the excision of the central Maoist problem of "bourgeois right," which was, at this very moment, being extinguished from political discourse. The formulation of labor humanism in terms of a vision of free labor, therefore, marked a problematic of "freedom" wholly different to that not only of Maoism but also He-Yin Zhen, for whom free labor was marked not by a plenitude of the human but by freedom from the wage-relation. The promulgation of free labor as unalienated labor in these terms provided the condition for the reabsorption of labor back into the wage form as the point of departure for a wholesale restoration of capitalism.

Zhu's elaboration of alienation as the foundational category of Marxism and concomitant closure of problems of socialist political economy provided the opening for Wang Ruoshui's 王若水 more famous interventions into the discussions around humanism, which were also responsible for popularizing a vocabulary of alienation. The terms in which Wang thought through the category of alienation similarly disclose the political imperatives that informed the whole discourse of which he was a part. In his famous 1980 article, entitled "The Human is the Point of Departure for Marxism," included in the major 1981 volume of the same name, Wang followed Zhu in arguing that Marx's discussions around surplus value in *Capital* were to be understood as the recurrent problem of alienated labor.[9] In doing so, he marked the closure of the socialist-era discussions around that problem of the wage form, accumulation, and remuneration which had been investigated under the conceptual framework of bourgeois right. The deployment of a language of alienation in these terms informed Wang's other interventions of the same period. In his "On Problems of Alienation," therefore, Wang argues that alienation is present in China, but its manifestations are, in his terms, the alienation of thought, politics, and the economy, above all phenomena of Mao worship from the Cultural Revolution. In taking stock of the problem of alienation under socialism, Wang argued that this problem demonstrates that "not all problems can be solved simply through the formation of a system of public ownership."[10] It was, in fact, precisely problems of this order that the theoretical vocabulary of "bourgeois right" had sought to address, especially through the theoretical discussions around precisely the problem of the state (and Mao's formulation of China as a bourgeois state) at the end of the Cultural Revolution, but which are here folded into a generalized category of alienation that is disjoined from the problematic of transition, including the division of labor, to which the Maoist period had addressed itself. Three years after Zhu himself had advanced an understanding of cultural production as itself labor, Wang also turned directly to the problem of the writer in his 1983 article "Labor—Knowledge—Wealth" to argue that the intellectual was also a laborer. Yet by this point Wang had no need to make recourse to Zhu's vocabulary of "spiritual labor" or labor as an aesthetic act; rather, he resorted to a quasi-biologized conception of labor: "Mental labor is also labor, it also creates value 价值, and possibly even greater value [than manual labor] . . . in actual fact according to scientific research, intellectual labor is by no means less than average manual labor in terms of the expenditure of physiological energy."[11]

The emergent biologization of labor as the basis on which to evade the problem of the transformation of writing marked a step away from the eloquent Marxist humanism of Zhu Guangqian and a shift toward the biologization of the human, developing, at the end of the decade, into a new quasi-evolutionary discourse in which the masculinized intellectual was marked not only as equal to the manual worker as a coparticipant in labor defined as an aesthetic or biological act, but rather as a more perfect instance of the human as such. The humanism of Zhu and Wang, to say nothing of the ideologue Li Zehou, was very far from an emancipatory critique of the revolutionary project, then. The cumulative effect of these intellectual shifts concerning the relations between writing, labor, and the tendency toward the reindividuation of cultural production became visible at the Fourth Writers Congress, held in 1984, where Hu Qili stated in his opening address that "literary creation is a kind of spiritual labor. The fruits of this work are the clear personal characteristics of the writer. Individual creativity, insight and imagination must therefore be brought into play." Furthermore:

> The writer must have a deep understanding and unique insights concerning life, as well as unique artistic skills. Therefore, creation must be free. This is to say, that the author must use their mind 头脑 in order to think 思维, they must have the freedom to select materials, their topic and means of artistic expression, and sufficient freedom to express their feelings, passions and express their thoughts, in order that they might write works capable of influencing and educating people.[12]

The positing in this context of writing as not only a form of "spiritual labor" but also the injunction that writers should use their "mind" as the point of departure for the practice of writing itself marks a decorporealization of writing, and the incorporation to that degree of the language of labor humanism otherwise associated with Zhu Guangqian and Wang Ruoshui. The shifts on the terrain of political economy to which these conceptual innovations corresponded in political terms consisted of a wholesale repudiation of the theoretical problem of the wage as thrown up by the socialist period and the Cultural Revolution in particular. The intellectual grounds for this repudiation proceeded in the form of a restoration of "remuneration according to labor" as the basic standard of remuneration under socialism, here conceived not as a totality of contradictory social forms and relations but as a stable mode of production that would enable a more rapid pace of economic development, and later divided into "primary" and "mature" stages. The effect of these arguments was to delink the problem of remuneration according to labor on the one hand from the problems of the wage form and bourgeois right on the other, effectively consigning the vocabulary of bourgeois right to the category of ultraleftism, and the "Critique of the Gotha Program" to a marginal status, as the basis for the Maoist reading of Marx that, unlike the *1844 Manuscripts*, could not be reconciled with the reform period.[13] So too did the anti-Maoist theorists at this juncture also seek to disentangle the socialist wage and capitalist wage from each other, arguing through the familiar vocabulary that wage payments under socialism differed in not being based on the sale of labor power as a commodity, marking a return to the Soviet orthodoxy of the early 1950s.[14] The impetus of these theoretical shifts was not only formally and historically parallel to the discourse around cultural production embodied in the ideas of labor humanism, but also, in turn, came to inform the reconstitution of the author in isolation from physical labor. Just as the entry of the vocabulary of bourgeois right in 1958 was intimately bound up with the problem of culture, so too did the recodification of remuneration according to labor in the late 1970s also have direct implications for the ongoing depoliticization of the relations between cultural and manual labor. In 1983, therefore, in an article titled "The Reform of Art and Literature and Artistic Quality" published in *Theoretical Trends*, Guo Rui drew on the language of "spiritual labor" to insist on the inviolability of writing and that authors and artists needed time under their own jurisdiction to conduct their craft: "A pressing question that must be solved by the reform of art and culture is the further implementation of the socialist principle of remuneration, 'from each according to their abilities, to each according to their labor,' whereby we might change the long-term policy of 'eating from the communal pot' and pursuing an irrational phenomenon of egalitarianism, and improve the material circumstances of culture workers."[15] These and other developments preceded the mass privatization of state enterprises in the 1990s, the full marketization of cultural production and its attendant soul-searching among intellectuals, the acceleration of the tempo of factory labor, or the conversion of the peasantry into a mobile supply of labor power for a new process of accumulation, but approaching labor after socialism from the angle of cultural production demonstrates the astonishing rapidity with which the politics of socialist labor were dismantled, enabled, to a very large extent, by a depoliticized discourse of labor humanism. Zhang Chunqiao and his comrades were right in arguing that social relations of labor are not reducible to a formal question of ownership and in their predictions that with the defeat of the alternative China would rapidly change its color and revert to capitalism. The fundamental moment of defeat for the Chinese Revolution was therefore the end of the Cultural Revolution in 1976 in the way that it marked the negation of the fundamental bases of the Maoist project of transforming society and life. Yet there remained those who resisted the total repudiation of the Maoist experiment.

The last Maoist

Ding Ling was present in Yan'an at the foundational moment of Maoist cultural politics, and so too do her interventions in that context, around the problem of the "double life," mark her sensitivity toward the challenges of overcoming the division between mental and manual labor. In ways true of no other intellectual figure, Ding Ling took seriously and grappled with the challenges, provocations, possibilities, and gaps of the Maoist cultural project.

Recognizing her in these terms provides a necessary counterpoint to the banal racialized and gendered discourse that cannot imagine the experiences of radical Chinese women under Maoism in any terms other than the liberal politics of moralized victimhood. This discursive apparatus marks a refusal to engage with the Ding Ling who wrestled with actually existing Maoism, to say nothing of her complex role in the literary system of the early 1950s, a literary system that so often turned her into a hack in the struggles that preceded her own downfall and expulsion from the ranks of professional writers. Her trajectory of writing over the 1960s, 1970s, and into the postsocialist 1980s therefore marks a subterranean current of struggles with a set of demands for the transformation of writing that ultimately proved irreconcilable. Central to this current is her late, fictional work "Du Wanxiang" (1979), which derived from her encounters of a real-life figure in the Great Northern Wilderness. In view of the ways that this book has stressed the problem of the temporality of writing, this work is distinguished by a temporality of writing that exceeds all others in its duration and recursive nature. Having begun writing this text in 1965, Ding Ling chose to rewrite it in 1977, being eventually published in 1979. The story of "Du Wanxiang" is suggestively simple, consisting of the tale of a single peasant woman, organized in linear fashion, charting her temporal and spatial movement from her rural home to the extremities of socialist China. Having been born to the countryside and losing her mother at a young age, Du Wanxiang is married into a family from Lijia Hollow, only to ultimately follow her husband, Li Gui, to the Great Northern Wilderness. The story takes up her emergence as a communist laborer. Yet the simplicity of the text simply at the level of the story contrasts with several formal features or even absences that attest to its importance as the last fictional work of Ding Ling's sustained encounter with the Maoist project.

These include, in the first place, the organization of the text according to a series of unnumbered chapter headings. Throughout the earlier part of the narrative, these headings also mark a series of key changes in the life of the protagonist that constitute the temporal organization of the text, and which bear directly either on Du's role as a woman born to a peasant society, or else on the key political shifts in the state history of the People's Republic. The second of the headings, for example, "Being a Wife," marks Du Wanxiang's shift from her birth home to that of her husband, in Lijia Hollow. In the second part of the narrative, that dealing with Du's experience of the Great Northern Wilderness, these headings come to mark not so much top-level political changes or life transitions as they do the different facets of Du's experience in the wilderness. In close tandem with the organization of the text in terms of temporality, however, is, as its second distinguishing formal feature, the distinct absence of any confident interrogation or narrative exposition of Du's life through practices of narrative interiority or subjectivity. At a formal level, there is a distinct absence of such conventional literary stratagems as interior speech, psycho-narration, free indirect style, or even much semblance of strict focalization. The stripping-away of the conventional trappings and devices of interior life—with scant exceptions—is rendered yet more visible by the fact that when instances of, for example, psycho-narration do emerge, they do so largely in relation to other characters. When, for example, in the first of the crucial transitions that mark Du Wanxiang's journey, she leaves for the home of her marital parents, her father is rendered as "thinking of how he had failed her deceased mother by not looking out for this young girl in accordance with her wishes." The same is true of free indirect style. When, for example, the village first learns of how Li Gui has been sent to the Great Northern Wilderness in 1958 and has requested via letter for Du Wanxiang to join him, there follow a series of unmarked interjections: "Could she really go? This Northern Wilderness, Northern Wilderness, where was it anyway? It was said that it was an extremely cold place, where it snowed in June, where people froze to death in winter or were blown away by the wind, where if you touched your nose or ears, they would fall off."[16]

The voice that emerges through these unmarked interventions is, in its narrative context, that of the village community as a whole rather than Du Wanxiang herself. The refusal, then, of interiority as it relates to Du Wanxiang derives its formal significance from what it means for her configuration as a communist laborer. This may be more closely observed at the level of content through the recurrent invocations of motherhood in the text, which in turn relates to how the use of chapter headings organizes the narrative of Du Wanxiang's life. It is by no means insignificant, in these terms, that Du Wanxiang is introduced in the first segment as having lost her mother at a young age. Motherhood thereafter appears repeatedly as a topos in the rest of the narrative, yet it does so in modes that refuse a narrowly biological or familial concept of motherhood, and instead invests motherhood—or, more appropriately, mothering—with a transformative, political significance. Even when, early in the narrative, Du Wanxiang departs for her marital family, it is compared explicitly to a mother figure: "as an orphan who had lost her mother, her parents, brothers and sisters in law were simply another kind of stepmother." Yet more significant is the invocation of motherhood in the following section, which, entitled "Mother Returns," announces the formation of the People's Republic and the ensuing transformation of the countryside through Du's relationship with a member of a work team: "at this time, a work team arrived to review the land reform. In the team there was a middle-aged woman who was lodged at the home of Wanxiang and slept with Wanxiang on the *kang*."[17] This encounter gives rise to a summary of Du's exposure to the revolution that is rendered explicitly in the language of motherhood and care: "Truly, it was as if Du Wanxiang had returned to her mother's embrace. Now, there were people to care for her, look after her, who were full of hope for her. She was like a child learning to walk before her mother, taking a step, then looking around, feeling that all around her there were people watching her closely, exerting themselves on her behalf, encouraging her."[18]

In this instance, the party, as actualized in the female work team member, assumes a mothering role in relation to Du Wanxiang herself, such that Wanxiang emerges as the object of maternal care. In the latter parts of the narrative, however, during her period in the Great Northern Wilderness, Du herself assumes the role of a laborer whose practice also becomes legible through a universal mode of motherhood. This is labor in the bodily mode as a form of care that Du Wanxiang assumes in her formal role as a family dependent, in the way that she volunteers, for example, to clean the latrines on behalf of other families, or when she assists sent-down youth despite their initial hostility against her. In the latter case, her conduct is explicated in the specific language of motherhood: "when it was necessary for her to sympathize with them, she was like a mother, when she had to be stern, she was like a teacher."[19] Du Wanxiang's shift toward communist labor in a maternal mode is in turn accompanied by a shift in the temporal framing of the narrative via a shift from singular events, such as Du Wanxiang's marriage, to the iterative, in which her labor takes on the form of a repetitive, daily process. The following passage is indicative of this shift, summarizing the role that she acquires in the Wilderness:

> As Du Wanxiang immersed herself in a labor full of happiness, there was no sense of exhaustion or hunger. When everyone else rested, she did not rest. When everyone else ate, her hands and feet did not cease. When it came to those workers and family dependents who participated in labor at the threshing floor, there were some whose wages were calculated on a piece work basis, others on a time basis, but her wages were not based either on time or on piece work. All those present at the threshing floor looked upon this woman with eyes of curiosity, a woman who was not tall in stature, whose body was by no means strong, but who always bore a faint smile. They wondered how she could be possessed of inexhaustible energy, wondered why there shone on her ordinary 平平常常 face such a sublime, solemn and pure light, such as to draw everyone's attention.[20]

The depiction of Du Wanxiang in these terms is posed, moreover, from the focalized position of other women, accompanied by fragments of psycho-narration—"they wondered"—that are similarly not the property of Du Wanxiang herself. The contents of this passage are distinguished by the way that Du Wanxiang's labor even in the agricultural context is articulated in terms of her refusal of the wage form and all standards of remuneration, being, therefore, labor unconstrained by bourgeois right. This passage also establishes a further distinct rhetorical topos of the text, which is that of the "ordinary" or "quotidian," a topos that is also marked at the formal level through the depiction of labor as an iterative, recurrent process, linked to the temporalities of the everyday. With the understanding that Du Wanxiang's husband was dispatched to the wilderness in 1958, any clear indication of how Du's ongoing pursuit of communist labor might be temporally mapped onto the formal calendrical year is left unclear until the final section, when Du Wanxiang is said to have started work at the Cultural Palace in 1964, which in turn sets up the conditions for the conclusion of the narrative in the form of a speech. In contrast to previous instances of speech-giving, Du Wanxiang reportedly insists that this speech should be of her own composition: "thereupon she decided to start a new draft, whereby she would draw out the threads from her thinking and use the words that she herself understood to speak forth the language of her heart." The invocation, in this context, of the contents of the heart marks a contrast to the otherwise consistent avoidance of any language or formal interrogation of subjectivity and interiority throughout the text. The speech as it is narrated, however, both through indirect and direct speech, makes manifest the extent to which the understanding of "heart" as posed here is precisely not that of a bounded subjectivity but rather consists of the invocation and articulation of those social relations in whose formation Du Wanxiang has come to play a key role. The opening segment of the speech, conveyed through indirect speech and concerned with Du Wanxiang's childhood, then, records that "she had dreamed of a different kind of world, a different kind of life 生活, and different kinds of relations between human beings 人与人的关系."[21] The climax to the speech marks the single most extended instance of direct speech from Du Wanxiang across the narrative:

> I am a common 普通 person and do ordinary 平凡 things of the kind that everyone 人人 can do. Anything I can understand, the fact that I am here today, is solely on account of you, you comrades who pursue diligent labor, and those people with ideals who have inspired me, encouraged me. All of us have received the education and cultivation of the party. I only hope that I will be able to commit my whole life to the communist enterprise under the leadership of the party, acting resolutely in accordance with the needs of the party and seeking truth from facts.[22]

The repetition here of various formulations of the ordinary is joined with a repudiation of any suggestion of Du Wanxiang's singular heroism and a willing abnegation of the self, a process recapitulated in the narrative commentary that follows, in the way that Du Wanxiang is herself said to have emerged from collective forms of communist labor, and to have actualized Mao's own classical injunctions: "Du Wanxiang had not simply cited the classics, but the ideas and formulations of those classical texts had rather come to be infused 融合 in her simple speech. Just like crops absorb the sunlight and rain, so too had good people, good things and good words come to seep into her soul and blood, rooting her in the soil, and allowing her to resist any ills that might assail her."[23] The fusion of communist ideas into the person of Du Wanxiang is, then, joined with the recurrent topos of motherhood and care work to make a claim on the contents of the communist new human. These narrative topoi can be read in conjunction with specific formal features, namely the refusal to construct Du Wanxiang in terms of the conventional devices of narrative interiority. There remains a studied distance between the voice of the narrator and the position of Du Wanxiang herself insofar as the narrator refuses to abrogate or assume any knowledge of Du Wanxiang's subjectivity or psyche. In these terms, this text marks Ding Ling's attempt to articulate the possibility of communist labor in terms that resist the falling back into a reified language of heroic subjectivity of the kind that emerges through the novels of the late Cultural Revolution, as well as the narcissistic modes of intellectual interiority that informed other texts of the early reform period. The articulation of communist relations of labor, then, it may be said from "Du Wanxiang," is not a singular but an iterative process, based on the everyday expansion of those sectors of life that are not governed by the wage form and for which the figure of a universal motherhood of care work provides a compelling model. The paratextual essay that Ding Ling wrote to accompany her fictional text, entitled "On 'Du Wanxiang,'" is distinguished by the extension of a language of universal motherhood into her own encounter:

> In the summer of 1964, when the wheat harvest was nearing completion, I took a visit to this farm from another farm, and the head of the farm took me to see the production team, above all in order to introduce me to the female crack troop of the seventh team, comrade Du Wanxiang. I was eager to see her, but when I went to her home during the day, she was not there. When the evening had come and the lamps had been lit, I went again, and she was there, with the whole family sitting around the *kang* eating dinner. Du Wanxiang greeted me with kindness, and at the same time carefully served her marital parents some food, which tasted dearly sweet to the mouth, clearly this was a virtuous woman.[24]

The presentation of Du Wanxiang in terms of being a "virtuous woman" as a rhetorical gesture here marks a gesture with which He-Yin Zhen would have been familiar, namely an appropriation of the organization of gendered labor around "livelihood" as that which is autonomous from the wage form, as the basis for imagining communist labor. Yet this echo with He-Yin Zhen registers, in turn, the contradictions and tensions of Ding Ling's turn to Du

Wanxiang, which is to say her status as an emblem of communist labor remains inextricably bound up with her formal status as a family dependent in the gendered division of labor. Ding Ling's late works sustain this contradiction as one that the prior history of socialist revolution did not overcome. So too does the suggestion of an intimate meeting between Du Wanxiang and Ding Ling recall Ding Ling's earlier, narrative instances of intimacy between women—not least her recollections of her encounters with Xiao Hong—as a point of departure for the reshaping of life. It is not surprising, then, that in this same essay, 'Concerning 'Du Wanxiang,' " Ding Ling also recapitulates the critical vocabulary that she mobilized in the 1940s and 1950s and which first emerged in her essay on Xiao Hong, namely the figure of "double life." The ultimate condition for writing, states Ding Ling, is that the writer "must first of all enter the hearts of those characters themselves, they must understand them, be familiar with them, experience them, and learn from them, and raise one's own feelings, otherwise writing will simply be impossible." She goes on:

> The raising of which I speak here means that one must rupture with the circle of one's old life, must constantly break through the circle of one's own life. My family background can hardly be considered as good, even though we were poor. When I was young I had some progressive education, and was committed to revolution, but there were also many old things bequeathed to me by feudal society. In the 1920s, I began writing in Shanghai, with some initial success. But even as I wrote I got bogged down in a particular place and could not further advance. Why? Precisely because I only lived within this kind of small circle of life, because those with whom I had contact, those things of which I gained experience, were restricted solely to this small circle, and I could not break out of that circle. Afterward I compelled myself, pressed myself, and forced myself to go to the worker districts, to go to the factories, to go to the worker dormitories. I did not go that much, but I did go somewhat, and broke through to some degree. Afterward, when I came to Shaanbei, I broke through to a greater extent.[25]

The invocation in this content of Ding Ling's attempt to break out of the narrow, small circle of life in which she was located amid the literary scene of the 1920s enacts, for the final time, the discursive trope that recurs in her earlier writing, namely the problem of how writing comes to be structured in a "double life" based on the bifurcation between the time of writing and the time of mass, collective life. Here, however, there is a specific temporal dimension to Ding Ling's insight in the way she stretches out the temporality of overcoming the bifurcation of the double life so that it comes to encompass her own, total life, becoming, in other words, the sustained, drawn-out project of a lifetime.

The increasing extent to which Ding Ling succeeded in breaking out of the circle of intellectual life has no definitive point of closure because it is incumbent in the very process of individual writing that it possesses its own rhythm, its own logic, that cannot be straightforwardly or permanently assimilated to the conditions of mass life. It marks, for Ding Ling, as for us, a communist horizon, that orients Maoist cultural practice, and one that is homologous with Du Wanxiang's extension through time of the labor of universal motherhood in the building of communism. These possibilities and aspirations ultimately cohere in Ding Ling's reflections published in her posthumous 1987 volume *Living Among Wind and Snow* with which this conclusion began, to pose a conception of labor as the basis of sociability. Her repeated desires to engage in labor emerge in the midst of this text as part of Ding Ling's descriptions of the violence abuse meted out during the Cultural Revolution, and her being consigned to the "cowshed," followed by her being permitted to engage in labor under mass supervision. She writes that amid the contradictions of this period:

> Yet I was still able to reassure and comfort myself with the fact that there remained a sliver of hope. It was nothing else, other than the fact that, no matter what might come to pass, I would no longer be cooped up inside a dark room, and that instead I would see the sun. I would be able to labor under the sun. Labor is exhausting, labor is bitter, yet in labor I can also derive happiness. Under the sun, too, the sunlight that I had desired for so long! In 1958 I had decided to leave Beijing to come to the Northeast to labor. In labor I had derived happiness. Now, I was once again going to labor. I truly wished that it should be so. I believe that when people engage in common labor 共同劳动 it is possible to generate a shared feeling 共同感情. Labor can break down those barriers erected by human beings and bridge the heart melodies 心曲 of the self and the other 彼此. This was what I desired.[26]

Labor, being exhausting, being bitter, is not the embodiment of a pregiven human essence, or the possibility of a plenitude of creative expression. It is, rather, for Ding Ling, as for the very best in the Chinese revolutionary tradition, the basis for the collective reproduction of the very conditions of our sociality, the site of practice that provides the possibility of new kinds of affective, social, and cultural relations to each other, including new relations—relations of friendship—between writers and the masses. It is also, in the same terms, the breaking down of any closed or atomistic subjectivity in favor of the melding of the self and the other. Labor in common enables a "we" in place of the "I." Ding Ling's emphatic statement—"this was what I desired"—is, like the instances invoked on the first page of this book, a mode of communist desire, the kind that cannot be buried, the kind that endures in spite of everything, the kind that demands the possibility of a life in common. Between

Ding Ling's late text "Du Wanxiang," her paratext relating her encounter with Du Wanxiang and her own history of writing, and her recollections of the Cultural Revolution, it becomes possible to glimpse the contours of a socialist or communist mode of temporality. Having foregrounded the problem of temporality at the outset, this book has nonetheless held at a distance the question of what a stable noncapitalist temporality might entail, let alone how it might be actualized. That this is so lies in the fact that any such attempts at operationalizing any such temporality too often ran the risk of falling into the very capitalist temporality from which Chinese revolutionaries sought to escape, not least through the coercive hypermobilization of labor or the impossible demands for feats of individual self-sacrifice.

Ding Ling's final work nonetheless sketches, in outline, a time of communism. This is no longer a unified or synchronized temporality unified under the state, including in the form of the Writers Association as ISA, in the interests of a project of development, but rather in the mode of a disjuncture from the state, and in the inauguration of a long, stretched temporality, in which we pursue the cultivation of islets of communist relations in the space of the everyday. Du Wanxiang, for Ding Ling, provides the contents of a communist practice and temporality of labor, in all its and her tensions and contradictions. This final attempt at writing communist time also encompasses a moment of tragedy, because Ding Ling's final work underlines that the overcoming of the temporal division between writing as cultural labor on the other hand and other forms of social practice could only remain a horizon, one that Ding Ling herself could pursue but never reach, stretched as it was over a whole life. It was the very persistence of the temporal autonomy of writing that provided the conditions for her imagining of the contents of a communist temporality. Her and our tragedy, then, lies in the fact that a capacity to sketch the time of communism—indeed, a communist horizon, which includes overcoming the division of mental and manual labor—reposed the irreducibility of writing as solitary, atomized, and too often devastatingly lonely cultural labor. As such, the possibility of overcoming her double life, that division between the life of the communist militant and the life of the solitary writer, remained, to the end, a question, a hope—her and our communist desire.

Communist pasts, communist futures

Ding Ling could not provide solutions to the multitude of challenges thrown up by the Chinese Revolution, because the problems to which she gestured—the double life that structured her experience as a writer and as a revolutionary—were and are ultimately irreconcilable. Nor can this book hope to provide answers to the contradictions and challenges with which Ding Ling grappled.

Yet her insistence on labor as nothing less than the conditions of the social, as the slow, ordinary working out of that which is common, as the basis of a universality not bound to the logic of capital, situates her as one who remained a part of the emancipatory promise of the Chinese Revolution. In this regard, insofar as much of the argument here has been concerned with excavating the contents of communist labor, as that which is truly universal, no longer being limited to the wage form, she reminds us of those glimpses of the world we want to see as they occur not only in her writing but also other moments in Chinese socialist culture. I have frequently returned here to moments in Chinese literary production of intimacy amid gendered labor: the household weavers of Yan'an, the reimagining of the factory in the fiction of Bai Lang in the early 1950s, the transformations of family life in the stories of Li Zhun during the Great Leap, the narratives of care and dependency of Ru Zhijuan in the early 1960s, and even those brief moments that inhabit the fiction of the Cultural Revolution. Their importance lies in the fact that, to a far greater extent than, for example, the moments of totalizing and hyperaestheticized heroism with which the novels of the Cultural Revolution conclude or the envisaging of male, factory labor as the basis of socialist production, it is these narrative texts that provide the grounds for feminist practices of labor embodying the possibility of the supersession of the wage form to which Maoist theorists such as Zhang Chunqiao aspired. This supersession emerges not through a singular moment of rupture but rather through the daily practices of care and lived dependency that assist in the mutual transformation of their participants. In this context, the failure, within the course of the Chinese socialist experiment, to solve the problem of reproduction in a meaningful way, or even to recognize the reproductive labor of women as labor, contributed to the defeat of the socialist project, and yet so too do the cultural inscriptions of this labor, by virtue of it being orientated toward the care of the other and always already outside of the wage relation, mark it as containing the possibilities for universalization that He-Yin Zhen recognized. The adequate model of communist labor is not ultimately that of the single moment of heroism but the repeated, normal, ordinary modes of caring labor that assist in enabling the capacities of the other and contain the hints of the world we want to see.

I have sought throughout this book to remind us of other worlds, other times, other rhythms of writing and labor. It is written in a spirit of critical—but unapologetic—solidarity with communist projects of past, present, and future. I hope and desire that I have therefore contributed in a small way to the renewal of a communist politics that might ultimately be able to draw on the revolutionary experiments of the past in order to pose new answers, if not definitive solutions, to the contradictions of their times and ours, so that future generations might one day cleanse life of all evil, oppression, and violence and enjoy it to the fullest.

NOTES

Introduction

Epigraph: Ding Ling 丁玲, "Xuexi di yi ge wunian jihua caoan de yidian ganxiang" 学习第一个五年计划草案的一点感想 (Feelings upon studying the draft of the first five-year plan), in *Ding Ling quanji* 丁玲全集 (Ding Ling collected works), ed. Zhang Jiong 张炯 (Shijiazhuang: Hebei renmin chubanshe, 2001), 7:439–41.

1. Ding Ling 丁玲, "Dao bei dahuang qu" 到北大荒去 (To the great northern wilderness), in *Ding Ling quanji*, 10:113–63.
2. The posing here and elsewhere of the problem of writing as a *relation* of literary production is intended to foreground writing as itself part of a constellation of social relations, as a counterpoint to a subjectivist conception of writing. For a further development of the category of the "literary mode of production" on this point, see Terry Eagleton, *Criticism and Ideology* (London: Verso, 1976).
3. Cai Xiang, *Revolution and Its Narratives: China's Socialist Literary and Cultural Imaginaries, 1949–1966*, trans. Rebecca Karl and Zhong Xueping (Durham, NC: Duke University Press, 2016), xiv.
4. The two landmarks of scholarship with respect to prose literature are Richard King, *Milestones on a Golden Road* (Vancouver: UBC Press, 2013), and Krista Van Fleit Hang, *Literature the People Love* (New York: Palgrave Macmillan, 2013). For a further exploration of the political underpinnings of modern Chinese literature as a discipline, see Kang Liu, "Politics, Critical Paradigms: Reflections on Modern Chinese Literature Studies," *Modern China* 19, no. 1 (1993): 13–40.
5. Louis Althusser, *Reading Capital*, trans. Ben Brewster (London: New Left Books, 1970), 99–100.
6. Althusser, *Reading Capital*, 105.
7. Caroline Levine, *Forms: Whole, Rhythm, Hierarchy, Network*. (Princeton, NJ: Princeton University Press, 2015), 53, 74.

8. Louis Althusser, *On the Reproduction of Capitalism: Ideology and Ideological State Apparatuses*, trans. G. M. Goshgarian (London: Verso, 2014), 91.
9. Althusser, *Reproduction*, 91.
10. Without here seeking to encompass a whole set of political debates, I would point out the radical departure from any alleged metaphysics of labor or political program based on the emancipation of labor in work such as Moishe Postone's *Time, Labor and Social Domination* (Cambridge: Cambridge University Press, 1996) versus the persistence of older traditions of Lukacsian-derived labor humanism, represented by Bruno Gulli, *Labor of Fire* (Philadelphia: Temple University Press, 2005).
11. He-Yin Zhen, "On the Question of Women's Labor," in *The Birth of Chinese Feminism: Essential Texts in Transnational Theory*, ed. Lydia H. Liu, Rebecca E. Karl, and Dorothy Ko (New York: Columbia University Press, 2013), 76.
12. He-Yin Zhen, "The Feminist Manifesto," in Liu, Karl, and Ko, eds., *The Birth of Chinese Feminism*, 180–81.
13. He-Yin Zhen, "Women's Labor," 77.
14. In these terms, He-Yin Zhen directly anticipates some of the most important observations of Marxist feminists. Mariarosa Dalla Costa, for example, in her famous essay "Women and the Subversion of Community," writes that "in precapitalist patriarchal society, *the home and the family* were central to agricultural and artisanal production. With the advent of capitalism, the socialization of production was organized with the factory as its center." Mariarosa Dalla Costa, *Women and the Subversion of Community* (Oakland, CA: PM Press, 2019), 20.
15. He-Yin Zhen, "Women's Labor," 78–81.
16. Liu Shipei 刘师培, "Lun zhongguo zuzhi laomin xiehui" 论中国组织劳民协会 (Concerning the desirability of an association of the laboring masses in China), in Liu Shipei 刘师培, *Guocui yu xihua Liu Shipei wenxuan* 国粹与西化 刘师培文选 (National essence and westernization: Liu Shipei selected works) (Shanghai: Shanghai dongyuan chubanshe 1996), 270.
17. Liu Shipei, "Lun nongye yu gongye lianhe zhi kexing yu Zhongguo" 论农业与工业联合制可行于中国 (Concerning the possibility of a unified system of agriculture and industry in China), in Liu, *Guocui yu xihua Liu Shipei wenxuan*, 282.
18. He-Yin Zhen, "Women's Labor," 91.
19. The significance of the framing of "free labor" in these terms, that is, in terms that interrupted the naturalization of wage labor, lies partly in the fact that the developmental discourse of nationalist modernization projects was characterized by precisely this naturalization. Andy Liu, then, writes in relation to Indian nationalist politics of the late nineteenth century that "Indian nationalists, living in an increasingly commercial and industrialized society, pushed for abolition [of indentured labor] on the reasoning that a free labor system was more economically rational than indenture," the campaign being defined by an opposition between "free versus unfree labor." The Indian valorization of contractual labor in these terms was accompanied by a Chinese reformist discourse of "productive" versus "unproductive" forms of economic activity that had a similar naturalizing function. Andy Liu, *Tea War: A History of Capitalism in China and India* (New Haven, CT: Yale University Press, 2020), 197.
20. Massimiliano Tomba, *Insurgent Universality* (Oxford: Oxford University Press, 2019).
21. Peter Kropotkin, *The Conquest of Bread and Other Writings* (New York: Cambridge University Press, 1995), 113–14.

22. He Zhen 何震, "Lun nvzi dang zhi gongchan zhuyi" 论女子当知共产主义 (What women should know about communism), in *Tianyi hengbao shang* 天义/衡报 上 (Natural justice, equity, part 1), ed. Wan Shiguo 万仕国 and Liu He 刘禾 (Beijing: Zhongguo renmin daxue chubanshe, 2016), 169.
23. Kathi Weeks, *Constituting Feminist Subjects* (Ithaca, NY: Cornell University Press, 1998), 123.
24. Susan Ferguson, "Intersectionality and Social-Production Feminisms: Towards an Integrative Ontology," *Historical Materialism* 2 (2016): 48.
25. Ferguson, "Intersectionality," 51.
26. Alberto Toscano, "Transition Deprogrammed," *South Atlantic Quarterly* 113, no. 4 (2014): 763, 766.
27. Toscano, "Transition," 769.

1. Learning to Write, Learning to Labor

Epigraph: Mao Zedong 毛泽东, "Wenyi gongzuozhe yao tong gongnongbing xiang jiehe" 文艺工作者要同工农兵相结合 (Culture workers must amalgamate with the workers, peasants, and soldiers), in Mao Zedong, *Mao Zedong wenyi lunji* 毛泽东文艺论集 (Mao Zedong collection of writings on art and literature) (Beijing: Zhongyang wenxian chubanshe, 2002), 90.

1. Mark Selden, *The Yenan Way in Revolutionary China* (Cambridge, MA: Harvard University Press, 1971), 177–87.
2. There were, to be sure, incipient critiques of the post–May Fourth conceptions of intellectual practice that emerged even before Mao's Yan'an talks, above all in the form of Qu Qiubai, who critiqued the formal and linguistic construction of even revolutionary literary works as beholden to "Europeanized" modes of writing that were in accessible to the masses.
3. It has been the major achievement of Chinese-language scholarship to tease out the complex relations between the talks and the Soviet literacy legacy on the one hand and the complex conjuncture of Yan'an on the other, with a view to resisting the dismissal or demonization of the talks in the postsocialist era. Li Yang, in an often-cited article, argues for a sustained dialectical movement between the generalized postulates of revolutionary literature and the nation-based project of New Democracy, which altogether constituted China's "antimodern modernity." The ultimate theoretical basis of the talks, they argue, lies in the preceding developments of the urban League of Left-Wing Writers and the Soviet legacy, such that the talks "can all be seen as a direct extension of left-wing literature [in the 1930s] and the proletarian literary theory of the Soviet Union." Li Yang 李杨, "'Jing' yu 'quan': Jianghua de bianzhengfa yu youling zhengzhixue" "经"与"权":《讲话》的辩证法与"幽灵政治学" ("Principle" and "provisional": The dialectics and hauntology of Mao's talks), *Zhongguo xiandai wenxue yanjiu congkan* 中国现代文学研究丛刊 (Modern Chinese Literature Studies) 1 (2013): 6. More recent scholarly interventions have followed Li Yang in resisting the treatment of the talks as a mere statement of policy, and by emphasizing their philosophical content on the subject/object relation between intellectuals and the masses. Zhou Zhanan summarizes this shift in a pithy formulation as follows: "thus, in order to overcome the state of affairs in which the talks have been emptied of their content, it is necessary to distinguish between their role as a 'policy text' and their role as a 'philosophical text,' and to shift from the former to the latter." This means, for Zhou,

situating the talks in a "dialogic" relation with the problem of the subject/object relation between writers and the masses as it arose amid the conjuncture of the War of Resistance, as well as the problem of "civilized" and "barbaric" cultural forms in the longer durée of Chinese history, which is to say the privileging of folks forms hitherto excluded from canonical modes of writing. Zhou Zhanan 周展安, "Zhuke yu wenye" 主客与文野 (Subject/object and civilized/barbaric), *Wenyi lilun yu piping* 文艺理论与批评 (Literacy Theory and Criticism) 3 (2022): 6. The writing of scholars in English altogether lacks any consideration of the talks as a theoretical or philosophical text. Kang Liu, in a study more sensitive than most English-language accounts, recognizes the importance of Mao's treatment of national form, only to argue that the codification of Mao's talks after 1949 inserted them back into the doctrinal straitjacket of socialist realism. Liu Kang, *Aesthetics and Marxism: Chinese Aesthetic Marxists and Their Western Contemporaries* (Durham, NC: Duke University Press, 2000), 92.

4. N. G. Chernishevski, "Life and Esthetics," *International Literature* no. 7 (1935): 55–56.
5. Chernishevski, "Esthetics," 56
6. While in this context Zhou Yang's translation clearly marked the proximate source for the introduction of Chernyshevsky in Yan'an, it is a matter of importance that as early as 1930 Lu Xun introduced Chernyshevsky to Chinese readers in the form of a translation of the first part of the chapter of Georgi Plekhanov, "N. G. Chernyshevsky's Literary Views," translated by way of the Japanese Marxist Kurahara Korehito. Plekhanov's article is a sustained explication of Chernyshevsky, including the relevant passages on the subject of the class-specific content of beauty. Plekhanov summarized Chernyshevsky: "The concepts of beauty in different social classes are, as we have seen, very different, occasionally even conflicting." Georgii Plekhanov, *Selected Philosophical Works* (Moscow: Progress Publishers, 1977), 5:328. In addition to translating Chernyshevsky, Zhou Yang was also responsible for the translation of Belinsky's essay "On the Natural School," which had been drawn from an English translation of Belinsky's extended work of criticism entitled "A Survey of Russian Literature in 1847."
7. Zhou Yang 周扬, "Women xuyao xin de meixue" 我们需要新的美学 (We need a new aesthetics), in *Zhou Yang wenji* 周扬文集 (Zhou Yang collected works) (Beijing: Renmin chubanshe, 1984–1994), 1:218.
8. Zhou Yang, "Xin de meixue," 221–22.
9. Zhou Yang, "Xin de meixue," 224.
10. Zhou Yang, "Xin wenxue yundong shi jiaoyi tigang (xu)," 新文学运动史讲义提纲 (续) (Outline of lectures on the history of the new literature movement [continued]), *Wenxue pinglun* 文学评论 (Literary review) 2 (1986): 109.
11. Zhou Yang, "Wenyi yu shenghuo mantan" 文艺与生活漫谈 (A casual discussion on literature and life), in *Zhou Yang wenji*, 1:325–26.
12. Zhou Yang, "Shenghuo mantan," 329.
13. Zhou Yang, "Shenghuo mantan," 330.
14. Zhou Yang, "Shenghuo mantan," 330, 332–33.
15. Zhou Yang, "Shenghuo mantan," 333.
16. Zhou Yang's translation was published in 1942 under the aegis of the Xinhua Bookstore, one of a limited number of such texts to be published in Yan'an given the fraught material conditions of printing. In the larger context of Zhou's engagement with Chernyshevsky, prior to the full-length book publication there also appeared two more restricted renditions of Chernyshesky's full text *The Aesthetic Relation Between Art and Reality*, translated by Zhou himself and drawn from the last portion

of the full work published in *International Literature*. The first appeared under the title "The Aesthetic Relation Between Art and Reality," published in the inaugural issue of *Spring Rain* in November of 1941 and corresponding to components of the sections "Art Is Not Life," "'Art Is a Copy of Nature," and "Form and Content." The second appeared under the title "On Poetry" and was published in *Literature Monthly* in April 1942, corresponding to the components "On the Question of Poetry" and "From Life?"

17. Zhou Yang 周扬, "Guanyu Che'ernixuefusiji he ta de meixue" 关于车尔尼雪夫斯基和他的美学" (Concerning Chernyshevsky and his aesthetics), in *Zhou Yang wenji* (1984) 1:359–79.
18. Zhao Haosheng 赵浩生, "Zhou Yang xiaotan lishi gongguo" 周扬笑谈历史功过 (Zhou Yang talks lightheartedly about historical contributions), *Xin Wenxue Shiliao* 新文学史料 (Materials of literary history) 2 (1979): 228–42. They did so, it should be noted, from a position of considerable material comfort. At this juncture and into the early 1950s the material needs of intellectuals were met through the "supply system" 供给制, whereby their food and accommodation were provided for. Chen Mingyuan 陈明远, *Zhishi fenzi yu renminbi shidai* 知识分子与人民币时代 (Intellectuals and the era of the Renminbi) (Shanghai: Wenhui chubanshe, 2002), 41–44.
19. Bonnie S. McDougall, *Mao Zedong's "Talks at the Yan'an Conference on Literature of Art": A Translation of the 1943 Text with Commentary* (Ann Arbor: University of Michigan Press, 1980): 61, subject to my adaptations.
20. McDougall, *Talks*, 61.
21. McDougall, *Talks*, 61.
22. It is in this sense, as in others, that Cheng Kai has insisted that during the revolutionary period of the 1940s to the 1970s, the talks marked not only a document guiding literary policy but also "a text relating to a theory of the subject (that is, how to transform, and constitute a revolutionary subject)" in the form, here, of a theory of class that passes beyond any antimony between the objective-sociological and subjective. Cheng Kai 程凯, "Cong geming zhuti lun ji lishi, xianshi de bianzheng guanxi kan jianghua" 从革命主体论及历史，现实的辩证关系看讲话 (Examining the talks from the dialectical relation between the theory of the subject, history, and reality), *Zhongguo xiandai wenxue yanjiu congkan* 5 (2022): 3.
23. McDougall, *Talks*, 70.
24. McDougall, *Talks*, 70.
25. This marks, then, a strictly nonrepresentational concept of the function of culture. Li Jiefei and Yang Jie summarize this function concisely via the definition of Yan'an culture as a form of "super-literature," expressing "an attitude of exceptionally high regard toward literature, in which literature operates at the same level as the life or death of political power and the state itself." Li Jiefei 李洁非 and Yang Jie 杨劼, *Jiedu Yan'an* 解读延安 (Reading Yan'an) (Beijing: Dangdai Zhongguo chubanshe, 2010), 164.
26. Kai Feng 凯丰, "Guanyu wenyi gongzuozhe xiaxiang de wenti" 关于文艺工作者下乡的问题 (Concerning the problem of culture workers undertaking xia xiang), in *Yan'an wenyi daxi* 延安文艺大系 (Yan'an art and literature collection), ed. Liu Runwei 刘润为 (Changsha: Hunan wenyi chubanshe, 2015), 3:171, 173.
27. Liu Qing 柳青, "Zai guxiang" 在故乡 (In the home village), in Liu Qing 柳青 *Liu Qing wenji* 柳青文集 (Liu Qing selected works) (Xi'an: Shaanxi renmin chubanshe, 1991), 2:594.
28. Liu Qing, "Guxiang," 594.

29. Liu Qing, "Guxiang," 596.
30. Liu Qing, "Guxiang," 596.
31. Liu Qing, "Guxiang," 597.
32. Liu Qing, "Guxiang," 599.
33. Liu Qing, "Guxiang," 602, 603.
34. Liu Qing, "Guxiang," 603.
35. Liu Qing, "Guxiang," 605.
36. Liu Qing, "Guxiang," 605.
37. Liu Qing, "Guxiang," 607.
38. Liu Qing 柳青, "Zhuanwan lu shang" 转弯路上 (On a winding path), in *Liu Qing zhuanji* 柳青专集 (Liu Qing special collection) (Fuzhou: Fujian renmin chubanshe, 1982), 6.
39. Mao Tse-Tung, "Get Organized!," in Mao Tse-Tung, *Selected Works* (Peking: Foreign Languages Press, 1965), 3:156.
40. Mao would repeat these formulas in other contexts, including in his 1945 address "We Must Learn to Do Economic Work," in which he stated, "since we are in the countryside, where the peasants are scattered individual producers employing backward means of production and where most of the land is still owned by landlords and the peasants are subjected to feudal rent exploitation, we have adapted the policies of reducing rent and interest and of organizing mutual aid in labor to heighten the peasants' enthusiasm for production and to increase the productivity of agricultural labor." Mao Tse-Tung, "We Must Learn to Do Economic Work," *Selected Works* 3:241.
41. Mao, "Get Organized!," 156.
42. Other writers in the base area were quick to extend Mao's formulations. In his article "Concerning Collective Labor," published in 1944, Ding Dongfang elaborated the disadvantages of atomized peasant labor, consisting of the fact that "the elements of production in the small peasant individual economy (that is, land, human and animal power, the instruments of labor, subsidiary production) are dispersed and weak" such that, when peasants lacked a given element, they could not engage in production. Moreover, "in the individual economy, there is [only] a domestic division of labor, and the waste of labor power is great and cannot be avoided," whereas "labor under collective mutual aid can develop a relatively beneficial industrial division of labor." Ding Dongfang 丁冬放, "Lun jiti laodong" 论集体劳动 (Concerning collective labor), in *Yan'an xiangcun jianshe ziliao* 延安乡村建设资料 (Yan'an village construction materials), ed. Sun Xiaozhong 孙晓忠 and Gao Ming 高明 (Shanghai: Shanghai daxue chubanshe, 2012), 2:452–61.
43. *Jiefang ribao* 解放日报 (Liberation Daily), "Ba laodong li zuzhzi qilai" 把劳动力组织起来) (Organize labor power), in *Yan'an xiangcun jianshe ziliao*, 2:391.
44. Zhonggong xibei zhongyang ju diaocha yanjiushi 中共西北中央局调查研究室 (Chinese Communist Party Northwest Central Government Investigation Research Bureau), "Shan gan ning de laodong huzhu" 陕甘宁边区的劳动互助 (Labor mutual aid in the Shan-Gan-Ning border region), in *Yan'an xiangcun jianshe ziliao*, 2:532.
45. Yanjiushi, "Huzhu," 536.
46. Liu Qing 柳青, "Mizhi minfengqu sanxiang lingdao biangongdui de jingyan" 米脂民丰区三乡领导变工队的经验 (An experience of leading a labor-exchange team in Mizhi), *Jiefang ribao* 解放日报 (Liberation Daily), June 3, 1945, 2.
47. Liu Qing 柳青, "Zhonggu ji" 种谷记 (A record of sowing grain), in *Liu Qing wenji*, 2:3.
48. Liu Qing, "Zhonggu," 4.
49. Liu Qing, "Zhonggu," 6.

50. Liu Qing, "Zhonggu," 11.
51. Liu Qing, "Zhonggu," 28.
52. Liu Qing, "Zhonggu," 28–29.
53. Liu Qing, "Zhonggu," 41.
54. Liu Qing, "Zhonggu," 57.
55. Liu Qing, "Zhonggu," 57.
56. Liu Qing, "Zhonggu," 70.
57. Liu Qing, "Zhonggu," 95.
58. In a 1950 discussion forum held on the novel, then, Li Jianwu commented that "the novel is seemingly rather long, but the period of days it covers does not even encompass two weeks. It begins in mid-March, and its climax is in Taohua township, on the 25th of March, encompassing chapter 16." Ba Jin 巴金 et al., "'Zhong guji' zuotanhui" 种谷记座谈会 (Discussion forum on Record of Sowing Grain), in *Liu Qing zhuanji*, 121.
59. Liu Qing, "Zhonggu," 164.
60. Liu Qing, "Zhonggu," 179.
61. Liu Qing, "Zhonggu," 200, 231.
62. Ding Ling 丁玲, "Fengyu zhong yi Xiao Hong" 风雨中忆萧红 (Remembering Xiao Hong amid wind and rain), in *Ding Ling quanji* (Shijiazhuang: Hebei renmin chubanshe, 2001), 5:135.
63. Ding Ling, "Fengyu," 135.
64. Ding Ling, "Fengyu," 135.
65. Ding Ling, "Fengyu," 136.
66. Ding Ling, "Fengyu," 137.
67. Ding Ling, "Fengyu," 137–38.
68. Ding Ling 丁玲, "Guanyu lichang wenti wojian" 关于立场问题我见 (My views on the problem of stand), in *Ding ling quanji* (2001) 7:68.
69. Ding Ling "Lichang," 68.
70. Ding Ling 丁玲, "Lun xiezuo" 论写作 (On writing), in *Ding Ling quanji* (2001), 8: 262.
71. The apparent shift away from a more distinctly feminist policy embodied in the 1943 decision has in turn been the point of intervention for feminist scholars examining the contradictions of women's policy in Yan'an, most directly exemplified by He Guimei: "the '1943 decision' and the new policy of the 'Yan'an Road' were tightly linked with one another, in that they no longer placed radical emphasis on 'opposing feudal forces' but rather took as their nucleus the mobilization of the masses, and formed a harmonious relationship with the rural ethical order that had patriarchal authority as its core." He Guimei 贺桂梅, "'Yan'an daolu' zhong de xingbie wenti" 延安道路中的性别问题 (The problem of sex in the Yan'an road), *Nankai xuebao* 南开学报 (Nankai Journal) 6 (2006): 19.
72. Jiefang Ribao 解放日报 (Liberation Daily), "Zhonggong zhongyang guanyu ge kangri genjudi muqian funu gongzuo fangzhen de jueding" 中共中央关于各抗日根据地目前妇女工作方针的 决定 (Decision of the Central Committee of the Chinese Communist Party concerning the present direction of women's work in every anti-Japanese base area) in Sun and Gao, *Yan'an xiangcun jianshe ziliao*, 1:335–37.
73. Mo Ai 莫艾, "Yi ye fufang fazhan shi" 一页妇纺发展史 (A page in the history of weaving women) in Sun and Gao, *Yan'an xiangcun jianshe ziliao*, 1:343.
74. Mo Ai, "Fazhan shi," 339.
75. Lu Zhi 鲁直, "Yan'an nanqu fazhan fufang de jingyan" 延安南区发展妇纺的经验 (The experience of developing women's weaving in Yan'an Southern District), in Sun and Gao, *Yan'an xiangcun jianshe ziliao*, 1:364–67.

76. Mo Ai, "Fazhan shi," 343.
77. In fact, "Recollections" was published in *Liberation Daily* only in 1945. However, Ding Ling began writing the text as her first project after Rectification, only then to conduct revisions over the period 1944–1945, after her other report, "Tian Baolin." See Ding Ling 丁玲, "Shanbei Fengguang jiaohou gan" 《陕北风光》校后感 (Thoughts after revising scenes of Shaanbei), in *Ding Ling quanji*, 9:53.
78. Ding Ling 丁玲, "Sanri zaji" 三日杂记 (Assorted recollections over three days), in *Ding Ling quanji*, 5:160.
79. Ding Ling, "Zaji," 160.
80. In these terms, as Lu Yang has observed, Ding Ling's text and other texts emerging from the talks also inaugurate a concern for the everyday as the condition for the transformation of the emotional world of intellectuals and social relations more generally: "[Ding Ling] does not only record the achievements of production or labor heroes, but rather the detailed, moving scenes of everyday life." Lu Yang 路杨, "Geming yu renqing: Jiefang qu wenyi xiaxiang yundong de qinggan shijian" 革命与人情：解放区文艺下乡运动的情感实践 (Revolution and sentiment: The emotional practice of the rural cultural movement in the liberated areas), *Zhongguo xiandai wenxue yanjiu congkan* 6 (2019): 103.
81. Ding Ling, "Zaji," 163.
82. Ding Ling, "Zaji," 165, 166.
83. Ding Ling, "Zaji," 166.
84. Ding Ling, "Zaji," 167.
85. Ding Ling, "Zaji," 168.
86. As Dong Limin notes, then, in part as a critique of He Guimei, "by means of 'female weaving' cooperatives and other such forms, it became possible to construct relations of mutual aid in labor that overcame individual forms, and in doing so explore new forms of public space that were at once both social and economic. Clearly differing from both the household-based model of weaving whose labor value was so often dismissed in the traditional small-peasant economic order, and the modern industrial system in which women textile laborers purely comprised labor power, collective textile production in Yan'an had the sense of a 'new woman.'" Dong Limin 董丽敏, "Zuizhi qilai: 'Xin nvxing' yu 'xin shehui' de goujian" 组织起来：新女性与新社会的构建 (Organize together: The rise of "new women" and the building of "new society"), *Funv yanjiu luncong* 妇女研究论丛 (Journal of Chinese Women's Studies) (6 (2017): 21.
87. Zhou Yang 周扬, "'Makesi zhuyi yu wenyi' xuyan" 《马克思主义与文艺》序言 (Preface to *Marxism and Literature*), in *Zhou Yang wenji*, 1:454, 457.

2. Lazy Peasants, Productive Proletarians

Epigraph: Zhou Yang 周扬, "Zhengdun wenyi sixiang, gaijin lingdao gongzuo" 整顿文艺思想，改进领导工作 (Rectify ideas of art and literature, enhance leadership work), in *Zhou Yang wenji* (Zhou Yang selected works) (Beijing: Renmin chubanshe, 1984–1994), 2:136–37.

1. In a related theoretical register, Li Jiefei and Yang Jie summarize this process in terms of the emergence of a distinct mode of literary production: "If one were to say that literature is not only a production process, but that, before this process, there is also a mode of production; then 1949 marks a turning point for the transformation of the Chinese literary mode of production, whereby literature was integrated into a mode

of production never before seen, and the arrival of this mode of production also engendered the re-construction of the literary superstructure." Li Jiefei 李洁非 and Yang Jie 杨劼, *Gongheguo wenxue shengchan fangshi* 共和国文学生产方式 (The literary mode of production in the republic) (Beijing: Shehui kexue wenxian chubanshe, 2011), 79.
2. Mao Dun 茅盾, "Zatan Sulian" 杂谈苏联 (Varied matters on the Soviet Union), in *Mao Dun quanji* 矛盾全集 (Mao Dun collected works) (Beijing: Renmin chubanshe, 1984), 17:301.
3. The results of the 1949 Soviet writers delegation were collected in a volume entitled *We and the Chinese People Together*, which includes the major speeches given by participants in the delegation, together with other records of the visit. These include, for example, a record of "Fadeev and Chinese Writers Exchange Literary Proposals," a discussion meeting at which Fadeev met with the luminaries of the Chinese socialist literary world, including Mao Dun, Ding Ling, Zhou Yang, and Ba Jin.
4. Mao Dun 茅盾, "Zhengqu fazhan dao geng ga de jieduan" 争取发展到更高的阶段 (Struggle to develop to a higher stage), in *Mao Dun quanji*, 24:156.
5. Zhou Yang, "Zhengdun," 139.
6. Chen Shunxin 陈顺馨, *Shehui zhuyi xianshi zhuyi lilun zai Zhongguo de jieshou yu zhuanhuan* 社会主义现实主义理论在中国的接受与转换 (The reception and adaptation of the theory of socialist realism in China) (Hefei: Anhui jiaoyu chubanshe, 2000), 244. Chen's text remains amongst the useful discussions of the history of socialist realism in China. See also *Wenyi bao* 文艺报 (Art and literary gazette), "Quanguo wenxie zuzhi shehuzhyi xianshizhuyi xuexi" 全国文协组织社会主义现实主义学习 (All-China Literature Association organizes the study of socialist realism), *Wenyi bao* 文艺报 (Art and Literary Gazette) 13 (1953): 7.
7. "Guanyu zhengli zuzhi gaijin gongzuo de fangan" 关于整理组织改进工作的方案 (A work plan for adjusting the organization and improving work), *Renmin wenxue* 人民文学 (People's Literature) 10 (1952): 94.
8. "Guanyu gaizu quanguo wenxie he jiaqiang lingdao wenxue chuangzuo de gongzuo fangan," *Zuojia tongxun* 作家通讯 (Writers Dispatch) 1 (1953): 38–43. See also "Quanguo wenxie chaungwu weiyuanhui juxing kuoda huiyi, tongguo gaizu quaanguo wenxie he jiaqiang lingdao wenxue chuangzuo de fangan" 全国文协常务委员会举行扩大会议 通过改组文协和加强领导文学创作的方案 (Standing Committee of the Literature Workers Association holds an expanded meeting, passes a work plan for the revision of the Literature Workers Association and the strengthening of leadership over literary creation), *Renmin ribao* 人民日报 (People's Daily), March 30, 1953.
9. Ding Ling 丁玲, "Sulian de wenxue yu yishu" 苏联的文学与艺术 (Art and literature in the Soviet Union), *Ding Ling quanji*, 7:136.
10. For a sustained discussion of the emergence and development of the manuscript fee system over the socialist period, see Huang Fayou 黄发有, "Gaochou zhidu yu 'shi qi nian' wenxue shengchan" 稿酬制度于'十七年'文学生产 (The manuscript fee system and literary production in the "seventeen years"), *Zhongguo xiandai wenxue yanjiu congkan* 中国现代文学研究丛刊 (Modern Chinese Literature Studies) 2 (2018): 65–81. Huang's work on literary institutions has proven invaluable for my own discussion here.
11. Li Jiefei and Yang Jie, *Shengchan fangshi*, 76.
12. The first issue of *Writers Dispatch* described the mission of the journal as follows: "*Writers Dispatch* is an internal periodical of the Writers Association. The aim of publishing this periodical is in order to enhance links between authors and circulate

experience in the work of literary creation. *Writers Dispatch* will regularly carry letters from writers and report on the experience of writers as they enter into life, the creation plans of writers, their conditions, and the different kinds of problems that emerge in the creation process. In doing so, it will be possible for the writers who are scattered across different locations to gain an understanding of each other, to have mutual discussions with one another, and so spur on competition in creation." Bianzhe 编者, ed., "Guanyu Zuojia Tongxun 关于作家通讯 (Concerning Writers Dispatch), *Zuojia tongxun* 1 (1953): 1. Copies of this internal publication are unfortunately not generally accessible to researchers. I have here made use of the issues for the years 1953–1954 that are available in the National Library. For a useful discussion, see Huang Fayou 黄发有,"'Shi qi nian' wenxue de jihua tizhi: Yi Zuojia Tongxun de xijian shiliao wei yiju" '十七年'文学的计划体制：以作家通讯的稀见史料为依据 (The planning system of literature in the "seventeen years": On the basis of the rarely seen historical materials in Writers Dispatch), *Wenxue pinglun* 文学评论 (Literary Review) 5 (2015): 155–64.

13. Shu Peide 束沛德, "Ji quanguo wenxie xuexi shehuizhuyi xianshizhuyi" 记全国文协学习社会主义现实主义" (All-China Literature Association studies socialist realism), *Zuojia tongxun* 1 (1953): 16–21; 2 (1953): 30–35. See also Shu Peide 束沛德, *Wo de wutai, wo de jia* 我的舞台我的家 (My stage, my home) (Beijing: Zuojia chubanshe, 2015). Shu Peide served as the secretary to the creation committee.

14. From this point onward, the Writers Association assumed a bureaucratic power different from other bodies that fell under the umbrella of the All-China Federation of Arts and Literary Circles. As Li Jiefei notes: "The Writers Association was, uniquely among all the cultural bodies otherwise subsumed under the Federation of Literary and Art Circles, turned into an independent administrative body, one with an administrative standing equivalent to that of the Federation of Literary and Art Circles." Li Jiefei and Yang Jie, *Shengchan fangshi*, 74.

15. In Li Jiefei's formulation: "Beyond the national-level Writers Association, there were also local associations. The local associations did not exist only at the provincial level; rather, the levels above prefectural cities all had writers associations. Each local association had a chairperson, vice chairpersons, and professional writers, and so too did provincial associations run their own periodicals, with sometimes more than one, and so too did many prefectural cities. In the era of the planned economy, these journals were primarily funded by the state." Li Jiefei and Yang Jie, *Shengchan fangshi*, 77.

16. "Zhongguo zuojia xiehui juban chuangzuo huokuan ji jintie zanxing banfa" 中国作家协会举办创作贷款及津贴暂行办法 (The Chinese Writers Association introduces temporary measures concerning payments and allowances), *Wenyi bao* 文艺报 (Art and Literary Gazette) 24 (1954): 77.

17. Zhang Xi 张僖, *Zhi yan pian yu: Zhongguo zuoxie qian mishuzhang de huiyi* 只言片语：中国作协前秘书长的回忆 (A few words: Memories of the former secretary-general of the Chinese Writers Association) (Beijing: Shiyue wenyi chubanshe, 2002), 36.

18. Hong Zicheng provides an effective summary of three groups among those writers who had membership in the Writers Association: "one kind consisted of writers who entered into universities, or research institutes (or they previously worked at universities and other such departments), or literary and cultural bodies and apparatuses to serve as leading personnel. This can be described as the 'second occupation' or 'dual occupation' (for some, they primarily worked as university professors, as researchers, as editors at publishing houses, or as officials in cultural institutions, such that writing became their 'second occupation'). There were also writers, who might have belonged to a certain organization or a group, yet this 'dual occupation' had no real

significance, and was purely a marker of honor. The third circumstance consisted of the 'professional writer' and 'resident writer' of the Writers Association and its local affiliates." Hong Zicheng, 洪子诚, *Dangdai wenxue gaishuo* 当代文学概说 (Summary of contemporary literature) (Nanning: Guangxi jiaoyu chubanshe, 2000), 80.

19. Zhou Yang 周扬, "Women bixu douzheng" 我们必须斗争 (We must struggle), in *Zhou Yang wenji*, 2:314.
20. Zhou Yang, "Zai di erci quansu zuojia daibiao dahui shang de zhuci" 在第二次全苏作家代表大会上的祝词 (Words of congratulation at the second Soviet Writers Congress), in *Zhou Yang wenji*, 2:331–32.
21. Cheng Kai perceptively notes that the radical ambitions of the Yan'an period were considerably diluted in the period after 1949. Thus, "after the formation of New China, in the 1950s, as compared to the period of the liberated areas, the radicalism in the state of literary production diminished significantly. The establishment of the system of literary production with the formation of New China was accompanied by the return and affirmation of the whole modern literary mode of production, especially under the template of the Soviet Union, consisting on the one hand of the provision of high manuscript fees and royalties, subsequently critiqued as forms of 'bourgeois right,' and, on the other, the institutionalized and official identity of the authors themselves." Cheng Kai 程凯, "Cong geming zhuti lun ji lishi, xianshi de bianzheng guanxi kan jiangua" 从革命主体论及历史，现实的辩证关系看讲话 (Examining the talks from the dialectical relation between the theory of the subject, history, and reality), *Zhongguo xiandai wenxue yanjiu congkan* 中国现代文学研究丛刊 (Modern Chinese Literature Studies) 5 (2022): 34.
22. Ding Ling 丁玲, "Dao qunzhong qu luohu" 到群众去落户 (Go among the masses), in *Ding Ling quanji*, 7:359.
23. Ding Ling, "Qunzhong," 361.
24. Ding Ling, "Zuojia xuyao peiyang dui qunzhong de ganqing" 作家需要培养对群众的感情 (Writers must cultivate feelings toward the masses), in *Ding Ling quanji*, 7:370.
25. Ding Ling, "Peiyang," 370–71.
26. He Jixian, among others, has underscored the emergent conflicts between Ding Ling's fidelity to the practices of Yan'an and the institutionalized literary system of the 1950s. In particular, "the principle of 'entering into life' as reconstituted by Ding Ling had its efficacy in terms of creation, and yet it also came into conflict with the requirement of 'reflecting reality in good time' as engendered by 'the subordination of culture to politics'" He Jixian 何吉贤, "Cong Yan'an zoulai de ren" 从延安走来的人 (The person from Yan'an), *Wenyi lilun yu piping* 文艺理论与批评 (Literary Theory and Criticism) 3 (2022): 41.
27. Zhou Yang 周扬, "Shehuizhuyi xianshizhuyi—Zhongguo wenxue qianjin de daolu" 社会主义现实主义—中国文学前进的道路 (Socialist realism: The path of advance for Chinese literature), in *Zhou Yang wenji*, 2:188–89.
28. Laurence Coderre provides a superb summation of these developments, with particular reference to Stalin's 1952 text, noting, that, for China and other new socialist countries, the experience of the Soviet Union "was essentially constitutive of what socialism was, and, therefore, what the future for these other states would necessarily be." Coderre, "A Necessary Evil: Conceptualizing the Socialist Commodity Under Mao," *Comparative Studies in Society and History* 61, no. 1 (2019): 30–31.
29. "Guanyu zuojia shenru shenghuo wenti de cankao ziliao" 关于作家深入生活问题的资料 (Consultation materials on problems of workers entering life), *Zuojia tongxun* 2 (1953): 24.

30. "Jin yi bu kaizhan gongkuang wenhua gongzuo" 进一步开展工矿文化工作 (Further develop cultural work in factories and mines), *Renmin ribao*, June 8, 1954.
31. Zhou Libo 周立波, "Guanyu xiezuo" 关于写作 (Concerning writing), in Zhou Libo 周立波, *Zhou Libo wenji* 周立波文集 (Selected works of Zhou Libo) (Shanghai: Shanghai wenyi chubanshe, 1982), 5:580.
32. "Zuojia shenru shenghuo he chuangzuo jihua de diaocha" 作家深入生活和创作计划的调查 (A survey on writers entering life and creation plans), *Zuojia tongxun* 1 (1953): 35.
33. Katerina Clark, *The Soviet Novel: History as Ritual* (Chicago: University of Chicago Press, 1985).
34. Zhou Libo 周立波, *Tieshui benliu* 铁水奔流 (Rivulets of steel), in *Zhou Libo wenji*, 2:7.
35. Zhou Libo, *Tieshui*, 7.
36. Zhou Libo, *Tieshui*, 7.
37. Zhou Libo, *Tieshui*, 37–38.
38. Zhou Libo, *Tieshui*, 43.
39. Zhou Libo, *Tieshui*, 88.
40. Zhou Libo, *Tieshui*, 89.
41. Zhou Libo, *Tieshui*, 154.
42. Zhou Libo, *Tieshui*, 161.
43. Zhou Libo, *Tieshui*, 246.
44. Bai Lang 白朗, *Weile xingfu de mingtian* 为了幸福的明天 (For a happy tomorrow), in Bai Lang 白朗, *Bai Lang wenji* 白朗文集 (Selected works of Bai Lang) (Shenyang: Chunfeng wenyi chubanshe 1983–1986), 2:132–33.
45. Bai Lang, *Mingtian*, 134.
46. Bai Lang, *Mingtian*, 145.
47. Bai Lang, *Mingtian*, 155.
48. Bai Lang, *Mingtian*, 158.
49. Bai Lang, *Mingtian*, 179, 189.
50. Bai Lang, *Mingtian*, 190.
51. Bai Lang, *Mingtian*, 243.
52. "Quanguo zong gonghui he zuojia xiehui lianhe zhaokai zuotan hui taolun wenyi chuangzuo ruhe biaoxian guojia gongye jianshe wenti" 全国总工会和作家协会联合召开座谈会 讨论文艺创作如何表现国家工业建设问题 (All-China Federation of Trade Unions and the Writers Association host a joint discussion forum, discussing how literary creation should express the problems of national industrial construction), *Renmin ribao*, June 9, 1954.
53. Li Fuchun 李富春, "Li Fuchun tongzhi zai Beijing wenyi gongzuozhe zuotanhui shang de jianghua" 李富春同志在北京文艺工作者座谈会上的讲话 (Comrade Li Fuchun's speech at the Beijing culture workers discussion forum), *Zuojia tongxun* 11 (1954), 1–8. See also Li Fuchun 李富春, "Li Fuchun tongzhi zai Beijing wenyi gongzuozhe zuotanhui shang de jianghua" 李富春同志在北京文艺工作者座谈会上的讲话 (Comrade Li Fuchun's speech at the Beijing culture workers discussion forum), in *Xuexi wenxuan* 学习文选 (Documents for study), ed. Zhongguo zuojia xiehui Wuhan fenhui 中国作家协会武汉分会 (China Writers Union Wuhan branch) (Wuhan, 1954), 305–6.
54. Lao She 老舍, "Wenyi gongzuozhe mang qilai ba" 文艺工作者忙起来吧 (Culture workers, busy yourselves), *Wenyi xuexi* 文艺学习 (Literary Study) 17 (1955): 4.
55. Lao She, "Gongzuozhe," 4.
56. Xiao Su 晓苏, "Tantan chuangzuo jihua" 谈谈创作计划, *Zuojia tongxun* 10 (1954): 47–49.

57. Ba Jin 巴金, "Ba Jin de fayan" 巴金的发言 (Speech of Ba Jin), in *Zhongguo zuojia xiehui di er ci lishi hui huiyi (kuoda) bagao fayan ji* 中国作家协会第二次理事会会议(扩大)报告发言集 (China Writers Association second expanded meeting of the Council of the Writers Association report and speech collection), ed. Zhonguo zuojia xiehui 中国作家协会 (China Writers Association) (Beijing: Renmin wenxue chubanshe, 1956), 167.
58. Ba Jin, "Fayan," 168.
59. Ba Jin, "Fayan," 169.
60. Mao Dun 茅盾, "Peiyang xinsheng liliang, kuoda wenxue duiwu" 培养新生力量，扩大文学队伍 (Cultivate new forces, expand the literary ranks), in *Mao Dun quanji*, 24:428.
61. Wenyi Bao 文艺报 (Art and literary gazette), "Zhongguo zuojia xiehui 1956 nian dao 1967 nian de gongzuo gangyao" 中国作家协会1956年到1967年的工作纲要 (The 1956–1967 work program of the Chinese Writers Association), *Wenyi bao* 文艺报 (Art and Literary Gazette) 7 (1956): 9.
62. Mao Tse-Tung, "Recruit Large Numbers of Intellectuals," in *Selected Works* (Peking: Foreign Languages Press, 1965), 2:303.
63. For an extended discussion of Ding Ling's role in the institute, see Xing Xiaoqun 邢小群, "Ding Ling yu wenxueyanjiusuo de xingshuai" 丁玲与文学研究所的兴衰 (Ding Ling and the rise and fall of the Literature Research Institute) (Zhengzhou: Henan wenyi chubanshe, 2013).
64. Ren Liqing 任丽青, *Shanghai gongren jieji wenyi xinjun de xingcheng* 上海工人阶级文艺新军的形成 (The formation of a new cultural army of the Shanghai working class) (Shanghai: Shanghai daxue chubanshe, 2010), 46.
65. The emphasis here is on the worker-writers who emerged from Shanghai. Yet a sense of the role of the Tianjin-based nexus of writers is given by an article published in *Art and Literary Gazette* in 1952 under the title "An Investigation Into the Conditions of Worker Writing in Tianjin," which, significantly, already emphasized the problem of the dislocation of worker-writers from production: "there are some worker-writers who, because they show some advance in their capacity with words, are promoted into staff workers or transferred to trade union cadres, and so depart from the workshop." Yang Zhiyi 杨志一, 天津工人写作情况调查 "Tianjin gongren xiezuo qingkuang diaocha" (An investigation into the conditions of worker writing in Tianjin), in *Yang Zhiyi shi wen xuan* 杨志一诗文选 (Yang Zhiyi selected works and poetry) (Nanning: Guangxi minzu chubanshe, 2007), 49.
66. Zhang Ying 张英, "Shouxian zuo ge jianshezhe, cai neng zuoge yeyu xiezuozhe" 首先做个建设者，才能做个业余写作者 (First a constructor, then an amateur writer), *Mengya* 萌芽 (Roots) 1 (1958): 7.
67. Tang Kexin 唐克新, "Gu xiaoju he ta de jiemei" 古小菊和她的姊妹 (Gu Xiaoju and her sisters), in Tang Kexin 唐克新, *Zhongzi* 种子 (Seeds) (Shanghai: Zuojia chubanshe, 1965), 214.
68. Tang Kexin, "Jiemei," 213.
69. Tang Kexin, "Jiemei," 218.
70. Tang Kexin, "Jiemei," 223.
71. Tang Kexin, "Jiemei," 223, 225.
72. As Erin Huang notes in relation to a different cultural text, then, the short story "depicts a self-contained society that never ventures outside the factory compound," or does so, rather, only in the movement between factory sites. Erin Huang, *Urban Horror: Neoliberal Post-Socialism and the Limits of Visibility* (Durham, NC: Duke University Press, 2020), 52.

73. Tang Kexin, "Jiemei," 227.
74. Zhou Yang 周扬, "Zai quanguo qingnian wenxue chuagzuozhe huiyi shang de jianghua" 在全国青年文学创作者会议上的讲话 (Speech at nationwide youth literature creator meeting), in *Zhou Yang wenji*, 2:369–90.
75. Liu Shaoqi 刘少奇, "Guanyu zuojia de xiuyang deng wenti" 关于作家的修养等问题 (Concerning the cultivation and other problems of writers), in *Dang he guojia lingdao ren lun wenyi* 党和国家领导人论文艺 (Party and state leaders discuss art and literature), ed. Zhonggong zhongyang shuji chu yanjiu shi wenhua zu 中共中央书记处研究室文化组 (Chinese Communist Party Central Committee Secretariat Research Bureau Culture Group) (Beijing: Wenhua yishu chubanshe, 1982), 81.
76. Lao She 老舍, "Qingnian zuojia yingyou de xiuyang" 青年作家应有的修养 (The appropriate training for young writers), in Lao She 老舍, *Lao She de huaju yishu* 老舍的话剧艺术 (The theatrical art of Lao She) (Beijing: Wenhua yishu chubanshe, 1982), 194.
77. Fei Liwen 费礼文, "Yao zuo shijian de zhuren" 要做时间的主人 (We must be masters of time), *Zhongguo qingnian* 中国青年 (China Youth) 6 (1956): 14–15.
78. Fei Liwen, "Zhuren," 14.
79. Fei Liwen, "Zhuren," 15. The vision of a scientific, rationalized practice of writing on the part of Fei Liwen also emerges in other advice given to amateur writers during this period. Writing in the journal for literary pedagogy *Wenyi xuexi* (Cultural Study), Wu Guan explicitly stated that "if you scientifically arrange your time," any conflict between the time of production and the time of writing could be dealt with. Wu Guan 吴灌, "Tan tan yeyu chuangzuo he hongzuo de maodun" 谈谈业余创作和工作的矛盾 (Concerning the contradiction between amateur creation and work), *Wenyi xuexi* 文艺学习 3 (1956): 28.
80. Tang Kexin 唐克新, "Rang wo zai huidao gongchang li qu ba!" 让我再回到工厂里去吧! (Let me once again return to the factory!), *Mengya* 10 (1957): 2.
81. Lu Yang appositely sums up this contradiction as follows: "just as worker-writers were called upon to ensure their close proximity to productive labor, such that they could not depart from their production station and conditions of labor, so too, as a result, did they have no means of ensuring the knowledge, training or plentiful time for creation that creative labor itself required." Lu Yang 路杨, "'Chuangzo laodong' ruhe keneng?" 创作劳动如何可能? (How might creative labor be possible?), *Wenyi yanjiu* 文艺研究 (Literary Research) 11 (2020): 87.
82. Li Fuchun 李富春, "Gongzi gaige de yiyi ji gaige de yuanze" 工资改革的意义及改革的原则 (The meaning of the wage reform and the principle of the reform), in Li Fuchun 李富春, *Li Fuchun xuanji* 李富春选集 (Selected works of Li Fuchun) (Beijing: Zhongguo jihua chubanshe, 1992), 157, 159. Li Fuchun's formulations are taken almost verbatim from the Soviet textbook on political economy. The chapter concerning wages under socialism from the revised English edition published in 1957, then, opens as follows: "wages in socialist economy are by their very nature quite different from wages under capitalism. Since labor power has ceased to be a commodity in socialist society, wages are no longer the price of labor power." The wage reforms in 1956 were accompanied by a widespread campaign in the periodical *Zhongguo Laodong* 中国劳动 (Chinese Labor) emphasizing the specific content of the socialist wage and warning against "egalitarianism."
83. "Gaoji nongye shengchan hezuo she shifan zhangcheng" 高级农业生产合作社示范章程 (Model regulations for an advanced producers cooperative), *Renmin ribao*, July 1, 1956.

84. Guo wu yuan 国务院 (State Council), "Guowuyuan guanyu guojia jiguan gongzuo renyuan quan shixing gongzi zhi he gaixing huobi gongzi zhi de mingling" 国务院关于国家机关工作人员全实行工资制和改行货币工资制的命令 (Order concerning the universal implementation of a wage system and the reform of the monetary wage system among state employees), in *Jianguo yilai zhongyao wenxian xuanbian* 建国以来重要文献选编 (Selection of important documents since the founding of the country), ed. Zhonggong zhongyang wenxian shi 中共中央文献室 (Chinese Communist Party Central Committee Textual Office) (Beijing: Zhongyang wenxian chubanshe, 2011), 7:132–34.

3. Time for Communism

Epigraph: Guo Moruo 郭沫若, "Bi he xianshi—Guo lao lai xin" 笔和现实—郭老来信 (The pen and reality—A letter from old Guo), *Renmin ribao* 人民日报 (People's Daily) September 9, 1958.

1. "Wenyi jie dui Ding Chen fandang jituan de douzheng shoude juda shengli Lu Dingyi, Guo Moruo, Mao Dun, Zhou Yang deng zai zongjie da hui shang zuo le jianghua" 文艺界对丁陈反党集团的斗争获得巨大胜利 陆定一、郭沫若、茅盾、周扬等在总结大会上作了讲话 (The cultural field wins a great victory in the struggle against the Ding-Chen anti-party clique, Lu Dingyi, Guo Moruo, Mao Dun, Zhou Yang, and others give speeches at the summation meeting), *Renmin ribao*, September 27, 1958.
2. "Shengli," 2.
3. "Shengli," 2.
4. "Yao you yi zhi qiangda de gongren jieji de wenyi duiwu 要有一支强大的工人阶级的文艺队伍 (We must have a great cultural detachment of the working class), *Renmin ribao*, November 12, 1957.
5. Zhonggong zhongyang 中共中央 (Chinese Communist Party Central Committee), "Zhonggong Zhongyang pizhun zhongyang xuanchuanbu guanyu zuojia xiaxiang xiachang wenti de baogao" 中共中央批准中央宣传部关于作家下乡下厂问题的报告 (Central Committee approves the report from the propaganda department on the dispatch of writers to the countryside and factories), in *Zhonggong zhongyang wenjian xuanji* 中共中央文件选集 (Selection of documents from the CPC Central Committee) (Beijing: Renmin chubanshe, 2013) 26:406–9.
6. "Zhongguo zuojia xiehui fachu xiangliang zhaohao: Zuojiamen! yuejin, dayuejin!" 中国作家协会发出响亮号召: 作家们！跃进，大跃进！(The Chinese Writers Association issues a clear call: Authors! leaps, great leaps!), *Renmin ribao*, March 8, 1958. *Art and Literary Gazette* carried a lengthy report on the discussions of this meeting, including the determination of professional culture workers to produce new novels and other texts according to a plan. Zhao Shuli, for example, is said to have committed to writing a sequel to his *Rhymes of Liu Youcai*. See "Yang fan gu lang, li zheng shang you" 扬帆鼓浪，力争上游 (Set sail and rouse the waves, strive for mastery), *Wenyi bao* 文艺报 (Art and Literary Gazette) 6 (1958): 20–23.
7. "Zuojiamen," 7.
8. The aims and theoretical coordinates of the folksong movement were registered by the April editorial published in the *People's Daily* under the title "Collect Folk Songs Across the Country on a Large Scale." The editorial suggestively mapped out a set of emergent relations between amateur writers of folk songs and professional poetry culture workers, urging, then, that "we must faithfully copy these folk songs down,

publish selections of them and conduct ordering and research, and also provide them to our poetry workers as materials through which they might supplement and enrich their own work." "Da guimo di shouji quanguo minge" 大规模地收集全国民歌 (Collect folk songs across the country on a large scale), *Renmin ribao*, April 14, 1958.

9. Hua Fu 华夫, "Wenyi fangchu weixing lai" 文艺放出卫星来 (Art and literature have released satellites), *Wenyi bao* 18 (1958): 2.

10. Yu Heiding 于黑丁, "Qunzhong chuangzuo shi shehui zhuyi wenyi yundong de zhuliu" 群众创作是社会主义文艺运动的主流" (Mass creation is the mainstream of the socialist cultural movement), in *Jianshe gongchan zhuyi wenxue di yi ji* 建设共产主义文学第一辑 (Build a communist literature, volume 1), ed. Huazhong shifan xueyuan zhongwen xi 华中师范学院中文系 (Central China Normal College Chinese Department) (Wuhan: Huazhong shifan xueyuan, 1958), 88.

11. The extent and diversity of amateur writing in the Great Leap is indicated by the publications that appeared under the "worker-peasant-soldier" (*gongnongbing*) series, which provided new visibility for worker and peasants who turned to writing during the Great Leap. For an overview of these publications, see Shi Jing 史静, "1958–1959 nian 'gongnongbing' congshu yanjiu" 1958–1959 年'工农兵'丛书研究 (Research on the "worker-peasant-soldier" series over 1958–1959), *Xin wenxue pinglun* 新文学评论 (Modern Chinese Literature Criticism) 3 (2012): 124–30.

12. Chen Baichen 陈白尘, "Guanyu jiti chuangzuo" 关于集体创作 (Concerning collective creation), *Wenyi bao* 9 (1958): 29.

13. Zhang Zhen 张真, "Jiti chuangzuo shi duo, kuai, hao, sheng de chuangzuo fangshi" 集体创作是多快好省的创作方式 (Collective creation is a varied, quick, economical and good creation method), *Zhongguo xiju* 中国戏剧 (China Drama) 18 (1958): 23.

14. Hua Fu 华夫, "Jiti chuangzuo haochu duo" 集体创作好处多 (The benefits of collective creation are many), *Wenyi bao* 22 (1958): 2, 3.

15. Chen Baichen, "Jiti," 29.

16. The movement to write factory histories took its inspiration from Maxim Gorky, who pioneered this form in the 1930s Soviet Union. Gorky's theoretical reflections on factory history writing were carried in the July 1958 edition of the Tianjin-based periodical *Xin gang* (New harbor), which facilitated the spread of the movement to the rest of the country, including communes and army brigades. For an extensive discussion of the history of factory history writing, see Xie Baojie 谢保杰, *Zhuti, xiangxiang yu biaoda: 1949–1966 nian gongnongbing xiezuo de lishi kaocha* 主体，想象与表达: 1949–1966 年工农兵写作的历史考察 (Subject, imagination and expression: A historical investigation of worker-peasant-soldier writing over 1949–1966) (Beijing: Beijing daxue chubanshe, 2015), chap. 6.

17. In *Writers Dispatch*, then, the Tianjin-based author Fang Ji observed with respect to writing factory histories: "We are, in intellectual terms, not without our doubts. One such doubt is why the Soviet Union did not sustain the activity of factory histories. There is surely a reason. Upon flipping through Gorky's writing on factory histories, the significance of factory histories was affirmed from a theoretical perspective. As for why the Soviet Union did not sustain this practice, there must be some other reason." Li Dan 李丹, "Lun 'dayuejin' shiqi 'qunzhong shi' xiezuo yundong" 论'大跃进'时期'群众史'写作运动 (Concerning the writing movement of 'mass histories' during the 'Great Leap Forward' period), *Wenxue pinglun* 文学评论 (Literary Review) 6 (2015): 7.

18. "Yao chuangzuo geng duo duan xiao de wenyi zuopin" 要创作更多短小的文艺作品 (We must create more literary works in short forms), *Renmin ribao*, April 26, 1958.

19. Zhang Chunqiao 张春桥 "Da yuejin de fengge" 大跃进的风格 (The style of the great leap forward), in *Kai yi dai shifeng: Lun shige chuangzuo de xinlu* 开一代诗风 论诗歌创作的新路 (Start a new poetic style: Concerning a new road for poetic creation) (Shijiazhuang: Hebei renmin chubanshe, 1958), 90. The demands for short forms generated by the Great Leap itself marks a common strategy across investigations of form during the period. Hei Tieding, for example, was able to write that the demands of the times "urgently require us to use the literary forms and weapons best able to speedily reflect reality, to deliver spiritual sustenance to the hands of the readers." He went on: "writing a novel requires rather more experience in writing, and it requires a relatively long time and expansive space to conduct concentration, refinement and summary." Hei Tieding 黑铁丁, "Tichang xie duanpian" 提倡写短篇 (Promoting short texts), in *Zhangchi ji* 张驰集 (Galloping collection) (Beijing: Zuojia chubanshe, 1959), 142–44.
20. Hu Wanchun 胡万春, "Cong 'duanpian bu duan' zhong suo xiang dao de" 从短篇不短中所想到的 (Thinking from "short is not necessarily short"), *Mengya* 萌芽 (Roots) 1 (1957): 31.
21. Mao Dun 茅盾, "Duan pian xiao shuo de fengshou he chuangzuo shang de ji ge wenti" 短篇小说的丰收和创作上的几个问题 (Questions concerning the creation and harvest of short stories), *Renmin wenxue* 人民文学 (People's Literature) 2 (1959): 4.
22. Mao Dun, "Duan pian," 4–7.
23. Hu Qingpo 胡青坡, "Women tichang xie xiaoxiao shuo" 我们提倡写小小说 (We support writing short short stories), *Changjiang wenyi* 长江文艺 (Changjiang Art and Literature) 9 (1958): 3.
24. Song Shuang 宋爽, "Qianlun 'xiaoxiao shuo'" 浅论'小小说' (A brief discussion of short short stories), *Wenyi bao* 7 (1959): 17
25. A powerful indication of the appeal of the "short short story" form is given by the proliferation of cultural competitions held between factories, parallel to production competitions. In March 1960, then, the editorial committee of *Sprouts* held a citywide "story and short short story" competition in tandem with the Yangpu District Mass Literature and Art Work Committee and the small theater of the Hudong Workers Cultural Palace, which is said to have involved almost three hundred amateur writers. Mengya benkan jizhe 萌芽本刊记者 (*Sprouts* reporter), "Shanghai sai gushi, xiaoxiao shuo huodong jieshao" 上海赛故事小小说活动介绍 (Introduction to Shanghai story competition and short short story activities), *Mengya* 9 (1960): 21.
26. Lao She 老舍, "Duo xie xiaoxiao shuo" 多写小小说 (We must write more short short stories), *Xingang* 新港 (New Harbor) 2–3 (1958): 4.
27. Lao She 老舍, "Yue duan yue nan" 越短越难 (The shorter, the more difficult), *Renmin wenxue* 人民文学 (People's Literature) 6 (1958): 21–22.
28. Xu Ming 徐明, "Tan xiaoxiao shuo" 谈小小说 (Discussing the short short story), *Renmin ribao*, May 26, 1959.
29. Ba Jin 巴金, "Xiao mei bian ge" 小妹编歌 (Little Sister compiles a song), *Renmin ribao*, July 9, 1958.
30. Lao She 老舍, "Dian Hua" 电话 (Telephone), *Xingang* 6 (1958): 3.
31. Li Zhun 李准, "Yi chuan yaoshi" 一串钥匙 (A chain of keys), in *Li Zhun zuopin xuan shang* 李准作品选 上 (A selection of Li Zhun's works, part 1), ed. Wang Hongying 王洪应 (Beijing: Dazhong wenyi chubanshe, 2004), 154.
32. Li Zhun, "Yaoshi," 157.
33. Li Zhun, "Yaoshi," 157, 158, 164.
34. Li Zhun, "Yaoshi," 164.

35. Li Zhun 李准, "Liang dai ren" 两代人 (Two generations), in *Li Zhun zuopin xuan shang*, 180.
36. Li Zhun, "Liang dai ren," 181.
37. Li Zhun, "Liang dai ren," 182.
38. Li Zhun, "Liang dai ren," 182, 183.
39. Li Zhun, "Liang dai ren," 183, 186.
40. Li Zhun, "Liang dai ren," 186–87.
41. Li Zhun, "Liang dai ren," 187.
42. Li Zhun, "Liang dai ren," 188.
43. Li Zhun, "Liang dai ren," 190.
44. Li Zhun, "Liang dai ren," 191.
45. Li Zhun, "Li Shuangshuang xiaozhuan," in *Li Zhun zuopin xuan shang*, 192. My translation here draws on Richard King's translation in *Heroes of the Great Leap Forward* (Honolulu: University of Hawai'i Press, 2010) for reference.
46. Tani Barlow, *The Question of Woman in Chinese Feminism* (Durham, NC: Duke University Press, 2004).
47. Li Zhun, "Xiaozhuan," 193.
48. Li Zhun, "Xiaozhuan," 193.
49. Li Zhun, "Xiaozhuan," 196–97.
50. Li Zhun, "Xiaozhuan," 200.
51. Li Zhun, "Xiaozhuan," 209.
52. Li Zhun, "Xiaozhuan," 222.
53. Li Zhun, "Xiaozhuan," 224.
54. Zhonggong zhongyang wenxian yanjiu shi 中共中央文献研究室 (Chinese Communist Party Central Committee textual research office), *Mao Zedong nianpu 1949–1976* 毛泽东年谱 (1949–1976) (Chronological biography of Mao Zedong 1949–1976) (Beijing: Zhongyang wenxian chubanshe, 2013), 3:414–17.
55. Zhonggong, *Nianpu*, 414–17.
56. Karl Marx, *Critique of the Gotha Programme* (Peking: Foreign Languages Press, 1972), 14–15.
57. Marx, *Critique*, 15.
58. Marx, *Critique*, 17.
59. Zhang Chunqiao 张春桥, "Pochu zichan jieji de faquan sixiang" 破除资产阶级的法权思想 (Smash the ideology of bourgeois right), *Renmin ribao*, October 13, 1958.
60. In the last three months of 1958, following Zhang's article, there were held six separate meetings on the problem of bourgeois right, whose participants were drawn overwhelmingly from the circles of philosophy and social science. The speeches were collected and published as an internal circulation document under the auspices of the Shanghai Municipal Philosophy and Social Science Academic Association.
61. Luo Gang is therefore right to argue that Mao's use of "bourgeois right" "was not restricted to Marx's original usage" in that he "expanded the [concept of] 'bourgeois right' that had initially been restricted to the field of distribution to the field of 'relations between human beings.'" Luo Gang 罗岗, *Renmin zhishang cong 'renmin dangjia zuozhu' dao 'shehui gongtong fuyu'* 人民至上 从"人民当家作主"到"社会共同富裕" (The people above all: From "the people are the masters" to "social common prosperity") (Shanghai: Shanghai renmin chubanshe, 2012), 164.
62. "Mao zhuxi zai Anhui" 毛主席在安徽 (Mao Zedong in Anhui), *Renmin ribao*, October 4, 1958.

63. This term defies straightforward translation. It had emerged throughout the 1956 discussions on the nationwide wage system, where it designated the simple use of differential wage scales for different categories of workers. In Zhang's usage, however, it seems to have posed the capacity of the wage system to constantly engender new forms of inequality, whereby rank as *dengji* might come to provide the material and ideological basis for the reemergence of antagonistic class formations.
64. As Luo Gang acknowledges with respect to the problem of consciousness, "if it may be said that [for Marx] 'bourgeois right' in 'the field of distribution' constituted the 'objectified form' of bourgeois right, then Mao further explored the 'subjective forms' appropriate to bourgeois right," consisting of the ongoing production of consciousness inimical to the development of communist social relations, as well as the need to engender a new consciousness of labor. Luo Gang, *Renmin*, 165.
65. Zhou Linzhi 周林知, "Ping Shanghai chuban wu zhong you guan laodong de fenpei wenti de yi xie cuowu guandian 评上海出版物中有关劳动和分配问题的一些错误观点 (Assessing some mistaken views concerning the problems of labor and remuneration in the Shanghai publishing world), *Jiefang* 解放 (Liberation) 9 (1958): 9.
66. Zhou, "Guandian," 11.
67. He Wei 何畏, "Nongcun shixing gonggei zhi de weida yiyi" 农村实行供给制的伟大意义 (The great significance of the countryside implementing the supply system), *Jingji yanjiu* 经济研究 (Economic Research) 11 (1958): 9.
68. Quan Zhili 全致力, "Dada tigao gongchan zhuyi de laodong taidu" 大大提高共产主义的劳动态度 (Greatly increase the communist attitude of labor), *Jiefang* 9 (1958): 1–4.
69. Yao Wenyuan 姚文元, "Lun gaofei" 论稿费 (On manuscript fees), *Wenhui bao* 文汇报 (Wenhui Daily), September 27, 1958.
70. On the same day that Yao's article was published, therefore, an expanded meeting encompassing the senior writers Zhang Tianyi, Zhou Libo, Ai Wu, and others pledged to reduce manuscript free payments, announcing "we are communist authors, and do not write simply for manuscript payments." Zhang Tianyi 张天翼, Zhou Libo 周立波, and Ai Wu 艾芜, "Women jianyi jiandi gaofei baochou" 我们建议减低稿费报酬 (We propose lowering manuscript payments), *Renmin ribao*, September 29, 1958. A series of reductions introduced in October under the aegis of the Culture Department were, however, reversed in the next year, on the grounds of their negative impacts on production.
71. Zhonggong, *Nianpu*, 527, 541.

4. Reproducing Revolution

Epigraph: Zhou Yang 周扬, "Zai wenyi gongzuo zuotanhui shang de jianghua" 在文艺工作座谈会上的讲话 (Speech at the art and literature work forum), in *Zhou Yang wenji* (Beijing: Renmin chubanshe, 1984–1994), 3:351.
1. Zhou Enlai 周恩来, "Guanyu wenhua yishu gongzuo liang tiao tui zoulu de wenti" 关于文化艺术工作两条腿走路的问题 (Concerning the problem of walking on two legs in art and literature work), in *Zhou Enlai Chen Yi lun wenyi* 周恩来陈毅论文艺 (Zhou Enlai and Chen Yi discuss art and literature) (Zhengzhou: Henan renmin chubanshe, 1980), 4.
2. Zhou Yang 周扬 et al, "Guanyu dangqian wenxue yishu gongzuo de yijian (xiuzheng cao'an)" 关于当前文学艺术工作的意见 (修正草案) (Proposals concerning current literary and artistic work [revised draft]), in *Wenyi zhanxian liang tiao luxian douzheng*

ziliao huibian 文艺战线两条路线斗争 资料汇编 (Two line struggle on the literary and artistic battle front collection of materials), ed. Xinan shifan xueyuan (chunlei) zao-fan bingtuan (hengkong chushi) 西南师范学院《春雷》造反兵团《横空出世》(Xinan Normal College Spring Thunder Rebel Corps) (Chongqing: Xinan shifan xueyuan, 1968), 430–32, 437–38.

3. Zhou Enlai 周恩来, "Zhou Enlai tongzhi tan yishu minzhu" 周恩来同志谈艺术民主 (Zhou Enlai on artistic democracy), in *Zhou Enlai Chen Yi lun wenyi*, 25.
4. Ru Zhijuan 茹志鹃, "Jingjing de chanyuan 静静的产院 (All quiet in the maternity clinic), in Ru Zhijuan 茹志鹃 *Ru Zhijuan xiaoshuo xuan* 茹志鹃小说选 (Ru Zhijuan short story collection) (Chengdu: Sichuan renmin chubanshe, 1983), 84–85.
5. Ru Zhijuan, "Chanyuan," 89.
6. Ru Zhijuan, "Chanyuan," 83–84.
7. Ru Zhijuan, "Chanyuan," 93–94.
8. Ru Zhijuan, "Chanyuan," 96.
9. Ru Zhijuan, "Chanyuan," 103
10. Hou Jinjing 侯金镜, "Chuangzuo geti he yishu tese—Du Ru Zhijuan xiaoshuo you gan" 创作个性和艺术特色-读茹志鹃小说有感 (Creative individuality and artistic uniqueness—feelings upon reading the short stories of Ru Zhijuan), *Wenyi bao* 文艺报 (Art and Literary Gazette) 3 (1961): 17.
11. *Wenyi bao* 文艺报 (Art and literary gazette), "Ticai wenti" 题材问题 (The problem of subject matter), in *Zhongguo xin wenxue daxi 1949–1976*中国新文学大系1949–1976 (New China literature series 1949–1976) (Shanghai: Shanghai wenyi chubanshe, 1997), 2:144.
12. Ru Zhijuan 茹志鹃, "Ah Shu" 阿舒 (Ah Shu), in *Ru Zhijuan xiaoshuo xuan*, 146.
13. Ru Zhijuan, "Ah Shu," 146–47, 150.
14. Ru Zhijuan, "Ah Shu," 158.
15. Ru Zhijuan, "Ah Shu," 161.
16. Li Zhi 黎之, *Wentan fengyu lu* 文坛风云录 (Record of happenings on the literary scene) (Beijing: Renmin wenxue chubanshe, 2015), 288–307.
17. Lin Mohan 林默涵, "Zongjie jingyan, jiuzheng cuowu, jixu qianjin" 总结经验，纠正错误，继续前进" (Rectify errors, correct mistakes, continue forward), in Lin Mohan 林默涵, *Lin Mohan wenlun ji* 林默涵文论集 (Lin Mohan essay collection) (Beijing: Dangdai zhonggu chubanshe, 2001), 421. While Lin does not specify his discursive antagonist here, the positions he describes suggest the ideas of Lukács, who argued for socialist realism as an extension of the achievements of the nineteenth-century realist novel.
18. Lin Mohan, "Jiuzheng cuowu," 426.
19. In the second half of 1962, then, those worker-writers such as Tang Kexin and Hu Wanchun who had been incorporated into formal literary institutions such as the Writers Association in the late 1950s underwent a process of reamateurization, in which they returned to their original sites of labor. "The worker-writer Hu Wanchun, having originally been a worker at the Shanghai Second Steel Factory, has now returned to this factory, to take up work at the party committee office, and so too is he preparing to enter the metal products workshop to engage in regular contact with the workers." "Chuangzuo fanying shehui zhuyi jianshe shiqi renmin qunzhong de huore douzheng" 创作反映社会主义建设时期人民群众的火热斗争 (Creation reflecting the fiery struggles of the masses in the period of socialist construction), *Renmin ribao* 人民日报 (People's Daily), December 26, 1962.

20. Mao Zedong 毛泽东, "Guanyu wenxue yishu de liang ge pishi" 关于文学艺术的两个批示 (Two directives concerning literature and art), in *Zhongguo xin wenyi daxi 1949–1966 lilun shiliao ji* 中国新文艺大系 1949–1966 理论史料集 (China new art and literature collection 1949–1966 collection of theoretical historical materials), ed. Zhang Jiong 张炯 (Beijing: Wenlian chubanshe, 1994), 13–14.
21. Hu Wanchun 胡万春, "Jiating wenti" 家庭问题 (A family affair), in Hu Wanchun 胡万春, *Xinsheng ji* 心声集 (Sounds of the heart) (Shanghai: Shanghai wenyichubanshe, 1981), 351.
22. The fame of these plays owes something to the fact that they were performed at the East China Drama Festival hosted in December 1963. Both Cai Xiang and Tang Xiaobing have subsequently interrogated these plays through the conceptual problem of the everyday. The analysis that follows here, however, differs from theirs in its choice of texts as well as attention to patriarchal displacement in the discourse of the everyday that emerged in tandem with the problem of revolutionary succession.
23. The fixation on hands was also central to Hu Wanchun's critical discourse during this period. Recounting an instance in which a young worker sought to preserve the elegant quality of their hands by wearing layers of gloves, Hu declaims that "currently among the youth there are two kinds of aesthetic perspective 审美观: are the hands of labor beautiful, or are the hands that do not labor beautiful? What is the class and social basis of such a perspective?" Hu Wanchun 胡万春, "Nuli fanying gongren jieji de douzheng shenghuo" 努力反映工人阶级的斗争生活 (Strive to reflect the life of struggle of the working class), *Guangming ribao* 光明日报 (Guangming Daily), April 1, 1964.
24. Xie Qipei 谢启沛, "Yao zhenxi yeyu shijian" 要珍惜业余时间 (It is necessary to treasure leisure time), *Zhongguo qingnian* 中国青年 (China Youth) 8 (1964): 47.
25. Hu Wanchun 胡万春, "Niandai" 年代 (Generations), in Hu Wanchun, *Xinsheng ji*, 444.
26. Hu Wanchun, "Niandai," 444.
27. Hu Wanchun, "Niandai," 445, 446.
28. Hu Wanchun, "Niandai," 451.
29. Hu Wanchun, "Niandai," 452.
30. Hu Wanchun, "Niandai," 452.
31. Hu Wanchun, "Niandai," 453.
32. Hu Wanchun, "Niandai," 454, 456, 457.
33. Hu Wanchun, "Niandai," 457, 460, 462.
34. Hu Wanchun, "Niandai," 465, 468.
35. Zhonggong zhongyang xuanchuan bu 中共中央宣传部 (Propaganda Department of the Central Committee pf the Communist Party of China), "Zhonggong zhongyang xuanchuan bu guanyu quanguo wenlian he ge xiehui zhengfeng qingkuang de baogao" 中共中央宣传部关于文联和各协会整风情况的报告 (Report from the Propaganda Department of the Central Committee of the Communist Party of China on the state of rectification in the cultural associations and varied bodies), in *Jianguo yilai zhongyao wenxian xuanbian* (Selection of important documents since the founding of the country) (Beijing: Zhongyang wenxian chubanshe, 2011), 19:8–14.
36. Mao Zedong, "Pishi," 13–14.
37. Li Zhi, *Wentan*, 345–52.

38. People's Daily, Red Flag, *On Khrushchev's Phony Communism and Its Historical Lessons for the World: Comment on the Open Letter of the Central Committee of the CPSU (IX)* (Peking: Foreign Languages Press, 1964), 7.
39. Lin Biao 林彪, "Dui budui wenyi gongzuo de zhishi" 对部队文艺工作的指示 (Directive on cultural work in army units), in Lin Biao 林彪, *Lin Biao wenji* 林彪文集 (Selected works of Lin Biao) (Xianggang: Zhongxiang chuanmei chubanshe, 2011), 402–3.
40. Kang Shanjin 康闪金, "'Zichan jieji faquan'—yi ge geming zhengzhi cihui de lishi kaocha '资产阶级法权': 一个革命政治词汇的历史考察 ("Bourgeois right": A historical investigation of a vocabulary of revolutionary politics), *Dangshi yanjiu yu jiaoxue* 党史研究与教学 (CPC History Research and Teaching) 1 (2015): 90.
41. "Quanguo dou yao xuexi jiefang jun" 全国都要学习解放军 (The whole country must study the People's Liberation Army), *Renmin ribao*, February 1, 1964.
42. "Ba san ba zuofeng chuanbo dao quanguo qu" 把三八作风传播到全国去 (Disseminate the three-eight work style throughout the country), *Renmin ribao*, February 23, 1964.
43. Chen Guangsheng 陈广生, *Mao zhuxi de hao zhanshi—Lei Feng* 毛主席的好战士—雷锋 (Lei Feng—good soldier of Chairman Mao) (Beijing: Zhongguo qingnian chubanshe, 1963), 80.
44. Hu Wanchun 胡万春, "Jianjue tong jiu shijie juelie" 坚决同旧世界决裂 (We must rupture with the old world), *Renmin ribao*, January 9, 1965.
45. Hu Wanchun, "Juelie," 6.
46. Hu Wanchun, "Juelie," 6.
47. Rebecca Karl, "Serve the People," in *Afterlives of Chinese Communism: Political Concepts from Mao to Xi*, ed. Christian Sorace, Ivan Franceschini, and Nicholas Loubere (Acton, ACT: ANU Press 2019), 248.
48. Zhang Jiong 张炯, "Wenxue yishu zhong de yingxiong he lixiang wenti" 文学艺术中的英雄和理想问题 (The hero and problem of the ideal in art and literature), in *Zhongguo xin wenyi daxi 1949–1966 lilun shiliao ji* 中国新文艺大系 1949–1966 理论史料集 (China new art and literature collection 1949–1966: Collection of theoretical historical materials), ed. Zhang Jiong 张炯 (Beijing: Wenlian chubanshe, 1994), 620.
49. For example, extracts of the novel were serialized across newspapers such as *People's Daily* and *Liberation Army Daily*. In one such extract, published in *People's Daily*, the editorial comment suggestively stressed that the narrative showed Yanghai's development "from desiring 渴望 to be a hero but not yet being a hero, to becoming a hero without being conscious of being so" under the tutelage of the party. Jin Jingmai 金敬迈, "Ou Yanghai zhi ge" 欧阳海之歌 (Song of Ou Yanghai), *Renmin ribao*, January 9, 1966. The notion of a *tempering* of desire as necessary for the formation of the hero is central to the analysis that follows.
50. Jin Jingmai 金敬迈, *Ou Yanghai zhi ge* 欧阳海之歌 (Song of Ou Yanghai) (Beijing: Jiefang jun wenyishe, 1979), 146.
51. Jin Jingmai, *Ou Yanghai*, 148–49.
52. Jin Jingmai, *Ou Yanghai*, 157.
53. Jin Jingmai, *Ou Yanghai*, 170.
54. Jin Jingmai, *Ou Yanghai*, 406.
55. Jin Jingmai, *Ou Yanghai*, 406.
56. Jin Jingmai, *Ou Yanghai*, 576, 592.
57. Zhou Yang 周扬, "Gaoju Mao Zedong sixiang hongqi, zuo you hui laodong you hui chuangzuo de wenyi zhanshi" 高举毛泽东思想红旗, 做又会劳动又会创作的文艺战士

(Raise high the banner of Mao Zedong thought, be a literary warrior capable of both labor and creation), in *Quanguo qingnian yeyu wenxue chuangzuo jiji fenzi dahui baogao, jianghua Ji* 全国抢年业余文学创作积极分子大会报告，讲话集 (Reports and speeches from the all-China meeting of youth amateur literary creation activists), ed. Zhongguo qingnian chubanshe 中国青年出版社 (China Youth Press) (Beijing: Zhongguo qingnian chubanshe, 1966), 23.

58. Zhou Yang, "Wenyi zhanshi," 27.
59. Zhou Yang, "Wenyi zhanshi," 27–28.

5. In and Out of Petersburg

Epigraph: Ren Du 任犊, "'Zouchu 'Bidebao!'—du Liening yi jiu yi jiu nian qi yue zhi Gao'erji de xin you gan" 走出"彼得堡!"—读列宁一九一九年七月致高尔基的信有感 (Get out of "Petersburg!"—feelings upon reading Lenin's 1919 July letter to Gorky), *Zhaoxia* 朝霞 (Morning glow) 3 (1975): 4.

1. The first intimations of a return to writing and the aspirations to produce a new mode of writing came in 1972 with the *People's Daily* editorial "Develop Socialist Literary Creation," which stressed that "worker-peasant-soldier amateur art and literature detachments must firmly use their free time in order to engage in literary activities, and they should not depart from productive labor." "Fazhan shehuizhuyi de wenyi chuangzuo" 发展社会主义的文艺创作 (Develop socialist literary creation), *Renmin ribao* 人民日报 (People's Daily), December 16, 1971. This shift was lent further momentum by the conclusions of the Publishing Work Forum held in 1971, which agreed to restore literary publications, subject to official approval. For a comprehensive listing of pre-1966 periodicals that eventually resumed publication (albeit often under new names) during the late Cultural Revolution, see Wu Shanzeng 武善增, *Wenxue huayu de jibian yu fumie: Wenge zhuliu wenxue huayu yanjiu* 文学话语的畸变与覆灭 (The aberration and destruction of literary discourse) (Zhengzhou: Henan daxue chubanshe, 2012), chap. 2.
2. The fictionalized diary of *Youth* has, to be sure, parallels with an earlier, pre–Cultural Revolution history of diary writing as a mode of pedagogy for the autoproduction of socialist subjects, grounded, as Shan Windscript notes, in "a ritual of daily self-transformation rooted in religious and revolutionary traditions," one oriented toward "self-discipline and daily introspective surveillance." Shan Windscript, "How to Write a Diary in Mao's New China: Guidebooks in the Crafting of Socialist Subjectivities." *Modern China* 47, no. 4 (2021): 423.
3. Zhang Changgong 张长弓, *Qingchun* 青春 (Youth) (Hohhot: Neimenggu renmin chubanshe, 1973), 9.
4. Zhang Changgong, *Qingchun*, 9.
5. Zhang Changgong, *Qingchun*, 53.
6. Zhang Changgong, *Qingchun*, 320.
7. Zhang Changgong, *Qingchun*, 159.
8. Zhang Changgong, *Qingchun*, 167–69.
9. Zhang Changgong, *Qingchun*, 168.
10. Zhang Changgong, *Qingchun*, 380.
11. Duan Ruixia 段瑞夏, "Tebie guanzhong" 特别观众 (Not just one of the audience), in *Zhaoxia* 朝霞 (Morning glow), ed. Shanghai wenyi congkan 上海文艺丛刊 (Shanghai art and literature collection) (Shanghai: Shanghai wenyi congkan, 1973), 3. My

translation here draws on Tuan Jui-hsia, "Not Just One of the Audience," *Chinese Literature* 9 (1973): 51–64.
12. Duan Ruixia, "Guanzhong," 13–14.
13. Duan Ruixia, "Guanzhong," 17.
14. Duan Ruixia, "Guanzhong," 17.
15. Shi Yanping 施燕平, *Chenfeng suiyue* 尘封岁月 (Years of dust) (Shanghai: Huadong shifan daxue chubanshe, 2014), 206–8.
16. Duan Ruixia 段瑞夏, "Zuo weida shidai douzheng shenghuo de jiluyuan" 做伟大时代斗争生活的记录员 (Serve as a recorder of the life of struggle of the great era), in *Jinzhong changming* (The long cry of the golden bell), ed. Shanghai renmin chubanshe 上海人民出版社 (Shanghai People's Publishing House) (Shanghai: Shanghai renmin chubanshe, 1973), 273–82.
17. Duan Ruixia, "Jiluyuan," 280.
18. Duan Ruixia, "Jiluyuan," 280–81.
19. The formulation of the "cake of a thousand people" also occurred elsewhere in the literary theory of the Cultural Revolution as an image of a collective writing subject, classified as an instance of a "new-born thing." Jin Mei, for example, also called for the release of literary creation from the mystified notion of individual genius and creativity. Jin Mei 金梅, "Cong 'qian ren gao' shuo qi" 从千人糕说起 (Speaking from a "cake of a thousand people"), in *Youya douzheng mingtian* 幼芽 斗争 明天 (New sprouts, struggle, tomorrow), ed. Tianjin renmin chubanshe 天津人民出版社 (Tianjin People's Publishing House) (Tianjin: Tianjin renmin chubanshe, 1976), 45–49.
20. As compared to *Morning Glow*, *Study and Criticism* has received more scholarly attention, not least due to its importance in the Critique Confucius Campaign. This journal was also distinguished by important theoretical debates and interventions around problems of "bourgeois right."
21. Duan Ruixia et al. 段瑞夏等, "Yangguang he turang" 阳光和土壤" (Sunlight and soil). *Xuexi yu pipan* 学习与批判 (Study and Criticism) 3 (1973): 58–62.
22. Duan Ruixia et al., "Yangguang," 60–61.
23. *Morning Glow* was by far the most significant literary journal to emerge during the late Cultural Revolution. Yet, in addition to those pre-1966 that resumed publication during the early 1970s, there are also intimations of further attempts to form new, revolutionary journals on the model of *Morning Glow*. From May 1975 onward there appeared a total of four issues of a literary series entitled *This Age* 今朝 in Tianjin. It is possible that this series was also intended to become a full, regular publication.
24. Shi Yanping, *Chenfeng*, 209–11.
25. Zhou Tian 周天, "Wenyi zhanxian shang de yi ge xinsheng shiwu—san jiehe chuangzuo" 文艺战线上的一个新生事物—三结合创作 (A newborn thing on the literary battle front: Creation through the three combinations), *Zhaoxia* 12 (1975): 69.
26. Zhou Tian, "Xinsheng shiwu," 70.
27. Ren Du, "Bidebao," 3.
28. Ren Du, "Bidebao," 4.
29. Ren Du, "Bidebao," 5.
30. Ren Du, "Bidebao," 4.
31. Ren Du, "Bidebao," 6.
32. Duan Ruixia 段瑞夏, "Chui yu shi" 锤与诗 (Hammer and poem), *Jiefang ribao* 解放日报 (Liberation Daily), May 18, 1975.

33. Duan, "Chui," 4.
34. Duan, "Chui," 4.
35. Duan, "Chui," 4.
36. Duan, "Chui," 4.
37. Duan, "Chui," 4.
38. Recreating the composition of the textbook has been greatly aided by the 1981 work of Peer Moller Christensen and Jorgen Delman, who unfortunately did not have access to the final published edition of the textbook that forms the basis of the analysis here. See Peer Moller Christensen and Jorgen Delman, "A Theory of Transitional Society: Mao Zedong and the Shanghai School," *Bulletin of Concerned Asian Scholars* 13, no. 2 (1981): 2–15.
39. Beyond the successive versions published in Shanghai under the aegis of the writing group, universities in Tianjin and Beijing also produced their own textbooks. More work is needed to discern the different theoretical trajectories that emerged during the Cultural Revolution, and the relations between them.
40. Fang Hai 方海, "Xuexi yi dian zhengzhi jingjixue" 学一点政治经济学 (Study some political economy), *Hongqi* 红旗 (Red Flag) 7 (1972): 36.
41. Shanghai Renmin Chubanshe 上海人民出版社 (Shanghai people's publishing house), *Xue dian zhengzhi jingjixue* 学点政治经济学 (Study some political economy) (Shanghai: Shanghai renmin chubanshe, 1972), 90–93, 104–5.
42. Shanghai Renmin Chubanshe 上海人民出版社 (Shanghai People's Publishing House), *Shehuizhuyi zhengzhijingjixue: Zhengqiu yijian gao* 社会主义政治经济学：征求意见稿 (Socialist political economy: Version for solicitation of comments) (Shanghai: Shanghai renmin chubanshe, 1972), 269.
43. Shanghai hudong zaochuan chang deng danwei tongzhi 上海沪东造船厂等单位同志 (Comrades from the Shanghai Hudong Shipyard and other work units), *Liang zhong shehui liang zhong gong zi* 两种社会两种工资 (Two kinds of society, two kinds of wage) (Shanghai: Shanghai renmin chubanshe, 1973), 12–13.
44. *People's Daily*, "Marx, Engels and Lenin on the Dictatorship of the Proletariat," *Peking Review* 9 (1975): 5. These commentaries were the product of a series of meetings held between Mao and senior political figures in late 1974, including Yao Wenyuan and Zhang Chunqiao. Mao's recorded oral comments are as follows: "as for why Lenin spoke of proletarian dictatorship, we should write some articles. Tell [Zhang] Chunqiao and [Yao] Wenyuan to find where Lenin discusses this problem in his works, have these extracts printed in larger characters, and send them to me. We will first read and then write some articles; [Zhang] Chunqiao must write these sorts of articles. If we don't get this question in order, we will turn revisionist." Zhonggong zhongyang wenxian yanjiu shi 中共中央文献研究室 (Chinese Communist Party Central Committee Textual Research Office), *Mao Zedong nianpu 1949–1976* 毛泽东年谱 (1949–1976) (Chronological biography of Mao Zedong 1949–1976) (Beijing: Zhongyang wenxian chubanshe, 2013), 6:572. It may be surmised that Zhang's article on proletarian dictatorship originated with Mao's request.
45. *People's Daily*, "Study Well the Theory of the Dictatorship of the Proletariat," *Peking Review* 7 (1975): 4–5.
46. *People's Daily*, "Marx, Engels and Lenin," 9.
47. Chang Chun-chiao, *On Exercising All-Round Dictatorship Over the Bourgeoisie* (Peking: Foreign Languages Press, 1975), 10.
48. Luo Gang is therefore right to note in this context that, in the late phase of the Cultural Revolution, under the impetus of Zhang's article, "the spearhead [of the critique

of bourgeois right] that had originally been directed against the 'privileged class' or the 'bureaucratic class' was instead turned against the common masses who were designated as 'small producers.'" Luo Gang, *Renmin*, 175.

49. Yao Wenyuan 姚文元, "Lun Lin Biao fan dang jituan de shehui jichu" 论林彪反党集团的社会基础 (On the social basis of the Lin Biao anti-Party clique), *Hongqi* 3 (1975): 27.

50. Fang Kang, "Capitalist-Roaders Are Inside the Party," *Peking Review* 25 (1976): 10. Adapted slightly from the official translation as published in *Peking Review*. The original official rendering is "a bourgeois state without capitalists," here replaced by the standard rendering of Lenin's formulation in *State and Revolution*, "a bourgeois state without the bourgeoisie."

51. This particular directive was, as Alessandro Russo has pointed out, without precedent in its conclusions, particularly in relation to the theoretical problematic of bourgeois right that had occupied Mao and other radicals over the late Cultural Revolution. Alessandro Russo, "How Did the Cultural Revolution End? The Last Dispute Between Mao Zedong and Deng Xiaoping, 1975," *Modern China* 39, no. 3 (2013): 239–79.

52. The theoretical knots notwithstanding, the direct appeal to Lenin's writings on the state in this context also underscores the extent to which the theoretical developments of late Maoism marked a direct and ultimately coherent critique of the Stalin-era Soviet Union for its theoretical and political degeneration. The small number of articles written specifically on this question evidence a close familiarity with theoretical developments from that period. Guo Zizuo, writing in 1976, wrote without compromise that "after the victory of the October Revolution, the Soviet government under Lenin's leadership adopted some measures to restrict bourgeois right in the areas of the ownership system, distribution and mutual relations. Yet in the 1930s, the Soviet government emphasized 'technique decides everything,' 'cadres decide everything,' and with respect to distribution and mutual relations they gradually restored and enlarged bourgeois right." Guo Zizuo 郭子佐, "Sanshi niandai sulian lilun jie guanyu zichan jieji faquan de taolun" 三十年代苏联理论界关于资产阶级法权的讨论 (1930s discussions in the Soviet theoretical sphere concerning bourgeois right), *Jiefang ribao*, March 15, 1976.

53. Shehuizhuyi zhengzhijingjixue bianxie xiaozu 社会主义政治经济学编写小组 (Socialist political economy editorial group), *Shehuizhuyi zhengzhijingjixue: Weiding gao di er ban taolun gao* 社会主义政治经济学: 未定稿第二版讨论稿 (Socialist political economy: Preparatory draft second edition discussion draft) (Shanghai, 1976), 46.

54. Xiaozu, *Taolun gao*, 73–74, 86–87.

55. Xiaozu, *Taolun gao*, 84.

56. The authors themselves were closely aware of the continued formal problems of the text, that is, the failure to organize the analysis of categories according to their purported aim of making the contradictions of socialism intelligible. They argued in the preface that "concerning the movement of a socialist economy, this book continues to divide its categories according to the external appearance of things rather than according to their internal relations. From the systematic structure of this book as well as from its analysis of individual categories of socialist production relations, the traces of Soviet textbooks of political economy from the 1950s are still visible" Xiaozu, *Taolun gao*, 6.

57. Xiaozu, *Taolun gao*, 379.

58. Xiaozu, *Taolun gao*, 384, 385.

59. Xiaozu, *Taolun gao*, 393.

60. Wu Zhanlei 吴战垒, "Cuihui linghun shenchu de Bidebao" 摧毁灵魂深处的彼得堡 (Destroy the 'Petersburg' in the depths of the soul), in *Haojiaoji* 号角集 (Bugle) (Shanghai: Shanghai renmin chubanshe, 1976), 18–19.
61. Fang Yun 方耘, "Shenru pipan wenyi lingyu de zichan jieji faquan sixiang" 深入批判文艺领域的资产阶级法权思想 (Deeply criticize the ideology of bourgeois right in the cultural sphere), in *Jianchi zou yu gongnong xiang jiehe de daolu* 坚持走与工农相结合的道路 (Firmly walk the path of integration with the workers and peasants) (Shanghai: Shanghai renmin chubanshe, 1975), 87–88.

Thermidor (By Way of Conclusion)

Epigraph: Ding Ling 丁玲, "Niupeng xiaopin" 牛棚小品 (Brief accounts from the cowshed), in *Ding Ling quanji* (Shijiazhuang: Hebei renmin chubanshe, 2001) 10:165–85.

1. Dai Jinhua, *After the Post-Cold War: The Future of Chinese History* (Durham, NC: Duke University Press, 2018), 29.
2. In yet more polemical terms, Kuang Xinnian notes: "as the discourse of 'human nature' 人性 replaced the discourse of 'class,' so too did the legitimacy of 'Enlightenment' replace the legitimacy of 'class struggle' constituting the surging trends of human nature and humanism in the 1980s. At the same time, the 'literature of the new period' also underwent a constant retreat from 'people's literature' to 'literature of the human,' and the 'literature of the human' came to replace 'people's literature.'" Kuang Xinnian 旷新年, "Renmin wenxue: Wei wancheng de lishi jiangou" 人民文学：未完成的历史建构 (People's literature: An incomplete historical project), *Wenyi liilun yu piping* 文艺理论与批评 (Literary Theory and Criticism) 6 (2005): 27–28. In close connection, Cheng Kai also observes that the distancing from the cultural experiments of the Cultural Revolution in the early 1980s was accompanied by a wholesale transmutation of the concepts of "politics" and the "people" as they appear in Mao's Talks. Through the interventions of Hu Qiaomu and others, there emerged a "negation of the revolutionary and struggle character of politics, whereby politics became purely institutionalized and functional (in the interests of legitimacy)." Cheng Kai 程凯, "Cong geming zhuti lun ji lishi, xianshi de bianzheng guanxi kan jiangua" 从革命主体论及历史，现实的辩证关系看讲话 (Examining the talks from the dialectical relation between the theory of the subject, history, and reality), *Zhongguo xiandai wenxue yanjiu congkan* 中国现代文学研究丛刊 (Modern Chinese Literature Research) 5 (2022): 6.
3. Dai Houying 戴厚英, *Ren a, ren* 人啊人 (Humanity, ah humanity!) (Guangzhou: Huacheng chubanshe, 1980), 260, 263.
4. The antagonistic theorization of aesthetics was consistently formulated with reference to Chernyshevsky from Yan'an onward. In the early reform period, then, Xia Zhongyi's famous 1988 article on Belinsky, Chernyshevsky, and Dobrolyubov marked an explicit attempt to contest the socialist theoretical genealogy around Chernyshevsky and to reformulate his ideas in terms of a depoliticized notion of realism. Xia Zhongyi 夏中义, "Bie, Che, Du zai dangdai Zhongguo de mingyun" 别、车、杜在当代中国的命运 (The destiny of Belinsky, Chernyshevsky, and Dobrolyubov in contemporary China), *Shanghai wentan* 上海文坛 (Shanghai Forum) 5 (1988): 4–19.
5. Zhu Guangqian 朱光潜, "Guanyu renxing, rendao zhuyi, renqing wei he gongtong mei wenti" 关于人性，人道主义，人情味和共同美问题 (On the questions of human

nature, humanism, human sentiment and universal beauty), in Zhu Guangqian 朱光潜, *Zhu Guangqian quanji* 朱光潜全集 (Zhu Guangqian collected works) (Hefei: Anhui jiaoyu chubanshe, 1989), 5:389.

6. Zhu Guangqian, "Renxing," 389.
7. Zhu Guangqian, "Yishu shi yi zhong shengchan laodong" 艺术是一种生产劳动 (Art is a kind of productive labor), in *Zhu Guangqian quanji*, 5:261. Zhu's formulation of a "world of objects" is taken directly from Marx's *1844 Manuscripts* and marks the actualization or "realization" of man's being in the world through unalienated labor. Consider Marx's formulation as follows: "in creating a *world of objects [gegenständlichen Welt]* by his personal activity, in his *work upon* inorganic nature, man proves himself a conscious species-being, i.e., as a being that treats the species as his own essential being, or that treats itself as a species-being."
8. Zhu Guangqian 朱光潜, "Makesi de jingjixue—zhexue shougao zhong de meixue wenti" 马克思的经济学哲学手稿中的美学问题 (Questions of aesthetics in Marx's economic and philosophical manuscripts), in *Zhu Guangqian quanji*, 5:412–62.
9. Wang Ruoshui 王若水, "Ren shi Makesi zhuyi de chufa dian" 人是马克思的出发点 (The human is the point of departure for Marxism), in Wang Ruoshui 王若水, *Wei rendao zhuyi bianhu* 为人道主义辩护 (In defense of humanism) (Beijing: Sanlian shudian, 1986), 216.
10. Wang Ruoshui 王若水, "Tan tan yihua wenti" 谈谈异化问题 (On problems of alienation), in *Wei rendao zhuyi bianhu*, 195.
11. Wang Ruoshui 王若水, "Laodong—zhishi—caifu" 劳动-知识-财富 (Labor—knowledge—wealth), in *Wei rendao zhuyi bianhu*, 99–100.
12. Hu Qili 胡启立, "Zai zhongguo zuojia di si ci huiyuan daibiao dahui shang de zhuci 在中国作家协会第四次会员代表大会上的祝词 (Congratulatory speech at the fourth congress of the Chinese Writers Association), *Renmin ribao* 人民日报 (People's Daily), December 30, 1984, 1.
13. This shift was marked in the apparently obscure problem of translation, in the shift from *zichanjieji faquan*/资产阶级法权 to *zichanjieji quanli*/资产阶级权利 as the formal translation for "bourgeois right," published in 1977 in *People's Daily* under the signature of the Communist Party Central Committee Marx-Engels-Lenin Stalin Translation Bureau.
14. Of special importance here are Su Shaozhi, Feng Youlan, and Yu Guangyuan. Su and Feng jointly published "Refuting Yao Wenyuan's Mistaken Theory That Remuneration According to Labor Gives Rise to the Bourgeoisie" in *People's Daily* on August 9, 1977, marking the direction of travel for the reform period. Su later became a "dissident" in the West, having served his intellectual function as a combatant against the radical left.
15. Guo Rui 郭瑞, "Wenyi gaige yu yishu zhiliang" 文艺改革与艺术质量 (The reform of art and literature and artistic quality), in *Lilun dongtai huibian ben 1983 nian di 3 ji* 理论动态 汇编本 1983年 第3辑 (Theoretical trends collected edition 1983, volume 3) (Beijing: Zhonggong zhongyang dangxiao chubanshe, 1983), 90.
16. Ding Ling 丁玲, "Du Wanxiang" 杜晚香, in *Ding Ling quanji*, 4:291, 294.
17. Ding Ling, "Du Wanxiang," 4:291, 293.
18. Ding Ling, "Du Wanxiang," 4:293.
19. Ding Ling, "Du Wanxiang," 4:309.
20. Ding Ling, "Du Wanxiang," 4:306.
21. Ding Ling, "Du Wanxiang," 4:311, 312.
22. Ding Ling, "Du Wanxiang," 4:313.

23. Ding Ling, "Du Wanxiang," 4:313.
24. Ding Ling 丁玲, "Guanyu Du Wanxiang" 关于杜晚香 (On "Du Wanxiang"), in *Ding Ling quanji*, 9:262.
25. Ding Ling, "Guanyu," 9:268.
26. Ding Ling, "Xiaopin," in *Ding Ling quanji*, 10:169.

SELECTED BIBLIOGRAPHY

Althusser, Louis. *On the Reproduction of Capitalism: Ideology and Ideological State Apparatuses*. Translated by G. M. Goshgarian. London: Verso, 2014.
——. *Reading Capital*. Translated by Ben Brewster. London: New Left Books, 1970.
Bai Lang 白朗. *Bai Lang wenji* 白朗文集 (Bai Lang selected works). 6 vols. Shenyang: Chunfeng wenyi chubanshe, 1983–1986.
Cai Xiang. *Revolution and Its Narratives: China's Socialist Literary and Cultural Imaginaries, 1949–1966*. Translated by Rebecca Karl and Zhong Xueping. Durham, NC: Duke University Press, 2016.
Chang Chun-chiao. *On Exercising All-Round Dictatorship Over the Bourgeoisie*. Peking: Foreign Languages Press, 1975.
Cheng Kai 程凯. "Cong geming zhuti lun ji lishi, xianshi de bianzheng guanxi kan jiangua" 从革命主体论及历史,现实的辩证关系看讲话 (Examining the talks from the dialectical relation between the theory of the subject, history, and reality). *Zhongguo xiandai wenxue yanjiu congkan* 中国现代文学研究丛刊 (Modern Chinese Literature Research) 5 (2022): 3.
Clark, Katerina. *The Soviet Novel: History as Ritual*. Chicago: University of Chicago Press, 1985.
Coderre, Laurence. *Newborn Socialist Things: Materiality in Maoist China*. Durham, NC: Duke University Press, 2021.
Dai Jinhua. *After the Post–Cold War: The Future of Chinese History*. Durham, NC: Duke University Press, 2018.
Ding Ling 丁玲. *Ding Ling quanji* 丁玲全集 (Ding Ling collected works). 12 vols. Shijiazhuang: Hebei renmin chubanshe, 2001.
He-Yin Zhen. *The Birth of Chinese Feminism: Essential Texts in Transnational Theory*. Translated by Lydia H. Liu, Rebecca E. Karl, and Dorothy Ko. New York: Columbia University Press, 2013.

Hong Zicheng 洪子诚. *Dangdai wenxue gaishuo* 当代文学概说 (Summary of contemporary literature). Nanning: Guangxi jiaoyu chubanshe, 2000.

Hu Wanchun 胡万春. *Xinsheng ji* 心声集 (Sounds of the heart). Shanghai: Shanghai wenyichubanshe, 1981.

Huang, Erin. *Urban Horror: Neoliberal Post-Socialism and the Limits of Visibility*. Durham, NC: Duke University Press, 2020.

Jin Jingmai 金敬迈. *Ou Yanghai zhi ge* 欧阳海之歌 (Song of Ou Yanghai). Beijing: Jiefang jun wenyishe, 1979.

Levine, Caroline. *Forms: Whole, Rhythm, Hierarchy, Network*. Princeton, NJ: Princeton University Press, 2015.

Li Jiefei 李洁非 and Yang Jie 杨劼. *Gongheguo wenxue shengchan fangshi* 共和国文学生产方式 (The literary mode of production in the republic). Beijing: Shehui kexue wenxian chubanshe, 2011.

Li Zhi 黎之. *Wentan fengyu lu* 文坛风云录 (Record of happenings on the literary scene). Beijing: Renmin wenxue chubanshe, 2015.

Li Zhun 李准. *Li Zhun zuopin xuan shang* 李准作品选 上 (A selection of Li Zhun's works, part 1) Beijing: Dazhong wenyi chubanshe, 2004.

Lin Biao 林彪. *Lin Biao wenji* 林彪文集 (Selected works of Lin Biao). Xianggang: Zhongxiang chuanmei chubanshe, 2011.

Lin Mohan 林默涵. *Lin Mohan wenlun ji* 林默涵文论集 (Lin Mohan essay collection). Beijing: Dangdai zhonggu chubanshe, 2001.

Liu Qing 柳青. *Liu Qing wenji* 柳青文集 (Liu Qing selected works). 2 vols. Xi'an: Shaanxi renmin chubanshe, 1991.

——. *Liu Qing zhuanji* 柳青专集 (Liu Qing special collection). Fuzhou: Fujian renmin chubanshe, 1982.

Liu Runwei 刘润为, ed. *Yan'an wenyi daxi* 延安文艺大系 (Yan'an art and literature collection). 28 vols. Changsha: Hunan wenyi chubanshe, 2015.

Liu Shipei 刘师培. *Guocui yu xihua Liu Shipei wenxuan* 国粹与西化 刘师培选文 (National essence and westernization: Liu Shipei selected works). Shanghai: Shanghai dongyuan chubanshe, 1996.

Luo Gang 罗岗. *Renmin zhishang cong "renmin dangjia zuozhu" dao "shehui gongtong fuyu"* 人民至上 从"人民当家作主"到"社会共同富裕 (The people above all: From "the people are the masters" to "social common prosperity"). Shanghai: Shanghai renmin chubanshe, 2012.

Mao Dun 茅盾. *Mao Dun quanji* 茅盾全集 (Mao Dun collected works). 40 vols. Beijing: Renmin chubanshe, 1984.

Mao Tse-Tung. *Selected Works*. 5 vols. Peking: Foreign Languages Press, 1965.

Mao Zedong 毛泽东. *Mao Zedong wenyi lunji* 毛泽东文艺论集 (Mao Zedong collection of writings on art and literature). Beijing: Zhongyang wenxian chubanshe, 2002.

Marx, Karl. *Critique of the Gotha Programme*. Peking: Foreign Languages Press, 1972.

McDougall, Bonnie S. *Mao Zedong's "Talks at the Yan'an Conference on Literature of Art": A Translation of the 1943 Text with Commentary*. Ann Arbor: University of Michigan Press, 1980.

Ru Zhijuan 茹志鹃. *Ru Zhijuan xiaoshuo xuan* 茹志鹃小说选 (Ru Zhijuan short story collection). Chengdu: Sichuan renmin chubanshe, 1983.

Shanghai Renmin Chubanshe 上海人民出版社 (Shanghai people's publishing house). *Shehuizhuyi zhengzhijingjixue: Zhengqiu yijian gao* 社会主义政治经济学: 征求意见稿 (Socialist political economy: Version for solicitation of comments). Shanghai: Shanghai renmin chubanshe, 1972.

Shanghai wenyi congkan 上海文艺丛刊 (Shanghai art and literature collection), ed. *Zhaoxia* 朝霞 (Morning glow). Shanghai: Shanghai wenyi congkan, 1973.

Shehuizhuyi zhengzhijingjixue bianxie xiaozu 社会主义政治经济学编写小组 (Socialist political economy editorial group). *Shehuizhuyi zhengzhijingjixue: Weiding gao di er ban taolun gao* 社会主义政治经济学：未定稿第二版讨论稿 (Socialist political economy: Preparatory draft second edition discussion draft). Shanghai, 1976.

Sun Xiaozhong 孙晓忠 and Gao Ming 高明, eds. *Yan'an xiangcun jianshe ziliao* 延安乡村建设资料 (Yan'an village construction material). Shanghai: Shanghai daxue chubanshe, 2012.

Tang Kexin 唐克新. *Zhongzi* 种子 (Seeds). Shanghai: Zuojia chubanshe, 1965.

Wang Ruoshui 王若水. *Wei rendao zhuyi bianhu* 为人道主义辩护 (In defense of humanism). Beijing: Sanlian shudian, 1986.

Xie Baojie 谢保杰. *Zhuti, xiangxiang yu biaoda: 1949–1966 nian gongnongbing xiezuo de lishi kaocha* 主体，想象与表达：1949–1966 年工农兵写作的历史考察 (Subject, imagination, and expression: A historical investigation of worker-peasant-soldier writing over 1949–1966). Beijing: Beijing daxue chubanshe, 2015.

Zhang Changgong 张长弓. *Qingchun* 青春 (Youth). Hohhot: Neimenggu renmin chubanshe, 1973.

Zhang Jiong 张炯 ed. *Zhongguo xin wenyi daxi 1949–1966 lilun shiliao ji* 中国新文艺大系 1949–1966 理论史料集 (China new art and literature collection 1949–1966: Collection of theoretical historical materials). Beijing: Wenlian chubanshe, 1994.

Zhonggong zhongyang wenxian shi 中共中央文献室 (Chinese Communist Party Central Committee Textual Office), ed. *Jianguo yilai zhongyao wenxian xuanbian* 建国以来重要文献选编 (Selection of important documents since the founding of the country). 20 vols. Beijing: Zhongyang wenxian chubanshe, 2011.

——. *Zhonggong zhongyang wenjian xuanji* 中共中央文件选集 (Selection of documents from the CPC central committee). 50 vols. Beijing: Renmin chubanshe, 2013.

Zhonggong zhongyang wenxian yanjiu shi 中共中央文献研究室 (Chinese Communist Party Central Committee Textual Research Office). *Mao Zedong nianpu 1949–1976* 毛泽东年谱 (1949–1976) (Chronological biography of Mao Zedong 1949–1976). 6 vols. Beijing: Zhongyang wenxian chubanshe, 2013.

Zhou Enlai 周恩来 and Chen Yi 陈毅. *Zhou Enlai Chen Yi lun wenyi* 周恩来陈毅论文艺 (Zhou Enlai and Chen Yi discuss art and literature). Zhengzhou: Henan renmin chubanshe, 1980.

Zhou Libo 周立波. *Zhou Libo wenji* 周立波文集 (Zhou Libo selected works). 6 vols. Shanghai: Shanghai wenyi chubanshe, 1982.

Zhou Yang 周扬. *Zhou Yang wenji* 周扬文集 (Zhou Yang selected works). 5 vols. Beijing: Renmin chubanshe, 1984–1994.

Zhu Guangqian 朱光潜. *Zhu Guangqian quan ji* 朱光潜全集 (Zhu Guangqian collected works) 17 vols. Hefei: Anhui jiaoyu chubanshe, 1989.

INDEX

accumulation, 11–12, 62, 70, 90, 97, 127, 134, 163, 223, 225; capitalist, 206, 210, 211; primitive, 13; surplus, 54, 70
aesthetic production, 6–7
aesthetics, 7, 24, 25–26, 28, 105, 167, 218, 220, 261n4; class, 30–31, 167; Hegelian, 22–23, 24; Kantian, 23; of labor, 57, 166; proletarian, 168, 179; realist, 22, 26; universal, 221, 222
Aesthetics, 220
agitation, 105, 199
agricultural experiment stations, 123
Ai Qing, 29; "Understand Authors, Respect Authors," 29
alienation, 4, 126, 218, 220, 222–23, 262n7
All-China Congress of Literary and Arts Workers (First Cultural Congress), 62, 63
All-China Federation of Literary and Arts Circles, 62, 63, 67, 244n14
All-China Federation of Trade Unions, 83
All-China Meeting of Youth Amateur Literary Creation Activists, 164, 174
Althusser, Louis, 6–9, 16, 17, 65, 178; on art, 7; on history, 6–7, 8; *Reading Capital*, 6. See also ideological state apparatuses (ISAs)

amateur, figure of the, 164, 187, 193
amateur writers, 68, 91, 92–93, 98, 101–2, 105, 109, 112, 149, 174–76, 187, 191–94, 195, 200, 249n8; worker-peasant-soldier, 174, 194
analepsis, 33–34, 37, 40–41, 43, 56, 72, 114, 116–18, 121–22, 139, 147, 159, 161–62
anarchism, 10
Anti-Japanese War, 20–21, 22, 25, 72, 238n3
Anti-Rightist Movement, 98
apprenticeship, 88, 158–59, 161
army of labor, 11, 12, 32, 38
Art and Literary Gazette, 102, 144; "The Problem of Subject Matter," 144
authorship, 101, 183, 184, 192; individual vs. collective, 193–95
autocritique, 112
automation, 88

Ba Jin, 84–85, 92, 107, 109, 111, 243n3; "Little Sister Compiles a Song," 107–9
backwardness, 46, 70, 90, 142
Bai Lang, 18, 77, 82, 83, 87, 90, 161, 234; *For a Happy Tomorrow*, 18, 77, 89
Balibar, Étienne, 17
Barlow, Tani, 120
base and superstructure, 149, 163, 203, 207

base areas, 2, 26, 29, 38, 59, 64, 69, 240n42
Beidaihe Conference, 127, 128
beauty, 25–26, 28, 30, 167–68, 221; conceptions of, 22–25, 167–68, 238n6
Beijing, 232
Belinsky, Vissarion, 23, 261n4 ; "On the Natural School," 238n6
bifurcation, 11, 12–14, 46, 68, 69, 134, 195, 211, 218, 231; of factory and domestic space, 12; of mental and manual labor, 12, 218; of orality and writing, 193; of politics and economics, 202, 213; of rural and urban spaces, 5, 12; of writing and labor, 197
big-character posters, 110, 111, 120–21, 122, 199
biography, 19, 79, 119–20, 122–24, 169; auto-, 123
"bitterness," 50, 140, 142, 145–46, 182
body, the, 11, 30, 51, 138, 149, 153, 160; proletarian, 78, 90; of the writer, 7
Border Region Mass News, 42
border regions, 20, 25, 33, 45, 181
bourgeois dictatorship, 177, 178, 195–96, 197
bourgeois elements, 165
bourgeois ideology, 163, 194, 196
bourgeois right, 98, 125, 126–27, 128–30, 164–65, 178, 197, 201–4, 206, 208–9, 213–16, 218, 222, 224–25, 228; emergence under socialism, 128, 210, 211; and the state, 206, 208
bourgeois state, 206, 223
bourgeoisie, 23, 30, 176, 177, 197, 199, 210; "inside the party," 210 ; petty, 2, 30, 85, 86
bureaucracy, 2, 29, 130, 207, 210
bureaucratism, 130

Cai Xiang, 3, 5, 255n22; *Revolution and Its Narratives*, 3
canteens, 97, 113, 120, 123–24, 129, 132
capital, 10, 12, 13–14, 208; intellectual, 215; logic of, 11, 234
capitalism, 10, 15–16, 94, 127, 130, 132, 165, 203, 206, 208; logic of, 211, 214
capitalist restoration, 195, 196, 206, 208, 209, 211, 213, 222
capitalist roaders, 208, 210, 213
capitalist world-system, 4

Central Committee, 31–32, 52
Central Military Commission, 165
Central Organization Department, 31–32
Changjiang Art and Literature, 104
"character," 71
Chen Baichen, 102
Chengdu Meeting, 126
Chernyshevsky, Nikolai, 22–25, 26, 28–29, 30, 55, 238n6, 238n16, 261n4; *Aesthetic Relation of Art to Reality*, 22, 28, 238n16
childbirth, 117, 138, 140, 142–43
childcare, 97
China Federation of Literature Workers (Literature Association), 63, 64–65, 66–67; "A Work Plan for Adjusting the Organization and Improving Work," 64; "Concerning a Work Plan for the Revision of the Nationwide Literature Workers Association and the Strengthening of Leadership Over Literary Creation," 65
China Youth, 157
Clark, Katerina, 72
class, 30, 144, 239n22, 261n2; aesthetics, 31, 238n6; background, 3, 184, 196; feeling, 171; forces, 23, 25; formation, 24, 30, 253n63; nature, 221; society, 59; status, 24; system, 11; transition, 30, 51, 178
class struggle, 147, 148, 167–68, 176, 199, 202–3, 218, 219, 222
collective creation, 101–3, 133, 181; "Collective Creation Is a Varied, Quick, Economical and Good Method of Creation," 102
collective drama, 102–3
collective labor, 38, 40, 54, 57–58, 87, 100, 119, 162, 172–73, 193, 199; aesthetics of, 57
collectivity, 49, 122, 212
collectivization, 38
commemoration, 48–49
commodity, the, 17, 94–95
commodity exchange, 53, 98, 128, 173, 215
commodity production, 10, 38, 98, 127, 129, 202, 205, 207–8, 215
communist labor, 14, 19, 96, 131, 133, 166, 178, 181, 184, 186, 192, 207, 212, 214, 227–29, 231, 234
Communist Party of China (CPC), 52, 181, 228

Communist Party of the Soviet Union (CPSU), 64; Nineteenth Congress, 64
communist social relations, 119
communist society, 59, 128
Communist Youth League, 119, 173
"Concerning a Decision to Implement the Party's Policy in Art and Culture," 32
consciousness, 30, 51, 72, 130, 134, 148, 166, 172, 210; bourgeois, 131, 197; communist, 131, 166, 178, 185, 210; feminist, 120; raising, 70; self-, 6
conservatism, 185, 204
consumption, 150, 152, 154–55
contradictions, 5, 15, 17, 19, 59; within socialism, 3, 69, 83, 97, 112–13, 126, 130, 202–3, 209–10, 212
cooperative labor, 37, 38, 53
cooperatives, 38, 120, 130, 242n86; advanced producer, 94; distribution of proceeds, 113
counterrevolutionaries, 185. *See also* reactionaries
Creation Society, 24
creative process, 31, 224
cultural labor, 2, 18, 20, 21, 61–62, 71, 83, 86, 93, 95, 102, 104, 111, 113, 125–26, 134, 147, 233
cultural level, 80
cultural politics, 22, 23; Maoist, 30, 47, 52, 225
cultural production, 2–4, 6–9, 16–17, 19, 21–22, 32, 61–63, 65, 67, 71, 83, 91, 97, 105, 108, 133, 168; collective, 194; forces of, 9, 65; institutions of, 164; marketization of, 225; militarization of, 175, 179; models of, 91; relations of, 2, 18, 177, 196, 197; revolutionary, 48
Cultural Revolution, 5, 9, 99, 129–30, 135, 164, 167, 169, 173, 176, 177–80, 186 190–92, 194–97, 201–2, 204, 207–9, 215–16, 217–18, 220, 223–25, 232–33; literature, 185, 188, 190
culture worker, 2–4, 10, 17, 21–22, 29, 31, 49, 56–58, 61, 64, 67, 69, 84–86, 91, 94, 100, 112, 133, 163–64, 187, 214–15, 225, 249n6, 249n8; abolition of, 175; class backgrounds of, 3; degeneration of, 167, 197; as figure of transition, 18, 59, 101, 133, 209; institutionalization of, 99; as laborer, 3, 37, 56, 62, 64, 83, 125; as privileged caste, 196; relations to the masses, 20; as social relation, 133; transformation of, 28, 30, 101, 137, 147, 164, 165, 169, 214

Dai Houying, 219 ; *Humanity, Ah Humanity!*, 219
Dai Jinhua, 5, 218
Decision of the Central Committee of the Chinese Communist Party Concerning the Present Direction of Women's Work in Anti-Japanese Base Areas, 52
deferral, 173
Deng Xiaoping, 208, 214; "three instructions," 208
Dengist coup, 214
"Destroy the 'Petersburg' in the Depths of the Soul," 214
development, 6–7, 17, 25, 78, 98, 134, 204, 207, 233; capitalist, 12, 13–14, 17; colonial, 10, 13, 17; economic, 224; industrial, 68; level of, 204; socialist, 129; stages of, 224; under-, 7; uneven, 7, 61
development (in narrative), 72–73, 77, 113; proletarian, 74, 79, 81, 87, 112
dictatorship of the proletariat, 177, 195, 205, 206, 207, 208
Ding Ling, 1–2, 18, 19, 29, 48, 55–58, 68–69, 85, 99, 217, 225–26, 230–33; "Assorted Recollections Over Three Days," 54; "Du Wanxiang," 226, 233, 234; exile, 2; "Go Among the Masses," 68; *Living Among Wind and Snow*, 217, 232; "My Views on the Problem of Stand," 51; "On 'Du Wanxiang'," 230–31; "On Writing," 52; posthumous texts, 19, 217, 232; "Remembering Xiao Hong Amidst Wind and Rain," 48, 51–52; "rightism" of, 99; "Thoughts on March 8," 29, 50; "Tian Baolin," 54; visit to the Soviet Union, 66; "Writers Must Cultivate Feelings Toward the Masses," 68
direct discourse, 79
"Directive on Cultural Work in Army Units," 165
"Directive on Strengthening Cultural and Artistic Work in Mines, Worksites and Enterprises," 71

"Directory Index Concerning Theses on Soviet Literature," 67
disability, 57
discipline, 71, 73, 77, 111, 166; in- 62, 110, 111; labor, 61, 62, 64, 83; temporal, 61
distribution, 126, 127–28, 203, 207, 211; according to labor, 129; communist, 134; mode of, 203
division of labor, 59, 130, 223, 231
Dobrolyubov, Nikolai, 23, 261n4
dogmatism, 204
domestic sphere, 79–80
"double life," 49, 50, 58, 69, 99, 157–58, 195, 225, 231, 233. See also Ding Ling
dream-images, 46
Duan Ruixia, 187–88, 190, 191–94, 197, 201; "Hammer and Poem," 197–201; "Not Just One of the Audience," 187–90, 191, 192, 197; "Serve as a Recorder of the Life of Struggle of the Great Era," 191, 192

economics, 16, 134, 202
editing, 42
education, 36, 150, 171, 184, 231; aesthetic, 168; ideological, 65, 153; political, 171; technical, 158
egalitarianism, 2, 94, 147, 225, 248n82
Eight Points on Art and Literary Work, 137, 147
eight-rank wage scale, 94, 205, 208
emancipation, 9, 13, 50; of labor, 10, 15, 236n10; through labor, 81; of women, 15, 81
employment, 11; women's, 11
energy, 223
Engels, Friedrich, 16, 59, 205, 206
"engineers of the human soul," 62, 63, 67–68, 69
enlightenment, 2, 22, 27
"entering into life," 3, 27, 30, 51, 66, 68–69, 71, 164, 178
"equal right," 127
everyday life, 12, 28, 48, 68–69, 125, 137, 144, 156, 158, 168–9, 172, 174, 233, 242n80; crisis of, 156; transformation of, 3, 150, 166
evolutionary discourse, 223
exchange value, 53–54; vs. use value, 53
experts. See technical workers
exploitation, 10–11, 211, 222

factory labor, 12, 15, 61, 75, 79, 82, 91, 123, 158, 160–61, 162, 225
factory histories, 103
"factory of literature," 194
Fadeev, Alexander, 63, 66; "The Labor of the Writer," 63; The Young Guard, 68
Family Affair, A, 151–56, 158, 159, 164
family, the, 28, 87, 88, 163; biological, 89; equality in, 118; nuclear, 77, 162; premodern, 11, 14; proletarian, 82; party as, 89; relations, 12, 113, 115; system, 120; as unit of production, 37, 130; as unit of reproduction, 88, 147
Fang Yun, 215; "Deeply Criticize the Ideology of Bourgeois Right in the Cultural Sphere," 215
fantasy, 108, 186
farce, 41, 42, 44
"feelings" (qing), 30, 51, 52, 68, 105, 167, 188, 224; class, 171; of the masses, 51; relation to "understanding," 51. See also sentiment
Fei Liwen, 86, 91, 92, 93; "We Must be Masters of Time," 92
femininity, 155, 156, 159
feminism, 10, 15, 16, 19, 50, 58, 120, 234; Marxist, 10; socialist, 77. See also social reproduction theory
Ferguson, Susan, 16
feudalism, 37, 173, 231
Feuerbach, Ludwig, 25, 28, 222
focalization, 40, 56, 72–73, 74–75, 76, 78, 198, 228; collective, 72
folk culture, 4
folk songs, 23, 101, 103, 149, 249–50n8; new folk song movement, 101
forces of production, 6, 128, 166, 207
form, literary, 22, 32, 47, 103–5, 112, 113; hierarchy of, 106, 179
formalism, 8
"Four Resolutions of the Central Committee of the Communist Party of the Soviet Union (Bolshevik) on Matters of Art and Literature and a Report of Zhdanov," 64
Fourth Writers Congress, 224
free labor, 14, 15, 222
friendship, 20, 48–50, 232; female, 50, 55, 87–90

"from each according to his ability, to each according to his needs," 15, 127, 128, 132, 133
"from each according to their ability, to each according to their labor," 94, 98, 225. *See also* remuneration according to labor
Fudan University, 201; Institute of Political Economy, 201
futurity, 46, 47

German Ideology, The, 59
German socialist movement, 127
"Get Out of 'Petersburg!'," 177–78, 195–96, 197, 214, 215
Gorky, Maxim, 59, 103, 195; collective histories, 103
Great Leap Forward, 96–97, 100–3, 106–8, 112–13, 116, 118, 119–20, 122, 125–27, 130, 132–34, 136–38, 144, 147, 157, 163, 194, 234; literature of, 104, 105, 110, 112, 115, 137, 151
Great Northern Wilderness, 217, 226–28
Guo Moruo, 96, 97–98, 101; "Mounting a Rocket," 96
Guo Rui, 225; "The Reform of Art and Literature and Artistic Quality," 225

Han Shaogong, 5
handicrafts, 88
Hao Jianxiu method, 88, 89
He Guimei, 5, 241n71, 242n86
He Sijing, 220
He Wei, 132
He-Yin Zhen, 10–14, 15–17, 222, 230, 234; "Feminist Manifesto," 11; "On the Question of Women's Labor," 10, 13; "What Women Should Know About Communism," 15
Hegel, G. W. F., 6, 222
Hegelianism, 6, 220; neo-, 6, 22–23, 24
hegemony, 82, 220; ideological, 178
heroism, 166, 213, 229, 234; communist, 188, 207. *See also* subjectivity: heroic
hierarchy, 9, 22, 130, 163, 165
holidays, 43
Hou Jinjing, 143–44; "Creative Individuality and Artistic Uniqueness," 143
household labor, 12, 14–15, 108, 114, 117, 122, 163

housework, 79, 97, 123, 132
Hu Feng, 86
Hu Qili, 224
Hu Qingpo, 105
Hu Wanchun, 86, 91, 149, 163, 167–68, 191, 195, 196; "A Family Affair" 149–50, 158, 159, 164; "Generations," 158–63; "We Must Rupture with the Old World," 167. *See also A Family Affair*
Hua Fu, 101; "Art and Literature Have Released Satellites," 101; "The Benefits of Collective Creation are Many," 102
human nature, 221
humanism, 7, 15, 220–23, 261n2; labor 10, 19, 218–20, 222, 224–25, 236n10; Marxist, 218, 220, 223; socialist, 221, 222

idealism, 22, 24, 30
ideological state apparatus (ISAs), 9, 63, 65, 68, 71, 100, 149, 163, 165 177, 195–96, 215–16, 233
ideology, 30, 210. *See also* bourgeois ideology
immediacy, 30, 105
imperialism, 170; American, 169–70
inequality, 27, 29, 126, 128, 131, 165, 204, 210, 253n63
indirect discourse, 121; free, 79, 89, 110, 121, 159, 170, 198–99, 227
individualism, 99, 165
industrialization, 12, 61–62, 68, 70, 97, 134; socialist, 62, 64, 65, 70, 71, 81, 90
industry, 11, 13, 171, 221; nationalization of, 94; rural, 97
Inner Mongolia, 180
intellectual labor, 22, 42, 126, 223
intellectuals, 1, 25, 28, 30, 49, 58, 219; bourgeois, 165, 177; capitalist, 98; class status of, 21–22, 24; as laborers, 223; petty-bourgeois, 29, 85, 214; reaction to Cultural Revolution, 217–19; reactionary, 177; transformation of, 18, 21, 30, 47, 50–51, 148, 178, 196, 220; worker-peasant, 85. *See also* culture worker
interiority, 35, 216, 226, 229
International Literature, 22–23, 238–39n16
International Women's Day, 116
intimacy, 81
irony (dramatic), 43

Jiang Qing, 148, 175
Jin Jingmai, 169; *The Song of Ou Yanghai*, 169–74, 186
journalism, 53, 190

Kai Feng, 32
Karl, Rebecca, 168, 169, 172
Ke Lan, 86
Ke Qingshi, 148, 149; "the thirteen years," 148
Kong Jue, 52
Korean War, 169
Kropotkin, Peter, 15; *The Conquest of Bread*, 15

labor: agricultural, 38, 42, 54, 94; agricultural vs. industrial, 74; anthropology of, 7; biologization of, 223; capitalist logic of, 131, 133; domestic, 47, 54, 75, 76, 80, 82; emotional, 55, 58; family, 44, 47; gendered organization of, 47, 52, 56; *gongzuo* vs. *laodong*, 4; individual, 115; industrial, 59, 75, 76, 125; productive vs. unproductive, 55, 106; proletarian vs. peasant, 62; rural, 59; skilled vs. unskilled, 94; social organization of, 125; surplus, 54, 212; tempo of, 103, 108; temporality of, 70, 233; unwaged, 163; withdrawal of, 155. *See also* collective labor; communist labor; cooperative labor; factory labor; intellectual labor; men's labor; reproductive labor; reserve army of labor; spiritual labor; women's labor
labor brigades, 39
labor exchange, 37, 39, 40, 42, 119
labor heroes, 54, 242n80
labor models, 52, 81, 121, 123
"Labor Mutual Aid in the Shan-Gan-Ning Border Region," 38
labor power, 11, 38–40, 53, 94, 132, 138, 204, 225, 240n42, 242n86; as commodity, 14, 94, 95, 204, 212, 224, 248n82; private, 163; reproduction of, 16, 19, 88, 149, 151, 156, 163; rural, 97
landlords, 33–35, 170, 240n40
Lao She, 83, 91, 106; "Culture Workers, Busy Yourselves," 83; "Phone Call," 109–11, 113; "The Shorter, the More Difficult," 106; "We Must Write More Short Stories," 106
Lassalle, Ferdinand, 127
law of value, 17, 70, 129, 202
League of Left-Wing Writers, 23, 237n3
Lei Feng, 168, 183; *The Diary of Lei Feng*, 166–67, 182–83
leisure time, 92, 156–57
Lenin, V. I., 9, 17, 38, 59, 131, 195, 205, 206, 208, 259n44, 260n52; on bourgeois right, 206, 208; "From the Destruction of the Old Social System to the Creation of the New," 131; interactions with Gorky, 195; *State and Revolution*, 206, 260n50
Levine, Caroline, 8
Li Fuchun, 83
Li Tuo, 5
Li Xifan, 148
Li Zehou, 223
Li Zhi, 148
Li Zhun, 18, 113, 115, 118, 119, 132, 138, 234; "A Chain of Keys," 113, 115, 119, 120; *A Minor Biography of Li Shuangshuang*, 119–20; "Two Generations," 115–16
Liang Shiqiu, 24
liberalism, 15, 99, 226
Liberation, 128, 132
Liberation Army Art and Literature, 104
Liberation Daily, 32, 59, 86, 87, 197
life (*shenghuo*), 3–4, 8, 9–10, 16, 18, 22–27, 28–29, 31, 47–49, 54, 58, 68–69, 92, 144, 178, 229; biological, 10; social, 3, 12, 13, 93; as totality, 144
life (*shengming*), 50
Lin Biao, 175, 205
Lin Mohan, 148, 164
line struggle, 176
literary criticism, 144
literary journals, 67, 86, 191
Literary Lecture Institute, 85
literary production, 7, 29, 138, 195, 201, 234; planning of, 100; reification of, 195
Literary Research Association, 24; "literature for life," 24
literary style, 143
literary theory, 104
Literature Association. *See* China Federation of Literature Workers

Literature Workers Association, 62, 65; Creation Committee, 65, 66; Literature Fund Management Committee, 65, 66. *See also* Writers Association

Liu Qing, 32, 44, 47, 52, 55; *The Creators*, 32; "Experience in Leading Labor Exchange Teams," 37; "In the Home Village," 32–37; *A Record of Sowing Grain*, 39

Liu Shaoqi, 91, 197

Liu Shipei, 12–13; "Concerning the Desirability of an Association of the Laboring Masses in China," 13; "Concerning the Possibility of Implementing a Unified System of Agriculture and Industry in China," 13

"livelihood" (*shengji*), 11, 12, 16, 230

Long March, 20

Lu Dingyi, 98, 125–26, 128, 133

Lu Xun, 32; "Hometown," 32, 35; "New Year's Sacrifice," 32

Lu Xun Academy of Art and Literature, 23, 26, 28

Lu Zhi, 54, 55; "The Experience of Developing Women's Weaving in Yan'an Southern District," 54

manuscript fees, 65–66, 94, 98, 133, 245n21

Mao Dun, 63–64, 65, 66, 67, 104–5; "Cultivate New Forces, Expand the Literary Ranks," 85

Mao Zedong, 52, 125–26, 128, 165, 205, 208, 214, 223; on class, 30; *Collected Works*, 31; "The Culture Workers Must Amalgamate with the Workers, Peasants and Soldiers," 20; "Get Organized!," 37; *Important Directives of Chairman Mao*, 208, 209 ; "On Khrushchev's Phony Communism and its Historical Lessons for the World," 165; "Rectify the Party's Style of Work," 29; on the state, 208–9; "Talks at the Yan'an Forum on Literature and Art," 47–48, 52, 58–59, 64, 200, 214

Mao Zedong Thought, 167, 181

Maoism, 18, 47, 130, 187, 200, 222, 225–26; late, 213–14

marriage, 76–77, 80

Marx, Karl, 59, 126, 127–28, 175, 204, 218; *1844 Economic and Philosophical Manuscripts*, 219–20, 221–22, 224; *Capital*, 127, 208, 222, 223; *A Contribution to the Critique of Political Economy*, 28; "Critique of the Gotha Programme," 127–28, 129, 204, 206, 224

"Marx, Engels and Lenin on the Dictatorship of the Proletariat," 205, 206

Marx-Engels Collected Works, 219

Marxism, 6, 7, 15, 59, 148, 219, 222; late, 222; Marxist feminism, 10; vulgar, 18. *See also* social reproduction theory

Marxism-Leninism, 167, 205

Marxism and Literature, 58–59, 175

masculinity, 73, 213; proletarian, 74, 80, 153–54, 159

Mass Production Movement, 21

masses, the, 2, 20–22, 28, 30, 51, 68–69, 99, 165, 200; orientation toward, 26, 49, 68, 97; serving, 103; understanding of, 30

materialism, 22, 23, 25, 26, 99

materiality, 6

maternity clinics/wards, 138–39, 140–43

May Fourth movement, 24, 26–27, 237n2; aesthetics, 26; tradition, 32, 37

means of production, 126, 240n40; ownership of, 126

mechanization, 88

mediation, 4, 6, 26–27, 31, 56, 187, 193

men's labor, 81, 82

mental vs. manual labor, 59, 60, 93, 94, 97–99, 113, 126, 128, 133, 149, 150, 164, 175, 178, 195–97, 215, 220–22, 225, 233

midwifery, 138–43

Military Arts and Literature Work Conference, 175

mind, 224

mis-en-scene, 151–52

Mizhi County, 37

Mo Ai, 53–54, 55; "A Page in the History of Weaving Women," 53

mobilization, 97, 120, 122, 132, 134, 138, 233; narratives, 144; political, 118; of women, 53–54, 97

model characters, 168

"Model Regulations for an Advanced Producers Cooperative," 94

model works, 179, 185, 187–88, 189; troupes, 187

modernization, 83, 236n19; socialist, 83, 139

modes of labor, 15, 40, 56, 59, 102, 108, 137; collective, 38–39; familial-patriarchal, 44
modes of production, 194, 215; coexistence of, 6, 10; individual, 43
Morning Glow Series, 194
motherhood, 227–28, 230, 232
mutual aid, 38–39

narration, 39, 114, 121, 149, 182; heterodiegetic, 190; I-narrator, 33–37, 54, 56, 58, 145–47, 181; psychological, 47, 56, 73, 75, 79, 89, 118, 143, 150, 227, 228; simultaneous, 145, 147
narrative: form, 5, 18, 32, 39, 66, 82; intradiegetic, 161–62, 189; practice, 5, 37, 47, 174; rhythm, 103, 119, 150; temporality of, 8, 36, 45, 169; time, 19, 32, 120, 121, 186–87; totality, 47
narratology, 8
National Resistance Association of Literary and Art Workers, 29
Nationalists (KMT), 20, 77, 172
Nationwide Art and Literature Work Forum, 136–37
Nationwide Meeting on Feature Film Creation, 137
Nationwide Youth Literature Creator Meeting, 91
Natural Justice, 10
Never Forget, 150, 152
New Construction, 220; "Alienated Labor," 220
New Culture Movement, 22, 26
New Democracy, 38, 237n3; as stage, 38
New Fourth Army Incident, 20–21
New Harbor, 104, 106
"new workers," 70, 87
novellas, 4, 107, 112, 119
novels, 4, 18, 77, 100, 107, 179; agrarian, 71; Cultural Revolution, 180, 184, 187, 216, 234; diary, 179; sent-down-youth, 179, 187, 189, 201, 202, 210, 213

obstetrics, 139
October Revolution, 177
opera, 189. *See also* model works
"Order Concerning the Universal Implementation of a Wage System and the Reform of the Monetary Wage System Among State Employees," 94
"Organize Labor Power," 38
output, 40
ownership: collective, 70, 207; private property, 38, 221; public, 70; socialist forms of, 126, 203, 207, 210; state, 211 ; transformation of, 126

pastoral, 46
patriarchy, 114, 117, 130, 163; patriarchal authority, 113–15, 156, 241n71
peasant associations, 40, 41, 45
peasantry, 21, 38, 59, 73, 76, 225; "backwardness" of, 46, 70; conservatism of, 70; industries, 13; representation of, 30, 47, 62, 83–84, 90, 167, 170; vs. proletariat, 77
pedagogy, 117, 172, 181 ; auto-, 181
People's Communes, 96, 113, 115, 123, 130; formation of, 96–97; movement, 119; production brigades, 146; supply system in, 130; transition to, 114; wage system in, 130; work teams in, 113
People's Daily, 100, 103, 166; "Authors! Leaps! Great Leaps!," 100; "Disseminate the Three-Eight Work Style Throughout the Country," 166; "The Whole Country Must Study the People's Liberation Army," 166; "We Must Create More Literary Works in Short Forms," 103
People's Liberation Army (PLA), 72, 79, 80, 165–66, 174
People's Literature, 106
People's Republic of China, 18, 226; establishment of, 61, 175, 227; First Five-Year Plan, 1, 18, 70, 71, 77, 82; literary system, 63–65, 68, 99, 137, 187, 195, 217, 226, 245n26; postsocialist period, 217, 218, 220, 226; reform period, 218, 224, 230; socialist period, 86, 92, 183, 218, 224
personification, 208, 210; personae, 210
Petofi Club 164
poetry, 198–200, 201
political economy, 69, 178, 187, 197, 205, 216, 224; aestheticization of, 202, 214; critique of, 202; of labor, 125; socialist, 201–3, 222; Soviet, 126, 129, 203, 211, 212; textbook, 201–5, 208–11, 213

Political Economy: A Textbook, 70
politics: as field of problems, 129–30, 206; in command, 135, 175; temporality of, 7; vs. economics, 129–30, 134, 202
popularization, 65
praxis (revolutionary), 49
production: collective, 54, 62, 162, 173, 193; factory, 11–12, 14, 85, 88, 92, 158, 159, 162; household, 53, 54, 121; tempo of, 84, 125; textile, 13, 52, 53, 87, 242n86. *See also* cultural production
production teams, 146, 230
professional writers, 60, 64, 67, 70, 87, 91–93, 99, 102, 112, 134, 167, 175, 178, 191, 197, 212–14; reproduction of, 71
professionalization, 31, 63–65, 67, 68, 70, 87, 91–93, 99–100, 101, 174, 195, 196
prolepsis, 72, 77, 79, 81, 82, 120, 122, 147, 198
proletarian subjectivity, 80
proletariat, 51, 62, 77, 182, 196; rural, 35
propaganda, 43, 105, 107
Propaganda Department, 148; Art and Literature Anti-Revisionism Writing Group, 148

Qu Qiubai, 49, 69; *Superfluous Words*, 49

Ranks, 77, 78
reactionaries, 179, 185
reading, 86, 103, 104–5, 111
rectification, 64, 164; "minor," 164
Rectification Campaign (1942), 21, 29, 31, 37, 52, 68
Rectification Campaign (1957), 100, 134
Red Army, 128
Red Flag, 165, 202, 206–7; "Study Some Political Economy" (Fang Hai), 202
Red Flag Ballads, 101
relations of production, 150, 211, 212, 219
"remnants," 212
remuneration, 94, 125, 127–28, 130, 208; according to labor, 70, 128, 129, 203–4, 205–6, 209, 211, 212, 224–25; piece rate, 132–33, 212, 228. *See also* eight-rank wage scale; wage, the
Ren Du, 177, 195. *See also* "Get Out of 'Petersburg!'"

"Report on Rectification Conditions in the National and Local Writers Associations," 164
"Report on the Problem of Writers Going Down to the Countryside and Down to the Factories," 100
reportage, 18, 53, 54, 101
reproduction, 12, 117, 123, 144, 155, 213; biological, 10, 14, 143, 144–45, 149; collective, 123; crisis of, 138, 163; ideological, 19, 66–67, 71, 147, 149, 156, 163, 178; of labor, 87, 88, 151, 163; political, 147; revolutionary, 147, 149; sexual, 117; of social forms, 4, 9, 205; socialization of, 123. *See also* social reproduction
reproductive labor, 47, 48, 58, 97, 112, 132, 155, 234
reserve army of labor, 11, 12
reservoirs, 73, 97, 120, 123
Resistance Association, 52
revisionism, 164, 196, 202; anti-, 148–49, 222
revolutionary strategy, 7
revolutionary succession, 19, 140, 149, 150, 163, 167, 255n22
rhythm, 2, 6–8, 38, 47, 104, 134, 137, 154; of writing, 97, 176, 232, 234
rightists, 98, 201, 219
Ru Zhijuan, 86, 138–40, 144, 147, 191, 234; "Ah Shu," 145–47; "All Quiet in the Maternity Clinic," 138–41, 145, 147; "The Second Step," 145
rumor, 45–46
rural transformation, 173

sabotage, 75, 76, 81
Salvation Association, 53
sent-down-youth, 180, 181–82, 228
sentiment, 86, 220, 221; petty-bourgeois, 86
sexuality, 77
Shanghai, 69, 85–86, 231; radical left in, 191
Shanghai Art and Literature Series, 191, 193–94; *The Long Cry of the Golden Bell*, 191; *Morning Glow*, 191, 194, 195, 201. *See also* Morning Glow Series
Shanghai (Writing) Group, 190–91, 192, 194, 195, 201, 202
Shijingshan, 71

278 Index

short forms, 103–4
short stories, 103–4; vs. "sketches," 105
slavery, 14
small producers, 70, 83, 215
social democracy, 127
social reproduction, 11, 19, 65, 76–77, 125, 151, 156, 163; theory, 16, 17
social support, 127
socialist construction, 2, 69, 116, 167
socialist culture, 3, 4, 47, 61, 97, 149, 176, 234
socialist labor, 95, 106, 212, 225
socialist realism, 22, 23, 64, 66, 70, 72
socialist transformation, 3, 91, 93, 94, 149, 169
sociality, 48, 56, 58
soliloquy, 88, 108, 139, 141
solipsism, 48, 59
Song Shuang, 105
Soviet Union, 23, 63, 66, 103, 131, 147, 165; degeneration of, 148; industrialization, 62; literary canon, 66; literary system, 63, 66; as model, 62, 83, 98, 129, 134; Supreme Soviet, 63
species-being, 218, 222
spinning, 53–54, 56–58
spirit mediums, 42
spiritual labor, 192–93, 194, 220, 222–24, 225
Spring Rain, 32, 48, 51–52
Sprouts, 91, 93, 104, 164
Stalin, Joseph, 64, 71, 126, 204; "A Letter to Comrade Demyan Bedny," 64; *Economic Problems of Socialism in the USSR*, 64, 70, 135, 204
Stalin Prize, 148
Stalinism, 135, 207–8, 210
stand(point), 29, 30, 196
State Planning Commission, 83
Story of Dong Cunrui, The, 169, 170, 174
stream of consciousness, 108
struggle sessions, 74
students, 40
Study and Criticism, 192, 194
Study Some Political Economy, 203; "How Individual Articles of Consumption are Distributed," 203
"Study Well the Theory of the Dictatorship of the Proletariat," 205
subbotniks, 131
subject matter, 48, 87, 143–44, 167, 198, 199
subject-object distinction, 27

subjectification, 149, 174; and objectivity, 27
subjectivity, 31, 69, 138, 180, 200, 214, 216, 226, 229, 232; bourgeois, 180; heroic, 174, 178, 184–85, 201, 210, 213, 216, 230; socialist, 139
sublime, the, 50
superfluousness, 49–50, 106, 112
superstition, 101
supply system, 94, 128–29, 130, 132, 134, 239n18
surplus value, 222, 223

Taking Tiger Mountain by Strategy, 187, 192
Tang Kexin, 86, 87, 90, 91, 93, 195; "Gu Xiaoju and Her Sisters," 87–90; "Let Me Return Once Again to the Factory!," 93; *Spring in the Workshop*, 87
Tazoe Tetsuji, 12
technical workers, 158–59, 187–88
"tempering," 51, 137, 166
temples, 41
temporality, 6–8, 10, 16, 37, 43, 72, 86, 139, 162, 186; acceleration, 142; biological, 143; capitalist, 233; collective, 41, 43, 44, 46; communist, 124, 233; industrial, 71, 90, 92; lived, 8; of social relations, 43; teleological, 6; temporal logic, 132, 173, 206; uneven, 131. *See also* rhythm; writing
"Temporary Measures Introduced by the Chinese Writers Association For Loans and Allowances," 67
Ten Points on Art and Literary Work, 137, 143, 147; "Encourage Greater Diversification in Style and Subject Matter," 137; "Strengthen Artistic Practice, Ensure Time for Creation," 137
Tenth Plenum, 147
textuality, 5
Theoretical Trends, 225
theory of the state, 206, 208–9
thought work, 166, 171
"three amalgamations, the," 165, 194
"three masteries, the," 165
"three prominences, the," 179
Tianjin, 85
Tibet, 169, 170, 171
timekeeping, 41
Tolstoy, Leo, 85
Tomba, Massimiliano, 14

Toscano, Alberto, 17
totality, 54; social, 126
trade unions, 71, 93
transition, 210, 213; communist, 59, 107, 128, 209; countryside-to-city, 77; peasant-to-worker, 77; socialist, 96, 186, 201, 202, 215, 218
transitional form, 18
treaty ports, 13
Triangle Hill, 169
Two Kinds of Society, Two Kinds of Wage, 204
typicality, 66

unified payment system, 94
Union of Soviet Writers, 63, 68; Second Congress, 68
universal exchangeability, 128

value, 127. *See also* exchange value; law of value; surplus value
victimhood, 217, 226
village government, 40
village heads, 55, 58
village schools, 40
village solidarity, 45
village teachers, 41
visual media, 104–5

wage, the, 94, 115, 129, 211, 224 ; form, 125, 132, 157, 202, 203–4, 209, 210, 218, 228, 230, 234; incorporation of women into, 132; reform, 94; -relation, 53, 130–31, 165, 206, 207, 211, 222; supersession of, 133–34, 207, 209, 216, 234; under capitalism vs. under socialism, 94, 130, 204, 206, 211–12, 224. *See also* remuneration
wage labor, 94, 212
"Waltz of the Youth," 107
Wang Guowei, 27
Wang Jie, 182, 183
Wang Ruoshui, 222–23, 224; "The Human is the Point of Departure for Marxism," 223; "Labor—Knowledge—Wealth," 223; "On Problems of Alienation," 223
Wang Shiwei, 29
"We Must Have a Great Cultural Detachment of the Working Class," 99

weaving, 52, 53, 56–58
Women of China, 138
Women of New China, 77
Women's Association, 53, 115
women's labor, 53–54, 80, 82, 97, 113, 151, 234
work of art, the, 25, 27, 28
work points system, 94, 114
work teams, 41, 43, 45, 227. *See also* labor-exchange teams
worker-peasant writers, 104
worker-peasant-soldier, 174, 181, 194, 250n11, 257n1
worker-writers, 18, 86–87, 91, 93, 99, 191, 195–97
working class, 62, 70, 73, 83, 85, 98, 153, 189, 190, 199; production of, 62–63, 77; socialist, 83, 90
working day, 157, 212
worldview, 148, 167; bourgeois, 167
writer, the: collective, 112; as engineer, 63, 67. *See also* amateur writers; professional writers; proletarian writers; worker-writers
writerly production, 7
Writers Association, 62, 67–68, 69, 83, 91, 93, 98, 195–97, 215–16, 233; "1956–67 Work Program," 85; Council, 84, 85
Writers Congress (1953), 68
Writers Dispatch, 66, 71, 84
writing: anonymization of, 101; autonomy of, 1, 85, 233; bourgeois conception of, 31, 59; deindividuation of, 194; individuation of, 197; literacy, 41, 80; methods, 32, 29; plans, 83; as occupation, 60, 67; organization of, 67, 103; physicality of, 48; and time, 49, 69; temporality of, 66, 69, 84, 87, 91, 92, 93, 103, 137, 193, 215, 236
Wu Manyou, 52
Wuchang Conference, 134

Xiao Hong, 48, 49–50, 55, 58, 231
Xie Qipei, 157; "It is Necessary to Treasure Leisure Time," 157
Xu Ming, 107

Yan'an, 21, 31, 48, 52, 55, 59, 68, 71, 85, 225, 234; inflation, 21; Nationalist blockade, 21. *See also* Mass Production Movement; Rectification Campaign

Yan'an Forum on Literature and Art, 52
Yao Wenyuan, 133, 204–5, 206, 208, 210; "On Manuscript Fees," 133; "On the Social Basis of the Lin Biao Anti-Party Clique," 206–7, 208
Yellow River, 180
yellow unions, 74
Young Generation, 150
youth, 149, 180; educated, 181
Yu Heiding, 101

Zhang Changgong, 19, 179; *Youth*, 19, 179, 180–6
Zhang Chunqiao, 103, 128, 130–31, 190–91, 195, 201–2, 204–5, 206–9, 210, 211, 213, 225, 234; critique of "the economists," 129; "On Exercising All-Round Dictatorship Over the Bourgeoisie," 206–7; "Smash the Ideology of Bourgeois Right," 128, 202; "The Style of the Great Leap Forward," 103
Zhang Guangnian, 148
Zhang Jiong, 168
Zhang Kangkang, 179; *Dividing Line*, 179
Zhang Ying, 86, 87
Zhao Shuli, 45; *San Li Wan*, 45
Zhao Wanshan, 53
Zhengzhou Conference, 135

Zhou Enlai, 136–37; "Concerning the Problem of Walking on Two Legs in Art and Literature Work," 136
Zhou Libo, 18, 71, 77–78; *Rivulets of Steel*, 18, 71–72
Zhou Tian, 194–95, 201; "A Newborn Thing on the Literary Battle Front," 194
Zhou Yang, 31, 48, 49, 59, 61, 64, 65, 67–68, 69, 82, 91, 136–37, 164, 174–75, 197; "A Casual Discussion on Literature and Life," 26, 28; "Art and Life," 24, 25; *rensheng*, 24, 25; "Materialist Aesthetics—An Introduction to Chernyshevsky's Aesthetics," 28; "Rectify Ideas of Art and Literature, Enhance Leadership Work," 61; "Socialist Realism: The Path of Advance for Chinese Literature," 70; "We Must Struggle," 67; "We Need a New Aesthetics," 24, 25
Zhu Guangqian, 220–22, 224; "Art is a Kind of Productive Labor," 221; *Letters on Aesthetics*, 221; "On the Questions of Human Nature, Humanism, Human Sentiment and Universal Beauty," 220–21; "Questions of Aesthetics in Marx's *Economic and Philosophical Manuscripts*," 222
Zong Baihua, 220

GPSR Authorized Representative: Easy Access System Europe, Mustamäe tee 50, 10621 Tallinn, Estonia, gpsr.requests@easproject.com